CONTEMPORARY THOUGHT ON NINETEENTH CENTURY SOCIALISM

CONTEMPORARY THOUGHT ON NINETEENTH CENTURY SOCIALISM

General Editors
Peter Gurney and Kevin Morgan

Volume III
Fabians, the ILP and the Labour Party

Edited by
Peter Lamb

LONDON AND NEW YORK

First published 2021
by Routledge
2 Park Square, Milton Park, Abingdon, Oxon OX14 4RN

and by Routledge
52 Vanderbilt Avenue, New York, NY 10017

Routledge is an imprint of the Taylor & Francis Group, an informa business

© 2021 selection and editorial matter, Peter Lamb; individual owners
retain copyright in their own material.

The right of Peter Lamb to be identified as the author of the editorial
material, and of the authors for their individual chapters, has been asserted
in accordance with sections 77 and 78 of the Copyright, Designs and
Patents Act 1988.

All rights reserved. No part of this book may be reprinted or reproduced or
utilised in any form or by any electronic, mechanical, or other means, now
known or hereafter invented, including photocopying and recording, or in
any information storage or retrieval system, without permission in writing
from the publishers.

Trademark notice: Product or corporate names may be trademarks or
registered trademarks, and are used only for identification and explanation
without intent to infringe.

British Library Cataloguing-in-Publication Data
A catalogue record for this book is available from the British Library

Library of Congress Cataloging-in-Publication Data
A catalog record for this book has been requested

ISBN: 978-1-138-49019-2 (set)
eISBN: 978-1-351-03570-5 (set)
ISBN: 978-1-138-32102-1 (volume III)
eISBN: 978-0-429-45234-5 (volume III)

Typeset in Times New Roman
by Apex CoVantage, LLC

Publisher's Note
References within each chapter are as they appear in the original complete work

CONTENTS

Introduction: the birth of British parliamentary socialism   **1**
PETER LAMB

PART 1
Work as it was and how it might be   **15**

1 *Land Lessons for Town Folk* (London: Clarion,
   1896), 1–12.   17
   WILLIAM JAMESON

2 "Dealing with the Unemployed: A Hint from the Past",
   Nineteenth Century, December, 1904, 1–14.   30
   J. KEIR HARDIE

3 *The Right to Work* (London: Independent Labour Party,
   c. 1908), 3–15.   44
   H. RUSSELL SMART

PART 2
Visions of the future   **59**

4 *The Progress of Socialism: A Lecture* (London: Modern Press,
   William Reeves and Freethought Publishing Company,
   c. 1888), 3–18.   61
   SIDNEY WEBB

CONTENTS

5 *The Claims and Progress of Labour Representation*
(Newcastle-on-Tyne: Labour Literature Society
[North England], c. 1894), 3–16.   **75**
FRED HAMMILL

6 "The Need for a Labour Party", in *Britain for the British*
(London: Clarion Press, 1902), 148–155.   **90**
ROBERT BLATCHFORD

7 *The Individual under Socialism: A Lecture* (London: ILP,
c. 1908), 3–14.   **96**
PHILIP SNOWDEN

PART 3
Concepts of political change   **109**

8 *What Socialism Means: A Call to the Unconverted – A Lecture
Delivered for the Fabian Society*, 3rd ed (London: William Reeves,
c. 1888), 2.   **111**
SIDNEY WEBB

9 *What Socialism Is* (London: Fabian Society, 1890), 1–3.   **113**
FABIAN SOCIETY

10 Poster for *Socialism!: The First of a Course of Four Lectures
Will be Given in the Co-operative Hall, High Street, on Tuesday,
Nov. 4, 1890, by Sidney Webb*, 1890.   **118**
SIDNEY WEBB

11 *On the Importance of Right Methods in Teaching
Socialism: A Paper Read to the Manchester and District
Fabian Society, February 10th*, 1891 (Manchester: R.J. Derfel,
1891), 1–15.   **120**
R.J. DERFEL

12 What is Socialism? A Discussion between Mrs. Annie Besant
and Mr W. J. Nairn (Glasgow: SDF, 1892), 1–8.   **130**
ANNIE BESANT AND W.J. NAIRN

CONTENTS

PART 4
Political economy   137

13   *Miners' Eight Hours' Bill. Speech by J. Keir Hardie, MP, in the House of Commons*, reprinted from *The Labour Leader* (London: John Penny, 1902).   139
      KEIR HARDIE

14   *The New Unemployed Bill of the Labour Party* (London: Independent Labour Party, c. 1907), 3–15.   142
      J. RAMSAY MACDONALD

15   *Socialism and Agriculture* (London: Independent Labour Party, 1908), 3–15.   155
      RICHARD HIGGS

PART 5
Ways of organising   169

16   *Manifesto of the Joint Committee of Socialist Bodies* (London: Twentieth Century Press, 1893), 1–8.   171
      JOINT COMMITTEE OF SOCIALIST BODIES

17   *Why We Are Independent* (London: Labour Representation Committee, 1903), 1–4.   177
      LABOUR REPRESENTATION COMMITTEE

18   *Why is the L.R.C. Independent?* (London: Labour Representation Committee, c. 1905).   183
      LABOUR REPRESENTATION COMMITTEE

19   *Labour and Politics: Why Trade Unionists Should Support the Labour Party* (London: Labour Party, c. 1907).   187
      LABOUR PARTY

20   *The Party Pledge and the Osborne Judgement* (Manchester: The National Press Ltd, 1910), 1–16.   192
      KEIR HARDIE

CONTENTS

PART 6
Democracy and the State

209

21   *The Law and Trade Union Funds. A Plea for "Ante-Taff Vale"*
(London: Independent Labour Party, 1903), 3–15.   211
J. RAMSAY MACDONALD

22   *The Women's Suffrage Controversy* (London: Adult Suffrage
Society, 1905), 1–4.   222
MARGARET BONDFIELD

23   *The Citizenship of Women: A Plea for Women's Suffrage*, third
edition (London: Independent Labour Party, 1906), 5–15.   227
KEIR HARDIE

PART 7
The new religion and the old

239

24   *A Socialist's View of Religion and the Churches* (London:
Clarion, 1896), 1–16.   241
TOM MANN

25   *The New Religion*, 2nd edition (London: Clarion, 1897), 1–12.   254
ROBERT BLATCHFORD

PART 8
Gender, sexuality and family relations

265

26   *Women and the Factory Acts* (London: Fabian Society, 1896),
3–15.   267
BEATRICE WEBB

27   *Socialism and the Family* (London: A.C. Fifield, 1906), 43–60.   281
H.G. WELLS

28   *Will Socialism Destroy the Home?* (London: Independent
Labour Party, c. 1907), 1–14.   288
H.G. WELLS

viii

CONTENTS

29   *Socialism and the Home* (London: Independent Labour Party, c. 1909), 1–11.   296
KATHARINE BRUCE GLASIER

30   *The New Children's Charter* (London: Independent Labour Party and Fabian Society, 1912), 3, 6–20.   307
C.M. LLOYD

PART 9
War, peace and internationalism   321

31   *Hands Across the Sea: Labour's Pleas for International Peace* (Manchester: The National Labour Press, c. 1910), 1–16.   323
G.H. PERRIS

32   *A Labour Case Against Conscription* (Manchester: National Labour Press, c. 1913), 3–14.   339
HARRY DUBERY

33   *The Origins of the Great War* (London: Union of Democratic Control, 1914), 3–17.   350
HENRY NOEL BRAILSFORD

Bibliography   363

INTRODUCTION

The birth of British parliamentary socialism

Peter Lamb

The present volume focuses on the early ideas, policies, strategies, actions of, and uneasy relations between three organisations: the Fabian Society, Independent Labour Party (ILP) and Labour Party, formed in 1884, 1893 and 1900 respectively. The Labour Party, which was originally the Labour Representation Committee (LRC) until it became a party in formal terms in 1906, continues to operate as a major player in British politics, the Fabian Society still functions as an influential think-tank of the moderate left, while the ILP declined, was revived in the mid-1970s and still plays a minor role as a pressure group today. In this introductory essay the context will be set for the reproduction and discussion in this volume of a range of pamphlets, leaflets and other documents produced by these organisations, or members of one or more thereof, included and discussed in the volume. Except for a few which help illustrate the key topics of the period, these items are far less easily accessible than many others which readers may have already studied.

Although it includes a few articles from journals and chapters from books, most of the items selected for this volume are shorter, freestanding pieces, written and published with the intention to agitate, mobilise and motivate activists to pursue the tactics and strategies advocated with specific goals in mind, and also to attract thus far inactive people to the political causes. The socialist and labour movement in general relied, as did other social and political movements of the period, on the short, printed medium to get the message out and frame it in an opportune manner. The Fabians became particularly adept and methodical in this respect with their pamphlets, or tracts as they called them, on a wide range of issues.[1] The references in this introduction to many other pamphlets and other documents of the period serve as further indication of the importance placed on short, printed pieces within the socialist movement during the period.

The reliance on such a medium gives the documents presented here a sense of urgency, reflecting the issues of the period. Pamphlets were particularly suitable for the introduction and propagation of new ideas on how to address the issue, tending to be less constrained by the publication line or approach than articles in journals and having a more ephemeral quality than books, the latter designed for a longer shelf-life. In that respect the pamphlet has been described as an anti-book.[2] Leaflets, printed speeches and posters can also have such an anti-book nature. Today, the Internet as a platform for websites, blogs and social media serves the purpose of many of the items included in this volume. Perhaps, this should be borne in mind as one seeks to appreciate the milieu of the writings reprinted here and thus to grasp their significance. The selection will demonstrate the close links but also significant differences between the Fabians, Labour and the ILP – differences which meant that British social democracy would, arguably, always lack firm foundations and thus harmony. The goals of trade union leaders and members would coexist in the same movement with those of socialists seeking major changes to the British and sometimes international economic structures, institutions and arrangements. Whether, moreover, the campaigns of the movement should be guided primarily by leaders and experts or benefit from significant contributions of the grassroots membership would be at issue.

An example of the relations between the organisations concerns the activity of the Fabian Society, which was largely conducted at the local level in the form of organised lectures and meetings. In his classic study of the first three decades of the Society, founding member Edward Pease, having been secretary for twenty-five years and thus knowing the leaders and other prominent members well, summed up the link with the ILP and Labour concisely. The local Fabian societies "were succeeded by and merged into branches of the Independent Labour Party, which adopted everything Fabian except its peculiar political tactics". When the Labour Party was formed a few years later, he went on, it was "more than Fabian in its toleration in the matter of opinions and virtually, although not formally, Fabian in its political policy".[3]

Pease's summary indicates not only the affinities but also some key points of contrast between the three organisations. A significant difference between the Fabians on the one hand and the two parties on the other was that the former was, as was mentioned above, what we would now call a think-tank. It was, in other words, an association of intellectuals seeking to influence opinions, views, policies and strategies. Two years after its foundation Annie Besant, one of the Society's most influential and controversial members, made a statement which serves to summarise the position of the Fabians as the leaders of British socialism, at least until the foundation of the ILP a few years later. "At present", she suggested, two years before her involvement in the successful London matchgirls' strike of 1888, for which she is probably best-known,

> the Socialist movement in England is far more a middle-class than a working-class one; the creed of socialism is held as an intellectual conviction by the thoughtful and the studious, and is preached by them to the workers who have everything to gain by accepting it, and some of whom have already embraced and are teaching it.[4]

INTRODUCTION

Having been formed in 1884 by a breakaway faction of an intellectual socialist group which styled itself the Fellowship of the New Life, later that year the Society published a manifesto in which its early commitment to extensive political and social change is plain to see. The manifesto condemned capitalism, profit-seeking, inequality and privilege. Its proposals included nationalisation of the land; state intervention to prevent neglect of children and to ensure a high standard of education and housing; equal rights for men and women; state involvement in industrial competition; and a direct tax to generate public revenue.[5]

Published in the name of the Society, the manifesto of 1884 was, as founding member Pease acknowledged, actually written by the prominent playwright and critic George Bernard Shaw.[6] The involvement of middle-class intellectuals such as Shaw reflected the broader nature of reformism in the United Kingdom. A tradition had begun to form within liberalism, and indeed among Liberals, based on concern for the conditions of the masses. This strand of liberalism suggested that the state should have a role in improving those conditions. Most well-known among liberals in this respect was, perhaps, T.H. Green. Among the many political philosophers influenced by Green was David G. Ritchie who was briefly a Fabian Society member. Of Green's famous conception of freedom as "a positive power or capacity of doing or enjoying something worth doing or enjoying, and that, too, something we do or enjoy in common with others", Ritchie wrote: "This is certainly a democratic, some would call it a Socialistic, sentiment". To achieve the end sought by Green, Richie went on, it would be necessary to rid society of the class barriers which many assumed had been broken down by Christianity.[7]

Liberals inspired by Green and even some conservatives gained the support of many working-class trade unionists. The political environment was thus not conducive to revolutionary socialism.[8] For intellectuals such as Shaw and Sidney Webb, the socialist theorising of the Fabian Society seemed far better suited than revolutionary ideas to their time and place.

Shaw and Webb had joined the Society in 1884, just a few months after its formation.[9] Underestimating or perhaps ignoring the disagreements between Society members including themselves which made the Fabian identity less than easy to pin down, they each portrayed the Fabians as practical socialists with clear aims and strategies, contrasting them with those they depicted as dreamers who remained in the Fellowship of the New Life.[10] Nevertheless, divisions between two wings of the Society, led by Shaw and Webb respectively, soon emerged. Having set out the Society's stall in the manifesto, Shaw began a campaign of persuasion, by means of which socialist ideas would permeate liberal circles. Radicals in the Liberal Party, he reasoned, would thereby be persuaded to leave and join a new socialist party within which Fabian permeation would continue. Webb, however, had a different strategy of permeation in mind, seeking instead to persuade the Liberal Party itself to adopt socialist policies.[11] Webb also attempted to attract other prominent politicians and administrators to the Fabian cause. He argued in an article of 1891 that intelligent people could not but convert from

3

individualism to socialism once they thought seriously about the conditions of a modern industrial society. He expressed this view as follows:

> Those who have forced directly upon their notice the larger aspects of the problem, those who are directly responsible for the collective interests of the community, can now hardly avoid, whether they like it or not, taking the Socialist view. Each Minister of State protests against Socialism in the abstract, but every decision that he gives in his own department leans more and more away from the Individualist side.[12]

Even five years later Webb reproduced the article as a Fabian pamphlet, almost identical to the original, and with the above quote intact.[13]

A very different interpretation of the debate between those who favoured permeation of the Liberal Party and those who advocated the formation of a new party was presented by Hubert Bland in the last chapter of *Fabian Essays in Socialism* which, edited by Shaw, was published in 1889. Bland warned that even those Liberals sympathetic to the socialist cause would, when private property ownership was challenged by the latter, draw back to their traditional positions. He put it as follows:

> Directly we feel ourselves strong enough to have the slightest chance of winning off our own bat we shall be compelled both by principle and inclination to send an eleven to the wickets. They will have to face the opposition, united or disunited, of both the orthodox parties... And whether our success be great or small, or even non-existent, we shall be denounced by the Radical wire-pullers and the now so complaisant and courteous Radical press. The alliance will be at an end.

It is perhaps significant that Shaw as editor allowed Bland to bring the collection of essays to a close with the following view. "The immediate result of this inevitable split will be the formation of a definitively Socialist party, i.e., a party pledged to the communalization of all the means of production and exchange, and prepared to subordinate every other consideration to that one end".[14]

Although Webb made a significant contribution to the *Fabian Essays* of 1889, his emphasis on the permeation of liberal and conservative parties and institutions for the purpose of developing a socialist society meant that the formation of the ILP in January 1893, at a conference in Bradford, did not have the enthusiastic support of the Society as a whole. In his Introduction to the 1920 edition of the *Fabian Essays* he insisted that the Fabian Society had not made the mistake of failing to see the necessity for a new socialist party.[15] This implication that he had seen the need for such a party may well have been sincere, but would have carried greater conviction had he been clear in presenting this view in the 1880s and 1890s. That there was, nevertheless, considerable overlapping between the

Fabians and ILP pioneers is evident from the authorship of the Programme and Policy published in September 1893. The author, H. Russell Smart, declared himself as both a Fabian and delegate to the Bradford Conference on the front cover.[16] The ILP programme called for a legal eight-hour day, productive, meaningful and useful work to avoid unemployment, a minimum wage which would have the effect of abolishing sweated labour, a guarantee that children enjoyed a high standard of living with a voluntary option of attendance at accessible and free boarding schools, and proper provision for the elderly including pensions. These measures would be paid for by a graduated income tax of unearned income.[17] This programme bore affinities and was thus compatible with the measures outlined by Shaw in the Fabian manifesto nine years earlier.

In June 1894 the ILP declared James Keir Hardie as President. Hardie was already becoming well-known as a working man who had won the parliamentary seat of West Ham with the intention of representing his class two years earlier. He would help form the LRC at the turn of the century and became the first parliamentary leader of the Labour Party in 1906. In 1894 Hardie, John Lister as Treasurer and Tom Mann as Secretary together published a greeting to the workers of Great Britain and Ireland. The experiences of a range of countries had, they argued, made clear that "so long as the Political Institutions and chief Industrial Agencies are owned and controlled by the landed aristocracy and the capitalist plutocracy, so long will it be impossible for the Democratic ideal to be realised".[18]

Furthermore, whilst being a party rather than a think-tank, the ILP shared the Fabian concern that an educative role was necessary for socialism to develop and gain a substantial following. That such a role would go hand in hand with the intention to engage in parliamentary politics rather than to influence the process from outside is clear in the introductory letter which party leader Hardie attached to the front of Smart's Programme and Policy. Hardie expressed this as: "the first serious attempt to teach the Democracy how to use the power of which it is possessed; and to use it in its own way, free from either patronage or dictation from the privileged classes of society".[19] Unless this could be accomplished, he went on, "the common people will remain enslaved and unrepresented however much the franchise may be extended". Looking ahead to commencing the programme, in their greeting the following year Hardie, Lister and Mann advocated an "Industrial Commonwealth" organised on a collectivist basis. The land, raw material and machinery would be "owned and controlled by the community for the common good of all".[20] Before this could be achieved it was, they stressed, necessary for working men and women to campaign for better wages and living conditions and, with a hint at a forthcoming internationalist stance, for the party to organise "the voting power of the populace so as to democratize the machinery of government, local and imperial".[21]

Hardie worked closely within the ILP with J. Ramsay MacDonald, who would become the first Labour prime minister for several months in 1924, hold that office again from 1929 but abandon his party upon the collapse of his government in 1931 and serve in the Conservative-led national government. In 1899 Hardie and MacDonald identified the decline of the Liberal Party and the significance of the ILP in the changing political landscape. The Liberals' time had passed. Once progressive, their party had now served its purpose of breaking the dominance of the aristocracy and had begun to operate on the basis of opportunity rather than principle. Liberalism had come to serve the purposes of a newly dominant business class, using its political emancipation to defend the interests of the few while obstructing the social emancipation of the many. The Liberal Party now opposed the ILP when the latter put forward its socialist candidates for election. As Hardie and MacDonald put it: "Socialism is to inspire the progressive forces of the twentieth century as Individualism inspired those of the nineteenth". The ILP alone was "able to interpret the spirit of the time".[22] Like Shaw and his allies in the Fabian Society, Hardie and MacDonald were stressing that the Liberals needed to be challenged rather than reformed.

Activists such as Hardie and MacDonald needed a substantial electoral base if their challenge to the Liberals was to be successful. Such a base existed among trade unionists, including officials such as Margaret Bondfield who were staunch socialists. In 1899, in her role as assistant secretary of the shopworkers' union, Bondfield, who would thirty years later become the first British female cabinet minister, recognised that while effective organisation by workers in their unions could achieve some gains, in other cases they would need to "look to the State". In the case of the members of her own union she argued that: "Nothing less stringent than legislation for the compulsory closing of shops will satisfactorily lessen their hours of labour".[23]

The relationships and shared interests of the Fabian Society, the ILP and some influential trade unionists led to brief and, frankly, over-optimistic prospects of socialist unity when in 1900 the LRC was formed. This was certainly not the sort of strong, clear-minded socialist party favoured by Fabians such as Shaw and Bland. It was, rather, a compromise.[24] The LRC was essentially an *ad hoc* alliance between the trade unions, the Fabian Society, the ILP and the Social Democratic Federation (SDF). These organisations each retained their independence, being represented at the founding conference that year as separate units and retaining this status thereafter. The trade unions, having a far greater presence than the other groups, became the dominant players in the LRC, influencing the nature of its policies and procedures.[25]

Meanwhile, although Sidney and Beatrice Webb had yet to give their full support to the Labour Party, in November 1901 there were signs that Sidney was moving away from his stance of permeating the established parties towards support for Labour. He stressed that month that neither of the two main parties was able to meet the demands of millions of ordinary people. Hence, "without a new grouping of the electorate, without the inspiration of some new thought, no virile and fecund Opposition, let alone an alternative Government, is conceivable". The "party and statesmen" whom millions of people would support, "the leaders for whom they are hungering", he added, "are those who shall convince them that above all other considerations they stand for a policy of National Efficiency".[26] His view was that workers in their trade unions, shopkeepers, merchants and others of the various classes in the United Kingdom were coming to think in terms of community rather than individualism, and that they sought a party to govern accordingly.[27] That he was overestimating perceptions of national interest in the country was already becoming evident as the pamphlet went to press. Four months earlier the House of Lords had upheld an injunction which made the railway workers' union liable for damages caused by their members' strike action in the Taff Vale dispute.[28] Many trade unionists consequently perceived division rather than community, and defence of their interests rather than national efficiency.

Furthermore, the non-trade union organisations in the LRC had, over the preceding decade, tended to disagree and quarrel with one another, not least because the SDF was a Marxist party, albeit a rather idiosyncratic one led by its authoritarian leader H.M. Hyndman who sought, unsuccessfully, to dominate it. This was a period in which the revisionist ideas of Eduard Bernstein and the moderate socialism of Jean Jaurès had begun to circulate among the left and subsequently to be opposed fiercely by the orthodox Marxists, including at the Amsterdam conference of the Second International Workingmen's Association in August 1904.[29] The class struggle doctrine of the SDF was opposed resolutely by MacDonald who, on return from the conference in Amsterdam in 1904, declared his support for Bernstein and Jaurès with whom he hoped the LRC and ILP would work constructively.[30] The SDF was, moreover, never going to be popular among the trade unions. The unions could not take on board a hardline socialist stance and so the SDF left the LRC after eighteen months.[31] The class conflict stance of the SDF would also have been unattractive to middle-class socialists. During his brief period as a Fabian Society member H.G. Wells referred to the party directly in this respect in 1906.[32] Wells was not, however impressed by the bureaucratic administrative nature of Fabianism, preferring the creative outlook of other middle-class socialists. The SDF continued to pursue class struggle and revolution by parliamentary means until 1911 when it merged with the British Socialist Party (BSP).[33]

The trade unions' interest in contributing to the foundation of the LRC stemmed from a lengthy period in the late nineteenth century in which the employers had enjoyed considerable success in court in deeming various cases of industrial action illegal.[34] Until 1901, however, this did not represent an urgent issue for the unions, as many of the legal verdicts determined as liable individuals such as union officials who could never afford to pay damages. This was to change with the decision in the House of Lords to uphold a verdict in court that the Amalgamated Society of Railway Servants (ASRS) was liable for the conduct of members who were deemed to have committed tort in their industrial action against the Taff Vale Railway Company. The decision removed the immunity of trade union funds from prosecution during industrial disputes. The ASRS was ordered to pay £40,000. This verdict set a precedent for other unions to be treated accordingly.[35] The political implications were summarised the following year by the eminent American statistician E. Dana Durand, who noted that a decision was made at the Trades Union Congress of 1902 that greater political action was required, including greater parliamentary representation. As he put it, the LRC, the functions of which had "heretofore been unimportant", immediately called a conference "the most significant fruit of which" was a request for unions each to donate one penny per member to promote the election and payment of labour representatives.[36]

Noting that the Trades Union Congress of 1902 decided parliamentary legislation was needed to protect the unions in future, Durand predicted that the unions would enjoy success in that respect.[37] The unions shared his view that such legislation would constitute the way forward, an unintended consequence of the Taff Vale decision being that trade union membership of the LRC doubled over the following two years.[38] The trade union movement thus put its weight behind the LRC as a vehicle not only to overturn the Taff Vale judgement, which was achieved through the Trade Disputes Act of 1906, but to protect against future suppression of organised labour.

In 1903 Hardie considered the implications of the Taff Vale decision, suggesting that British workers and their representatives, whether or not they were socialists, were generally in favour of transforming the LRC into an actual Labour Party. He carefully distinguished between the LRC and ILP in this respect, stressing that the latter was firmly socialist, concerned with issues beyond the representation of the working class and, as he had emphasised from the start, that it had an educative purpose and function.[39] In previous campaigns for representation in parliament, the unions, many members of which had no time for the socialism of the ILP, had, Hardie suggested, put forward candidates through the Liberal or Conservative parties. This having proved ineffective the unions had "practically cut themselves adrift from their old political moorings, and they are heading direct for the open sea of Labor Representation and a Labor Party".[40] Hardie seems to have been overstating the formal links between the Conservatives and trade unions. By 1903 the Conservatives had indeed gained considerable support from "the Tory workingman" since the 1880s, and even adopted trade unionists as candidates in municipal elections.[41] The Conservatives by and large, however, had attracted working-class people to clubs which encouraged them to make the best of their lives rather than campaign for change through trade unions.[42] It is indeed the case, nevertheless, that as Hardie argued, the LRC was beginning to take support from working-class people who had sympathised with the Conservatives and the Liberals. The LRC had already won two parliamentary seats and he expressed confidence, predicting that many more of its candidates would contest the next general elections. Although by the nature of the LRC not all would be socialists, they would all be committed to forming a parliamentary Labour Party pledging to raise the condition of the people in general.[43]

Hardie's optimism turned out to have been well-placed. At the general elections of 1906 the LRC returned thirty members to the House of Commons, including one who had officially entered the contest as an independent labour candidate. The LRC was helped by an arrangement with the Liberal Party which did not enter candidates in a number of constituencies, meaning that twenty-four of the LRC's thirty were helped in this way. Also elected were a number of Liberal MPs sponsored by the trade unions. The LRC was renamed the Labour Party which supported the Liberal majority on many issues, especially after the Liberals helped reverse the Taff Vale judgement by means of the Trade Disputes Act that year.[44]

By this time the Webbs had warmed to the Labour Party and, moreover, become powerful voices within. A factor which began to influence the party's approach in this period was Beatrice Webb's argument in her minority poor law report of 1909 that relief of destitution should require those who were able to do so to seek work or training.[45] This communitarian socialist vision, with its emphasis on national efficiency and the expectation of individuals to benefit from their responsibility to contribute by means of labour, envisaged a level of social unity that was soon overtaken by events. If socialists and trade unionists thought the reversal of the Taff Vale decision had put the labour movement in a strong position, a legal judgement of 1909 brought them firmly down to earth. This was the Osborne decision. The case was brought to court by Walter Osborne who was not only a branch secretary of the ASRS but also a Liberal Party supporter. Osborne opposed both his union's political levy and what he considered to be the socialism of the Labour Party. The decision disallowed the levy which funded the organisational and electoral efforts of the party. This persuaded many that the party needed the full support of trade unionists and socialists to defend working-class interests. Two years later, Webb wrote a substantial article on the consequences of the Osborne decision in which he insisted that trade unions could not avoid political involvement given the effects of legislation on their members.[46] The decision was overturned by the Trade Union Act of 1913 but, as will be discussed below, this reversal was conditional.

The year before Webb's article on the Osborne decision, fearful that trade union unrest would lead to increased support for the ailing SDF, MacDonald wrote an article attacking Hyndman and his party for being outdated in terms of what British workers wanted.[47] The unrest which MacDonald feared materialised the following year as a period began, only brought to a close by the beginning of the world war in 1914, in which dissatisfaction with parliamentary politics grew.[48] The unrest was not simply in response to pay, conditions or other traditional trade union issues, but also more broadly the role of the state, the loss of confidence in parliamentary politics, equality and distributive justice in society.[49]

One result of the unrest was negative in terms of gains for the labour movement, in that the reversal of the Osborne decision in the Trade Union Act 1913 was limited. Although the reversal restored the legitimacy of trade union funding of a political party, members would thereafter be able to opt out of paying into a political fund that the unions were required to have for the purpose of parliamentary funding. Unions would each ballot all their members on whether to have the fund, allowing those who objected to the levy to opt-out. One reason for the limitation was that the unrest had hardened the attitude of the employers' organisations, which began to put pressure on the government to repeal the Trade Disputes Act of 1906. Fearful that this pressure would prevail, the Labour leaders accepted the compromise. Another reason for taking this approach was that many union leaders were losing interest in reversing the Osborne decision, as their minds were on the unrest which seemed far more urgent.[50]

If cautious regarding trade union rights, the Labour Party was equally indecisive and still more divided regarding the position of women in society and politics. It was not until 1912 that the party committed itself to reject any bill to extend the suffrage which did not include a specific assurance that this would include women's suffrage on the same basis as that of men.[51] That this had not been decided earlier reflected a more general disinterest in, and even disrespect for, the rights and demands of women in the socialist and labour movement of the late nineteenth and early twentieth centuries.[52] The fear of appearing too radical, which would frustrate the British left throughout the twentieth century, had already begun to shape Labour policy.[53]

The turbulent period which began around 1910 was interrupted by the outbreak of war in 1914, when the unrest petered out as millions of workers went to fight. Although war had been dreaded by some on the British left, it had not been a prominent theme among socialists in the country. This perhaps reflects a more general lack of international perspective in many of the writings in this volume, and even in some cases ignorance regarding non-British people. Even the more cosmopolitan-minded ILP member Henry Noel Brailsford had until the outbreak in 1914 considered full-scale war between the major powers unlikely now that international capitalism could exploit around the world, firms gaining and importantly maintaining investment projects in part by having their states' advanced armaments to support and defend projects without actual fighting. When war did begin, however, he conceded that he had underestimated the possibility of armed peace turning into actual conflict, but defended his main argument in which he criticised the role of the state in supporting capitalist investment.[54] In the years leading to the outbreak of war in 1914 some, especially among the pacifist ILP, campaigned against conscription should war begin, and warned that planning to maintain peace needed to be taken far more seriously. Although the case against conscription was not universal on the British left, MacDonald and Philip Snowden maintained the anti-conscriptionist stance during the war.[55]

At the end of the war in 1918 the broader political issues once again began to emerge in debate, not least because workers were now aware of a revolutionary uprising in Russia. However, in part because of the fear of revolutionary action far better-organised than that of the pre-war unrest, the major political parties, including Labour, encouraged citizens to take a milder approach to politics.[56] The links between the Fabian Society and Labour Party in the development of British social democracy led to the important moment when in 1918 the Labour Party leader Arthur Henderson and Sidney Webb wrote a new report on reconstruction of the party which criticised capitalism and distanced Labour from the conservative and

10

liberal parties.[57] This criticism would, however, be conducted from within parliamentary politics.

Later that year Henderson and Webb wrote a new constitution for the party which, as Webb (1918) declared in a pamphlet, for the first time had distinctly socialist objectives. Webb declared that the constitution included the following objective:

> to secure for the producers, by hand or by brain, the full fruits of their industry and the most equitable distribution thereof that may be possible upon the basis of the common ownership of the means of production, and the best obtainable system of popular administration and control of each industry or service.[58]

This, of course, was the famous Clause IV that survived until the 1990s. In 1918, moreover, he and Beatrice Webb published a pamphlet on the principles of the party, outlining its socialism in terms of common ownership, equality and devolved governance rather than centralisation.[59] The Webbs and Henderson thus contributed to a distinctive British socialist tradition of the twentieth century based on Clause IV. The major theorists of the tradition such as R.H. Tawney, Harold Laski, and G.D.H. Cole offered more sophisticated political philosophy than one finds in the works of those on the left who were prominent and influential in the thirty-five years before the First World War.[60] Nevertheless, the British socialist tradition in practice has not lived up to the promise of either Clause IV or the work of the theorists. As Gregory Elliott suggested shortly before the original Clause was abandoned for one far less ambitious in 1995, the Labour Party has never really been genuinely socialist. Acknowledging that he was adopting the critique of the party pioneered in the 1960s by Ralph Miliband which still applied three decades later, Elliott insisted that Clause IV had bred an illusion that the party was committed to the goal of socialism. As the critique suggested, the party was labourist rather than socialist, being committed to parliamentary election in order to implement social and economic reform that would ameliorate capitalism. Socialists within the party were in a minority.[61] Of course, this was a thesis that depended on a particular interpretation of socialism. Tony Blair who abandoned the old Clause IV and led a very moderate Labour government from 1997 to 2007 (followed immediately after his resignation by another moderate one by Gordon Brown until 2010) argued that his amelioration of capitalism was itself a form of socialism – or social-ism as he put it.[62]

Whether Blair was a socialist in his own way is subject to debate, and the same goes for the pre-Clause IV work of the Webbs, Shaw, Wells, Besant and others, whom nobody could credibly accuse of being incapable of sophistication, albeit in a very different way than Tawney, Cole and Laski. However, with exceptions such as one finds in some of Snowden's work, their political writings were experimental in a practical rather than philosophical sense, both instigating and responding to fast-moving political and social events. It is, in part, this that makes the sources to be found in the present volume so fascinating.

INTRODUCTION

Notes

1 Jon Lawrence, 1992. "Popular Radicalism and the Socialist Revival in Britain". *Journal of British Studies* 31 (2): 182.
2 Nicholas Thoburn, 2016. *Anti-Book: On the Art and Politics of Radical Publishing.* Minneapolis: University of Minnesota Press, 61–62, 97–101.
3 Edward R. Pease, 1916. *The History of the Fabian Society.* New York: E.P. Dutton and Company, 97.
4 Annie Besant, 1886. "Why I am a Socialist". *Our Corner* (September): 161.
5 Fabian Society, 1884. *A Manifesto*, Fabian Tracts No. 2. London: Geo Standring.
6 Pease, *History*, 273.
7 David G. Ritchie, 1891. *Principles of State Interference.* London: Swan Sonnenschein & Co, 151.
8 John Callaghan, 1990. *Socialism in Britain Since 1884.* Oxford: Basil Blackwell, 3–9.
9 Max Beer, 1929. *A History of British Socialism*, Volume II. London: G. Bell and Sons, 274–275.
10 Kevin Manton, 2003. "The Fellowship of the New Life: English Ethical Socialism Reconsidered". *History of Political Thought* 24 (2): 282.
11 Mark Bevir, 1996. "Fabianism, Permeation and Independent Labour". *Historical Journal* 39 (1): 179–196; Bevir, 2011. *The Making of British Socialism.* Princeton N.J.: Princeton University Press, 195–214.
12 Sidney Webb, 1891. "The Difficulties of Individualism". *The Economic Journal* 1 (2): 380.
13 Sidney Webb, 1896. *The Difficulties of Individualism.* London: Fabian Society, 18.
14 Hubert Bland, 1889. "The Outlook". In *Fabian Essays in Socialism*, edited by George Bernard Shaw, 217. London: Fabian Society.
15 Sidney Webb, 1931. "Introduction to the 1920 edition". In *Fabian Essays in Socialism*, edited by George Bernard Shaw, xxx. London: Fabian Society and George Allen and Unwin.
16 H. Russell Smart, 1893. *The Independent Labour Party, Its Programme and Policy.* Manchester: Labour Press Society Ltd, 1.
17 Smart, *Independent Labour Party*, 6–13.
18 Independent Labour Party, 1894. "To the Workers of Great Britain and Ireland, Greeting". *Economic Journal* 4 (14): 369.
19 J. Keir Hardie, "Introductory Letter" in Smart, *Independent Labour Party*, 2.
20 "To the Workers of Great Britain and Ireland".
21 "To the Workers of Great Britain and Ireland".
22 J. Keir Hardie and J.R. MacDonald, 1899. "The Liberal Collapse, III: The Independent Labour Party's Programme". *The Nineteenth Century: A Monthly Review* 45: 25.
23 Margaret Bondfield, 1899. "Conditions Under which Shop Assistants Work". *Economic Journal* 9: 286.
24 David Howell, 1980. *British Social Democracy: A Study in Development and Decay.* London: Croom Helm, 26–27.
25 Lewis Minkin, 1978. *The Labour Party Conference: A Study in the Politics of Intra-Party Democracy.* London: Allen Lane, 3.
26 Sidney Webb, 1901. *Twentieth Century Politics: A Policy of National Efficiency.* London: Fabian Society, 7.
27 Webb, *Twentieth Century Politics*, 3–4.
28 Henry Pelling, 1976. *A History of British Trade Unionism*, 3rd edition. Harmondsworth: Penguin, 123–124
29 Donald Sassoon, 2014 edn. *One Hundred Years of Socialism: The West European Left in the Twentieth Century.* London: I.B. Tauris, 17–18.

INTRODUCTION

30 J. Ramsay MacDonald, 1904. "The International Socialist Congress". *The Speaker*, 77 (August): 490–491.
31 Keith Laybourn, 1994. "The Failure of Socialist Unity in Britain c. 1893–1914". *Transactions of the Royal Historical Society* 4: 153–175.
32 H.G. Wells, 1906. "Socialism and the Middle Classes". *Fortnightly Review* (November): 786.
33 Graham Johnson, 2000. "Making Reform the Instrument of Revolution: British Social Democracy, 1881–1911". *Historical Journal* 43 (4): 977–1002.
34 Michael J. Klarman, 1989. "The Judges Versus the Unions: The Development of British Labor Law, 1867–1913". *Virginia Law Review* 75 (8): 1487–1521.
35 Klarman, "The Judges Versus the Unions", 1516–1521.
36 E. Dana Durand, 1902. "The British Trade Union Congress of 1902". *The Quarterly Journal of Economics* 17 (1): 183–184.
37 Durand, "The British Trade Union Congress", 184.
38 Klarman, "The Judges Versus the Unions", 1578.
39 J. Keir Hardie, 1903. "Federated Labor as a New Factor in British Politics". *The North American Review* 177 (561): 233, 240–241.
40 Hardie, "Federated Labor", 236.
41 Frank Bealey, 1956. "The Electoral Arrangement Between the Labour Representation Committee and the Liberal Party". *The Journal of Modern History* 28 (4): 372; Martin Pugh, 1988. "Popular Conservatism in Britain: Continuity and Change, 1880–1987". *Journal of British Studies*, 27 (3): 271, 273, 278.
42 David Thackeray, 2011. "Rethinking the Edwardian Crisis of Conservatism". *The Historical Journal* 54 (1): 195; Martin Pugh, 2002. "The Rise of Labour and the Political Culture of Conservatism, 1890–1945". *History* 87 (288): 517.
43 Hardie, "Federated Labor", 238.
44 Bealey, "The Electoral Arrangement".
45 Ben Jackson, 2007. *Equality and the British Left: A Study in Progressive Political Thought, 1900–64*. Manchester: Manchester University Press, 45–46.
46 Sidney Webb, 1911. "The Osborne Revolution". *The English Review* (January): 380–393.
47 J. Ramsay MacDonald, 1910. "The Trade Union Unrest". *English Review* (November): 728–739.
48 Keith Middlemas, 1970. *Politics in Industrial Society: The Experience of the British System Since 1911*. London: André Deutsch, 51–67.
49 James Thompson, 2014. "The Great Labour Unrest and Political Thought in Britain, 1911–1914". *Labour History Review* 79 (1): 37–54.
50 Michael J. Klarman, 1989. "Parliamentary Reversal of the Osborne Judgement". *Historical Journal* 32 (4): 922–923.
51 Caroline Rowan, 1982. "Women in the Labour Party, 1906–1920". *Feminist Review* 12: 78–79.
52 Mary Davis, 2009. *Comrade or Brother? A History of the British Labour Movement*. London: Pluto Press, 136–140.
53 Ralph Miliband, 1972 edn. *Parliamentary Democracy: A Study in the Politics of Labour*. London: Merlin Press, 36–38.
54 Peter Lamb, 2011. "Henry Noel Brailsford's Radical International Relations Theory". *International Relations* 25 (4): 479–498; Peter Lamb, 2017. "Henry Noel Brailsford: Neglected Cosmopolitan". *International Politics* 54 (1): 104–117.
55 Kevin Morgan, 2009. "Militarism and Anti-Militarism: Socialists, Communists and Conscription in France and Britain 1900–1940". *Past and Present* 202: 218–229.
56 Lawrence, "Popular Radicalism".
57 *Labour and the New Social Order: A Report on Reconstruction*. London: Labour Party, 1918, 5.

INTRODUCTION

58 Sidney Webb, 1918. *The New Constitution of the Labour Party*. London: Labour Party, 3.
59 Sidney and Beatrice Webb, 1918. *The Principles of the Labour Party*. London: Labour Party.
60 Matt Beech and Kevin Hickson, 2007. *Labour's Thinkers: The Intellectual Roots of Labour from Tawney to Gordon Brown*. London: Tauris, 9.
61 Gregory Elliott, 1993. *Labourism and the English Genius: The Strange Death of Labour England?* London: Verso, xi.
62 T. Blair, 1994. *Socialism*. London: Fabian Society, 4; for a discussion see Peter Lamb, 2019. *Socialism*. Cambridge: Polity Press, 5–6.

Part 1

WORK AS IT WAS AND HOW IT MIGHT BE

1

LAND LESSONS FOR TOWN FOLK (LONDON: CLARION, 1896), 1–12.

William Jameson

[William Jameson's pamphlet *Land Lessons for Town Folk* of 1896 contributed to a debate within the British left on land reform (Tichelar, 1997). An intellectual campaigner for a radical form of land nationalisation and the prevention of famine, Jameson (1896) offered idiosyncratic support for Clarion socialism. Formed in 1891 by Robert Blatchford, the *Clarion* newspaper and pamphlets presented socialism in ethical terms, employing religious ideas and terminology. The *Clarion* opposed liberalism, avoided Marxism, presented cooperation and healthy recreation in the countryside as natural features of humanity, but also voiced Blatchford's militarism, nationalism and crude antisemitism in some articles (Callaghan, 1990: 53–58; Prynn, 1976: 65–67 and 75). The Clarion movement was based and predominantly active in the North and North Midlands. There were some members in the South-East, upon which Jameson's pamphlet focused. Unlike the more chauvinistic Clarion writers, Jameson stressed that his belief in brotherhood did not distinguish between race, creed, sex, caste or colour.

In *Land Lessons for Town Folk* Jameson recommended the reduction of London's population to help ease poor living conditions and the better, socialistic, use of the countryside. Small groups of socialists would move to the countryside to take control, initially drawing on the Local Government Allotments Act of 1894, of production in areas of land linked to villages. Villagers would see that they could improve their lives by working with the socialists as members of their settlements.

Jameson's preference for small-scale agricultural communities was shared by the Independent Labour Party (ILP) while the Social Democratic Federation (SDF) advocated large-scale control of agriculture and ownership of the agricultural means of production (Tichelar, 1997: 131–133). In this pamphlet Jameson criticised the SDF for focusing on owning and controlling the instruments of production, thus neglecting the more basic and important issue of controlling the means of life with which such instruments worked. For Jameson, the most hopeful sign of the times came from the scout crusade of bicyclists, by which he meant the Clarion scouts who had begun to travel by bicycle to the countryside, selling socialist literature and holding open-air meetings and lectures in the villages

(Prynn, 1976: 67–69). Jameson was keen to declare himself a Londoner several times in the pamphlet, thus promoting the cause of the Clarion movement beyond its northern heartlands.]

(1)   "Why Should London Grow?"
(2)   "Guardian Angels."
(3)   "Cockneyfied Socialism."

WHY SHOULD LONDON GROW?

I hold strongly to the view that a solution of the rural Labour problem will help materially to solve the Labour problem in towns. Indeed, I look upon each step taken towards the industrial reorganisation of the village as a step towards easing the condition of the over-crowded workshop. But a line must be drawn at London, which is far and away the biggest workshop in the world. It is so vast, in fact, and its people are so closely wedged together, that attractive forces exercised by a reorganised rural industry upon the workers in an ordinary town would not be strong enough in themselves to pull many people out of London. Or, to state the case in another fashion, getting away from the industries of an average town into country industries may be compared to crossing a river—if a man cannot swim, he can easily be ferried across by people from the country side of it who know him. On the other hand, getting out of London is like crossing the ocean; crossing to reach an unknown shore! Therefore, an exodus of Londoners, in sufficient numbers to tell, effectually and lastingly, upon the condition of those who remain behind, must necessarily be organised from within the Metropolis.

But, stop. I see I am almost taking it for granted that London workers are likely to desire a change of situation. Unhappily, such is far from being the case at present. Our leaders here are very hot upon the question of taxing ground rents, and appropriating unearned increment. This is their *minimum* demand. Their *maximum* is, to socialise our Cockney institutions all round! Compared with men of equal thought and earnestness outside the huge city, the "advanced" people in London are careless to indifference about their birthright in the soil of the country. They seem to think that it is only necessary somehow or other to give the Capitalist "the dirty kick-out" to make London an industrial paradise—the envy of the civilised world!

Now, I entirely challenge this view of the case. And in asking the question "Why should London grow?" I am merely expressing, in a roundabout way, my most earnest belief that, not only should London cease growing, but that, in order to become an industrial paradise—or a paradise of any kind, its population, within its present area, ought to be diminished by just a million or two. As I want to justify this belief of mine to practical men, I shall, without apology, give a few dry facts and statistics straight away.

SIZE AND POPULATION.

Greater London, which is the area controlled by the Metropolitan Police, comprises 441,587 acres, or about 690 square miles. Within its limits dwell a population of six million souls, which is pretty nearly a sixth part of the entire population of the United Kingdom. But I do not intend to say much about this Greater London, for it is not a unity, such as is the area governed by the London County Council. In a sense, there are countrified spots here and there within its boundaries. Bricks and mortar do not in all directions extend from centre (say, the General Post Office) to circumference. Still, eastward, bricks and mortar do thus practically extend; for at Stratford Greater London swells out into the municipality of West Ham—tenth in size of the big towns in the United Kingdom, and continues in at least one direction with an almost unbroken line of buildings as far as Ilford. Here, I am personally thankful to say—for I live in the place—you get to the country at last. And between this and the westward limit of our bricks and mortar line, which is somewhere about Putney, lies a space of at least twenty-two miles! South and north Greater London stretches itself to almost the same degree.

But Lesser London is what I want to talk about now. This is very much smaller in area than the former (74,672 acres; roughly, 120 square miles). Within this region, however, exist—it were a mockery to say live—three-fourths of the entire number of those who have to yield to the sway of the Metropolitan Police. Packed within these limits are the *four and a half millions*[1] whose health is, or ought to be, the first consideration of the London County Council. And here I would remark that although, as a Londoner born (thank heavens, I have no London blood in me!) I am duly grateful to the above body for that thousand acres of green space which they have given to us all during their rule; this addition only brings the *total area* of our parks and play lands up to 3,656 acres—about a mile and a quarter of the article per million of population. Such are the boasted "lungs of London"!

Now let us, for a moment, compare London's enormous population with others. To begin with, the population of all Lancashire is *less* by about a quarter of a million, and Lancashire can claim a population nearly equal to that of all Scotland! Ireland's population, which has been steadily diminishing for years past, just about matches London's at this present period; while the population of entire Wales is *less* by nearly three-fifths. "Neglected" Cockneys are entitled to note

WORK AS IT WAS AND HOW IT MIGHT BE

these facts, in view of current complaints about "neglected nationalities." For, as I shall endeavour to show presently, Cockneys are a sort of nation, a peculiar people, with the brand of death marked upon their foreheads.

Finally, the total population of the next ten largest towns in the United Kingdom is less than that of Lesser London. And if we add together the population of every single town in the three kingdoms containing 100,000 inhabitants or more, this total is only from a half to three-quarters of a million bigger than that of the district embraced by the widespreading arms of the Metropolitan Police.

Now, are these facts to exult over? Proud patriots generally have not hitherto bothered their heads about them, although the question of London is, as I shall endeavour to point out, supremely a question of maintaining the Empire. Proud County Councillors—Progressive or otherwise—do I fancy, in their secret hearts rejoice to have a share in the management of such an enormous concern; "Nothing like it for size, in the wide world, you know!" Am I wronging them to say that their municipal ideal at this point reminds me of an old sketch in *Punch?* A self-made man wants an eminent artist to paint a picture for him. The artist is to fix his own price, but the price is to be reckoned by the square feet of canvas covered. On these conditions he can paint a picture as big as he likes—in fact, a quantity of picture suited to the importance of his customer. Ah! who of those who sit in council at Spring Gardens prefer quality to quantity? A smaller but artistic London (I am not now speaking of area but of population) in place of the present enormous daub? "No," I fancy they will one and all say; "keep it big, only do let us try to make it better." Better! Another park or two? A few more lunatic asylums?

CONDITIONS.

We will now study some of the conditions of metropolitan life, just to see what sort of "bettering" is possible.

It is a well-accepted fact that twelve hundred and fifty thousand of London's industrial population earn less than 21 shillings per week. And, what a hideous mockery this pittance really is may be seen in the light of a statement made some years ago by a School Board inspector, Mr. Marchant Williams, viz., that *88 per cent.* of London poor pay more than *one-fifth* of their income in rent! And for what sort of shelter do they pay this proportion? Alderman Fleming Williams has told us—and he, if I mistake not, has been Chairman of the Council's Housing Committee—that 828,941 people live in London in a state of overcrowding. Light is thrown on this statement by another which I have among my notes; that 386,973 Londoners live in single-room tenements. Yes, the head of a family, so situated, pays four shillings, or more, out of every twenty he earns, for the right to live in what can be little better than a piggery.

I pass on to think of his children. It seems to me not an unfair estimate to suppose that out of the eight hundred and odd thousand who live under overcrowded conditions, at least *five* hundred thousand are children. That is to say, two-thirds of the children in London Board schools go home to live as here described. Now, no less an authority than Mr. John Morley told us some years ago that 40,000 children went to Board schools in a condition of starvation, and Mr. Sidney Webb has put the same fact in a different way when he speaks of thirty thousand children going to school breakfastless. Evidently, then, only a minority, a considerable minority, of the poor darlings who sleep in overcrowded rooms, suffer the inconvenience of chronic hunger as well. This is something to be thankful for! Still, starving or not starving, here we have in our midst a population of children equal to the entire population of Birmingham, who are sheltered in a fashion which every person possessed of sound moral instincts most utterly condemn. We talk about

The fresh heart of a simple child.

What sort of freshness, what sort of simplicity can exist amid circumstances such as these?

To conclude this list of the horrors of London life, I may casually mention that there were in 1894 sixty-six thousand indoor paupers—more than the total number for the rest of England and of Wales. Also, that according to a recent census made by the County Council, we have 22,000 "dossers" in our midst—persons who have no registered address, and are too proud to find a night's lodging in the workhouse so long as they have fourpence or a little more in their pockets.

Then London has 8,000 epileptics among its people. How many inhabitants are contained by the *five* lunatic asylums governed by our Council I am unable to say. But evidently there is some slight overcrowding even here, for the Council is busy now in providing London with another lunatic asylum, although the vast establishment at Claybury was opened only three or four years ago.

Nor can I say definitely what is the *cost* of London's lunacy, since both the Council and Boards of Guardians contribute to the amount. However, it will be useful at this point to put in the fact that our London poor-rate is a trifle of five millions sterling annually. Such are a few of the conditions under which Londoners *live*. The manner of their death I leave to the imagination of my readers, after giving just one item of documentary evidence. The Registrar-General for London reported in 1888 that twenty-two and a half per cent. of the total deaths in London took place in workhouses, hospitals, &c. Is it unreasonable to assume that now—eight years later, with such evidence as I have given, of increasing misery and destitution—is it unreasonable to assume that *one out of every four* of those who die in London die thus?

CONSEQUENCES.

Before studying the consequences of the present state of social life in London I have just one more statistical fact to set forth. Dr. Alfred Russel Wallace, in his presidential address to the members of the Land Nationalisation Society in 1885, stated, as the result of carefully examining the census returns for 1871-81, that there was a "total of nearly *two millions of people* who, in ten years only, had been forced by the struggle for existence to leave the country for the towns." For the purposes of this article I have studied the census returns for 1881-91, and have come to the conclusion that, at the very lowest, *twelve hundred thousand people* have been similarly forced into the towns during this later period. A superficial glance at the returns might suggest that as many migrated during the later decade as during the earlier one, for the general conditions were unchanged. But I have taken into account the fact that there was a relatively smaller population to draw upon, and accordingly have made a liberal allowance for this.

Now, how is the question of growth of London affected by statistics such as these? The answer shall be given in the words of Mr. Charles Booth ("Life and Labour in London").

"London is nourished by the literal consumption of bone and sinew from the country." He further states that Essex is the chief recruiting ground for East London.

In these statements of his, the result of most laborious research, we have a clue to the puzzle of London's *growth,* despite the horrible conditions under which multitudes of its inhabitants crawl despairingly to a pauper's grave. Londoners are *dying out fast;* but "bone and sinew from the country" accumulate in the Metropolis faster still. It is the countrymen who do all the "show business" in metropolitan life. It is the stalwart countrymen who, on every side, are driving the "natives" harder and harder against the wall, in the fierce industrial struggle by which Capital alone thrives and waxeth fat.

Now, I am not "guessing at truth" when I say that Londoners are dying out fast. There is sound medical authority for the assertion. Mr. James Cantlie, F.R.C.S., stated publicly some years ago that:—

> "It is absolutely impossible to find a fourth generation of pure Londoners, the progeny ceasing, partly from want, partly from physical decline and inability of continuance."

How, I ask, is the County Council of London prepared to deal with a statement of this sort? After all, Dr. Cantlie's assertion is but the natural climax to those sad statistics which have been quoted so abundantly earlier in this article. How, then, is the *new* Council going to face the situation? Two years ago one could have respectfully warned our municipal rulers, as patriotic men, against making London *more* attractive, since thereby they were but preparing a grave for the nation. At this moment such a warning appears to me to be needless, for the situation has changed. I am hopeful that Parish Councils will keep the countrymen at home; that, so far as country bone and sinew is concerned, London will "cease to draw." But on this assumption it is self-evident that the Londoners of the future will, to use Bismarck's famous phrase about besieged Paris, "have to stew in their own juice!" If this is the fate before us it doesn't really much matter, so far as I can see, whether we have "Progressive" cooks or are only "Moderately" done. Anyhow, on the face of it, the "Cockney" appears to be doomed to extinction like the mammoth and the cave bear! Unless——

LAND LESSONS FOR TOWN FOLK

Unless the London County Council is resolutely prepared to study the problem "How to grow Londoners."

This growing of Londoners cannot, I most strongly contend, be accomplished by simply carrying out the policy of the last Council to its logical issues. Wonders were done, I freely and gratefully acknowledge, by Sir John Hutton and his colleagues. They socialised the government of the Metropolis with almost bewildering speed. I trust that the pace may be maintained. Yet in the direction in which the most progressive of the Progressives is moving I see nothing that will help us to grow Londoners.

"Not in improved sanitation? Healthier dwellings?" No. There are plenty of villages in England which in these features are worse off than London. Still, somehow or other, the village type of humanity has persisted. Their environment evidently fails to kill them off in three generations. "Not by aiming at a 'subsistence wage' for all sorts and conditions of Londoners?" No. The villagers have been without it ever since the reign of Queen Elizabeth, yet—to be somewhat Irish—they have contrived to subsist.

The cause of the decay of Londoners is not to be found in this or that particular condition, but in their *total environment*. I cannot better express my contention than by quoting the words of a far-seeing man, written nearly fifty years ago. I pray that the new Council will enter them (for instruction) on the minutes of their meeting one of these days:—

> "Is it to be credited that this crowding together of men in houses dovetailed into each other, with everything of Nature—winds, flowers, verdure, the healthy smell of earth—shut out and replaced by a thousand miasms—is it, I say, to be credited that this is the normal condition of beings born with natural cravings for activity and pure air, with an intelligent eye for Nature's manifold picturesquenesses, with bodies requiring to be exercised, no less than heads? The very necessity for drains tells against us. All manure was meant directly to nourish the land it accumulates on—not to pollute our streams and rivers. Cities as they now are, and must probably always be, are abscesses of nature. The soil and terrestrial space are not meant for the rearing of food only, but to be dwelt and moved about on, to be daily enjoyed in all the variety of wholesome sights, sounds, and odours they afford us."

Now, it must not be forgotten that the primary duties of the London County Council are those of a Board of Health. If vitality—continued vitality—be *impossible* for the Londoner born, situated as he is, then the Council ought, as a matter of duty, to vitalise him *elsewhere*. This is a question going far beyond that of providing for the needs of the poor in our midst. It affects every single citizen who cannot, of his own free will, place himself outside of London to become thoroughly and permanently vitalised. In a word, the rulers of London ought, as a matter of duty to their constituents, to establish a claim for the use and enjoyment of the green fields of England. And the Council ought to repress any ambition it may have in the direction of governing the "biggest population in the world," and be content with having two or two and a half millions of Londoners "*in residence,*" so to speak, at any one period, upon the existing area. Then, for the health's sake of those Londoners "in town," all Whitechapel, for example, might be turned into cheerful wilderness.

This, I admit, is a somewhat "large order." I contend, however, that it is eminently practicable. I don't suppose it could be executed in a day; but with the splendid organising faculty some of our councillors are showing, it ought to be accomplished within the next ten years. But how? Simply by establishing *London Colonies* in every English county. These, in order to prevent competition with rural industries as they at present exist, would of necessity be self-contained. They would need to be "insulated," as it were, for industrial purposes. In plain language, they would have to be *socialised* institutions, remaining permanently attached to the "Mother City." The size of such rural colonies is a mere detail. So is the length of years during which Londoners should have a title to remain in them. The power to obtain land for their establishment is the only matter, I fancy, that the County Council need trouble Parliament about. At present, rural land can be obtained for sewage farms and lunatic asylums—purposes of health, in short. For this infinitely more important object of "growing Londoners," surely the Metropolis should have a right of entry upon the national estate?

In conclusion, I don't wish to go beyond my brief, by discussing the rights of the community generally in connection with this "estate." I am, however, as I said at the beginning, London born, and therefore feel that I have a right to speak for my fellow-Cockneys. They are, even if they don't last four generations, a sharp lot. I trust that they are sharp enough to see that along the lines I have indicated they can not only save themselves, but *save the nation.* For what will rural magnates be able to do to resist the Parish Councils Act and its necessary developments, when there is an independent Cockney colony looking on and "taking notes"? Why, the very *example* of a colony' (organised by Mr. Sidney Webb, for example,) will be enough to "bust up the whole show" of landlordism in its immediate neighbourhood!

GUARDIAN ANGELS.

———

"Dirt," remarks a practical philosopher, "is merely matter in the wrong place." Our standing army of paupers represents in the main so much industrial dirt, which may be described as aforesaid. But, regarded as human beings, those who compose this standing army ought to be treated—so the public conscience is beginning to realise—with more kindness and consideration than has hitherto been customary. And the improved method of electing Guardians which is declared in the Local Government Act of 1894, certainly makes it *possible* to recognise the human claims of that waste product of our civilisation, the pauper.

Yet, while there is thus opportunity for the stern Guardian of popular imagination to become translated into a kind of elementary Guardian Angel, the average

Briton, however well disposed, won't stand this sort of thing very long (that is, angelic treatment of the pauper), if it means *addition to the rates*. Therefore, it were well, perhaps, to anticipate the danger of reaction, by endeavouring to arrange for the said angelic treatment on the lowest possible terms.

My object in this article will be to suggest how *a start may be made* in the direction of economical, and, at the same time, humane treatment of the poor by those who now have their guardianship. Indeed, the method which I propose to suggest may very well be urged on the ground of economy alone. Still, provided that those who give effect to it exercise reasonable social wisdom, they can scarcely avoid showing practical kindness to the poverty stricken; while, concurrently, they may save the rates to a very marked degree—thus killing two birds with one stone.

Before going further into this matter, however, let me furnish a few samples of the present cost of pauperism. In Cornwall, dividing the amount collected under poor rate by the number of paupers, we find the cost per head to be £13 per annum; in Somerset it is £14; in Essex £19; in Lancashire £22; while London pays a heavy penalty for its overgrowth in the shape of a cost per head of £37! This is nearly double as much as any other crowded centre of population, and it is well on to three times as much as the average cost in distinctly rural counties.

It will be seen then by these figures, that the crowded areas, and especially London, have a very serious interest in reducing the cost of pauperism. In fact, it would pay London to create a three per cent. stock and allot £1,000 of this stock to each pauper, supposing it could thereby permanently get rid of him. On the other hand, it certainly is against the interest of the rural areas to receive into their midst any portion of the surplus population of towns who are likely to be chargeable upon the rates. But, if a scheme could be devised by which these particular rates would be simultaneously reduced in town and country alike, surely this were occasion enough for all sorts and conditions of Guardian Angels to shout for joy?

Now, I make this modest demand upon Guardians, especially in London. I claim that in the exercise of their calling they should do what is expected of every business man worth his salt—try to anticipate the market. If they do this much, if they recognise it as essential to the proper discharge of their duties, that they should boldly anticipate the pauper market, then the ideas I respectfully submit to them may possibly be turned to permanent account. Not otherwise; not if the pottering policy of the past be adopted by the new type of Guardian, however greatly it may be characterised by the fresh spirit of kindliness. With this proviso, I have no hesitation in saying that Guardians can, out of the powers they are already furnished with by the existing Poor Laws, devise a method that will not simply lessen local charges, but will increase the wealth of the nation.

Now, it is a general direction of these Poor Laws that a person reduced to pauperism should be ultimately chargeable upon the parish of his birth. There are, however, sundry qualifications to this general direction. I took pains to ascertain from a relieving officer what these were before writing this article. He very kindly told me that a person claiming relief in the parish where he resided, must have resided more than a twelvemonth in that parish to have any title whatever. Three years' residence made his claim absolute. Failing this, the custom was to pass him on from parish to parish until he reached the parish in which he was born. It is evident that this practice, so far as it relates to destitute persons who, when earning a living, do not settle for long in any particular spot (and trade statistics will show that there are thousands of workers, usually earning fair wages, who are thus conditioned), it is evident that this is calculated to bear rather severely upon the rates of the birth parish. On the other hand it is very hard on London, for example, that a man attracted to this great labour mart from rural districts should, if able to make a struggle for a livelihood that lasts three short years, become a liability upon metropolitan ratepayers for the rest of his days. There is, consequently, a perpetual conflict of interests between town and country unions.

I suggest that peace can be restored, that "industrial dirt" can become useful "industrial matter" in the following way. And as a concrete illustration will, perhaps, make my meaning clear, I will suppose the case of two warring Unions, Romford and Hackney. Let Hackney, in view of next winter's destitution, invite Romford to hire land whereon to plant able-bodied men, *born within the Romford Union,* who happen to cast themselves upon the Hackney rates. The metropolitan Union would, it seems to me, be making a good bargain if it paid, by way of consideration for this transfer of industrial dirt, the whole cost of cottage building, and also make a small grant of capital (of course, through the hands of the rural Union) for every able-bodied pauper whom it thus got rid of. On the other hand, Romford would show a profit by "the deal" in two ways. First, it would add to its own stock of ratepayers; *e.g.,* a farm of one hundred acres cut up into twenty small holdings, with an inhabited cottage on each, would be worth more to the rates than before. Secondly, it would be checking at the fountain head, *i.e.,* London, that inevitable stream of pauperism that nowadays flows towards Romford as the "birth parish." Apply this method of exchange to every Union in London, or other crowded centre, and every Union in rural England, and possibly, before long, those Guardian Angels would be the only persons left who had "got no work to do."

Here I can bring in with effect those remarks of mine about anticipating the pauper market. Urban Guardians, once they had established friendly in place of hostile relations with their rural *confrères,* might do well to offer the facilities of this transfer to working men of country origin who were unemployed, but had hitherto kept their heads above the pauper level. Or they might cast an eye over the "out-of-work" list of the various trade unions. All this kind of thing could, I contend, be done on strictly business lines, with this main object in view, *of saving the rates,* by Guardians with a dash of the angel in them.

COCKNEYFIED SOCIALISM.

"THE Socialised Administration of Slum Property" does not strike one as an attractive theme. Nor does "Philosophical Anarchy for Footmen" seem a better one. Yet, a recent experience of mine, when lecturing to some members of the S.D.F. on the very practical subject of "London's Interest in the Land Question," inclines me to think that a vehement discourse on superfluities, such as "Slums" and "Footmen," will please some sort of advanced people a great deal more than a sober statement of facts concerning one of the prime necessaries of existence, namely, Mother Earth. For my audience, although they gave me a very hearty reception, did not seem at all to realise that the control of the land was a matter of first importance.

Nationalisation of railways and of the instruments of production, was the chief interest in their view. This strikes me as equivalent to saying that the control of a parish pump is more important than the control of the spring that supplies it. Or, to use an illustration that may appeal more directly to the town dweller, my friends, the Social Democrats who criticised me, were really in the position of those who would ask for London's water pipes to be under municipal control, without first making sure of the water supply itself.

It ought to be obvious to anyone who reflects, that pumps, water pipes, railways, and other instruments of production, are, to a large degree, but the *conveniences* of human life; while water and land are absolute necessaries. To attach greater importance to the former than to the latter shows a cockneyfied mind—a mind warped or obscured by unwholesome environment. London is not alone in exhibiting this mental type. All great cities tend to cockneyfy. Hence our Cockney Socialism.

It, has, I grant, enormous energy and vast aspirations. But these qualities show themselves too often in relation to things of a purely ephemeral character—the products of a civilisation that is rooted in injustice, and sustained only by fraud. The injustice shows itself in the denial of an elementary human right—*i.e.,* the personal use of land, to nearly every resident in the British Islands; and the fraud is seen in the consequent spoliation of Labour wherever it is exercised—either in husbandry or manufactures. Remedy that injustice, and the fraud becomes impossible; unless working men are such fools as to voluntarily submit to robbery. On the other hand, I see no hindrance to the fraud in Socialism of the Cockney sort.

"Oh, you are a mere Land Nationaliser," says the indignant Cockney. "I believe in something more advanced. We ought to nationalise Capital, you know." Then my friend explains away Capital as being those instruments of production already noted; and so we get back into the old rut!

Well, I'll just put in my confession of social faith at once, so as to avoid misunderstanding. I, too, believe in something more advanced than Land Nationalisation. I believe in Brotherhood; in "Brotherhood of Humanity, without distinction of race, creed, sex, caste, or colour." This involves Socialism of a far more sweeping character than the town-made article, since it necessarily involves the destruction of that Capital which is Labour's enemy. For the "instruments of production" are not, I contend, the "Capital" in question; they are, after all, simply *land moulded into convenient forms by human labour*. [In this definition of land, minerals and wood are, of course, included.] And the forms thus moulded—railways, factories,

27

houses, machinery, tools, &c.—are constantly wearing away: so that fresh human labour is needed to repair or replace them.

What, then, is the Capital that I wish to see destroyed?

It consists merely of a variety of *claims* upon Labour. And the sole reason why these claims can be enforced is that Labour is shut out from the direct use of land. Now, I say without the slightest hesitation, that were land monopoly abolished to-morrow, this claim-capital (which is really the main part of capital of the money market and banking houses) would all disappear within a twelvemonth. The claimants, *i.e.,* capitalists, would not be able to make good their claims upon Labour, for the very plain reason that Labour would no longer be compelled, by the *dread of starvation,* to yield up any part of its earnings.

The capitalist, so far as he is now the superintendent of the labour he controls, would receive an income—the wages of superintendence; but there would be nothing left over in the way of profit or dividend payable to *idleness*—Labour would absorb it all.

Now, personally, I should not like to see land monopoly destroyed at a single stroke. For one reason, that I should not care, on the grounds of brotherhood, to have those capitalists suddenly paid in the coin they have been paying Labour. I want them to be treated with such wise consideration as will induce them to loyally assist in making "Merrie England." Another reason for preferring that the destruction of land monopoly should be gradual is, that the toilers themselves— the wage-earners—would suffer by the shock of sudden change. We need one and all of us to work out our own salvation, social or otherwise.

But where shall we begin the work? In town or country? I say, most earnestly, *in the country*. For the sake of the sickly wives and children, if for no other reason, I would urge upon those who have but Cockney ideals of Socialism, to turn their thoughts and their energies towards the green fields of England. Socialise the Parish Councils. Break the moulds of the rural mind.

This means that Socialists themselves should set their faces country wards; should invade the rural districts. I don't for a moment suggest that every man of them should, when he got there, start cabbage growing. But this has to be borne in mind: Once in a given village for a twelve month, the Socialist has a claim to use at least four acres of land. Ten or a dozen Socialists in that village—if they were selected men of a practical sort, could dominate its municipal life; they could, step by step, socialise it industrially. Thus while the farmer and squire were still looking on and wondering what this invasion of new ideas meant, that farmer and squire would get a sharp lesson in the shape of scarce, and therefore dear, labour; for the villagers would throw in their lot with the Socialists. All the rural workers would become "independent"! Independent, not of each other; in fact, leaning more than ever they did upon each other in a fraternal spirit of give and take; but independent of the employer of labour. Consequently, that particular capitalist, the farmer, would not be able to make good his claims upon Labour. To carry on business at all, he would need to make a claim upon the landlord instead; namely, for a considerable reduction in rent and reliable conditions of tenure. Well, just imagine this kind of thing going on in say *ten per cent.* of the rural parishes of England;—it would mean, unless I have altogether mistaken the action of economic laws, the speedy fall of rural rent in all parts of the country.

Simultaneously, there might be an organised exodus of socialistic workers from the big towns. They need not abandon the trades they were brought up to, unless these trades happened to be injurious or unnecessary to a socialised community. No; they would simply carry their town arts and crafts into the country, and for the future exercise these, not competitively, but in accordance with the ideals of the socialised village. And their exodus from the towns would tell *pro rata* upon the capitalists and ground landlords in towns. Gaps in the labour market, and emptied houses, would materially ease the situation for town Socialists in their work of organising urban industry upon fraternal lines.

To me, as one standing apart somewhat from Socialist activities, among the most hopeful signs of the times, is the "Scout" crusade of Bicyclists. I wish God speed to their efforts. They are likely to become the travelling prophets of the new era. They are getting to like the country themselves; they are waking up the villagers to the truths of Socialism. If they only carry their efforts a step farther, and look about for convenient spots whereon to establish Clarion settlements of the sort I have been indicating, they may thereby furnish object-lessons of permanent value to that unhappy Cockney Socialist of mine. In a word, they may start the work of socialistic evolution as opposed to revolution, and thus peacefully and fraternally lead all England to higher levels of life.

WILLIAM JAMESON.

LOCAL GOVERNMENT ACT, 1894, SEC. 10; ALLOTMENTS ACT, 1887, SEC. 2.

The *modus operandi* is for "any six registered parliamentary electors or ratepayers resident" to address the Parish Council in writing, and declare that there is a demand for allotments. If satisfied that the facts are so, the Council has first of all to use its persuasive powers with land-holders to let to it the land required. If persuasion doesn't succeed, then force does the business, *i.e.,* the land can be hired compulsorily for from fourteen to thirty-five years, and (I quote words of the Act) "The Council may let to one person an allotment or allotments exceeding one acre; but, if the land is acquired compulsorily, not exceeding in the whole four acres of pasture, or one acre of arable and three acres of pasture." I frankly admit that there is enough rigmarole in these Acts to make it practically impossible for the timid agricultural labourer to live up to the land privilege they grant him.

Note

1 In making estimates, I have naturally taken into account normal increases in population since the census of 1891.

2

"DEALING WITH THE UNEMPLOYED: A HINT FROM THE PAST", *NINETEENTH CENTURY*, DECEMBER, 1904, 1–14.

J. Keir Hardie

[One of the founders of the Independent Labour Party in 1893 and MP for Merthyr Tydfil since 1900, the year he helped form the Labour Representation Committee (LRC), Keir Hardie wrote "Dealing with the unemployed: A hint from the past" for the journal *Nineteenth Century* in 1904. Having previously been an independent MP for West Ham South between 1892 and 1895, he had become established as a major figure of the British left.

The formation of the LRC as a parliamentary force to represent the British working class is part of the context of Hardie's article, another being the failure of the Liberal Party to live up to developments in British liberal ideology in the late nineteenth century. The new liberal theory held that the *laissez-faire* approach championed by the ideology earlier in the century had legitimated conditions which made the liberal goals of individual self-realisation and self-development unattainable for most people. Government intervention, new liberals such as T.H. Green argued, was necessary for individuals to have the opportunity to flourish.

Hardie (1904) named John Morley as a Liberal politician who did not feel obliged to relieve the condition of the unemployed. Morley had in the 1880s opposed regulation, while the classical liberal Herbert Spencer described the same processes as restriction (Barker 1997, 15–16). In 1892 Morley declared that he would rather not govern than regulate working hours (Greenleaf 1983, 84). In his article Hardie acknowledged the efforts of the existing Liberal government to provide relief for the unemployed.

For Hardie, genuinely helpful relief, while very welcome, did not deal with the underlying problem of unemployment. The state had usually disregarded its responsibility to ensure authorities have the means of finding decently paid, permanent work for the capable. A proper Department of Labour was needed with funding to create public works and labour bureaus to arrange necessary work such as reclamation of wastelands, protecting coasts and building harbours. A geographical network of bureaus would, preferably, be managed by the working classes themselves to alert the willing, able and needy to suitable opportunities around the country. Hardie insisted that unemployment and poverty should not be considered punishable crimes, as was so at the time by means of the poor law.

The broader point of the article appears at the end. The *laissez-faire* doctrine should be abandoned. Poverty, according to Hardie, was a disease. He illustrated the effects of unemployment upon health. For much of the century liberals had considered health the responsibility of individuals, and thus not a concern for public policy funded by taxation (Pearson and Williams 1984, 165). The revised liberal theory had yet to produce significant change in this respect. For Hardie, the possibility of 30 to 40 Labour Party MPs who looked set to emerge from the LRC meant the campaign for the new era of work was imminent.]

WHAT shall we do with the Unemployed? The question is no new one. So familiar was the spectacle of men standing idle in the market-place of Jerusalem 2,000 years ago because no man had hired them that Jesus used it for one of his most striking illustrations. The prophetic books of the Old Testament teem with references to something suspiciously like an unemployed problem as having existed some thousands of years before the coming of Christ, and now, at the beginning of the twentieth century of the Christian era, it is still with us in all its pathetic fulness. Statesmen like the late Lord Salisbury and the Right Hon. John Morley have pictured in moving language the pathos of the lonely figure who, moving in the midst of wealth which his labour has assisted to create, begs in vain for some 'brother of the earth to give him leave to toil.' Strange as it may appear, these men ask nothing more than an opportunity to work for a living. They lack food and clothing and shelter for themselves and their children; they have the skill and the strength and the will to produce all these, but in all our wondrous civilisation no man has yet been found to tell us how capable honest men may be assured of a livelihood in return for their work. Statesmen and municipal councillors are faced from time to time with this strange problem, and many of them, like Mr. Morley, have given up in despair even the attempt to find any solution. They shelter themselves behind the comfortable thought that the matter is not one with which the State can, or should, interfere. Fortunately, this counsel of desolation is beginning to give way before the assaults of men who refuse to be bound by the traditions of a school of thought which served its day, but is now ceasing to be.

During the reign of Henry the Eighth 72,000 sturdy beggars for whom no work could be found were, it is said, hanged, because no one could think of any other method of dealing with them. Deprived of the land from which they had been used to look for their living, thieving and begging were the only methods left them of obtaining food, and as it was no one's affair to find them work the halter was the quickest way of getting rid of them. We have travelled a long way since then in the

WORK AS IT WAS AND HOW IT MIGHT BE

matter of civic responsibility, but many a sturdy knave would still find the halter or its modern equivalent his best friend.

The total number unemployed cannot be accurately given, but that it is very large the numerous agencies and activities now at work to cope with the distress bear only too convincing testimony. Ministers of the Crown do not readily commit themselves to an acknowledgment that something in the nature of a national crisis, due to bad trade, is upon us. This, however, is what Mr. Walter Long, as representing the Government, has done by his sympathetic action in calling into being new machinery for dealing with the distress, and Royalty itself has countenanced his efforts by subscribing to the London fund which Mr. Long has initiated. I estimate the minimum number of unemployed during this month to be 700,000. This figure is reached by deducting from the total number of wage-earners those trades not specially affected by the depression: to wit, agricultural labourers, textile workers, those engaged in the carrying and transit service, miners and domestics. Many of these, particularly colliers, shoemakers, and hatters, are working short time, but not being totally unemployed I leave them out of my calculation. The remainder number roughly ten millions, and of these I reckon an average of 7 per cent. as being out of work from causes for which they are not personally responsible. Allowing for women and children, this will represent over two million persons. The Labour Department of the Board of Trade reports that during November the unemployed in the Unions which pay out-of-work benefit, and which represent mostly the higher-paid, skilled artisan class, averaged 7 per cent., and the proportion in the unskilled trades is always higher than in the skilled. Seven per cent. is thus a very moderate estimate. Some of these, such as painters, are season trades and are always affected during the winter months, but nine-tenths of the total are idle because their trade is slack and not from seasonal causes. It is a very remarkable fact, and one which has not been satisfactorily explained, that the over-sea trade, imports and exports alike, shows a healthy increase for the first eleven months of the year despite the prevailing gloom in the labour market. It has been stated publicly by a writer who poses as an authority on economics that the 7 per cent. reported as unemployed by the 100 biggest trade unions, as published in the *Labour Gazette,* include 'trade unionists incapacitated from all causes, including sickness, accidents, strikes, lock-outs, seasonal influences, drink, &c.' This statement, with the exception of the reference to seasonal causes, is wholly misleading. The 7 per cent. represent only those members of the trade unions who have been dismissed owing to bad trade. Those receiving strike or lock-out pay, or sick or accident benefit, are all classed under separate headings and are shown on the returns distinct and apart from the unemployed. The unemployed are those who, being fit for work, have been discharged for causes for which they were not personally responsible: that is to say, slackness of trade.

In addition to those totally unemployed, as stated above, there are the casually employed, such as dockers and others. Of the latter the over-supply is seldom less than one-third of the effective demand. At the London Docks there are during these months 20,000 workmen always available, whereas the number at work on any one day varies between ten and fifteen thousand. Some skilled trades are affected in much the same way, although in their case it happens that the factory or shop is put on short time, so that although all the workers may be in employment their earnings may be only one-half, or even less than that of their nominal wages. These, however, do not figure in the unemployed returns, although they are no whit better off than those members of a union out of work who receive 12*s*. or 14*s*. per week as out-of-work pay.

To a better understanding of what follows one or two other facts require to be borne in mind. Sir Henry Campbell-Bannerman recently made himself responsible for giving currency to the statement that some twelve millions of people are always on the borderline which separates poverty from starvation. They are in this condition because the wages they receive when fully employed and during a period of prosperous trade will not maintain them in the same standard of physical efficiency as we provide for our paupers. It is this fact which makes it so difficult to tide the masses over a period of bad trade. These people who form 28 per cent. of the working-class population are always at close grips with poverty and have no resources upon which they can fall back when overtaken by sickness, accident, or unemployment. How can they when their wages, even when fully employed, leave no margin for saving, do not, in fact, provide them with a sufficiency of the things needful for a healthy existence? Comforts and luxuries are beyond their reach, or, if indulged in, are purchased at the expense of some of the necessaries of life. They constitute a great reservoir of poverty which on the slightest pressure of bad times overflows into the bog of destitution. Their condition is largely the outcome of the perpetual congestion of the labour market in the lower-paid occupations, a condition which even the drain of 250,000 men for South Africa scarcely appreciably affected. No outline of the unemployed difficulty would be complete which did not take account of this hapless mass of almost unrelieved misery. With them also the question is how to find work which will yield them a decent living. Unless we can reduce the number of those who compete for jobs which will not bring them in even paupers' fare when obtained, there cannot be any hope of ever improving their lot. The inexorable laws of supply and demand operate in the lower strata of society with unbridled ferocity, and it is only by reducing the supply of workers for these lower-grade callings that we can ever hope to improve their condition, either physically or morally. Unless, therefore, we resort to the hanging expedient, we are under the necessity of enlarging the area of employment and absorbing the permanently surplus labour supply which alone is responsible for keeping one-third of the population on the borderland which separates poverty from starvation.

Before proceeding to a consideration of the powers possessed by various Authorities for dealing with the Unemployed and of amendments thereto, I propose briefly to outline the scope of the voluntary agencies for dealing with distress already at work. First in the order of importance come the Trade Unions. In nearly all the Unions of skilled artisans provision is made for out-of-work benefit being paid from the funds. The sum paid weekly to members out of work depends upon the amount of the contribution paid when in work, and varies from 5s. to 15s. per week. As a rule out-of-work benefit is only paid for a limited number of weeks, ranging from twelve to twenty-six, and is intended to tide members over the period which must elapse between the loss of one job and the finding of another. In this connection they are of great value to the members, but fall woefully short of meeting the necessities of the case when a period of trade depression lasting two or three years throws thousands out of employment. So long as out-of-work benefit continues there is a certainty that money for the rent will be forthcoming and the home kept together, but sooner or later the benefit limit expires, and with it the last resource is gone.

This side of the Trade Union movement is a form of insurance against bad trade. For 1903 the sum paid in respect of unemployment, as distinct from strike, lock-out and accident, and sick benefit, by the 100 principal Unions was 504,214*l.*, whilst the total so expended during the past twelve years aggregates 4,200,000*l.* For season trades affected by the weather this form of insurance is most valuable. In France, Belgium, and Switzerland, special grants from public funds are made to Unions of a sum almost equal to that raised by the members for out-of-work pay.

One day this country may also show its appreciation of this form of thrift in like manner. In this same connection membership in a co-operative society is helpful, as usually there is a small accumulation of capital at the credit of a member which may be drawn upon during a time of stress. Soup-kitchens and so-called relief works have hitherto bulked largely in the methods of those who have sought to deal with the problem of poverty resulting from lack of employment, but the experience gained has not been favourable to their continuance, and these methods are now being generally discarded, particularly when dealing with the respectable poor. These resent bitterly being classed with loafers and wastrels, and frequently prefer starvation to relief offered at the cost of their manhood and self-respect. A much more hopeful movement in this direction is the provision of meals for school children, particularly when the arrangements are made directly by the Education Authority, the necessary funds being provided by the charitable. Bradford Corporation carried a resolution to provide the money for the free meals for school children from the city funds, but rescinded it again at a subsequent meeting. In Bradford, Leeds, Manchester, Halifax, and other industrial centres, one or two meals each day are being provided for school children by the Educational Authority, provision being made to supply children with free tickets where the circumstances warrant this being done. In this the school authorities are but following the example set by France and Italy, with this difference, that in these countries the money mostly comes from the corporation funds.

DEALING WITH THE UNEMPLOYED

The Joint Committees which have been formed in London and elsewhere on the initiative of Mr. Walter Long, President of the Local Government Board, are a hopeful and helpful development of the machinery of relief. True the opposition of the City and of some of the wealthier parts of the metropolis has prevented Mr. Long, for the present at least, from carrying out his original intention to confer upon the Committee power to levy a rate, and reduced it to dependence upon voluntary contributions for the carrying through of the schemes which it may undertake, but even with this handicap we may still hope for some good results from its workings. It will at least introduce system and order into the methods of giving relief, and by employing men upon the land for wages weed out the deserving from the loafers.

It will also discourage the overlapping of relief agencies which has been fruitful of so much mischief in the past. Such committees will also, it is to be hoped, give permanency to the machinery for dealing with distress arising from lack of work. The weak spot in all this relief work is that it is dealing with distress due to unemployment, and not with the central point in the problem, which is unemployment itself. It is obvious that the proper solution of the unemployed difficulty lies in keeping men constantly employed. To deal with the unemployed and not with unemployment is to deal with an effect and leave the cause untouched. It cannot be too often repeated that the unemployed question does not consist of giving relief to the destitute, but of finding work for the capable. Spasmodic attempts at relief when the crisis becomes acute, and when despair is beginning to make men desperate, is but a poor substitute for that systematic and carefully thought-out effort which all who have had dealings with the unemployed difficulty know to be necessary to any adequate solution.

In a very real sense, the unemployed problem is always with us, but it is only when it becomes dangerous to the safety of the lieges, or the peace of the realm, that we notice its existence.

To deal effectively with the unemployed two reforms are necessary:

1. The creation of such new machinery as will enable the responsible authorities to act promptly in offering work, not relief, to those thrown out of employment by depression in trade;
2. To open up permanent and remunerative employment for at least one million workers who are at present overcrowding the labour market.

The first of these objects could be secured by the creation of a Department of Labour under a responsible Minister of Industry, who would be charged, *inter alia,* with the duty of making adequate provision for tiding the workers over a period of bad trade. This would entail the preparation, during times of prosperity, of great public works of necessity or utility, such as reclamation of foreshores and waste lands, building harbours and breakwaters, protecting threatened coasts against the encroachments of the sea, and the like. For giving the proper effect to this idea a system of labour bureaus or registries would be indispensable. In

WORK AS IT WAS AND HOW IT MIGHT BE

Germany the bureau system has reached its greatest perfection. There the Labour Registry offices, partly, by the way, under the management of the working classes themselves, are so federated and linked up by means of clearing-houses that unemployed workmen even in remote villages are put in touch with employers in search of workmen, almost irrespective of distance.

Lists showing the numbers of unemployed for each occupation are posted up side by side with lists of vacant situations, and the telephone is freely used for bringing employers and workmen, mutually in need of each other, into touch. The whole of Bavaria, which covers 29,000 square miles and has nearly 6,000,000 inhabitants, is grouped under one system, and in 1903 the Munich registry found situations with private employers for 51,664 applicants, being 65 per cent. of the names on the books. Those familiar with the peddling manner in which labour bureaus are worked in this country, where each one occupies a position of impotent isolation within its own borough or township, will see how much we have to learn from Germany in respect to their proper management. In the case of applicants unable to find employment, the bureau, if properly established, would investigate the case of each applicant for work, and when forwarding him to the nearest public undertaking in operation, would also state his qualifications, so that his services might be turned to profitable account.

Labour colonies, as a means of dealing with the genuine unemployed, are of very doubtful value. That they have their part to play, and a very useful part, I do not dispute; but their value lies chiefly in the fact that they deal with a class of the unemployed who require special treatment. For reclamation purposes, and also as a means of training people to work upon the land, they are in the latter case useful, in the former indispensable; but as a means of dealing with the genuinely unemployed they have not been a success. In a 'Report on Agencies and Methods for Dealing with the Unemployed in certain Foreign Countries' just issued by the Board of Trade, and which is in continuation of a similar report published in 1893, the compiler of the report states, as the result of the fresh investigations, that he confirms the conclusion arrived at in 1893 concerning labour colonies—viz. 'That whatever be the object of these colonies, the great bulk of material with which they deal consists not of efficient workmen out of work, but of tramps, ex-prisoners, and others whose distress is caused by personal defects. They are not colonies of unemployed so much as receptacles for social wreckage.' In Holland, it is reported, the tendency is for these colonies to breed a semi-pauper dependent class deficient in energy and lacking in initiative. Since there are such people in the world, it is doubtless necessary that provision should be made for them; but these do not constitute even an appreciable proportion of the unemployed, and no one wishes to multiply their numbers. In addition to the powers of preparing schemes of public works and organising an efficient system of labour bureaus, our Minister of Industry would be empowered to assist and co-operate with local authorities in carrying out local improvements at a time when they would be of most service.

36

Before outlining my proposals for enlarging the area of permanent and profitable employment, it will be instructive to look at the methods adopted by some of the monarchs who followed bluff King Hal when dealing with the unemployed. This is all the more necessary since what I propose is to revert to their principles, merely adapting them to meet the requirements of these our times. It is a popular and widespread fallacy that no one is responsible for finding work for the able-bodied unemployed. The State in the past not only decreed that work should be found for the willing, and provided the necessary administrative machinery for giving effect to its decree, but actually made failure on the part of the responsible authorities a penal offence, punishable by fine and imprisonment.

The first recorded effort which Parliament made to deal with the unemployed is contained in the Act of 43 Elizabeth, chap. 2, and dated 1601. It forms the foundation upon which the whole superstructure of the Poor Law has been subsequently erected, and leaves no doubt in the mind of the reader as to the intention of the statesmen responsible for its enactment. The helpless poor were to be relieved, and the able-bodied unemployed set to work. Clause I. sets forth the manner in which this was to be accomplished. The clause is of sufficient interest at present to bear being quoted entire:—

> Be it enacted by the authority of this present Parliament, that the church-wardens of every parish, and four, three or two substantial household-ers there, as shall be thought meet, having respect to the proportion and greatness of the same parish and parishes, to be nominated early in Easter week, or within one month after Easter, under the hand and seal of two or more Justices of the Peace in the same county, whereof one to be of the quorum, dwelling in or near the same parish or division where the same parish doth lie, shall be called overseers of the poor of the same parish; and they, or the greater part of them, shall take order from time to time, by and with the consent of two or more such Justices of Peace as is aforesaid, for setting to work the children of all such whose parents shall not, by the said churchwardens and overseers, or the greater part of them, be thought able to keep and maintain their children; and also for setting to work all such persons, married or unmarried, having no means to maintain them, and use no ordinary and daily trade of life to get their living by; and also to raise weekly or otherwise (by taxation of every inhabitant, parson, vicar, and other, and of every occupier of lands, houses, tithes impropriate, propriations of tithes, coal mines, or saleable underwoods in the said parish, in such competent sum and sums of money as they shall think fit) a convenient stock of flax, hemp, wool, thread, iron, and other ware and stuff to set the poor on work; and also competent sums of money for and towards the necessary relief of the lame, impotent, old, blind, and such other among them being poor, and not able to work; and also for putting out of such children to be apprentices, to be gathered out of the same parish, and to do and execute all

WORK AS IT WAS AND HOW IT MIGHT BE

other things, as well for the disposing of the said stock, as otherwise concerning the premises, as to them shall seem convenient . . . upon pain that every one of them absenting themselves without lawful cause as aforesaid from such monthly meeting for the purpose aforesaid, or being negligent in their office or in the execution of the orders aforesaid, being made by and with the assent of the said Justices of Peace or any two of them before mentioned, to forfeit for every such default or absence or negligence twenty shillings.

The italics are not to be looked for in the original Act. It would appear that the Act was being but indifferently administered, as in 1694 'Salisbury, a Secretary of State,' and another, issued a reminder to the Overseers wherein, after reciting their powers under the Act, he concluded, 'if you be found negligent, or shall fail to meet once a month to confer together for the purpose aforesaid, then you are to forfeit 20s. apiece for every month that you shall be found remiss or careless therein. And therefore see that you fail not in these premises at your peril.' Clause II. stipulates that if 'the inhabitants of any parish are not able to levy themselves sufficient sums of money for the purposes aforesaid' the said two Justices of the Peace 'shall and may tax, rate and assess' any parish within the same hundred, and if the hundred was not sufficient they might extend their taxable area, by a resolution passed at Quarter Sessions, to include an entire county. The idea of making the poor rate a national charge is thus no new thing. Mayors and bailiffs of cities and corporations and aldermen of the City of London were endowed with the same power and authority as justices of the peace for the purposes of the Act. I would not have dealt at such length with this old statute but for the fact that it has never been repealed, is still in force, and presumably could be enforced by J.P.'s in counties, and mayors and aldermen in cities and boroughs. The law of England makes it compulsory on the guardians and the other authorities named to provide work for the able-bodied unemployed. On that point there can be no dispute. Sir Henry Fowler, when President of the Local Government Board, replying to a question of mine in the House of Commons (12th of September 1893) said, 'Boards of Guardians have power to purchase or rent land not exceeding 50 acres for any parish, and to open workshops for setting destitute able-bodied poor to work, and to pay such persons reasonable wages for their labours.' I quote this lest anyone should say these powers have either been taken away or lost by disuse. They still exist, and can be made operative.

The next landmark on our voyage of inquiry is the Act 59 Geo. III. chap. 12 (31st of March 1819). After dealing with various matters affecting the administration of the Poor Law, Clause 12 recites the provisions of the Act of Elizabeth and proceeds:

And whereas by the laws now in force sufficient powers are not given to the churchwardens and overseers to keep such persons fully and constantly employed, be it further enacted that it shall be lawful for the churchwardens and overseers of the poor of any parish, with the consent of the inhabitants thereof in vestry assembled, to take into their hands any land or ground which shall belong to such parish, or to the churchwardens and overseers of the poor of such parish, or to the poor thereof, or *to purchase or to hire and take on lease, for and on account of the parish, any suitable portion or portions of land within or near to such parish,* not exceeding twenty acres in the whole, and to employ and set to work in the cultivation of such land, on account of the parish, any such persons as by law they are directed to set to work, and to pay to such of the poor persons so employed *as shall not be supported by the parish* reasonable wages for their work; and the poor persons so employed shall have such and the like remedies for the recovery of their wages, and shall be subject to such and the like punishment for misbehaviour in their employment as other labourers in husbandry are by law entitled and subject to.

The reference to the 'poor persons so employed as *shall not be supported by the parish*' is significant as distinguishing them from paupers, a point to which I shall revert when I come to deal with the question of disfranchisement. Clause 13 of the same Act introduces a new power in dealing with the land. It reads:

Provided, and be it further enacted, that for the promotion of industry amongst the poor, it shall be lawful for the churchwardens and overseers of the poor of any parish, with the consent of the inhabitants in vestry assembled, to let any portion and portions of such parish land aforesaid, or of the land to be so purchased or taken on account of the parish, to any poor and industrious inhabitant of the parish, *to be by him or her occupied and cultivated on his or her own account, and for his or her own benefit* at such reasonable rent and for such term as shall by the inhabitants in vestry be fixed and determined.

The special mention of women in the above clause is notable. Here also, as in Clause 12, it is clearly not pauper relief which is contemplated, but the provision by a public authority of land to be let on the usual terms of hiring to the able-bodied poor out of work.

In 1831 Parliament found time, despite the excitement and turmoil connected with the passing of the Reform Act, to carry still further the provision which had then already been made for providing work on the land, for 'poor and industrious inhabitants.' The twenty acres which the parish might acquire for this purpose under the former Act was extended to fifty acres, and power was also given to enclose (apparently) another fifty acres of common land 'in order to extend the salutary and benevolent purposes' of the Act. Fifty acres of 'forest or waste lands belonging to the Crown' might also be taken for the same purpose. The year following (1832) the overseers of the poor were empowered to take fuel allotments belonging to the poor and let them to be cultivated in portions of 'not less than one fourth of a statute acre,' and not exceeding one acre to one individual, at a fair rent. These were to be allotted to 'such industrious cottagers of good character, being day labourers or journeymen,' as should apply for the same. The holders were 'held bound to cultivate it in such a manner as shall preserve the land in a due state of fertility.' All the powers herein set forth are still possessed by guardians or parish councils, although the Local Government Board claims the right to say how, when, and upon what conditions they may be exercised. How far the Department is justified in this attitude, particularly in those portions relating to setting the unemployed to work, is an open question which has never been put to the test. Nor is there anything to show that the powers conferred upon justices, mayors, and others, for having these portions enforced have ever been either transferred or taken away. The one thing which can be said with certainty is that the unemployed are deprived by the Local Government Board of the very ample protection which the law throws around them.

Sir Henry Fowler, when replying as quoted above, added:—'The law officers further advised that wages so paid would be parochial relief, and would involve the same disfranchisement as other relief under the Poor Laws.' Mr. Walter Long has since, in substance at least, said the same thing. I do not attach much weight to these opinions. Twelve years ago the Local Government Board, backed by the 'law officers of the Crown,' denied that the guardians had any such powers as those quoted above. I admit that the question of disfranchisement in this connection is a moot-point which has never been tested at law. Clause 35 of the Reform Act of 1832 states that no person shall be entitled to be registered (as a voter) who shall have, within twelve calendar months, . . . received parochial relief.' The point of my contention is that work provided at reasonable wages, or allotments let at a fair rent, is not parochial relief. However, it is to be hoped that on an early day Parliament itself will settle the matter by drawing a clear distinction between the dissolute loafer and the willing worker, driven by a hard and cruel necessity to invoke the aid of the Poor Law.

I set out on this incursion to prove my contention that the law of England asserts, by implication at least, the right of every citizen to claim work as a right, and imposes upon the guardians of the poor and the justices of the peace the responsibility, under a penalty for failure, of providing that work. For sixty years the guardians have been administering the Poor Law in such a way as to lead to the conclusion that poverty is a crime to be punished with great severity. Every humane tendency has had to be rigorously repressed, and they have been encouraged to transform the workhouse from a refuge into a penitentiary. So steeped have they and their officials become in this theory, so hardened are they from having to deal constantly with the clever impostors and shiftless wastrels of our social wreckage, that they are totally unfitted for dealing with the case of the decent man out of work. Some new authority is needed for this task, either specially-elected Councils of Industry or some combination of existing authorities fully equipped to deal with the organisation of labour and charged with the responsibility of bringing work within the reach of every applicant. Should this result in the guardians being abolished and the relief of the destitute poor being transferred to some other authority, few will regret the change.

To afforest the waste, and plant a race of yeomen on the fertile land of Britain, would be a profitable task. Not only might our idle surplus population be thereby absorbed in the ranks of the army of industry, but our dependence upon oversea nations for supplies of food and timber very much reduced. And it is to the State we must look for the realisation of this ideal. It alone has the continuity of purpose and the financial resources necessary for such a vast undertaking. This remark applies in a special manner to afforestation, and the success which has been won in India should be an encouragement to even the timid to press forward. Germany, however, affords the best illustration of the value of afforestation. The forests of the German Empire, mostly under public control, cover 55,000,000 acres, maintain a population of 400,000, and yield a yearly revenue of about £18,000,000. Experiments on a small scale made in this country show that wood-growing would be no less profitable if undertaken with intelligence and spirit. In 1885 a Royal Commission considered the question, and in 1902 a departmental committee of the House of Commons was appointed 'to inquire into and report as to the present position and future prospects of Forestry and the planting and management of Woodlands in Great Britain,' &c. This committee reported *inter alia* that 'it is shown on the highest authority that there is in these islands a very large area of waste, heather, and rough pasture or land out of cultivation, amounting in all to 21,000,000 acres, on a large proportion of which afforestation could be profitably undertaken.' Here we have a vast national asset lying unused, which might be turned to good account. The timber supply of the world is giving out, and already prices are rising in consequence. Last year we imported firewood valued in the Board of Trade returns at £23,000,000. But for the almost criminal neglect of our opportunities, every stick of this might have been grown within our own shores, giving healthy occupation to thousands, and yielding ultimately a handsome addition to the nation's income.

Afforestation cannot be safely left to the caprice of individual landlords. Only the very wealthy, who could afford to wait twenty or thirty years for a return upon their investment, would care to put money in wood-growing, and even were the State to advance the money to landlords on easy terms there would not be the same guarantee that the work would be properly done as would be the case if it were being done directly by the Government itself.

The same argument, though not perhaps to the same extent, justifies us in claiming that the creation of a peasant-yeoman class is a duty which should press heavily upon the collective conscience. From every point of view, moral, physical, industrial, and economic, the cultivation of the soil is desirable. Since 1850 the number of people directly employed upon the land has gone down by 1,250,000, whilst the area of land under cultivation grows yearly more circumscribed. To this fact is to be traced largely the increasing difficulty of the military authorities to find recruits of the necessary strength and stamina. It is a long time ago now since the present Viscount Wolseley pointed out the impossibility of recruiting an army

WORK AS IT WAS AND HOW IT MIGHT BE

from the slums, and since then our town and country population has kept growing, whilst the rural has been declining.

It is, however, the industrial aspect of the case which appeals to me most. The beginning of that organisation of industry, on the basis of each nation supplying its own people with at least the fundamental necessaries of life, which the rapid growth of machine production all over the world will make inevitable at no distant date, can best be begun upon the land. Economically, the big farm has not been a success, whilst *per contra* peasant cultivation has been proved to be so by the most irrefutable evidence. Profitable employment for the best part of a million families could be found in providing Great Britain with the garden, dairy, and barnyard produce we now import from abroad to the value of over 50,000,000*l.* a year. The effect upon the labour market of adding one million to the number of workers in constant employment will be evident to even the most obtuse. By relieving the pressure of over-supply from the lower-grade callings, wages, and with them social conditions, would begin to move upwards. To aim at such a result is no chimera impossible of attainment. With proper facilities for teaching and training people of both sexes to work upon the land, and the provision of small holdings of, say, from three to twenty-five acres, with security of tenure and a reasonable rent, wonders would be accomplished in the lifetime of one generation. It is a serious question with thoughtful members of the working class to know what to do with their children when they are ready to begin work, and it would be a great relief if they knew that the land offered a safe and certain means of earning a livelihood, and that every facility would be given the youth for becoming a settler. And here let me say that I am more hopeful of something of this kind being attempted with success in industrial counties than I am of those wholly given over to agriculture. One, and not the least, of the difficulties of keeping young men in the country is the unvarying monotony of village life. Were it possible, however, to have villages large enough to maintain their own library, theatre and music-hall, and to have a responsible system of government, the difficulty would be largely got over. If, in addition, the villages were within easy reach by rail or tram of the big centres of population, so close in fact as to be in touch with them, the success of the effort I am suggesting would be doubly certain. Besides, the town would provide a market for the produce, a factor of no mean importance in estimating the chances of success.

Our new Councils then would be empowered to acquire land to be used for any purpose necessary for setting the poor on work. Existing administrative authorities have certain powers to acquire land for allotments, small holdings, cottages, which they may also build, and for technical instruction. Some of the formalities necessary to be gone through before these powers may be exercised are cumbrous and circumlocutory, and obviously intended to discourage any real attempt at putting the powers to use. It would be an easy matter for any Government to codify the existing Acts, conferring such powers upon local councils as those referred to above. Strengthen these powers where necessary, simplify the procedure, and then call into being the new authority for dealing with the entire question of land

and labour, and make it responsible, as the overseers of the poor were of yore, for providing employment for every poor applicant.

I repeat that sooner or later the work of organising industry as a national concern will require to be faced. Free trade has not solved the social problem; protection would but add fresh horrors to it. But the doctrine of *laisser faire* will no longer hold good in industry. Poverty is a disease for which a remedy must be found. It is like some cancerous growth eating its way into the vitals of the nation, and which, if not removed, will sooner or later prove fatal. Despite all that is said to the contrary, poverty is growing amongst the poor just as lavish display is assuredly on the increase amongst the rich. The body politic is thus threatened from both sides. Poverty in our midst is chronic, and an unemployed crisis is but an acute stage of the disease. It is this fact which must be faced resolutely. No half-hearted temporising semi or wholly charitable measures will suffice. The grim phantom of want will not be exorcised by such means. Bold statesmanlike handling is called for, and fortunately, with the advent of a Labour party thirty or forty strong in the next Parliament, there are good grounds for hoping and believing that the effort will not now be long delayed.

J. KEIR HARDIE.

3

THE RIGHT TO WORK (LONDON: INDEPENDENT LABOUR PARTY, c. 1908), 3–15.

H. Russell Smart

[Senior Independent Labour Party (ILP) member Russell Smart was also a Fabian and had been a less than enthusiastic member of the Marxist Social Democratic Federation. Soon after writing the pamphlet *The Right to Work* of around 1908 he became very critical of the ILP and Labour Party leaders, including Keir Hardie with whom he had been a close colleague, for their failure to present radical, innovative policies. He feared socialism would be abandoned in favour of unambitious, reformist policies (Laybourn 1994, 174).

Only socialism, Smart (c. 1908) argued in *The Right to Work*, could provide genuine solutions to unemployment, the sweating industries (long hours at home in unsuitable conditions for low pay) and the absence of worthwhile work for reasonable pay in decent conditions. His intention was to publicise the ILP's plan to achieve such solutions. The plan was not simply to provide the usual temporary relief to those who cannot find work. Workers on short-term contracts were desperate to accept work for low pay and in poor conditions. Drawn into temporary work, they lacked economic security and experienced neither emancipation nor self-development. He advocated legislation to regulate both public and private employers, thus eliminating exploitation.

Smart included a casually racist example of the sort often found in literature of the period, referring to the "black tribes of South Africa" as an "uncivilised community", where there were neither landlords nor game laws. They thereby had the economic freedom to decline the opportunity to work for mine owners and farmers if "primitive freedom" could produce for them a better standard of life. The employers thus had to offer reasonable wages and conditions. White labourers, according to Smart, did not enjoy such economic freedom. Such instances of casual racism and Eurocentrism were widespread. Even the leading Fabian Sydney Olivier, who would later take a paternalist approach in helping the exploited and oppressed people of the colonies to become socialist, had at around the time

Smart wrote his pamphlet, used offensive language to describe black people (El Amin 1977). Smart's view differs from both the early and later views expressed by Olivier. Employing John M. Hobson's categories, one can consider Smart an anti-paternalist Eurocentrist who assumed non-European peoples will evolve naturally into civilisation following the path pioneered by Europeans (Hobson 2012, 6). Smart believed that the black South Africans could choose employment by Westerners to gain a better life than they had in their kraals. On the other hand, the "civilised" workers could catch up with the Black Africans in terms of economic freedom.]

IT is frequently stated that Socialism is impracticable, and the organised state a dream of visionary enthusiasts. Whether this be so or not, it is at least certain that every suggestion for dealing with social problems that has gained public approval has originated from Socialists, and is based on the principles of collectivism. So it is with the problem of the unemployed, the sweating industries, and the whole of those social diseases that are summed up in the Labour question. There is neither remedy nor hope of remedy save in Socialist organisation.

It is indisputable that modern poverty is artificial. It is neither the result of Divine anger nor of the niggardliness of Nature. It is the product of the private ownership of land and capital by which men are prevented from earning their livings unless the proprietary class can make profit from their labour. The inevitable result of this system is that in all industries and at all times there are more men seeking employment than there is employment for. The consequent competition for work forces wages down to bare subsistence, causes hours of labour to be prolonged till they reach the limit of endurance, drags the wife from the home, the children from the playfield, and produces those horrors of physical and moral destitution that are the unsolved problems of modern industrial states.

The Independent Labour Party has put forward in its programme a method by which this evil may be remedied. It refuses to be satisfied with the temporary expedients that are hastily adopted by State or voluntary agencies in times of exceptional distress. No system of merely finding work for unemployed men can be successful while unemployment is being manufactured in increasing volumes. Even were the whole of the workless million transported to Canada or sunk in mid-ocean on the voyage, our unregulated industrial methods would soon produce another million to take its place. Not only must State agency be evoked for the provision of work, but private industry must be so regulated that it will afford constant work and humane conditions to all those whom it employs. This may be effected partially by direct legislation, of which the Eight Hours Bill is the chief measure, and partially in an indirect manner by giving the alternative of State employment, or right to work.

The principle it is desired to establish may be illustrated by an example from an uncivilised community. Among the black tribes of South Africa there are neither landlords nor game laws. The natives have access to veld and forest, and can support themselves by simple industry. They possess economic freedom without which the political liberty of the white labourer is but a mockery. This system has fixed in a very complete manner the conditions for the employment of black labour, for the mine-owners and farmers, instead of paying wages based upon the competition of starving men, have had to offer a rate sufficient to induce the natives to leave their kraals.

The purpose of the Right to Work is to establish a civilised equivalent for this primitive freedom. Every citizen able and willing to work should be endowed with the privilege of demanding

STATE EMPLOYMENT,

under conditions of which the following are the chief:—

(1) The work should be within the capacity of the average man to perform without special skill or previous training.
(2) It should be free from degrading conditions and insulting enquiries.
(3) It should be obtainable by all adults whether unemployed at the time of application or not.
(4) The labour time should not exceed forty-eight hours a week.
(5) A minimum wage should be definitely specified.

This last clause requires careful consideration, for it would affect the conditions of life of all engaged in British industry. Its indirect effect would be to make the minimum apply to every worker. It should therefore be fixed at such a sum that whilst it would be sufficient to support life on a scale of decency it would not unduly tax the resources of the capitalist system to afford it. Its money value should vary in localities according to the cost of living, but the purchasing power should be the same in all cases. Food and clothes cost practically the same in all districts. The chief items that cause a variation in the cost of living are rent and transit. These are generally a question of density of population, and the wage might be varied accordingly.

Both the London County Council and the Manchester City Council have fixed

A MINIMUM LIVING WAGE

for their employees of 24/- and 25/- a week. The former amount is the lowest sum upon which a man can support a family in a large town. Even then it must be a continuous wage, reckoned not by the week, but by the year, as all incomes should be calculated.

The object of the Right to Work is not merely to provide for the unemployed. Beyond the workless million there are twelve other millions living in a condition of penurious toil for which the term slavery is an understatement. The Right to Work would effect a revolution in the lives of these unhappy people. So soon as they were provided with the opportunity of honourable employment they would begin to leave their occupations to take advantage of their new social rights. Employers, therefore, would be unable to retain labour except by offering terms equivalent to those provided by the public authority. The indirect effect of the Right to Work would therefore be to establish

Constant employment,
A normal working week of forty eight hours,
A minimum living wage,

for all workers, and these conditions would form the low water mark of British industry.

The question arises as to how the practical enforcement of these restrictions would affect production. It is evident that if

THE COST OF MANUFACTURE

be seriously increased prices must rise and production be curtailed, with a consequent increase of unemployment. It is therefore necessary to show that private industry has a capacity of adaptation to the new set of circumstances.

The question of an eight hours' working day has been subjected to a searching economic analysis. Experience has proved the truth of the theory, that the reasonable shortening of the hours of labour need not increase the cost of production. The economic effect in those industries that permit of work being quickened either by greater effort or improved apparatus is likely to be very slight.

Nor should the minimum wage increase the cost of production. Economic science has established the economy of high wages, and that there is no labour so dear as cheap labour. Skilled English labour is more productive than that of the Continent for the reason that it is more highly paid, that is, the standard of living is higher.

It is a commonplace saying that thirty years ago the wages of the agricultural labourer were so low he was not even worth the miserable pittance he received.

The well-fed, well-housed operative with moderate hours is more physically fit for his work, goes at it with greater pluck and energy than the under-fed, discontented drudge. The higher wages also stimulate the introduction of labour-saving appliances and cause greater managerial efficiency. Cheap Labour is not worth saving.

The earnings of skilled workmen in

THE STAPLE TRADES

already average more than £60 a year, even with the average amount of unemployment, and usually the labourer who waits on the artisan receives the minimum of 24s. a week. Thus the chief alteration would be the provision of constant work. It would be necessary for an employer to keep a sufficient staff to cope with busy periods for there would be no "reserve army of labour" upon which to draw. Fluctuations of trade would have to be met by varying the work time of the whole factory instead of the present method of discharging a number of men and working the others full time. These variations would not be unmanageable. The Trade Union returns to the Board of Trade show that unemployment due to Trade causes fluctuates between 2·2 and 8 per cent. No doubt the proportion among the less efficient non-unionists is higher, but even with these the maximum percentage will not exceed 12. The percentage over unionist and non-unionists probably never exceeds 10 even in the worst times. The variation therefore would not be greater than from 48 to 42½ hours a week, and a whole instead of half-holiday on Saturday would meet the difficulty in times of depression.

THE RAILWAYS AND TRANSPORT TRADES

This group, in which no greater efficiency can result from a reduction in hours, would have to face a considerable increase in the wages bill, nor could they recoup themselves by higher charges. The method the Railway Companies adopt in fixing rates is to disregard altogether the cost of working and to charge the traffic "all that it will bear." In 1904, the total Railway receipts were £111,883,000, of which £69,100,000 was absorbed in working expenses, leaving nearly £42,800,000 to be divided among the shareholders.

The cost of establishing a 48 hours week among the 500,000 employees, and raising the wages of the 150,000 men who receive less than the proposed minimum wage would be as nearly as can be guaged, £6,000,000 a year. There would still be left 36½ millions profit as an inducement for the directors to continue the national services until such time as the nation might see fit to undertake these duties for itself.

The profits of tram and omnibus companies would also suffer dimunition. Still the wages and hours that would be enforced approximate to those prevailing in municipal service where a considerable excess of revenue over expenditure is being earned.

THE SWEATED TRADES AND HOME INDUSTRIES

could not bear even a slight increase in the cost of production. The workers in these industries not only compete with each other but have a more powerful rival in the machine equipped factory. Any advance in the wages bill would place them at a hopeless disadvantage.

But though their occupations would be extinguished there would be no decrease in the volume of trade. The "goods," if the term may be permitted, for these products, are generally necessary commodities for which the demand would be increased rather than diminished. Instead of being manufactured by starving people in insanitary slums they would be produced under the relatively well-paid and healthy conditions of factory life. Casual labour also would disappear. Concerns like the Dock Companies, which employ a large number of men for short periods, would have to engage permanent staffs, sufficiently numerous to cope with normally busy periods. Casual labourers form the most numerous class in the army of the unemployed. The alternate periods of overwork and underwork cause physical and moral degradation. Many of the unhappy victims of these demoralising conditions become incapable of sustained industry and deteriorate into the street corner loafers who maintain a precarious existence by odd jobs eked out by charity. The public knowledge that there was employment available for every able bodied man would dry up this stream of demoralizing doles. Such of them as were capable of efficient labour would seek public or private work in order to maintain themselves. The others would form a pathological problem of industrially deseased, which would have to be dealt with by other agencies.

AGRICULTURE.

It is possible that many farmers would find the increased cost of labour a greater burden than they could bear under existing conditions of rent and tenure. If so a much needed system of land reform would be hastened, that will otherwise need legislative compulsion. The land of Britain is steadily going out of cultivation. The area under crops of all kinds in 1880 was 48,850,000 acres, in 1901 it had decreased to 40,400,000 acres. The number of agricultural labourers declined from 1,200,000 in 1881, to 870,000 in 1901, a reduction of more than 25 per cent. in face of a general increase in the population of nearly 20 per cent.

This decline in the most important of our national industries is largely due to our feudal methods of land tenure and the reluctance of both landlord and farmer to allow the labourers to get possession of land by which they could sustain themselves in an independent position. Every expert observer, foreign or colonial, tells the same tale of neglected opportunities. Yet there is no inherent incapacity in either our soil or climate to produce food largely in excess of our present crops.

Prince Krapotkine states[1]: "If the soil of the United Kingdom were cultivated as it was 35 years ago, 24,000,000 instead of 7,000,000 could live on home grown food, and that agriculture while giving occupation to nearly 750,000 people, would give nearly 3,000,000 wealthy home customers to British manufacturers. If the cultivatable area of the United Kingdom were cultivated as the soil is cultivated on the average in Belgium, the United Kingdom would have food for at least 37,000,000 inhabitants . . . . and finally, if the population of this country came to be doubled, all that would be required for producing the food for

80,000,000 inhabitants would be to cultivate the soil as it is cultivated on the best farms of this country, in Lombardy, and in Flanders."

The European countries where agriculture prospers are those where there is a numerous body of small cultivators. Should the capitalist farmers be compelled to relinquish their holdings in any numbers, the landlords would still desire to let their land and would divide it into smaller tenancies. The success that has already attended such a policy where it has been adopted warrants the belief that the revival of agriculture is to be looked for largely in this direction.

But it is not by any means certain that even under our present system of farming there is not sufficient margin of gross profits to pay the equivalent of the town wage of 24/-.

In 1894 a Parliamentary return was issued on "The Relation of Labour to Cost of Production." A list of twelve farms was given showing the value of the produce, total expenditure, cost of labour, &c. In these the labour bill figures at £5,975, and rent at £7,779. In the same return the total amount paid in wages to the agricultural labourers is estimated at £58,000,000 in 1878, and £50,000,000 in 1888. Schedule A of the Income Tax gives the rentals paid to the owners of agricultural land for these two years as £69,300,000, and £61,300,000. In the census of 1901 there were 715,138 males returned as farm workers. Mr. Wilson Fox reported to the Board of Trade in 1905 that the average wages of agricultural workers was 18/- a week. On the basis of these figures the total wages of the men engaged in agriculture for 1901 was £35,750,000. Schedule A of the Income Tax gives the rent of agricultural land for that year as £52,463,000. All these figures correspond and tend to prove that the rent of agricultural land considerably exceeds the cost of the labour engaged in cultivating it.

This evidence indicates that there is sufficient margin to allow of rents being adjusted to meet the increased cost of labour. A farmer will not offer more for land than he thinks he can afford to pay. If the labour bill be high the rent must be low, and vice versa. Strong contributory evidence is afforded by the fact that the wages of agricultural labourers in the mining districts are considerably higher than the average. Mining is an occupation for which the agricultural labourer is well fitted. Employment is constant and wages nearly double the rural rate, consequently mining partially affords the labourer that alternative employment which would be established for all by the Right to Work. The average wages of agricultural workers in Great Britain are 18/-, but in Durham, Glamorgan, Renfrew, and Lanarkshire they average over 22/-,[2] which is about the rural equivalent of the proposed city minimum. It would appear that the farmer finds no difficulty in adjusting rent to meet this increased labour bill.

The argument has gone far enough to establish a prima-facie proof that the proposed conditions would place no intolerable burden upon production, and would offer no insuperable difficulties for employers to overcome.

The effect of the Right to Work being to make employment constant, there would be a large number of workers excluded from private industry. These would seek the public work.

They would be composed of all sorts and conditions of men. Along with the capable out of works there would be the loafer, the drunkard, the broken-down professional man, the semi-criminal, the aged, the intellectually and physically degenerate. This wretched mass of poverty and vice is Labour's vanquished army. It forms the unemployables—creatures who once were men. The product of an evil social and industrial environment, it swells the ranks of the efficient unemployed, and forms the excuse by which plutocratic parliaments have hitherto evaded their responsibilities.

These inefficients would have to be weeded out. The applicants must conform to

A STANDARD OF EFFICIENCY.

This would be necessary both for the preservation of self-respect and the success of the principle. The public work must not be regarded as a rate-aided refuge for the destitute, or the evils of the old Poor Law will reassert themselves.

Yet the public authority must not be entrusted with the power of free selection and dismissal, or the whole intention of the proposal would be defeated. A method must be devised by which the community may be protected from the wasters, and the capable workers from excessive tasks set by an unsympathetic authority. This two-fold difficulty may be met by establishing a labour test. This should be some definitely specified task capable of accurate measurement. Probably stone-breaking best fulfills the required purpose. It is not suggested that the public authorities should actually employ the applicants at this unpleasant and expensive task, which, when necessary, may be better performed by machinery. The public authority should be invested with powers to undertake any alternative industries it considered suitable for employing the applicants. Neither side would have the power either to enforce or demand this alternative work, though both would be anxious to adopt it. The public authority, as the representative of the ratepayers—especially the property owning ratepayers—would be unwilling to set men at a comparatively high rate of wages to work on unproductive undertakings. Assuming they had a reasonable regard for their own interests, they would seek means whereby the labourers might produce wealth more or less equal in value to their wages. On the other hand, the disagreeable nature of the test-work would cause the men eagerly to accept any other work of a pleasanter character. This alternative work would be therefore a matter of ready agreement between the public authority and the applicants. When it was established, the various managers and foremen would weed out those whose quality or quantity of work was not up to the average standard. They would not have the power of dismissal, but could send them on to the test-work. If a man loafed at the pleasanter occupation, he would almost certainly shirk his allotted task, in which case he could then be dismissed. On the other hand, should the public authority attempt to evade the Act by exacting more than a fair day's work, the labourers could refuse to perform it, in which case also the agreement would be ended, and the public authority would be compelled to provide the test-work. The threatened expense of this would be sufficient to cause a relaxation of the onerous conditions, while its unpleasant nature would prevent the demand being made if the grievance were not genuine. The specified task would thus form a measuring rod by which the value of every other form of labour could be arrived at. It would be at once a safeguard by which loafing or sweating could be prevented. It would weed out the unemployable, and ensure that the remaining labourers were up to the ordinary standard of industry. It would then be a question of organising capacity on the part of those responsible as to whether

THE PUBLIC INDUSTRIES SHOULD BE SELF-SUPPORTING

or a charge upon the community. This is a matter of the utmost importance, not only from the ratepayers' point of view, but for the ultimate success of the scheme. In a criticism of the Unemployed Workmen's Act, Mr. Harold Cox, M.P., the late Secretary of the Cobden Club, made use of the following argument:—"There can be no increase in the volume of employment unless there be an increase in the total mass of exchangeable commodities." This essential fact is continually overlooked in the provision of work. Road making, laying out parks, afforestation, foreshore reclamation, and the other methods that are advocated and adopted add nothing to the exchangeable wealth of the community until a considerable number of years have elapsed, and therefore do not increase the total volume of employment. The maintence of the men and their families has to be borne by the citizens either by voluntary charity or the enforced contributions of the rates. In either case the result is a diminution in the spending power of the contributors. If 24/- a week be taken as the average wage, every person who is in possession of that sum commands minute portions of the labour time of a multitude of workers to the equivalent of one man's labour for a week. If he spend it in a coat he sets spinners, weavers, and tailors at work; in food, agriculturalists, butchers, and bakers; if he saves it, it is invested in a railway or buildings, and he gives work to bricklayers, masons, navvies, and plate-layers. In each case the resultant amount of employment is the same. It is evident, then, that if the wages of the men on the relief works are paid by the citizens their powers of employing labour is diminished by the amount of employment that is given. As a temporary expedient this course may have some success, for its action is not immediate, and it shifts the burden on to the shoulders of others better able to bear it, but the ultimate effect is to reduce employment in other directions. It would be equally useless producing goods for which there is no effective demand. To manufacture commodities for which there would be no sale, or which, if sold, would displace others, is for practical purposes unproductive work.

All social reformers are agreed that the only hope of a revival of industry is to be sought in a return to agriculture. But here a practical difficulty occurs. The majority of the applicants would be town labourers and quite unfitted for farming on their own account. But agriculture may be successfully conducted on properly equipped farms by inexperienced labourers under expert direction. Mr. Rider

THE RIGHT TO WORK

Haggard, the Commissioner appointed by the Government to report on the Colonies of the Salvation Army in this country and America, states:—

"The lesson to be learned from it (Fort Amity Colony, Colorado) is one of great importance. It shows that unskilled and untrained persons can be taken from towns, put upon land, and thrive there even when the land is of a nature not very suitable to such settlements."[3]

"The Hadleigh Settlement is to my mind an instance of the extraordinary results which can be attained by wretched men working on land the ordinary agriculturalist would also call wretched. . . . . It shows what could be done with much cold English soil if only sufficient capital and labour were applied to that soil."[4]

Both small holdings and large farms have their places in agriculture. There are some forms of produce that are more economically raised by extensive methods of culture, and others by the small holding system. Probably cereals, meat, dairy produce, and tree fruit may be better dealt with on large areas, while vegetables, poultry, soft fruit, and the like, requiring more individual care and hand labour, may be produced more successfully by the peasant cultivator. Municipalities have considerable experience in agriculture. Many of them farm large tracts of land for the disposal of the town waste, and the results are not discouraging. There is a growing demand for the municipalization of the milk supply. Pure milk is necessary for the health of the community. At present the supply is a source of contagion and disease. No amount of inspection can cope with the dishonesty or carelessness of private profit makers. The only safe method is for the local authorities to take over the whole service from the originating cow to the consumer's milk jug. Cow keeping involves cattle breeding, and also growing the food necessary for winter support. There thus seems to be ample scope for the establishment of communal farms, as well as small holdings, where able bodied labourers without previous experience may be trained to the agricultural industry.

When the crops were put on the market additional purchasing power would be given, causing the demand for other necessaries to become effective. Some of this demand might very well be supplied by the public authorities. Clothing factories, building departments, and other productive industries might then be established, and the circle of municipal enterprise might gradually widen out until it would embrace a very large number of operations.

Into this development it is unnecessary to enter. Sufficient evidence has been given to show that the Right to Work need neither break down the commercial system, nor prove a burden upon the community, and that there is ample opportunity of employing our surplus labour in productive industries.

The Right to Work makes no provision for

THE UNEMPLOYABLE.

Possibly it might make their case harder than at present, for its effect would certainly be to stop at once the stream of semi-charity upon which so many of them eke out a precarious living. The term is frequently used to indicate what the Swiss

WORK AS IT WAS AND HOW IT MIGHT BE

call 'workshies'—the Weary Willies and Tired Tims of our comic journals. It is probable this class is less numerous than is generally imagined. Undoubtedly differences in habits of industry exist, but it is very questionable if there be any man, who, having the ability to work, and having no other means of support, would refuse to work under decent conditions. At any rate no man can be termed loafer, until he has been offered and has declined the opportunity. Even the actual inefficients are many of them only temporarily so. A man is frequently dubbed lazy when he is merely disabled by hopelessness and starvation. Intermittent work demoralizes its victims. Steady, regular occupation becomes as distasteful to them as it does to the rich idlers of the West End.

Better opportunities will reform most of these unfortunates. It has been freely admitted by those responsible for finding work for the unemployed, that at first the work performed is inefficient and costly, but with every week both speed and quality increase until it is up to the general average. The real unemployables— those physically or mentally incapable of working—are probably reared as such from childhood. Cradled in a slum, schooled in the gutter, underfed from birth, stunted in body, preternaturally sharpened in cunning, they become incapable of honest toil.

Society, which has allowed this evil growth, must bear the cost of its own neglect, and must maintain these people even though irreclaimable. It may be a consolation that the expense can never be as great as the maintenance of the unemployables of wealth and fashion, who at the popping of every champagne cork cost the community a sum equal to a week's support of each of their poorer imitators.

With the establishment of better conditions the unemployable would no longer be bred and reared and in the lapse of time would disappear.

There is some diversity of opinion as to

WHAT AUTHORITY SHOULD BE RESPONSIBLE

for providing employment. There are four alternatives:

(1) The Central Government.
(2) The new Committees formed under the Unemployed Workmen's Act, 1905.
(3) The Boards of Guardians.
(4) The Municipalities and County Councils.

There are many objections to making the Government the responsible authority. If a comparison be made between State and Municipal organization of labour, the balance in favour of economical and successful administration is preponderatingly on the side of the latter. The organizing of industry on so vast a scale as the State is apt to become rigid and uniform. The control exercised by Parliament over the Government departments is merely nominal. Even the titular chief is frequently but a figure head. The real authority lies with the permanent officials. On the other hand the control by a municipality over its officers is real. The method of governing by Committees is far more effective than by a single minister, whose selection is generally made for party or social reasons, and whose term of office is necessarily temporary. Unless, therefore, there is some overwhelming reason in favour of the State being the unit of administration, as in the case of the Post Office or a nationalized Railway system, the development of communal activity is better carried on through the agency of the smaller bodies.

The Distress Committees are not popularly elected, and are likely to be wanting in energy and initiative. Their rating power is necessarily limited, it would be an intolerable indignity and wrong to allow a nominated and inferior Committee unlimited powers of levying rates over a municipal area. Yet this very limitation coupled with the non-representative character would be likely to cause inefficient administration. The requisition would become a permanent charge and would be regarded as an alternative poor rate over the expenditure of which the citizens would have little control.

The same objections apply largely to the Boards of Guardians added to which there is the strong popular prejudice against them. So far from it being desirable to increase their powers it would tend both to efficiency and economy to abolish them, and vest their responsibilities in

THE MUNICIPALITY OR COUNTY COUNCIL.

Evidence points to these authorities as on the whole the most suitable bodies on whom the onus of providing work should fall. They are already large employers and conduct a number of important social industries. In many cases a better adjustment of hours and work would absorb the effective unemployed. In efficiency and economy they are superior to all other communal or industrial organizations. In a comparison of Electric Undertakings by private companies and Local Authorities compiled by the Accountant of the Durham County Council, figures are given which prove that municipalities obtain more from their plant and manage their undertakings more economically than the private companies, and a similar enquiry shows the same general result to be true with regard to Gas, Water and Tramways. The area most conveniently adapted as the unit of administration is that covered by the Education Authorities. There has been a desire expressed by many interested in the unemployed question that the cost should either be borne entirely by the State or supplemented by a grant from the Exchequer. This appeal would be reasonable if the maintenance of the unemployed is to be a permanent charge on the community. It should certainly apply to the Colonies for the reformation of the unemployable, but the Municipal industry that has been recommended is on a different footing.

It has been shown that employment can only be increased by the extent that the public industries are self-supporting, and every inducement should be put upon the Municipality to make them so. There can be no greater inducement to the average property owner than to make him pay for the loss. It should be taken for granted that efficient labour applied to land and capital can produce value equal to the cost of its maintenance. If it did not, the fault would lie with the management and organization, and the State should no more be expected to make up the deficiency than it is now called on to do, when Municipal Trams, or Gas Works fail to pay.

Every reasonable protection should be given to the public authority for this purpose. In particular,

TEMPORARY EMPLOYMENT.

which is always inefficient and costly, should be dispensed with, and conditions imposed which would render it somewhat difficult for men to re-enter the public service after they had left it. It is no intention of the Right to Work to give temporary employment in times of stress. Certainly it is not desirable that the ratepayers should maintain workmen from starvation until the capitalists could, again, make profits from their labour. In order to qualify for the work, a period of residence in a district should be imposed, six months would be a reasonable term, and this should be extended to a year in order to regain the privilege. Employers who wanted to attract men from the public work, would then not only have to offer equivalent wages and hours but a year's engagement.

This is a reasonable requirement. It is a consequence of the enslaved condition of the manual-working classes that the very moment their labour can be dispensed with they are discharged and thrown on their own resources. Yet the official classes, whose services are largely non-productive, are dealt with in a different fashion. Their salaries are paid by the year, and no professional or commercial man ever calculates his earnings by the week.

Employers, when embarking in an industry, undertake many fixed annual charges—rent, interest on capital, salaries of official staff, and find no difficulty in meeting these current expenses. It is but just and reasonable that the subsistence of the workers, upon whom all the other classes depend, should be made the first charge upon production.

The ultimate justification of all social reform lies in the

MORAL AND INTELLECTUAL IMPROVEMENT

of the people. The demoralisation of labour is due less to its poverty than its servitude. The absolute dependence of the wage-earning classes, black-coated or fustian-clad, upon the capitalists saps their manhood and destroys self-respect. Give the people the right to live without permission of a master, even though it be but bare shelter and a crust of bread, and a mental revolution will be effected that will exceed the economic in the degree that the spiritual transcends the physical. No other reform holds out the promise of social betterment like the right to work. The existence of the unemployed constantly defeats the intention of legislative reform. Measures designed to mitigate some of the effects of poverty frequently produce other forms of suffering. The Workmen's Compensation Act has increased the amount of unemployment among the elderly. Old Age Pensions will probably lower the wages of light occupations. Even the transference of industries to the community does not solve the difficulty. Trams may be municipalised, mines and railways made national services, even a complete industrial organisation established, and yet the worker will be enslaved. While there exists a man, whether capitalist or communal employer, who possesses the power of dismissal over a body of workmen, servitude, with its mental and moral degradation, will exist.

The Right to Work is the charter of industrial freedom, the emancipation of Labour from capitalist tyranny. Till it is obtained there can be neither social nor moral progress. When it is obtained all other things become possible.

Notes

1 "Fields, Factories, & Workshops." Swan & Sonnenshein.
2 Wilson Fox, Labour Department, Board of Trade.
3 "Report on the Salvation Army Colonies," C.D. 2562, June, 1905, p. 35.
4 Ibid, p. 69.

Part 2

VISIONS OF THE FUTURE

4

THE PROGRESS OF SOCIALISM: A LECTURE (LONDON: MODERN PRESS, WILLIAM REEVES AND FREETHOUGHT PUBLISHING COMPANY, c. 1888), 3–18.

Sidney Webb

[Sidney Webb's pamphlet *The Progress of Socialism* was published in 1888, four years after the formation of the Fabian Society. Portraying himself as an "avowed socialist", Webb defines socialism in a distinctively Fabian way as a principle of social organisation. If socialism can very broadly be considered as an ideology based on compatible tenets of community, equality and freedom (Lamb 2019, 24–46), early Fabianism emphasises the first two of those three. Webb (c. 1888a) discusses progress in terms of the growing field of services now taken out of the control of private enterprise by means of governmental legislation introducing regulation by the state.

Webb writes that the material condition of the mass of people can be raised if they resume control of industry. His interpretation of resuming control was, how-ever, control of industry by the state on behalf of those people. This was a view which characterised early Fabianism, made clear by George Bernard Shaw in his preface to the ground-breaking *Fabian Essays in Socialism* the following year. According to Shaw (1889, iv), the authors of the chapters, including Webb, "are all Social Democrats, with a common conviction of the necessity of vesting the organization of industry and the material of production in a State identified with the whole people by complete Democracy".

Early Fabianism had little faith in the ability of workers, especially those other than the highly-skilled, to organise themselves and thus fulfil the freedom tenet of socialism. The London dock strike of 1889, in which unskilled workers did assert their strength, was a key factor in the labour movement. In *The Progress of Socialism* the previous year Webb mentioned the insecurity of the dockers. What he overlooked in this pamphlet and neglected in his later work on the

VISIONS OF THE FUTURE

history of trade unionism was that several other groups of unskilled workers had already begun to organise themselves when he wrote the pamphlet (Duffy 1961, 306–309).]

IT is a sign of the times when so eminently respectable a body as the Council of the Sunday Lecture Society arranges for a lecture on Socialism, and invites an avowed Socialist to expound to you its influence on social welfare. We are rapidly getting to the third of the stages through which every notion has in England to pass: It's impossible: It's against the Bible: We knew it before. "We are all Socialists now," says one of Her Majesty's late Ministers, and, in sober truth, there is no anti-Socialist political party. What has long formed part of the unconscious basis of our practice is now formulated as a definite theory, and the tide of European Socialism is rolling in upon us like a flood. All the authorities, whatever their own views, can but note its rapid progress. If we look back along the line of history, we see the irresistible sweep of the growing tendency: if we turn to contemporary industrial development it is there: if we fly to biological science we do not escape the lesson: on all sides the sociologic evolution compels our adherence. There is no resting place for stationary Toryism in the scientific universe. The whole history of the human race cries out against the old-fashioned Individualism.

Economic Science, at any rate, will now have none of it. When the Editor of the new issue of the Encyclopædia Brittanica lately required from some eminent Economist an article on Political Economy, fully representing the present position of that science, it was to an avowed Socialist that he addressed himself, and the article took the form of an elaborate survey of the inevitable convergence of all the economic tendencies towards Socialism. At the present moment (December, 1887,) out of a total of 14 courses of lectures on Economics being delivered under the auspices of various public bodies in London, eight, to my knowledge, and possibly more, are being given by professed Socialists. I have been told that one of the University Extension Societies lately found some difficulty in obtaining young economist lecturers sufficiently free from what some of its older members thought the Socialistic taint. And this is not to be wondered at when we learn that Professor Marshall has at various times declared himself a Socialist, and when we find Professor Sidgwick, that most careful of men, contributing an article to the *Contemporary Review*,[1] to prove that the main principles of Socialism are a plain deduction from accepted economic doctrines, and in no way opposed to these.

Indeed, those who remember John Stuart Mill's emphatic adhesion to Socialism, both the name and the thing, in his "Autobiography,"[2] cannot be surprised at this tendency of economists. The only wonder is, at the way in which the interested defenders of economic monopoly are able to persuade the British public that Political Economy is against Socialism, and to make even the Bishop of Rochester believe that its laws "forbid" anything but the present state of things.

It is, however, time to give a plain definition of Socialism, to prevent any mistake as to meanings. Nothing is more common than the statement, "I can't understand what Socialism is." But this is sheer intellectual laziness. The word is to be found in our modern dictionaries. The Encyclopædia Brittanica contains exhaustive articles upon its every aspect. There are enough Socialist lectures in London every week, good, bad, and indifferent, to drive the meaning into every willing ear.

The abstract word "Socialism" denotes a particular principle of social organisation. We may define this principle either from the constitutional or the economic standpoint. We may either put it as "the control by the community of the means of production for public advantage, instead of for private profit," or "the whole community obtaining all rent and interest." In either case, its opposite is the control of the means of production for individual ends, and the individual consumption of rent or interest.

But this definition does not satisfy some people. They want a complete description of a Socialist State, an elaborately worked out, detailed plan, like Sir Thomas More's "Utopia" or Gulliver's Travels. Such fancy sketches have, indeed, at times been thrown off by Socialists as by all other thinkers, but with the growing realisation of social evolution, men gradually cease to expect to be able to devise a perfect and final social state, and the dreams of Fourier and Cabet, like those of Godwin and Comte, become outworn and impossible to us. There will never come a moment when we can say, "*Now* let us rest, for Socialism is established:" any more than we can say, "*Now* Radicalism is established." The correct principles of social organisation must already have secured partial adoption, as a condition of the continued existence of every existing social organism, and the progress of Socialism is but their more complete recognition, and their conscious adoption as the lines of advance upon which social improvement depends.

Looking back along the whole line of human progress, we see one main economic characteristic underlying every form of society. As soon as production is sufficiently advanced to furnish more than maintenance, there arises, wherever two or three are gathered together, a fierce struggle for the surplus product. This struggle varies in outward form according to the time and circumstances, but remains essentially alike in economic character. The individuals or classes who have possessed social power, have at all times, consciously or unconsciously, made use of that power in such a way as to leave to the great majority of their fellows practically nothing beyond the means of subsistence according to the current local standard. The additional product, determined by the relative differences in productive efficiency of the different sites, soils, capitals, and forms of skill above the margin of cultivation, has gone to those exercising control over these valuable but scarce productive factors. This struggle to secure the economic rent is the key to the confused history of European progress, and the underlying, unconscious motive of all revolutions. The student of history finds that the great world moves, like the poet's snake, on its belly.

The social power which has caused this unequal division of the worker's product has taken various forms. Beginning, probably, in open personal violence in the merely predatory stage of society, it has passed in one field, through tribal war, to political supremacy, embodied, for instance, abroad in a "Jingo" foreign policy, and at home in vindictive class legislation. A survival in England at the present time is the severity of the punishment for trifling offences against property compared with that for personal assaults, and its effect is curiously seen when the legal respect for person and that for property are, to some extent, opposed to each other, as in the case of wife-beating.

The social power does not, however, always take the forms of physical strength or political supremacy. From the Indian medicine man and the sun-priests of Peru down to the Collector of Peter's Pence and the Treasurer of the Salvation Army, theological influences have ever been used to divert a portion of this rent to spiritual uses, nourishing (like the meats offered to idols), whole classes of non-producers.

But by far the most important means of appropriating the surplus product has been the organisation of labour. The industrial leader, who can cause his fellows to organise their toil under his direction, is able thereby to cause an enormous increase in their productivity. The advantages of co-operative or associated labour were discovered long before they were described by Adam Smith or Fourier, and human history is the record of their ever-increasing adoption. Civilisation itself is nothing but an ever-widening co-operation.

But who is to get the benefit of this increased productivity? In early times it turned upon the political condition of the labourer. The universally first form of industrial organisation is chattel slavery. At a certain stage in social development there seems to have been possible no other kind of industrial co-operation. The renunciation of personal independence is, as Darwin observed of the Fuegian, the initial step towards civilisation.

As a slave the worker obtained at first nothing but bare maintenance at the lowest economic rate. Cato even advises the Roman noble that the bailiff or foreman need not have so large a ration as the other slaves, his work, though more skilled, being less exhausting. On the other hand, the surplus value was not yet differentiated into its component economic parts, and went in an undivided stream of profit all to the master.

Advancing civilisation, itself rendered possible only by chattel slavery, gradually made this form of servitude incompatible with intellectual and moral development, and inadequate to industrial needs. The slave became the feudal serf or the tribal dependent. As a chattel he had ceded all but his maintenance to his master; as a serf he rendered to his lord three or four days' unpaid labour per week, maintaining himself on the product of the rest.

The further development of the social organism proved no more favourable to feudalism than to chattel slavery, and the politically free labourer came into existence. But the economic servitude of the worker did not cease with his political fetters. With the chains of innate status, there disappeared also its economic privileges, and the free labourer found himself, especially in England, in a community where the old common rights over the soil were being gradually but effectually extinguished. He became a landless stranger in his own country.

The development of competitive production for sale, and the industrial revolution of the past century, has involved, moreover, in order to live, not merely access to the land, but the use, in addition, of increasingly large masses of capital, at first in agriculture, then in foreign trade, then in manufacture, and now, finally, also in distributive industries. The mere worker became steadily less and less industrially independent as his political freedom increased. From an independent producing unit, he passed into a mere item in a vast industrial army, over the organisation of which he had no control. He was free, but free only to work at the market wage or starve. Other option he had none, and even now the freedom to work at any wage is denied to many at a time for varying periods, and we have the constantly recurring phenomenon of the unemployed. When it suits any person having the use of land and capital to employ the worker, this is only done on condition that two important deductions, rent and interest, can be made from the product, for the benefit of two in this capacity absolutely unproductive classes, those possessing the legal ownership of land and capital. The reward of labour being thus reduced on an average by at least one-third, the remaining eightpence out of the shilling is then shared between the various classes who *have* co-operated in the production, including the inventor, the managing employer, and the mere wage-worker—but shared in the competitive struggle in such a way that at least fourpence goes to a favoured set of educated workers numbering one-fifth of the whole, leaving four-fifths to divide less than fourpence out of the shilling between them. The consequence is the social condition we find around us. A fortunate few, owing to their legal power over the instruments of wealth-production, are able to command the services of thousands of industrial slaves whose faces they have never seen, without rendering any return whatever to them or to society in exchange. A larger body of persons contribute some labour, but are able, from their education or their cultivated ability, to choose occupations for which the competition wage is still high, owing to the relatively small number of possible competitors. These two classes together number only one-fifth of the whole. On the other side is the great mass of the people, the weekly wage-earners, four out of every five[3] of the nation, toiling perpetually for less than a third of the aggregate product of labour, at an annual wage averaging at most £35 per adult, hurried into unnecessarily early graves by the severity of their lives, and dying, as regards, at least, one-third of them, destitute or actually in receipt of poor law relief.

To-morrow morning, in London alone, twenty to twenty-five thousand adult men will fight like savages for permission to labour in the docks for fourpence an hour—and one-third of them will fight in vain, and be turned workless away.[4] With their families these men make up 100,000 souls, a whole Norwich or Brighton, in the single class of casual dock labourers in this one city.

Tomorrow morning thirty to thirty five thousand London children will go to school in the bitter blast absolutely breakfastless; this is the average number at school without food at all since the previous day.[5] How many in addition have had an insufficient breakfast we know not. But this we know—they die—the infants at any rate, in appalling heaps around us, of virtual starvation. Three times as many young children per thousand die in the working class as in the upper class. In my own parish is a naturally healthy area, inhabited by the poor, where the total death-rate is four times that of the other parts of the same district, even when no epidemic rages.[6] It is not enough that we of the middle and upper classes should demand the unceasing labor of our poorer brethren, that we should shorten their lives, and afflict them with disease for our comfort. We must also sacrifice the little children to our greed and harrow up in our unthinking cruelty all the most sacred feelings of our bondsmen.

And then, when we have bound the laborer fast to his wheel, when we have practically excluded the average man from every real chance of improving his condition, when we have virtually denied to him the means of having any share in the higher feelings and the larger sympathies of the cultured race, when we have shortened his life in our service, stunted his growth in our factories, racked him with unnecessary disease by our exactions, tortured his soul with that worst of all pains, the constant fear of poverty, condemned his wife and children to sicken and die before his eyes, in spite of his own perpetual round of toil—then we are aggrieved that he often loses hope, attempts to drown his cares, and driven by his misery irresistibly down the steep hill of vice, passes into that evil circle where vice begets poverty, and poverty intensifies vice, until Society unrelentingly stamps him out as vermin. And then we lay the flattering unction to our souls that it was his own fault, that he had his chance, and we preach to his fellows thrift and temperance, prudence and virtue, but always industry, that industry of others which keeps the industrial machine in motion, so that we can still enjoy the opportunity of taxing it. Nay, so that we may not lose his labour, we keep him when we can from absolute starvation, and when the world has taken his all, we offer him the pauper's dole. Nothing gives a more striking picture of his condition than the official statistics of our pauperism. We have clogged our relief with irksome and humiliating conditions, so that the poor often die lingering deaths rather than submit to them. Yet there is a class in receipt of this bitter bread during any one year, numbering between three and four millions, one in ten of the whole population, one in eight of the wage-earning class.[7] In some rural districts *every* aged labourer is a pauper. When the Queen, last June, passed in review the whole population of London, she may, perhaps, have reflected that for one in every five of that whole crowd, a pauper's death was waiting. One fifth of the population of the richest city in the world die in the workhouse or the hospital (not including recipients of out-door relief,) and the proportion for the wage-earning class alone must, of course, be much greater.[8]

To anyone who knows the silent anguish of the long struggle before the workhouse is reached, how the iron enters into the soul in that desperate losing fight down the hill of poverty, what a sum of misery is here depicted. These people, our brothers, were not *born* paupers. They, too, had their entry into life, dark and unpromising it may have been, but never without hope, and some youthful aspirations. Then comes the check, and the cold world quenches at last, after more or less soul-agony, both hope and aspiration, and our fellow-man once erect is borne down by *our* pressure into a pauper's grave.

This is the nett result of our social arrangements after a generation of gradual *improvement,* greater, we are told, than England ever before knew. The distress is only normal. The condition of the people exhibits a marked advance in prosperity. It may be that this is true; nay, owing to the silent progress of Socialism it probably is true; yet the problem for *us* is no lighter. Are things *now* such as we can dare to be responsible for? Let a sober, non-Socialist authority of weight answer. Mr. Frederic Harrison, writing just three years ago says:—"To me at least, it would be enough to condemn modern society as hardly an advance on slavery or serfdom, if the permanent condition of industry were to be that which we now behold, that 90 per cent. of the actual producers of wealth have no home that they can call their own beyond the end of a week; have no bit of soil or so much as a room that belongs to them; have nothing of value of any kind except as much old furniture as will go in a cart; have the precarious chance of weekly wages which barely suffice to keep them in health; are housed for the most part in places that no man thinks fit for his horse; are separated by so narrow a margin of destitution that a month of bad trade, sickness or unexpected loss, brings them face to face with hunger and pauperism. . . . . This is the normal state of the average workmen in town or country." (Report of Industrial Remuneration Conference, 1886, p. 429.)

Such then is our position to-day. Those who believe it possible that the festering evils of social ulceration can be cured without any fundamental change in property relations, rely mainly on three leading remedies, Trades Unions, Co-operation and a general recrudescence of a Christ-like unselfishness. What does the dry light of science say to these homeopathic "pills against the earthquake"?

The belief in universal Trades Unionism as a means of raising wages all round must be at once dismissed as involving a logical fallacy. Certainly, the workers in some few skilled trades have managed to improve their economic position by strict Trade Unions. We are never allowed to forget the splendid incomes earned by these aristocrats of labour, a mere thirteenth of the whole labour class. But those who merely counsel the rest to go and do likewise forget that Trade Union victories are only won by strict limitation of the numbers in the particular trade, and the excluded candidates necessarily go to depress the condition of the outsiders. The Trades Unionist does but raise himself on the bodies of his less fortunate comrades. If all were equally strong, all would be equally powerless—a point clearly proved by Prof. Cairnes,[9] and obvious to all Trade Unionists themselves.

Co-operation is a more seductive means of escape, and most social reformers cannot, even now, refrain from keeping alive lingering hopes that some solution may here be found. But a whole generation of experiment has done little more than show the futility of expecting real help from this quarter. Less than one four hundredth part of the industry of the country is yet carried on by co-operation. The whole range of industrial development seems against it, and no ground for hope in Co-operation as a complete answer to the social problem can be gained from economic science. It fails to deal even with the real elements of the case. It may claim to obviate competition, but "the deepest root," says Mill,[10] "of the evils and iniquities which fill the industrial world is *not* competition, but the subjection of labour to capital, and the enormous share which the possessors of the instruments of production are able to take from the produce." Co-operation can make no real defence against the continuance of the exactions of this "enormous share"—rent and interest—the continued individual enjoyment of which it, indeed, actually presupposes. It affords a valuable moral training, a profitable but somewhat hazardous savings bank for small investments, and a temporary means of interesting the worker in the industrial affairs of his country. But it is merely a survival from the days before Joint Stock Companies existed, and ordinary joint stock investment is now rapidly elbowing it out of the field, and is already a hundred and sixty times as great as Co-operation. Now even the most enthusiastic believer in the virtues of association will hardly expect salvation merely from a régime of Joint Stock Companies, and this, and not co-operation, is clearly the line in which our industrial development is rapidly travelling. It will, of course, be some time before the more enthusiastic co-operators realise this, or even become aware that modern economic science turns regretfully against them, but such eminent authorities as Cliffe Leslie, Professor Walker, Mr. Leonard Courtney, and Dr. J. T. Ingram, concur in dismissing the idea of universal co-operation as chimerical.[11]

There remains the ideal of the rapid spread of a Christ-like unselfishness. Of this hope I desire to speak with all the respect which so ancient a dream deserves; if it were realised it would, indeed, involve an upset of present property arrangements, compared with which Socialism is a mere trifle, yet science must perforce declare that the notion of any but the slowest real improvement in general moral habit is absolutely without warrant. Forms of egoism may change, and moral habits vary, but constituted as we are, it seems inevitable for healthy personal development that an at best instructed and unconscious, egoism should preponderate in the individual. It is the business of the community, not to lead into temptation this healthy natural feeling, and so to develop its social institutions that individual egoism is necessarily directed so as to promote only the well-being of all. The older writers, led by Rousseau, in the reaction against aristocratic government, saw this arrangement in absolute freedom. But that crude vision has long been demolished. "It is, indeed certain," sums up Dr. Ingram,[12] "that industrial society will not permanently remain without a systematic organisation. The mere conflict of private interests will never produce a well-ordered commonwealth of labour."

Is there then no hope? Is there no chance of the worker ever being released from the incubus of what Mill called,[13] "the great social evil of a non-labouring class," whose monopolies caused the "taxation of the industrious for the support of indolence, if not of plunder."[14]

Mill tells us that he found a sure and certain hope in the Progress of Socialism which he foresaw, and so energetically aided. We who call ourselves Socialists today, largely through Mill's teaching and example, find a confirmation of this hope in social history and economics, and see already in the distance the glad vision of a brighter day, when, practically, the whole product of labour will be the worker's, and the worker's alone, and at last social arrangements will be deliberatedly based upon the Apostolic rule ignored by so many Christians, that if a man do not work, neither shall he eat.

But it must clearly be recognised that no mere charitable palliation of existing individualism can achieve this end. Against this complacent delusion of the philanthropist, Political Economy emphatically protests. So long as the instruments of production are in unrestrained private ownership, so long must the tribute of the workers to the drones continue: so long will the toilers' reward inevitably be reduced by their exactions. No tinkering with the Land Laws can abolish or even diminish Economic Rent. The whole series of Irish legislation, for instance, has not altered its amount by a single penny, however much it has resulted in its redistribution. The *whole* equivalent of every source of fertility or advantage of all land over and above the very worst land in use, is necessarily abstracted from the mere worker. So long as Lady Matheson can "own" the island of Lewis, and "do what she likes with her own," it is the very emphatic teaching of Political Economy that the earth may be the Lord's, but the fulness thereof must, inevitably, be the landlord's.

There is an interesting episode in English history among James the First's disputes with the City Corporation, then the protector of popular liberties. James, in his wrath, threatened, as a punishment upon London, to remove the Court to Oxford. "Provided only your Majesty leave us the Thames," cleverly replied the Lord Mayor. But economic dominion is more subtle than king-craft—our landlords have stolen from us even the Thames. No Londoner who is not a landlord obtains one farthing of economic benefit from the existence of London's ocean highway; the whole equivalent of its industrial advantage goes to swell our compulsory tribute of 35 millions sterling—London's annual rental.

And it is precisely the same with industrial capital. The worker in the factory gets absolutely no advantage from the machinery which causes the product of his labour to be multiplied a hundredfold. He gets no more of that product as wages for himself, in a state of free and unrestrained competition, than his colleague laboring at the very margin of cultivation with the very minimum of capital. The artisan producing shoes by the hundred in the modern machinery works of Southwark or Northampton gets no higher wages than the surviving hand cobbler in the bye street. The whole advantage of industrial capital, like the whole advantage of superior land, necessarily goes to him who legally owns it. The mere worker can have none of them. "The "remuneration of labour, as such," wrote Professor Cairnes in 1874,[15] "skilled or unskilled, can never rise much above its present level."

Nor is it the increase of population which effects this result. During the present century, indeed, in spite of an unparalleled increase in numbers, the wealth annually produced in England *per head* has nearly doubled.[16] If population became stationary to-morrow, other things being equal, the present rent and interest would

VISIONS OF THE FUTURE

not be affected; our numbers determine indeed how *bad* the margin of cultivation will be, and this is of vital import—but, increase or no increase, the unrestrained private ownership of land and capital necessarily involves the complete exclusion of the mere worker, as such, from all the advantages of the fertile soil on which he is born, and of the buildings, railways, and machinery he finds around him.

So much the orthodox economists tell us clearly enough. Where then is the Socialist hope?

In the political power of the workers. The industrial evolution has left them landless strangers in their own country, but the political evolution is about to make them its rulers. If unrestrained private ownership of the means of production necessarily keeps the many workers permanently poor, from no fault of their own, in order to make a few idlers rich, from no merit of their own (and this is the teaching of economic science) unrestrained private ownership will inevitably go. In this country large inroads have already been made in it, and this is the Progress of Socialism.

Three hundred years ago, for fear of the horde of "sturdy beggars," which even hanging had failed to extirpate, the wise Cecil was led to institute the general system of poor relief, a deduction from rent and interest for the benefit of those who were excluded from directly sharing in them. But the industrial evolution had not yet made this condition universal, and little further progress was made in Socialism until the beginning of this century. Then, indeed, the acme of individualism was reached. No sentimental regulations hindered the free employment of land and capital to the highest possible personal advantage, however many lives of men, women, and children were used up in the process. Capitalists still speak of that bright time with exultation. "It was not five per cent. or ten per cent.," says one, "but thousands per cent. that made the fortune of Lancashire." But the tide turned against *Laisser faire* fifty years ago, mainly by the heroic efforts of a young nobleman, who lately passed away from us as Lord Shaftesbury, a really effective Factory Act was won, and the insatiate greed of the manufacturers was bridled by political power, in the teeth of their most determined opposition. Since then the progress has been rapid. Slice after slice has, in the public interest, been cut off the profits of land and capital, and therefore off their value, by Mines Regulation Acts, Truck Acts, Factory Acts, Adulteration Acts, Land Acts. Slice after slice has been cut off the already diminished incomes of the classes enjoying rent and interest, by the gradual shifting of taxation from consumption to incomes above £150, the average family income of the Kingdom. Step by step the political power and political organisation have been used for industrial ends, until one Minister of the Crown is the largest employer of labor in the country, and at least 150,000 men, not counting the army and navy, are directly in the service of the community, without the intervention of the profit of any middleman. The mere list of separate industrial operations which the local or national government has rescued from the private capitalist, and now conducts for the public benefit, fills three crowded pages of my manuscript. Besides our international relations and

70

the army, navy, police and the courts of justice, the community now carries on for itself, in some part or another of these Islands, the post office, telegraphs, carriage of small commodities, coinage, surveys, the regulation of the currency and note issue, the provision of weights and measures, the making, sweeping, lighting and repairing of streets, roads and bridges, life insurance, the grant of annuities, shipbuilding, stockbroking, banking, farming, and money-lending. It provides for many thousands of us from birth to burial, midwifery, nursery, education, board and lodging, vaccination, medical attendance, medicine, public worship, amusements, and burial. It furnishes and maintains its own museums, parks, art galleries, libraries, concert-halls, roads, streets, bridges, markets, fire engines, lighthouses, pilots, ferries, surfboats, steamtugs, lifeboats, cemeteries, public baths, washhouses, pounds, harbours, piers, wharves, hospitals, dispensaries, gasworks, waterworks, tramways, telegraph cables, allotments, cow meadows, artisans' dwellings, schools, churches and reading rooms. It carries on and publishes its own researches in geology, meterology, statistics, zoology, geography and even theology. In our Colonies, the English Government further allows and encourages the communities to provide for themselves railways, canals, pawnbroking, theatres, forestry, cinchona farms, irrigation, leper villages, casinos, bathing establishments, and immigration, and to deal in ballast, guano, quinine, opium, salt and what not. Every one of these functions, including even the army, navy, police and courts of justice, was at one time left to private enterprise, and was a source of legitimate individual investment of capital. Step by step the community has absorbed them, wholly or partially, and the area of private exploitation has been lessened. Parallel with this progressive nationalisation or municipalisation of industry, there has gone on outside the elimination of the purely personal element in business management. The older economists doubted whether anything but banking could be carried on by joint stock enterprise; now every conceivable industry, down to baking and milk-selling is successfully managed by the salaried officers of large corporations of idle shareholders. More than one-third of the whole business of England, measured by the capital employed, is now done by joint stock companies, whose shareholders could be expropriated by the community with little more dislocation of industry than is caused by the daily purchase of shares on the Stock Exchange.

Besides all its direct supersession of private enterprise, the State now registers, inspects, and controls nearly all the industrial functions which it has not yet absorbed. In addition to births, marriages, death, and electors, the State registers all solicitors, barristers, notaries, brokers, newspaper proprietors, playing-card makers, brewers, bankers, seamen, captains, mates, doctors, cabmen, hawkers, pawnbrokers, tobacconists, distillers, plate dealers, game dealers; all insurance companies, friendly societies, endowed schools and charities, limited companies, lands, houses, deeds, bills of sale, compositions, ships, arms, dogs, cabs, omnibuses, books, plays, pamphlets, newspapers, raw cotton, trademarks, and patents; lodging-houses, public-houses, refreshment houses, theatres, music-halls, places of worship, elementary schools, and dancing rooms.

Nor is the registration a mere form. Most of the foregoing are also inspected and criticised, as well as all railways, tramways, ships, mines, factories, canalboats, public conveyances, fisheries, slaughter-houses, dairies, milkshops, bakeries, babyfarms, gasmeters, schools of anatomy, vivisection laboratories, explosive works, Scotch herrings and common lodging houses.

The inspection is often detailed and rigidly enforced. The State in most of the larger industrial operations prescribes the age of the worker, the hours of work, the amount of air, light, cubic space, heat, lavatory accommodation, holidays, and mealtimes; where, when, and how wages shall be paid; how machinery, staircases, lift holes, mines, and quarries are to be fenced and guarded; how and when the plant shall be cleaned, repaired, and worked. Even the kind of package in which some articles shall be sold is duly prescribed, so that the individual capitalist shall take no advantage of his position. On every side he is being registered, inspected, controlled, and eventually superseded by the community, and is compelled in the meantime to cede for public purposes an ever increasing share of his rent and interest.

This is the rapid progress of Socialism, which is so noticeable in our generation. England is already the most Socialist of all European communities, though Prince Bismarck is now compelled by the uneasy ground swell of German politics to emulate us very closely. But as the oldest industrial country we are likely to keep the lead, although old-fashioned politicians will doubtless innocently continue to regard Socialism as a dangerous and absolutely untried innovation. Are there not still, in obscure nooks, disbelievers and despisers of all science? The schoolmaster never penetrates into *all* the corners in the same generation.

But some will be inclined to say, "This is not what we thought Socialism meant? We imagined that Socialists wanted to bring about a sanguinary conflict in the streets, and then the next day to compel all delicately nurtured people to work in the factories, at a fixed rate of wages."

I confess I should not like to be made responsible for all the notions about Socialism which even this audience entertains. It is not only in the nursery that bogey-making continues to be very general though quite unnecessary source of mental anxiety. We know how the English country folk regarded Napoleon Buonaparte, and just such a bogey is now being made of Socialism. All I can say is, look into it for yourselves. We do but declare unto you the line upon which English evolution is rapidly developing, and it needs nothing but a general recognition of that development, and a clear determination not to allow the selfish interests of any class to hinder or hamper its free scope for Socialism to secure universal assent. All other changes will easily flow from that state of mind, and need not be dwelt upon at present.

"But will not Socialism abolish private property." It will certainly seriously change the definition of what the community will lend its force to protect as private property.

It is already clear that no really democratic government, whether consciously Socialist or not, will lend its soldiers or its police, to enforce the "rights" of a Lord

Clanrikarde. Even Mr. Matthew Arnold declares the position of the mere landlord to be an "anachronism." The gradual limitation of the sphere of private property which has been so steadily progressing will doubtless continue, and just as courts of justice, private mints, slaves, public offices, pocket boroughs, votes, army commissions, post offices, telegraph lines, and now even continental telegraph cables landing on English shores, have ceased to be permissible personal possessions, so will the few remaining gasworks, waterworks, docks, tramways, and schools be quickly absorbed, and an end be also made to private railways and town ground-rents. Ultimately, and soon as may be possible, we look to see this absorption cover all land, and at least all the larger forms of industrial capital. In these, as Herbert Spencer pointed out 36 years ago as regards land, private ownership will eventually no more be possible than it is now with a post-office or a court of justice, both once valuable means of individual profit. Beyond the vista of this extension of collectivism, it is at present unprofitable to forecast; but we may at any rate be sure that social evolution will no more stop there than at any previous stage.

This is the Progress of Socialism. To an evergrowing number of students of history and science, the rapid increase of this progress appears at once our evident destiny and our only hope. Political Economy, at least, whatever the economist may think of Socialism, now recognises no other alternative. So long as land and industrial capital remain unrestrained in private ownership, so long must what Mill calls[17] "the subjection of labour to capital, and the enormous share which the possessors of the instruments of industry are able to take from the produce" inevitably continue, and even increase. The aggregate product may continue to grow, but "the remuneration of labour as such, skilled or unskilled, can never rise much above its present level," says Cairnes.

The *only* effectual means of raising the material condition of the great mass of the people, is for them to resume once more that control over their own industry which industrial evolution has taken from them, and to enter once more into the enjoyment of the fertile lands and rich mines from which they are now so relentlessly excluded. This is the teaching of economic science; and the workers are rapidly coming to appreciate it.

In this direction, too, is the mighty sweep and tendency of social evolution. Without our knowledge, even against our will, we in England have already been swept far along by the irresistible wave. What Canute will dare to set a limit to its tide? One option we have, and one only. It is ours if we will, to recognise this rising force, to give it reasonable expression, nay, within limits, even to direct its course. This is why we are Socialists, and why you must become so. But if the conscious intelligence of the natural leaders of the community lags behind the swelling tide beneath them, if we ignore the vast social forces now rapidly organising into common action, if we leave poverty and repression and injustice to go on breeding their inevitable births of angry brutality and the savage ferocity of revenge—then, indeed, social evolution will necessarily be once more accomplished by a social cataclysm. From this catastrophe, the Progress of Socialism is the path of escape.

The Buddhists have a beautiful story of the Veil of Maya, which hides from the worldly mortal the blessed Nirvana. We, too, have our Veil of Maya, woven partly of our selfishness, but even more of our prejudice and ignorance, which hides from us the True Path to which we are so near. But by patient searching of heart and diligent enquiry, we too may be purged of our prepossession and error, our Veil of Maya may be rent, aad we may enter consciously on the right track. The road may be dark and steep, for we are still weak, but the Torch of Science is in our hands: in front is the glow of morning, and we know that it leads to the mountain tops where dwell the Spirits of the Dawn.

Notes

1 "Economic Socialism," *Contemporary Review,* Nov., 1886.
2 Pages 231–2.
3 Prof. Leoni Levi, *Times,* 13th January, 1885; and see "Facts for Socialists" (Fabian Society Tract, No. 5).
4 Mansion House Relief Committee Report, 1886, p. 7.
5 Founded on partial census taken in various Board Schools, 1887–8.
6 The Shelton Street and Bloomsbury Sub-Districts respectively, of the parish of St. Giles and St. George. See Report of Vestry, 1887.
7 Mulhall's Dictionary of Statistics, p. 346; see also "Facts for Socialists."
8 In 1884, out of 81,951 deaths in London, 9,909 were in workhouses, 6,559 in hospitals, and 278 in public lunatic asylums. The deaths of paupers in receipt of outdoor relief are not included.—*Registrar-General's Report,* 1886, C—4,722, *pp.* 94 *and* 118.
9 "Some Leading Principles of Political Economy," p. 293.
10 "Principles of Political Economy," last edition (1865), p. 477 (quoting from Feugueray).
11 Article on "Political Economy" in Encyclopædia Brittanica, by Dr. J. T. Ingram, vol. xix, p. 382.
12 Encyclopædia Brittanica, vol. xix, p. 382.
13 "Principles of Political Economy," p. 455.
14 "Principles of Political Economy," p. 477.
15 "Some Leading Principles of Political Economy," p. 348.
16 Mulhall's "Dictionary of Statistics," p. 245.
17 "Principles of Political Economy," p. 477.

5

THE CLAIMS AND PROGRESS OF LABOUR REPRESENTATION (NEWCASTLE-ON-TYNE: LABOUR LITERATURE SOCIETY [NORTH ENGLAND], c. 1894), 3–16.

Fred Hammill

[Fred Hammill's pamphlet *The Claims and Progress of Labour Representation* of 1894, which is a revised edition of an article he had published in the *Fortnightly Review* earlier that year, is significant for a number of reasons. First, it reflected a major dispute in the Fabian Society, on the executive of which Hammill served. The two opposing sides were led by George Bernard Shaw and Sidney Webb respectively. Shaw and his supporters favoured the formation of a new socialist party. Webb argued that the Fabians should permeate existing parties and organisations and thereby influence Liberal and even Conservative party members (Bevir 2011, 195–214). The position presented by Hammill (c. 1894) was consistent with that of Shaw.

The pamphlet also reflected a dispute in the Independent Labour Party (ILP). In the first few months after the formation of the ILP in 1893, a number of activists, including Hammill, were deterred from joining because of the involvement of H.H. Champion and Maltman Barry (Duffy 1962). Champion had held office in the Social Democratic Federation (SDF) which was influenced by its leader H.M. Hyndman's distinctive combination of Marxism with Toryism, while Barry was a member of the Conservative Party with a history of funding SDF candidates to help them defeat Liberals (Barnes 2005). Hammill's opposition to Champion and Barry is plain to see in the pamphlet.

A third reason why the pamphlet is of interest is that Hammill insisted that the trade unions should help form a new Labour Party and fund its parliamentary and other electoral candidates. Hammill's pamphlet is thus important in the campaign which brought about the Labour Representation Committee in 1900, which in turn became the Labour Party six years later. Hammill did not live to see the latter development.]

VISIONS OF THE FUTURE

THE Claims of Labor for full and direct representation in Parliament, on County Councils, Municipalities, Local Boards, School Boards, Vestries and Boards of Guardians, are now being more vigorously forced to the front than at any previous period. All ministers, politicians, and public men have to listen to the claims, and to reckon with the Labor forces behind them, for any real glory or prosperity our country can boast of has come through industry by labor; and the workers, forming the great majority of the nation, are becoming conscious of this, and are discriminating more and more as they emerge from the darkness of ignorance, between the hypocritical disguises which class Governments invest their maladministration, misrepresentation, and tyranny, and that which makes a nation great and its people prosperous. They are clamouring for a more equal division of enlightenment, comfort, leisure, recreation, and liberty. But clamour by itself will never attain that end, and Labor must put its own shoulder to the wheel if the political waggon is to be got out of the rut in which it is now sticking; and it is this conviction which is producing the growing determination of the working classes to be directly represented in Parliament and on governing bodies by men of their own class. They have never been represented on any of our public bodies in any real sense, directly or indirectly. Their representation has been the employé by the employer, the sweated worker by the sweater, poverty by the capitalist and the philanthropist, slum-life by the slum-owner, the agricultural labourer by lords, landlords, and country squires; while their general welfare, of both body and soul, has been entrusted to the Church, and all acting together have made "England the paradise of the rich, the purgatory of the wise, and the hell of the poor."

Whichever party may be in office, landlords and capitalists are always in power; and they use it to lay hands for themselves on the nut of labor, obtain the nut of Labor while the working classes are expected to remain content with the husks, washed down by promises from the rival political leaders who, once in power, do as little as they can beyond taking care of the interests of their class until the next election, when the old round of promises and pretentious friendship by both Liberal and Tory begins again with the same result as before. Can the workers be wondered at if, in taking off the blinkers of ignorance and putting on the spectacles of education and intelligence, they take a leaf out of the book of "their betters" and imitate their determination to be represented in Parliament by men of their own set?

The Liberal and Conservative parties representing as they do, and being as they are, part of the class depending on Rent, Interest, and Profit, are, from the working class point of view, really not two political parties at all but an organised concentrated ring, representing everything but Labor or the class that lives by wages. They have no hunger for food, no pawning of Sunday clothes to pay rent, no fireless grates, no bare floors or clotheless beds, no fear of unemployment, and no paupers' coffins awaiting their well-nourished corpses. All those needs which are matters of life and death being satisfied for them, they have no such terrible "spur to prick the sides of their intent" as Labor has. Whatever mere readjustments of the present system, whatever fanciful speculative ideals they may occupy themselves with, their only real need in Parliament is to protect their own incomes; and this they can only do by keeping things in the main just as they are.

Hence the demand for direct independent Labor representation, meaning independent of, but not indifferent to, already existing political parties. North, South, East and West of England this demand is increasing in volume and in strength with startling rapidity, and is already recognised by the Conservative and Liberal parties as a "dangerous" factor in politics. It is true that the organisation of the workers educationally, socially, and politically is as yet only in its infancy; but the infancy of a giant is more formidable than the maturity of a person of ordinary stature, and the infant hand is making its power known and felt.

The education of the masses during the past ten years, in the direction of direct representation of Labor in Parliament and collective ownership and control of industry, has been effected partly by the object lessons of experience—and very bitter and barbarous lessons have they been—and partly by the propaganda carried on by Socialistic and Democratic political societies. Among the forces at work in this way, the following are worth specifying:—

(a) Compulsory (and now free) education.
(b) Trades Unionism and Organization.
(c) Strikes and Lock-outs.
(d) Unemployment.
(e) The Social Democratic Federation.
(f) The Fabian Society.
(g) Labor Electoral Associations, National and Local.
(h) The Independent Labor Party.
(i) The Champion-Barry Tory Independent Labor Party.
(j) The Red Vans of the English Land Restoration League.

(a) Compulsory education, as was predicted by its most far-sighted opponents in 1870, is arming the working population with a weapon which will finally effect their complete emancipation. As long as education was on the side of the classes and ignorance on that of the masses, the struggle between them could have only one issue; and the upper and middle classes knew this well enough to maintain their advantage by keeping the people ignorant, until it became apparent that no modern State could hold its place in the industrial markets of the world unless its workmen were educated. The age of popular ignorance is rapidly passing away, and the new educational policy is being pushed by Labor leaders

VISIONS OF THE FUTURE

who do not merely say, Agitate, Organize, but Agitate, *Educate,* Organize. The best proof that this advice is being acted upon may be found in the questions which candidates now have to answer at elections for Parliament, Municipalities, Local Boards, Vestries, &c. These questions are often the means of educating the candidates, who find in them more knowledge of the duties and powers at stake than they themselves possess.

(b) The Trades Union Congress is the recognised trumpet of trades organization throughout this country. This Congress, held annually in different parts of the United Kingdom, gives a collective opinion on all questions affecting organized Labor—the members of each trade organization expressing their opinion by the vote of their trade delegate. For many years the political representation of Labor has been neglected, and by many of the older trades unionists purposely ignored, they having no hope of ever forming an independent Labor party, or perhaps preferring to support one of the two already existing political parties as the easiest way of making the best of a weak position. This is surprising enough, for on perusal of the Annual Reports it appears that at least two-thirds of their annual resolutions are asking the Government to do for them what they are unable to do for themselves. Recently, however, all this has been changed. The delegates of different trade societies, skilled and unskilled, express an almost unanimous desire for direct Labour representation. Foremost among these bodies which have already taken action is the Amalgamated Society of Engineers, which in June, 1893, decided:—"If at any time it should appear to the Council desirable to contribute towards the expenses of a member of the society as a candidate for election as a member of the House of Commons, they shall have power, after submitting the question to a vote of the members, to cause a levy to be made for payment of such contributions, and of an annual allowance to such member if elected; such levy not to exceed threepence per year per member." This small levy, if based on the 74,000 members, will bring in an annual income of £900, enough to support at least two members in Parliament until such times as payment of members by the State and election expenses from the rates become a reality. The important point in this resolution is the one empowering the Council to "contribute towards the expenses of a member of the Society AS A CANDIDATE for election as a member of the House of Commons." This means the initiation of a policy of endeavour to win a seat for direct Labor representation by providing funds for the propagation of the candidature previous to entering Parliament. The supporters of this resolution foresaw that direct independent Labor seats in the future must be won by fighting and not by begging.

The General Railway Workers' Union decided on a policy of direct Labor representation in the year 1890, and have reaffirmed their decision since then. Many others, too numerous to mention, are advancing in the same direction; and at the annual Trades Union Congress, held in Belfast in September, 1893, and

CLAIMS & PROGRESS OF LABOUR REPRESENTATION

composed of 380 delegates, representing 900,000 trades unionists, definite action was decided upon for the selection and financing of Parliamentary candidates. The two following clauses were adopted by a very large majority:—

> "SELECTION OF CANDIDATES.—(1) The selection of candidates in every case to rest with the localities in the first instance. If, at any time, however, it should be impossible to secure a suitable local candidate, a candidate may then be selected by the locality from a list of persons approved by the committee. (2) All candidates receiving financial assistance must pledge themselves to support the Labor programme as agreed upon from time to time by the Congress.
>
> "FINANCIAL.—(1) That a separate fund be established for the purpose of assisting independent Labor candidates in local and Parliamentary elections. (2) Each Society desiring to affiliate with the movement shall subscribe annually to the election fund the sum of 5s. per 100 members. (3) The administration of the aforesaid fund to be entrusted to a committee of thirteen persons (including secretary and treasurer), who shall be elected annually at the Congress by and from the delegates representing the contributing societies. A statement to be made of money received and expended during the year."

This independent policy, if skilfully and resolutely handled by capable and determined men on behalf of the trade organisations, would play havoc in the ranks of both the Conservative and Liberal parties.

(c) The many strikes and lock-outs since the strike of the London Gasworkers in 1888, have given a marked political impetus to the Labor cause. To take two prominent instances: the Manningham strike led to a Parliamentary Labor candidature in Bradford in opposition to Mr. Alfred Illingworth, and the Hull strike forced the Hull dockers and workmen generally to the conclusion that they could no longer depend on a dock-owner to represent them in Parliament. During the past year the Cotton strike and the Miners' lock-out, though costing the workers considerably over half-a-million pounds, with much sacrifice, suffering, and loss of life, have done more for independent Labor action than five years of energetic educational propaganda could have been expected to accomplish. So continuously have the workers been at war with the employers, that there is not a single organised worker in England who has not been either directly involved or called upon to assist those who were. The misery and suffering that women and children have been helplessly called upon to endure in such barbarous warfare has so hardened the heart of the father against the strike weapon, that he now needs little argument to persuade him to look in another direction for help. The political machine at Westminster, too long the weapon of his opponents, lies ready to his hand if only he will make up his mind to seize it.

VISIONS OF THE FUTURE

(d) Unemployment, with its accompaniment of hunger and want, is the natural breeder of discontent, crime, violence, and anarchy. The unemployed worker with no redress, without hope, sullenly examines his position and compares it with that of others "who toil not, neither do they spin." Be he Tory or Liberal in politics, he soon finds violent anarchism more reasonable than it seemed when he was in work; and by the time he has discovered that anarchism can do nothing for him but get him into mischief, he is at least thoroughly weaned from the political pap that formerly sufficed him. When trade revives, he returns to employment with his opinions ripe for an independent Labor policy.

(e) The Social Democratic Federation of England persistently holds itself aloof from all other bodies. It acknowledges no candidate as a Socialist, or as a genuine representative of the working classes, unless he joins its ranks. At elections, when the members can muster money enough to run a candidate, they select him without consulting the rest of the constituency, and send him to the poll win or lose, whether he is wanted or not, supporting him by vigorous and impartial abuse of all opinions and organisations except their own. This they call a "no compromise" policy; and they carry it out so thoroughly that up to the present moment their candidate seldom secures as many votes as would accredit him as a representative of the company in a village taproom. Nevertheless the Social Democratic Federation is a force which makes for independent Labor representation. Ludicrously as its attempts at electioneering have failed, still its socialist propaganda, which it carries on with extraordinary energy and assiduity considering the insignificance of its numbers, has unquestionably had a telling and permanent effect on the minds of the workers; and as this propaganda is always associated with unsparing denunciation of both Conservatives and Liberals, the impression it leaves is always favourable to independent political action by the working class, and strongly hostile to the old Radical policy of attaching the workers to the skirts of the Liberals. The Social Democratic Federation, or rather its members, mostly agree that no organisation other than their own is the one that can ultimately emancipate the workers, and no person can possibly be a Socialist unless he be a member of their body; and any Socialist, however uncompromising, however violent or destructive he may be, unless he be a member of their body, is called a "milk and water Socialist;" the more rabid, violent, and destructive he be—apart from common sense, reason, principle, honour, or constructive ability—he is hailed as a jolly good fellow, and his membership sealed with enthusiastic cheers. This spirit ought not to be either present or engendered; for if Socialism means anything, it means the establishment and promotion of a closer, higher, and more honourable fellow-feeling between us all, which ought to exist and must exist if we are to succeed.

(f) As to the Fabian Society I must excuse myself a little, as my position as a member of the Executive Council of that body disqualifies me from giving an unbiassed account of it. However, I will quote the opinion of no less an authority than the official organ of the Gladstonians. The

Fabian Society, says "The Speaker" (4th November, 1893), consists of "a few nobodies banded into a society. . . . . . The blend of individual peculiarities which would thus be produced would account for the collective type with which students are familiar under the name of Fabianism—a mixture of dreary, gassy doctrinairism and crackbrained farcicality, set off by a portentous omniscience and flighty egotism not to be matched outside the walls of a lunatic asylum." This is quite enough to prove that the Fabian Society is pretty active and influential in the direction which the older Whigs most dread. The peculiarity of the Fabian Society is that it is a purely propagandist body, taking no direct political action in its own name, running no candidates, making no attempt to enlist its converts in its own ranks, but permeating all existing political and social organisations with socialistic and democratic doctrines, stirring them up to action, pointing out the best opportunities to them, and supplying them with information, documents, a policy, and, if necessary, brains. The Fabians are, in fact, the Jesuits of the Labour movement; and they have had a finger in more pies than is supposed, including some which even "The Speaker" has swallowed with unsuspecting relish. In electioneering tactics they have always denounced the policy of abstention from voting. Where there was no possibility of a successful Labor candidature, they have joined the Liberal Associations in order to bring about the selection of as advanced a Liberal as possible; and when they succeeded in this, they backed the candidate vigorously at the election. At the last general election this led to an impression that the Fabian Society was a section of the Liberal party. But the support they gave to all properly organised and really hopeful independent Labor candidatures ought to have removed this very erroneous impression. At any rate, it was not the fault of the Fabians if the Liberals were surprised at the demand for an independent Labor campaign which the Society published in "The Fortnightly Review" in November, 1893, a demand which has now been elaborated into "A Plan of Campaign for Labour," under which title it has been circulated in great numbers throughout the country, thanks to the invaluable advertisements it received from the attacks of the Gladstonian press. What the influence of the Fabian Society may be worth it is not for me to say; but there can be no question that such as it is, the Fabians have thrown it with all their might on the side of independent Labor at the next general election.

(g) Labor Electoral Associations, national and local, have been formed with a special leaning towards Labor—some favourable to independent action, others as auxiliaries to the Liberal party. The members of the Labor Electoral Association have long relied on the sympathy and promises of the bountiful Liberal party, and while relying have in many ways assisted the Liberal party into possession of the three P's—Pay, Position, and Power. While they were willing to assist the Liberal party they were smiled on and flattered, and to goad them on to greater support a few of their members were created J.P.'s, with promises of more deserts to follow. This has proved to be the end

VISIONS OF THE FUTURE

of Liberal sympathy and support. The Labor Electoral Association has now found out, as instanced by the Attercliffe bye-election and the South Shields jugglery, that so long as the Association will remain subordinate and be a good boy by doing as its Liberal foster-mother tells it, so long can it remain under the Liberal wing; but as soon as it says "We want a *bona-fide* candidate to run for Parliament, a man of our own choice, a man of independent principles and policy", the Liberal party and Labor Electoral Association not only part friendship, but fly at each others throats like political tigers—the Liberal party fighting for authority, the Labor Electoral Association fighting for sympathy. While the fight is going on it is dangerous to prophesy what may happen. What we may hope for, work for, and fight for is, that those who are more Liberal than Labor shall be forced into the Liberal camp, while those who are more Labor than Liberal will be brought over by their own intelligence and common sense into the Independent line. Events seem to show that under equally capable management those which pursue the Independent policy survive, whilst the others will disappear or shunt on to the Independent line. Generally speaking, these associations are only useful educationally; their direct political action amounts practically to nothing.

(h) The Independent Labor Party was formed in January, 1893, when 125 delegates from local Independent Labor Clubs, Workman's Federation, Trades Unions, Trades Councils, Labor League, Labor Church, Scottish Labor Party, Social Democratic Federation, Fabian Society, Eight Hours League, and other bodies throughout the country met in conference at Bradford, under the presidency of Mr. Keir Hardie, M.P., merged their separate forces into the organisation, which is now known as the Independent Labor Party, under the control of a National Administrative Council. The second General and Annual Conference was held in 1893 in Manchester, where the secretaryship was accepted by Mr. Tom Mann, and important changes were made in the *personnel* of the Council. It is too soon to estimate the full effect of these changes; but anyone who has done any political work in the Labor interest in the North of England lately must admit that the opportunities of the Independent Labor Party are very great, and only need good management to be turned to immediate account.

(i) What I have called the Champion-Barry Tory Independent Labor Party consisted of two persons, Mr. H. H. Champion and Mr. Maltman Barry, who published a monthly organ named *The Labour Elector,* which they described as "the organ of the Independent Labor Party." The paper was, of course, simply the organ of the two gentlemen who published it. Some years ago, under the editorship of Mr. Champion, it did splendid work in forwarding the Eight Hours Question, in connection with which Mr. Champion may fairly claim as much credit as any living person; but *The Labour Elector* even at that time was not a representative organ of Labor. It has lately ceased to be published, but while

82

it was under the sole editorship of Mr. Maltman Barry it scurrilously attacked every prominent person in the Labor movement, unless he was prepared to oppose Home Rule and support Protection, Imperial Federation, and what is generally known as Tory Democracy. Mr. Champion, however, freely invited well known Labor men or Socialists to contest Parliamentary seats, promising pecuniary support, which, if they accepted, gave him a considerable hold over them. Nothing is easier than to find money for a Labor candidate. This Labor candidate, who was run not with the intention of winning a seat for Labor, but of making the return of the Conservative sure. Whether the suspicions which have been expressed that the subsidies negotiated are of this nature are well founded, need not be discussed here; but it cannot be too thoroughly understood that *The Labour Elector* and the "party" of which it professed to be the organ, are in no way representative of the general Labor or Socialistic movement. The Independent Labor party has expressly repudiated them, and the current opinion in Labor circles seems to be that the Independent Labor party in doing so took a very politic step.

(j) I have mentioned the red vans of the English Land Restoration League as among the bodies which have been educating the workers politically for some years past. These vans go from village to village, forming county unions among the agricultural labourers, and preaching the doctrines of Land Nationalization and the Labor programme. When I add that the lecturer, who has to live in the van and rough it a bit, doing plenty of hard work for nothing, is almost always an enthusiastic member of the Fabian Society or some other Socialistic society, it will be understood that the labourers do not hear much party politics of the conventional pattern from him.

Closing this summary of the different bodies, strong, weak, and pretentious, that are encouraging direct Labor representation, it may be taken for certain that Labor in the future will have a much louder voice in the political world than heretofore. How little chance it has had hitherto may be judged from the following analysis of the present House of Commons:—

* Landholder M.P.'s (including the sons or heirs of great landed proprietors	130
Lawyer Interest	148
Shipowners	25
Liquor Interest	24
Money Interest	30
Railway Interest	22
Coalowners	21
Ironmasters	24
Employing and Manufacturing Interests (excluding Shipowners)	116
LABOR INTEREST	15

VISIONS OF THE FUTURE

But the application of these figures becomes more emphatic when we observe the interests excluded from the House of Commons, thus:—

450,000 Railway Shareholders have of their number in Parliament. 22

380,000 Railway Servants have no direct representative.

The Landowning Classes (in addition to their own select chamber, the House of Lords), have of their number in Parliament. 130

800,000 Agricultural Labourers have only one direct representative. 1

220,000 British Merchant Sailors have only one direct representative in the "People's House," while the trades employed in shipbuilding have none; but the limited class of Shipowners and Shipbuilders are represented in Parliameut to the number of. 25

66,000 Persons connected with the Legal Peofession have members in the House. 148

655,000 Miners have only 7 direct representatives in Parliament, while the very small and limited class of Coalowners have fully 21

There are fifteen Millowners in Parliament, but not one representative of the Cotton Operatives; twenty-four Ironmasters, but not one Iron-worker. There are twenty-five Directors in addition to Railway Directors; forty-four Professional Men; twenty-one Heirs to Titles, and fifty-four belonging to the Fighting Interest. Twenty-seven Members of the Government and Officials draw £72,587 per year out of the State, some of whom are against payment of members.[1]

The anomaly presented by these figures can only be appreciated in view of the fact that in 400 constituencies a majority of the voters belong to the working class. An analysis of the voting at the last general election will show the weak position of the two political parties at the present time, and how easily this will become weaker if Labor asserts itself.

At the last general election 204 members were elected with majorities less than 500.

Conservative small majorities:—107 Conservatives or Liberal Unionists were elected with majorities less than 500. Twenty of these had majorities between 500 and 400; 25 ranged from 400 to 300; 22 from 300 to 200; 21 from 200 to 100; 8 ranged from 100 down to 50, and eleven had majorities less than 50.

Liberal small majorities:—97 Liberals (excluding Ireland) were elected with majorities less than 500; 80 had majorities less than 400; and 68 of these had less than 300 majority; 44 less than 200; 19 less than 100, and 10 less than 50.

In all these constituencies, and with very little organisation, Labor, through the industrial population, can give the casting vote as between Conservative and Liberal, even when they are not prepared to run a candidate of their own.

The political ball is already at the feet of Labor, and only waits for Labor to kick it. When this is realised, the Labor representation of fifteen in the year 1893 will be increased to fifty.

England is far behind other countries in direct Labor representation. In Germany, for instance, the attempts of the German Government since 1878 to stop the progress of the Social Democratic movement have proved a farce. Obtaining its anti-Socialistic law, from October 21st to December 17th, 1878, it suppressed 174 societies, 44 journals, and 157 periodicals. It issued 375 edicts, and paid over 1,000 domiciliary visits. In spite of this persecution, Social Democratic representation in the Reichstag has increased from nine in 1878 to forty-four in 1894.

Australia has gone further than this, as the following table will show:—

AUSTRALIAN LABOR MEMBERS, AUGUST, 1893.

COLONY.	Number of Seats in Parliament.	Number of Labor Members in present Parliament.	Number of Labor Members in last Parliament.	Increase.
New South Wales.......	139	37	0	37
Victoria......................	95	12	6	6
South Australia...........	54	13	2	11
Queensland.................	65	17	4	13
New Zealand..............	70	15	(?)	15

Ireland, helped by what is virtually Payment of Members from America, has gone so far as to secure 86 seats by members pledged to a policy of Home Rule. Mr. Michael Davitt, in his article in the December number of the "Nineteenth Century," states:—"Home Rule has over seventy solid votes in Parliament as much at the service of the British toilers as for the advancement of the interests of the labouring masses of Ireland." As this assurance forms part of a bitter attack by Mr. Davitt on the protest recently made on behalf of these same British toilers by the Fabian Society, it can hardly be received with much conviction.

The Labor movement has become far too strong and determined to lie down quietly in the gutter of the political arena, while Home Rule continues to walk over it crying, "Wait." Labor will no longer be content to wait for Home Rule, even at the request of Mr. Michael Davitt. Ireland cannot complain of want of sympathy from Labor. That sympathy was voluntarily extended at a time when Liberal Governments were not the plausible friends of Ireland, but her implacable and coercive foes. I trust, then, that a friendly and honourable alliance will be formed between the Irish party and the Labor party. The autocratic power and attitude of the Lords on the Home Rule question, and the obstinate opposition of the Unionists in both Houses towards the political progress of Labor, points clearly to such an alliance. As the struggle of Democracy against class domination developes, new difficulties will arise which will make the need for union still plainer. It is not quite safe to predict, but at any rate I may conjecture that with such an alliance the Irish and Labor parties combined will be master of the situation in the House of Commons. The Whigs and moderate Liberals will in that case be forced across the floor of the House to the friends of monopoly; the Radicals will merge into the Irish, Labor, or Socialistic party, which will represent Labor and the masses as against capital and the classes. This is likely to happen much earlier than is generally expected. How long will be decided by how far and how soon Labor will force her way into Parliament.

The Parliamentary Committee of the Trades Union Congress can set to work at once to prepare for the next general election, if it is as unfettered by political partisanship as it ought to be. Initiative and energy on their part is all that is necessary: the support of the organised workers behind them is already guaranteed. The psychological moment has come; and the only question is whether Trade Union officialdom will be equal to the emergency. Labor never need be hampered by want of funds. The workers can afford all that is needed; and if they are not in earnest enough to provide it, they deserve to be non-represented and misrepresented. A national subscription or levy of a penny a year from every male worker in this country would bring in £35,000 a year. If weekly wage workers of all ages and both sexes were levied, or subscribed one penny a year each, we might rely on an annual income of at least £60,000. A levy of a penny a week from every London worker represented on the London Trades Council would bring in £10,000 a year. The London Trades Council have lately decided to establish a Labor Representation Committee to act for all London constituencies, and sub-committees are to be formed in every constituency for supporting and controlling Labor representation on all governing bodies, and will probably become affiliated with the National Independent Labor party. The expenses will be borne by the local committees, the central committee paying for postage, printing, and stationery. These expenses are to be met by a voluntary subscription of 10s. per 1,000 members for local elections, and 10s. per 100 members for Parliamentary candidates. If the 65,000 members endorse this policy by giving it practical support much outside help will be forthcoming, and London representation can be revolutionised in a very short time. A gentleman writing in the "Contemporary Review" of December last, intimates that the idea of financing Labor candidates by means of a special fund is "out of harmony with the steady resolve of the Parliamentary Committee of the Trades Union Congress to steer clear of election funds, and to put all its force into the movement for democratising Parliament by payment of members." If this be true, it is entirely *out* of harmony with the vigorous "resolve" of the Trades Union Congress itself, which at Belfast declared by 145 votes against 78 in favour of "establishing a separate fund, and that each society shall subscribe annually to the election fund the sum of 5s. per 100 members." This "resolve" was decided by those who evidently fully believe the statement that payment of members was erased from the last Budget but one by Mr. Gladstone, who, like all the Liberals of his school, is more Conservative in his attitude to the new Labor movement than many of the Conservatives themselves. If this Government is to proceed on Gladstonian principles, it would be interesting and instructive to Labour to know how Parliament is to be "democratised" other than by a special election fund for payment of Labor representatives. No doubt I shall be called a "Fabian wrecker" for daring to question the revolutionary order of the Liberal Cabinet. Sir William Harcourt is still promising payment of members; he evaded it entirely in his Budget speech, and no doubt the Liberal candidates will come before the constituencies with the same salve of promise. Promise everything; give nothing until they are compelled. The workers will be prepared to meet these political promises as they deserve. We have no indication of the Liberal party further redeeming its Newcastle Programme pledges, especially as to the "free breakfast table," by repealing the tax on tea, coffee, cocoa, chicory, chocolate, currants and raisins. If Sir William Harcourt had wished to eradicate the prevailing impression that Labor has placed its trust in false hopes and false friends, instead of a Budget disappointment he could have given a spur to Labor representation, and thereby helped to banish that apathy which is the most dangerous of all the political vices of the workers.

For my part, I have no faith in any real help coming to labor except from labor itself; and that is fast becoming the growing opinion all round. That labor is asserting itself, that labor will be directly and independently represented in Parliament, is only a question of time. The Independent Party, the New Party, the heterogeneous party composed of brain-workers, mental workers, all workers, is solidifying itself, is concentrating its energy and its force preparatory to raising a united demand for immediate remedies for the social evils that surround us on all sides.

It may be useful to here give some proof how many of our statesmen in England see equally with us as to what is happening and what is coming.

Lord Rosebery, speaking at St. James' Hall, March 21, 1894, said:

> —"I am certain that there is a party in this country, unnamed as yet, that is disconnected with any existing political organisation—a party that is inclined to say "A plague on both your houses, a plague on all your unending discussions that yield so little fruit."

This is exactly what we are saying, what we are tired of saying, and we now intend to act for ourselves.

Lord Salisbury, speaking at Covent Garden, April 21, 1894, said:—

> "They looked round them and saw a growing mass of poverty and want of employment, and, of course, the one object which every statesman who loved his country should desire to attain was that there might be the largest amount of profitable employment for the mass of the people. He did not say that he had any patent or certain remedy for the terrible evils which beset us on all sides, but he did say that it was time they left off mending the constitution of Parliament, and that they turned all the

wisdom and energy Parliament could combine together in order to remedy the sufferings under which so many of their countrymen laboured."

The Right Hon. John Morley, M.P., speaking at Newcastle on May 21, 1894, said:—

"Gentlemen, I am not blind to the signs of the times. I see new ideas, new principles, new aims, new social ideals, new industrial methods and hopes coming above the horizon. I am not afraid of them—I welcome them. I believe that out of this great ferment good will come."

"Now I dare say the time may come—sooner than some think—when the Liberal party will be transferred or superseded by some new party."

I may here quote some extracts from a shilling work called "Merrie England," by Nunquam. I would it could be read by every man and woman in England. We will endeavour to see that every boy and girl does read it. He says—

"At present the working people of this country live under conditions altogether monstrous. Their labor is much too heavy, their pleasures are too few; and in their close streets and crowded houses decency, and health, and cleanliness are well-nigh impossible. It is not only the wrong of this that I resent—it is the *waste*. Look through the slums, and see what childhood, girlhood, womanhood, and manhood have become. Think what a waste of beauty of virtue, of strength, and of all the power and goodness that go to make a nation great is being consummated there by ignorance and by injustice. For, depend upon it, every one of our brothers or sisters ruined or slain by poverty or vice, is a loss to the nation of so much courage and skill, of so much glory and delight. Cast your eyes, then, over the Registrar-General's returns and imagine, if you can, how many gentle nurses, good mothers, sweet singers, brave soldiers, clever artists, inventors and thinkers, are swallowed up every year in that ocean of crime and sorrow, which is known to the official mind as 'the high death-rate of the wage-earning classes.' Alas! the pity of it."

Do the two great political parties ever think like this? Do any of the members ever write like it? Have they in their sphere any real knowledge of it? Do they not rather cloak it, hide it, ignore it, or try to forget that such is the practical side of the wage-earner's lot. I would they could respond to the same author who in the same work invitingly says:—

"Come with me and I will show you where men and women work from morning till night, from week to week, from year to year, at the full stretch of their powers, in dim and fœtid dens, and yet are poor, aye, destitute—have for their wages a crust of bread and rags. I will show you where men work in dirt and heat, using the strength of brutes for a dozen hours a day, and sleep at night in styes, until brain and muscle are exhausted, and fresh slaves are yoked to the golden car of commerce, and the broken drudges filter through the union or the prison to a felon's or pauper's grave! And I will show you how men and women thus work and suffer, and faint and die, generation after generation; and I will show you how the longer and harder these wretches toil, the worse their lot becomes; and I will show you the graves, and find witnesses to the histories of brave, and noble, and industrious poor men whose lives were lives of toil and poverty, and whose deaths were tragedies. And all these things are due to *sin;* but it is to the sin of the smug hypocrites who grow rich upon the robbery and the ruin of their fellow-creatures."

Here we have presented the result of a system of selfish individualism, grinding competition, rent, interest and profit extraction, assisted by over a century's patchwork legislation horrible to behold; and to any close observer or reasonable investigator, the position in the near future is doubly horrible to contemplate. That this question is a broad humanitarian question, that it ought to be considered equally by either Liberal, Conservative, Whig, or Socialist, cannot be denied. The intelligent, the unselfish, do care, do consider, and *are* anxious for a new order of things. The two parties, Liberal and Conservative alike, as parties, don't care, don't consider, and are not anxious for a new order of things, but rather prefer and encourage the old order of lackadaisical progress, not for our benefit, only for theirs. Because this is so, because we have the power to be honestly, earnestly, and disinterestedly represented in Parliament apart from the old gang is why I want to see, with the setting of the nineteenth century and the dawning of the twentieth, the long-hoped-for realisation of a real representative Labor or Socialistic party in the British House of Commons.

FRED HAMMILL.

Note

1 Labor Electoral Association Report, 1893.

6

"THE NEED FOR A LABOUR PARTY", IN *BRITAIN FOR THE BRITISH* (LONDON: CLARION PRESS, 1902), 148–155.

Robert Blatchford

[At times a member of the Fabian Society and Independent Labour Party (ILP), at other times Robert Blatchford was one of their most prominent critics. He was also, notoriously, a nationalist and supporter of war to defend the British Empire. These were traits which many socialists found inconsistent with their ideological commitment to the empowerment of the international working class (Callaghan 1990: 73).

There is no direct or substantial discussion in Blatchford's book *Britain for the British* of the exploitation of people in the Empire for either the benefit of the rich or concessions for the less wealthy in the British Isles. Blatchford (1902) mentioned trade between Britain and India and said, disapprovingly, that the employers of the British poor are often those who also exploit the Indian poor. However, he also suggested that the Empire should be defended. His reluctance to elaborate is a case of neglect in which the key socialist principle of community is restricted to a degree which many socialists could not accept.

To grasp the point of Blatchford's chapter of *Britain for the British* selected for this volume one needs to understand his views on the Labour Representation Committee (LRC). Blatchford had been pressing for the formation of a single British socialist party since the early 1890s, stressing in his newspaper *The Clarion* in 1894 that there were non-socialists in the ILP, but that a genuine Labour Party would consist exclusively of socialists (Laybourn 1994: 156–157). The ILP put its efforts into supporting the trade unions, with which it and the Fabians joined in 1900 to form the LRC. The Social Democratic Federation also joined but soon broke away. The LRC, with its Fabian and ILP influences, was driven by trade union interests and prepared to collaborate with the Liberal Party. As Blatchford's chapter makes clear, for him a proper Labour Party would need to be

THE NEED FOR A LABOUR PARTY

a party exclusively of working-class socialists. It would campaign for the nationalization of industry rather than trade union-inspired reform and exclude middle-class Liberals.]

I AM now to persuade you, Mr. John Smith, a British workman, that you need a Labour Party. It is a queer task for a bookish man, a literary student, and an easy lounger through life, who takes no interest in politics and needs no party at all. To persuade you, a worker, that you need a worker's party, is like persuading you that you need food, shelter, love, and liberty. It is like persuading a soldier that he needs arms, a scholar that he needs books, a woman that she needs a home. Yet my chief object in writing this book has been to persuade you that you need a Labour Party.

Why should Labour have a Labour Party? I will put the answer first into the words of the anti-Socialist, and say, Because "self-interest is the strongest motive of mankind."

That covers the whole ground, and includes all the arguments that I shall advance in favour of a Labour Party.

For if self-interest be the leading motive of human nature, does it not follow that when a man wants a thing done for his own advantage he will be wise to do it himself.

An upper-class party may be expected to attend to the interests of the upper class. And you will find that such a party has always done what might be expected. A middle-class party may be expected to attend to the interests of the middle class. And history and the logic of current events prove that the middle class has done what might have been expected.

And if you wish the interests of the working class to be attended to, you will take to heart the lesson contained in those examples, and will form a working-class party.

Liberals will declare, and do declare, in most pathetic tones, that they have done more, and will do more, for the workers than the Tories have done or will do. And Liberals will assure you that they are really more anxious to help the workers than we Socialists believe.

But those are side issues. The main thing to remember is, that even if the Liberals are all they claim to be, they will never do as much for Labour as Labour could do for itself.

Is not self-interest the ruling passion in the human heart? Then how should *any* party be so true to Labour and so diligent in Labour's service as a Labour Party would be?

What is a Trade Union? It is a combination of workers to defend their own interests from the encroachments of the employers.

Well, a Labour Party is a combination of workers to defend their own interests from the encroachments of the employers, or their representatives in Parliament and on Municipal bodies.

VISIONS OF THE FUTURE

Do you elect your employers as officials of your Trade Unions? Do you send employers as delegates to your Trade Union Congress? You would laugh at the suggestion. You know that the employer *could* not attend to your interests in the Trade Union, which is formed as a defence against him.

Do you think the employer is likely to be more useful or more disinterested in Parliament or the County Council than in the Trade Union?

Whether he be in Parliament or in his own office, he is an employer, and he puts his own interest first and the interests of Labour behind.

Yet these men whom as Trade Unionists you mistrust, you actually send as politicians to "represent" you.

A Labour Party is a kind of political Trade Union, and to defend Trade Unionism is to defend Labour representation.

If a Liberal or a Tory can be trusted as a parliamentary representative, why cannot he be trusted as an employer?

If an employer's interests are opposed to your interests in business, what reason have you for supposing that his interests and yours are not opposed in politics?

Am I to persuade you to join a Labour Party? Then why should I not persuade you to join a Trade Union? Trade Union and Labour Party are both class defences against class aggression.

If you oppose a man as an employer, why do you vote for him as a Member of Parliament? His calling himself a Liberal or a Tory does not alter the fact that he is an employer.

To be a Trade Unionist and fight for your class during a strike, and to be a Tory or a Liberal and fight against your class at an election, is folly. During a strike there are no Tories or Liberals amongst the strikers; they are all workers. At election times there are no workers; only Liberals and Tories.

During an election there are Tory and Liberal capitalists, and all of them are friends of the workers. During a strike there are no Tories and no Liberals amongst the employers. They are all capitalists and enemies of the workers. Is there any logic in you workers? Is there any perception in you? Is there any *sense* in you?

As I said just now, you never elect an employer as president of a Trades' Council, or a chairman of a Trade Union Congress, or as a member of a Trade Union. You never ask an employer to lead you during a strike. But at election times, when you ought to stand by your class, the whole body of Trade Union workers turn into black-legs, and fight for the capitalist and against the workers.

Even some of your Labour Members of Parliament go and help the candidature of employers against candidates standing for Labour. That is a form of political black-legging which I am surprised to find you allow.

But besides the conflict of personal interests, there are other reasons why the Liberal and Tory parties are useless to Labour.

One of these reasons is that the reform programmes of the old parties, such as they are, consist almost entirely of political reforms.

But the improvement of the workers' condition depends more upon industrial reform.

The nationalisation of the railways and the coalmines, the taxation of the land, and the handing over of all the gas, water, and food supplies, and all the tramway systems, to Municipal control, would do more good for the workers than extension of the franchise or payment of members.

The old political struggles have mostly been fought for political reforms or for changes of taxation. The coming struggle will be for industrial reform.

We want Britain for the British. We want the fruits of labour for those who produce them. We want a human life for all. The issue is not one between Liberals and Tories; it is an issue between the privileged classes and the workers.

Neither of the political parties is of any use to the workers, because both the political parties are paid, officered, and led by capitalists whose interests are opposed to the interests of the workers. The Socialist laughs at the pretended friendship of Liberal and Tory leaders for the workers. These party politicians do not in the least understand what the rights, the interests, or the desires of the workers are; if they did understand, they would oppose them implacably. The demand of the Socialist is a demand for the nationalisation of the land and all other instruments of production and distribution. The party leaders will not hear of such a thing. If you want to get an idea how utterly destitute of sympathy with Labour the privileged classes really are, read carefully the papers which express their views. Read the organs of the landlords, the capitalists, and the employers; or read the Liberal and the Tory papers during a big strike, or during some bye-election when a Labour candidate is standing against a Tory and a Liberal.

It is a very common thing to hear a party leader deprecate the increase of "class representation." What does that mean? It means Labour representation. But the "class" concerned in Labour representation is the working class, a "class" of thirty millions of people. Observe the calm effrontery of this sneer at "class representation." The thirty millions of workers are not represented by more than a dozen members. The other classes—the landlords, the capitalists, the military, the law, the brewers, and idle gentlemen—are represented by something like six hundred members. This is class representation with a vengeance.

It is colossal *impudence* for a party paper to talk against "class representation." Every class is over-represented—except the great working class. The mines, the railways, the drink trade, the land, finance, the army (officers), the navy (officers), the church, the law, and most of the big industries (employers), are represented largely in the House of Commons.

And nearly thirty millions of the working classes are represented by about a dozen men, most of whom are palsied by their allegiance to the Liberal Party.

And, mind you, this disproportion exists not only in Parliament, but in all County and Municipal institutions. How many working men are there on the County Councils, the Boards of Guardians, the School Boards, and the Town Councils?

VISIONS OF THE FUTURE

The capitalists, and their hangers-on, not only make the laws—they administer them. Is it any wonder, then, that laws are made and administered in the interests of the capitalist? And does it not seem reasonable to suppose that if the laws were made and administered by workers, they would be made and administered to the advantage of Labour?

Well, my advice to working men is to return working men representatives, with definite and imperative instructions, to Parliament and to all other governing bodies.

Some of the old Trade Unionists will tell you that there is no need for parliamentary interference in Labour matters. The Socialist does not ask for "parliamentary interference"; he asks for Government by the people and for the people.

The older Unionists think that Trade Unionism is strong enough in itself to secure the rights of the worker. This is a great mistake. The rights of the worker are the whole of the produce of his labour. Trade Unionism not only cannot secure that, but has never even tried to secure that. The most that Trade Unionism has secured, or can ever hope to secure, for the workers, is a comfortable subsistence wage. They have not always secured even that much, and, when they have secured it, the cost has been serious. For the great weapon of Unionism is a strike, and a strike is at best a bitter, a painful, and a costly thing.

Do not think that I am opposed to Trade Unionism. It is a good thing; it has long been the only defence of the workers against robbery and oppression; were it not for the Trade Unionism of the past and of the present, the condition of the British industrial classes would be one of abject slavery. But Trade Unionism, although some defence, is not sufficient defence.

You must remember, also, that the employers have copied the methods of Trade Unionism. They also have organised and united, and, in the future, strikes will be more terrible and more costly than ever. The capitalist is the stronger. He holds the better strategic position. He can always outlast the worker, for the worker has to starve and see his children starve, and the capitalist never gets to that pass. Besides, capital is more mobile than labour. A stroke of the pen will divert wealth and trade from one end of the country to the other; but the workers cannot move their forces so readily.

One difference between Socialism and Trade Unionism is, that whereas the Unions can only marshal and arm the workers for a desperate trial of endurance, Socialism can get rid of the capitalist altogether. The former helps you to resist the enemy, the latter destroys him.

I suggest that you should join a Socialist Society and help to get others to join, and that you should send Socialist workers to sit upon all representative bodies.

The Socialist tells you that you are men, with men's rights and with men's capacities for all that is good and great—and you hoot him, and call him a liar and a fool.

The Politician despises you, declares that all your sufferings are due to your own vices, that you are incapable of managing your own affairs, and that if you were intrusted with freedom and the use of the wealth you create you would degenerate into a lawless mob of drunken loafers; and you cheer him until you are hoarse.

The Politician tells you that *his* party is the people's party, and that *he* is the man to defend your interests; and in spite of all you know of his conduct in the past, you believe him.

The Socialist begs you to form a party of your own, and to do your work yourselves; and you call him a *dreamer*. I do not know whether the working man is a dreamer, but he seems to me to spend a good deal of his time asleep.

Still, there are hopeful signs of an awakening. The recent decision of the miners to pay one shilling each a year into a fund for securing parliamentary and other representation, is one of the most hopeful signs I have yet seen.

The matter is really a simple one. The workers have enough votes, and they can easily find enough money.

The 2,000,000 of Trade Unionists could alone find the money to elect and support more than a hundred labour representatives.

Say that election expenses for each candidate were £500. A hundred candidates at £500 would cost £50,000.

Pay for each representative at £200 a year would cost for a hundred M.P.s £20,000.

If 2,000,000 Unionists gave 1s. a year each, the sum would be £100,000. That would pay for the election of 100 members, keep them for a year, and leave a balance of £30,000.

With a hundred Labour Members in Parliament, and a proportionate representation of Labour on all County Councils, City, Borough, and Parish Councils, School Boards and Boards of Guardians, the interests of the workers would begin, for the first time in our history, to receive some real and valuable attention.

But not only is it desirable that the workers should strive for solid reforms, but it is also imperative that they should prepare to defend the liberties and rights they have already won.

A man must be very careless or very obtuse if he does not perceive that the classes are preparing to drive the workers back from the positions they now hold.

Two ominous words, "Conscription" and "Protection" are being freely bandied about, and attacks, open or covert, are being made upon Trade Unionism and Education. If the workers mean to hold their own they must attack as well as defend. And to attack they need a strong and united Labour Party, that will fight for Labour in and out of Parliament, and will stand for Labour apart from the Liberal and the Tory parties.

7

THE INDIVIDUAL UNDER SOCIALISM: A LECTURE (LONDON: ILP, c. 1908), 3–14.

Philip Snowden

[Often regarded, along with Ramsay MacDonald, Keir Hardie and John Bruce Glasier, as being among the most prominent and influential members of the Independent Labour Party (ILP) and the Labour Party, Philip Snowden also made a significant contribution to socialist theory in the early years of the twentieth century. A key theoretical feature of socialism is social freedom, arguments for which can each be categorised in terms of either negative freedom, which is broadly freedom from interference, or positive freedom. The term "positive freedom" refers to either effective freedom or freedom as autonomy (Lamb 2019, 39). Snowden's belief in social freedom is clearly in the positive category, in terms of autonomy. Socialism, for him, would prevent people from harming not only others but also themselves. To do what was required for the common good would constitute true liberty. As is the case with many positive libertarians, he described the freedom he was advocating as a type of individuality very different than that which drove capitalist society. People under socialism would not continually seek more material gains, as they would be satisfied with their good standard of living. Educated to appreciate the benefits of meaningful work, people would, being free from irrational desires, act according to their communal, cooperative nature. Positive libertarians call this condition autonomy.

Much of the ILP literature drew on Christian morality, even when particular members were irreligious (Bevir 2011, 304–308). As a devout Christian, Snowden emphasised not just the morals but also the religion of Christianity. His pamphlet *The Individual under Socialism* of 1908 is a clear example of his Christian socialism (Snowden c. 1908).

Snowden's reputation tends to be that of a moderate in the British socialist movement. Some even regard him as a traitor because of his support nearly twenty years later for MacDonald's formation and leadership of the national government following the electoral collapse of 1931 after the economic crisis which brought down the Labour government that year. Snowden did not contest a parliamentary seat in the subsequent elections but gained a peerage and thereby was enabled to participate in the national government, which he did until September 1932 (Skidelsky 1994, 385).]

A COMMON objection against Socialism is that a Socialist State would involve the sacrifice of individual liberty, and that there would be no opportunity for the satisfaction of individual ambition.

Socialism, it is urged by these opponents, considers only the satisfaction of mere physical needs. Socialism, they tell us, lacks the moral element, it ignores human nature, it is meat and drink and nothing more. Such an objection as this betrays an ignorance of Socialism and the Socialist movement which would be irritating if it were not amusing. "Socialism merely meat and drink and material conditions and nothing more!" And were it so, surely is there not need enough to-day for a movement which seeks to provide these things for the millions who are lacking meat and clothing and homes? With, according to the latest investigations made in an industrial English town, about 80 per cent. of the working class living in houses which do not fulfil the barest needs of health and decency; with 52 per cent. of the working class families unable, by long hours of toil, to gain an income sufficient to obtain enough food to satisfy the needs of the body; with one man in every twenty begging for leave to earn his bread but denied the opportunity; with old age dependent on the starvation doles of a heartless Poor Law system; with children going breakfastless to school and mumbling on empty stomachs the Apostles' Creed; with these things on the one hand, and on the other, idleness satiated with luxury and debauchery, there is surely little need to sneer at a movement, did it confine its energies solely to setting these material wrongs right.

But it is further urged that if such an organisation of industry could be established as would ensure work for all willing workers, and satisfy the physical requirements of all, that such an organisation would be obtained at the cost of all that makes life worth living. Remove the incentive of gain, and we are told the motive force of all progress would be destroyed. Socialism would reduce all to one dead level of mediocrity. The individual would lose his identity in a cast iron State. Men would be converted into mere machines, life would be an intolerable servitude, the nation would be converted into one huge prison house. The great principle of Socialism, these objectors remind us, is Equality; and to ensure a condition of perfect equality would be the work and function of the State. Aye, the State—a monster more terrible in its strength and more tyrannical in its despotism than ever the genius of a Frankenstein created! To ensure this condition of perfect equality, the State will allot to each individual his appointed task, and the whip of the State taskmaster will enforce its full discharge. Intellectual equality would be secured by depriving superior ability of all encouragement to excel, the mental condition of the lowest would be the standard to which all would be degraded to maintain a condition of perfect equality. The State would decide and direct the minutest details of each individual life. The work, the place of abode, the dress, the food, the home, the amusement, the recreation—all would be directed by the

VISIONS OF THE FUTURE

State, leaving the individual no freedom but to obey. For the certainty of being fed and clothed, we are to sacrifice the glorious privilege of individual liberty and the blessings of a civilisation won for us by the efforts of gifted free individuals in all past ages. And in the end, it is further predicted, this dead mass of equality would sink into a condition of squalid animalism spurred on to effort only by the whip of the State taskmaster. Socialism, which promised liberty, equality and plenty, will end in a cataclysm of slavery, barbarism, and want.

Surely, but this is a terrible picture, and should give us pause. Who could have thought such terrible consequences lay concealed in such innocent proposals as the national ownership of land, the State control of the railways, every adult one vote, and the enforcement of the Pauline law, that if a man will not work neither shall he eat.

The powers of human imagination are very limited. It is impossible to imagine any new thing. Our pictures of a future society are tainted by what we know of the present. This picture of the individual under Socialism, drawn by our opponents, is an illustration of the difficulty of getting away from familiar ideas, for it is a very faithful representation of the condition of the individual of to-day under a system of boasted individualism. What to-day, under our vaunted individual freedom, is the type of the developed individual? If you would see the works of Competition, and the play of the Incentive of Gain, look around! You will find their monuments everywhere. Surely but it must be in grim irony we are told that Socialism will destroy individual liberty and close the avenues for intellectual development. Let those who fear that Socialism will destroy individual liberty and hinder intellectual development go with their talk to the machine workers of our great industrial towns, who are chained for eleven hours a day to a monotonous toil, with the eye of the overseer and the fear of dismissal spurring them on to an exertion which leaves them at the end of their day's work physical wrecks, with no ambition but to restore their wasted energies at the nearest public house. Let them go with their talk of the blessings of civilisation to the pottery and chemical workers, whose systems are poisoned, whose sight is destroyed, where through the bodies of the parents being saturated with poison, half the children are born dead, and of the rest not one in four lives to be five—tell *them* to hold fast to their share of the blessings of our glorious civilisation. Or go to the sweaters' victims, living, eating, working, dying in one room for which a grasping landlord will take in rent one-half of all the family can earn by working day and night—talk to them of individual liberty and warn them of the tyranny of the coming Socialism. Or go on a bitterly cold winter morning to the dock gates of one of our great ports, and see thousands of men waiting in the hope of a day's job; and watch how a few here and there of the strongest are selected, and the rest left to another day of hunger and despair; or wait still and see how a few remain behind in the hope that their mate may meet with an accident and "they can snatch at the work he had." Or go with your talk of the individual liberty of to-day and the tyranny of Socialism, to practically the whole of our working class population, who live and work not for

THE INDIVIDUAL UNDER SOCIALISM: A LECTURE

themselves, but for a master at whose whim they can be turned adrift to starve, or to tramp the country in search of another master who may employ them so long as he can make a profit by so doing, but who, when he finds it no longer profitable to do so, turns them away to perish, he knows not, nor often cares not, where or how. He has paid his hirelings their wages at the market rate, and there the duty of the master and the right of his servant end. Oh yes, we need the warning. We must be careful not to destroy individual liberty nor to close the avenues for individual ambition, which are now open wide to every man who has only sufficient pluck and ability to push his way in the world! Why, to talk of individual freedom and equality of opportunity, under a system of cannibalistic competition like this, is like the mocking laughter of a raving maniac gloating over the torture of the victim it holds in its murderous grip.

There can be no individual liberty where land, the absolute essential to man's existence, is the property of a few and is used by this few to dictate to the many the terms on which they shall be permitted to live. There can be no individual liberty so long as machinery which has been made by the associated labour of all the workers becomes the property of the class, and is used by that class to keep themselves in idleness and to pay the workers wages by wealth taken from them. Under such a system, where the common needs of life are the object of a competitive struggle in which all goes to the victors, leaving nothing to the vanquished; in which the sole object in life is to secure a monopoly of what all need so that by this monopoly one may get his fellows into his power to use them for his own selfish ends,—under such a system as this there can be no individuality. There can be no individuality where men work not for themselves, and where they have no voice whatever in determining the way in which the work shall be done. When a man worked with his own tools in his own workshop, and was his own master, he put his individuality into his work. He made what articles he liked, he made them as he liked, he sold them as he liked, and every blow the workman struck left the mark of his freedom and individuality.

But now a workman has no voice whatever in the management of the business in which he is employed. He is a "hand"—a mere cog in the capitalistic machine. He cannot make what articles he would like, he cannot use any genius or individuality he may possess in fashioning the work according to his own ideas. He has to do mechanically the work to which he is set, and he must do it as he is told. The mechanic, "a skilled workman," is employed year after year in making a machine turn out identical pieces of iron from the same model—a model made by somebody else. The weaver is employed in watching a loom turn out hundreds of pieces of the same design. The workman to-day has no opportunity to display any originality or individuality in his work; and as practically all his waking hours, and indeed all his energies, are absorbed in this monotonous soul-killing work— the inevitable result is, that he becomes devoid of individuality and becomes just a mechanical reproduction of his conditions of work and life. This is why there is practically no such thing as individuality or originality in the mass of the people to day. Their mechanical work, the slavery of thousands to the instructions of one, makes the people of the same class all of one mould.

Look where we will in our life to-day and we find everywhere this lack of individuality, a slavery to fashion, to conventional ideas. In personal attire, where we might expect to find the display of originality or individuality, it is everybody's effort to be in fashion—that is to be dressed like everybody else. To be out of fashion, especially for a woman, requires a courage before which the heroism of a martyr sinks into insignificance. And if there were such a thing as individuality among the masses, where could there be found a more fitting place for its expression than in the homes of the people. Look at the homes of the people! Long rows of houses, bare and inartistic, every house just like its neighbour, every street the counterpart of the next. And inside the house, in nine cases out of ten, where the people can afford it, we find just the same articles of machine-made furniture, and in every house arranged just in the same symmetrical positions against the walls. In scarcely a working-class home do we see any evidences of literary taste or artistic bent. In the middle and upper class homes we find the same slavish submission to conventionality, though more expensively but not more artistically expressed. Look where we will to-day and the material world we have created for ourselves is the reflex of a people's character devoid of individuality, dead to beauty and to art, without the inspiration of one elevating ideal. The sordid materialism of our mammon worship has laid its sacrilegious hands on every worthy institution and degraded all to its own depths. It is impossible that there can be an elevated character among a people whose whole life is taken up in seeking after the mere material things of life. This all-absorbing competition to secure material things inevitably destroys all the finer feelings of humanity, and abnormally develops all the animal and baser instincts of our nature. The struggle for material things is animal and develops only animal characteristics. But as man's wits have been developed by this struggle he has brought his wits to aid him in the struggle for material acquisition. Competition is now a battle of wits. Instead of men robbing each other by brute force as formerly, they now cheat each other "by the lying tricks of trade." The man who is the most successful in such a struggle is the man whose animal instincts are most highly developed. The necessities of the people afford the opportunity for seeking to gratify this animal desire for supremacy and acquisition. The object of production is to make profit; not to produce articles which are good, useful, and morally elevating. Consequently the markets are full of adulterated rubbish, cheap imitations of everything—made to sell at a profit. And so far have we been demoralised by this cheap production that we shamelessly justify it all by declaring that a good article lasts too long, while the making of a bad article "finds work," and is "good for trade." Just as former ages have been known from their chief characteristic, as the Age of Stone, the Age of Iron, so this age will be known from its chief characteristic, as the Age of Shoddy.

The outcome of this struggle to get hold of riches is that individuals best fitted for such a struggle survive: those who have most animal acquisitiveness, least consideration for the feelings and sufferings of others, and most of that kind of smartness and unscrupulousness which can make a good bargain. As our ideal of the development of individuality is getting rich by these means—which are the only means by which a man can get rich—we conventionally honour the men who are successful; and so selfishness, cheek, cunning wit, smart business methods—those qualities which are essential to a "good" business man—have come to be admitted as the most desirable individual qualities. Consequently, as it pays better to live by one's wits than by the work of one's hands, society honours the man who lives by his wits; and useful toil is so despised that a man is ashamed to let it be known that he has only sufficient wit to earn an honest living by the work of his hands and the sweat of his brow.

John Bunyan tells us how the Interpreter showed Christiana and her company a man who could look no way but downwards, and who had a muck rake in his hand. And there stood one holding over the man's head a celestial crown which the man might have in exchange for his muck rake. But the man was so intent on raking together the dust, the sticks, and the stones, that he never raised his eyes to see the heavenly crown above his head. To-day we are like the man with the muck rake—grovelling in the dust of materialism—seeking the satisfaction of a carnal mind in things which degrade men's souls and keep their eyes chained to the dust of the earth. Our ideal of individual liberty is freedom to develop those qualities which will enable a man to get rich. It is true that Socialism will destroy such individual liberty as that—the liberty of brute force and cunning wit to crush the weak and rob the innocent.

Socialism means the elevation of the struggle for existence from the material to the intellectual plane. Competition for material things—which are limited in supply—must result in extremes of poverty and riches, for the more one appropriates the less there must be for the rest. But Socialism will raise the struggle for existence into a sphere where competition shall be emulation, where the treasures are boundless and eternal, and where the abundant wealth of one does not cause the poverty of another. The time has passed when men need struggle against each other for their physical needs. We have a command over natural forces capable of supplying every need without the necessity for arduous toil—a command which increases more rapidly than our capacity for its rational use. By the sensible organisation of industry all might be provided with the necessaries of a comfortable existence with the expenditure of a little time and labour. The struggle for existence, instead of being a struggle by individuals against each other, should be a struggle by men united together to subdue the external forces of nature for the service of humanity.

Socialism will justify God's way to man. That divine instinct of affection in human nature has through all the ages rebelled against the merciless slaughter of the weak, for tho'

Nature red in tooth and claw with ravine
Shrieked against our creed . . . .
We felt that God is love indeed
And love Creation's final law.

VISIONS OF THE FUTURE

And now Socialism comes as the Angel of Light bearing to mankind this message of truth. Socialism, equipped with all the learning of the ages, takes up the ripest teaching of the poet, the philosopher, the economist, the scientist, the historian, and joins the conclusions of each together into one harmonious whole, which tells us that the weak are necessary, the uncomely are not to be despised, that not competition but the co-operation of all is the law of life. Now we have the knowledge of the truth of Browning's words:—

All is law,
Yet all is love.

And now we know that suffering, misery, and poverty are a violation of God's will; now we know that the fulness of time has come for us to cast the last relic of our fallen nature from us and to follow the beckoning angel who is waiting to lead us back through the gates of Paradise into an Eden of intellectual joys.

Socialism, by making land and machinery the common property of all, and using these instruments to supply material needs, will completely change the business and object of life. Socialism will change human nature. The opportunity makes the man. Socialism will take away the desire for accumulating riches. To-day men struggle for riches because the possession of riches gives the command of those things men most desire—social position, honour, independence, freedom from arduous toil and the horror of poverty and starvation. But under Socialism the possession of riches will cease to be a ruling passion, for honest labour will be a guarantee against want, and riches will no longer be the passport to social position. Under such conditions the possession of riches will be a superfluous burden which no sane man will wish to bear. Crimes of property must inevitably disappear. The age of shoddy will be passed, for then it will be to no man's profit to poison another with adulterated rubbish. The demoralisation of present day business methods will be removed, for just as the conditions of employment and the methods of competition of to-day reflect themselves in the character of the people, so the fact that men are engaged in work they know to be good, useful, and honourable will have an elevating influence upon their character.

When the acquiring of riches has ceased to be the object of life; when men's minds are free from the carking care of providing for the morrow; when the perpetual fear of poverty is removed; then men will seek for fresh avenues for the satisfaction of their individual desires. When men have leisure, and they are not enervated by exhausting toil, nor demoralised by superfluous riches, they cannot help themselves from following their natural instincts. Man, under natural, that is under favourable material conditions, is an intellectual being, and his intellectual aspirations will manifest themselves when his material needs are satisfied. Just as the nightingale sings in the evening shades, or the lark trills in the summer sky, so man in natural surroundings will seek to gratify his higher nature. The instances of men of exceptional ability who, against adverse circumstances have risen to intellectual eminence, are proof of the fact that this higher nature of man is constantly striving to burst through the obstacles to gain the intellectual life for which men were created.

And Socialism will create a condition of things favourable to the development of the higher type of individuality. The organisation of industry, the saving of the present waste of competition, will reduce the labour of supplying the physical needs to the narrowest limits, leaving abundant leisure for the satisfaction of individual desires. And the conditions under which this necessary work will be done will be healthy, pleasant, and elevating. Men and women will be educated to take an intelligent interest in their work. Society will have discovered that it is best for society and for the individual to put him to the work he can best do, and this will transform his labour from a drudgery to a perpetual joy. John Ruskin truly says: "When a man is rightfully employed, his amusement grows out of his work as the colour petals out of a fruitful flower." Socialism will realise that desirable condition.

Socialism will provide all the conditions which are necessary for the gratification of every reasonable desire. Even if the acquisition and enjoyment of material wealth were a desirable object, Socialism will gratify that better than our present system. Under competition it is certain that but a few individuals can realise the sordid ambition of getting rich. To-day nineteen persons out of every twenty who die leave no property behind them. But under Socialism—and Socialism, it may be said, does not involve the abolition of private property; under Socialism a man will be permitted to possess just as much private property as he can honestly earn; but he will not be permitted to use that private property to rob others of their private property. Under Socialism nineteen-twentieths of the people will be better off materially than they are to-day, for they will be equal partners in all the productive and distributive wealth of the community.

Socialism will establish the moral conditions which are necessary for the development of true individuality, and the exercise of true liberty. The moral basis of Socialism is the recognition of the eternal moral law, that the individual as a member of society is limited in his development by the development of the society of which he is a member. Herbert Spencer puts it in this form: "The individual development in a given period is determined by the corresponding development of the social organism." In other words, the civilisation of the mass determines the condition of the individual. For instance, we do not find a Shakespeare among the Hottentots, a Gladstone among the Malays, an Edison among the Feugeans. The individual cannot rise above the highest civilisation of his own race or society. For example, the nearest approach to the ideal state of which history has any record was in Ancient Greece. The Greek ideal was the perfect state. In reality it was not a democratic state, but an oligarchy based on slavery. But within the oligarchy where the state ideal was recognised there were produced as a consequence, individuals of every sphere of intellect—poets, orators, philosophers, artists, who have never since been equalled, let alone surpassed. After two thousand years, in spite of the vast increase in the sum of human knowledge which has come by natural evolution, we have not raised the type of the individual man. And the

VISIONS OF THE FUTURE

reason is because we have not raised the condition of society; and the dead weight of society has prevented the development of the individual. What we need is an answer to Browning's prayer—

Oh God, make no more giants,
Elevate the race.

Socialism will raise the dead weight of society which now crushes the development of the individual. Socialism aims at making the ideal state as a necessary condition to making the ideal individual. And when men realise this great fact that their own development depends on the development of all, then a perfect society will come to be regarded as the ideal to the attainment of which all individual effort should be directed. The recognition of this great fact will show individuals the folly of seeking the gratification of their own individual desires except by promoting the welfare of all. The well-being of all will now be seen to be necessary, not merely as a sentimental thing but as a scientific fact. When it is recognised that the common life is the source of the individual good, then love for the common life will take the place of love of self. The desire to serve the common life, to advance its welfare, will be the highest ambition of the individual; and in this service he will find abundant scope for the satisfaction of his aspirations. This love for the common life will manifest itself in making all common things beauteous and joyful.

Men should be simple in their homes,
And splendid in their public ways;
Filling the mansions of the State,
With music and with hymns of praise.

And this claim that in a moral state love for the common life will take the place of love of self, is no mere dreaming sentiment. It is that love for the common life which has been the inspiration of every noble life whose memory is enshrined on the hearts of men. What has kept alive the worship of the Christ through the persecution of nineteen hundred years? Not the knowledge of his kingly rank, but because He, being rich, for the common good became poor. Self-sacrifice for the common good has in every age appealed to the highest admiration of men. It has been instinctively felt that this is the highest trait of human nature, and men have accorded to it their highest meed of honour. Selfishness, we are often told, is in human nature. If this be so, then there is no reason to be ashamed of selfishness. And yet where is the man or woman who is not ashamed to be considered selfish. Our feelings are better than our creed. Deep down in our hearts we know that selfishness is not human nature, and we express our real human nature when we deprecate selfishness and honour self sacrifice.

And when we find so much of this love of the common good manifested in the past and to-day under conditions not favourable to its development, is it not

104

reasonable to expect, that when we have established industrial and social conditions, favourable to its growth, that we shall see a love of the common life, and a pride in the common life, the dominating motives of individual action?

The fear of the tyranny of the State, under Socialism, which is felt by some opponents, though quite unfounded, has some excuse from past experience. In the past, the State has always been the representative of the oppressing and exploiting class. Under slavery the State was the slave owner, under feudalism the State was the baronage; under capitalism the State is the capitalist. But under Socialism the State as we have known the State in the past, will have disappeared; for under Socialism, there will be no classes, but all the people will form one class, and the government and organisation will be democratic, each individual having an equal voice in directing the affairs of the common life. And as Socialism postulates an intelligent democracy, this discloses at once the absurdity of the fear that Socialism will result in the oppression of the individual. When all the power will be in the hands of the whole people: when the condition of things is what the common sense of an intelligent, self-governing community makes it, is it not foolish to suppose that such a people will voluntarily inflict upon themselves the terrible condition of things the opponents of Socialism profess to fear?

Those who fear that Socialism will destroy individual liberty, fail to distinguish between liberty and licence. Individualism is licence—it is the freedom of the individual to do as he likes without regard to the effect of his action on others, or even without regard to his own best welfare. Socialism is liberty; for it will restrict the freedom of the individual to inflict injury upon others, or to do what is morally injurious to himself. Socialism is the observance of law. "Government is eternally and in all things the law of life," says Ruskin. It is only through the observance of law that men can enjoy individual happiness. Just as physical health is maintained only by obeying every law of health, so individual liberty, the true development of individual character, can only be secured by obedience to all those moral restraints which govern the conduct of individuals and society. Law is slavery only when the law is inflicted by a class upon another class. When all submit to law imposed by all for the common good, then law is not slavery, but true liberty. For do we not sing sometimes:—

> *True liberty it is to share*
> *All the chains our brothers wear;*
> *And with heart and hand to be,*
> *Earnest to make others free.*

Socialism is something more than meat and drink, and food and clothing. It attaches so much importance to industrial reform, because we must first establish the material base of life on a moral foundation before we can raise up a society of moral and intellectual men and women. Material conditions are the soil out of which the intellectual life of the people grows. Socialism seeks first the kingdom of industrial righteousness, and then all else shall be added to it.

VISIONS OF THE FUTURE

Instead of Socialism being merely a material movement, seeking only satisfaction of physical needs, it is a movement which is seeking to subordinate materialism to the intellectual life, and Socialists are working for the industrial commonwealth because they realise that only by such an industrial organisation can there be individual liberty and opportunity for true individual development. And when Socialism has freed the individual from the all engrossing task of supplying his material wants; when all have independence and equal opportunity, then we shall find that what we have regarded as exceptional natural gifts is not the endowment of a favoured few only, but the normal condition of all humanity, and that in more ways than we have yet dreamt of the Father of all is no respecter of persons. What man may become under favourable conditions is beyond human imagination to conceive.

> *For man is not man as yet;*
> *Nor shall we deem his genuine aim put fairly forth,*
> *While here and there a towering form*
> *O'erlooks its prostrate fellows:*
> *While here and there a star dispels the darkness,*
> *Not until the whole host is out at last,*
> *Then, and not till then,*
> *Begins man's general infancy.*

And in conclusion may we point out that the moral spirit which Socialism will generate will not be confined within the selfish limits of nationality. Socialism is brotherhood; and brotherhood is as wide as the heaven and as broad as humanity. The growth of international Socialism is the promise of the realisation of the angels' natal song: "On Earth, peace; Goodwill toward men." Socialism will remove the causes of international antagonism, and make the interest of all nations the same. And when Socialism has joined the people of every nation and of every tongue into one human brotherhood, then the dream of the noblest spirits of all ages will be realised—for then

> *War shall cease and ancient fraud shall fail,*
> *Returning Justice lift aloft her scale,*
> *Peace o'er the earth her olive branch extend,*
> *And white-robed Innocence from Heaven descend.*

That is the work which Socialism has set before it, and whether the day of its realisation be near or far depends upon us. If we are determined that it shall be, then the day of its coming shall not be long delayed. The ideal is in the future, but our work lies in the present. The Age of Chivalry is not past. To-day we all may win our knighthood spurs in a nobler chivalry than tilting a lance before the Queen of Beauty. If you would win this nobler knighthood, come with us, and help us to take the children out of the fœtid slums into the pure air of God's own

THE INDIVIDUAL UNDER SOCIALISM: A LECTURE

country. Come with us to the man with the muck rake and tell him to lift his eyes from the earth, and to seize the celestial crown above his head. Come with us and help us to abolish poverty, sin, and suffering, and to bring hope and health, and joy and liberty to every child of our common Father.

Oh, who would not a champion be
In this the knightlier chivalry;
Up, rouse ye now brave brother band
With honest heart and willing hand:
For there are those that ache to see
The day dawn of our victory;
Eyes full of heart-break with us plead,
And watchers weep and martyrs bleed,
Work, brothers, work, work hand and brain,
We'll win the Golden Age again,
And love's millennial morn shall rise
In happy hearts and blessed eyes;
We will, we will, brave champions be,
In Labour's knightlier chivalry.

Part 3

CONCEPTS OF POLITICAL CHANGE

8

WHAT SOCIALISM MEANS: A CALL TO THE UNCONVERTED – A LECTURE DELIVERED FOR THE FABIAN SOCIETY, 3RD ED (LONDON: WILLIAM REEVES, c. 1888), 2.

Sidney Webb

[First delivered as an address to the two-year-old Fabian Society in May 1886, this lecture by Sidney Webb (c. 1888b) originally appeared in print the following month in Volume 1, No. 6 of the monthly magazine *The Practical Socialist*, produced by the radical socialist publisher William Reeves. The excerpt reprinted in this volume constituted the first page of the revised edition published as a pamphlet in 1888. Reeves became well-known in the late nineteenth century for his publication of radical and Utopian books such as William Morris's *News from Nowhere* and the English edition of Edward Bellamy's *Looking Backward*. Nevertheless, in the early 1880s he was involved in more practical activities of the left, such as prominence in the Land Nationalization Society (LNS), which pressed for state-purchase of land and a heavy single tax on landowners until the achievement of this aim. At around the time he first published Webb's lecture Reeves changed allegiance to the rival Land Reform Union (LRU), which took a more pragmatic and less class-specific approach than the LNS (Beaumont 2003). The LRU was, indeed, a more reformist organisation. Having joined the Fabian Society in May 1885, Webb also joined the LRU later that year (Bevir 2011, 179), attracted by its stance of reform rather than nationalisation which he opposed.

One can understand why Reeves was enthusiastic in publishing the work of the reformist Webb as one of the most prominent writers of the newly-formed Fabian Society. In this lecture and pamphlet Webb stresses that Fabian socialists do not pursue a dogmatic programme of nationalisation. Although taking a definite direction in line with the capabilities of humans in society which were becoming potentially ever-greater by means of the industrial revolution, he stressed, socialists work for social reform without a final goal of social evolution. As Mark Bevir suggests (2011, 173–174), Webb's approach can be categorised as ethical positivism, combining a humanitarian ethic with rationalism and a belief in evolutionary progress.]

Nothing is more universal than the widespread illusion as to what Socialism really means, and as to how Socialists intend to obtain its adoption. It seems almost impossible to bring people to understand that the abstract word "Socialism", denotes like "Radicalism", not an elaborate plan of Society, but a principle of social action. Socialists easily recognise that the adoption of the principle can only be extended by bringing about a slowly dawning conviction in the minds of men; it is certain that no merely forcible "revolution" organised by a minority, can ever avail, either in England or elsewhere. We seek therefore to influence only convictions, so as thereby to bring about the great bugbear of our opponents, the "Social Revolution"—a revolution in the opinions men form of the proper Society in which to live, and in the kind of action to which these opinions lead them.

There are many who desire to help in social reconstruction, but who are not quite decided to act; many who sympathise, but who are timid; many, indeed, who are Socialists, but are not conscious of their Socialism. It is to these especially that we must address ourselves asking them always to remember that Socialism is more than any Socialist, and its principles more than any detailed system or scheme of reform. The Fabian Society has no such plan or scheme; its members are led by their Socialist principles to work for social reform in a certain definite direction, but the future evolution of Society no man can exactly forecast, and to human evolution no final goal can be set. The moment will never come when we can say, "Now Socialism is established; let us keep things as they are," Constant evolution is the lesson of history: of endings, as of beginings, we know nothing.

Socialism inevitably suffers if identified with any particular scheme, or even with the best vision we can yet form of Collectivism itself. In this, as in many other cases, the public are so much concerned with details, that they miss the principle: they "cannot see the forest for the trees." But it is no more fair to identify Socialism with any modern prophet's forecast of it, than it would be to identify Christianity with the "New Jerusalem" of the Swedenborgians. Nevertheless, such misconceptions will inevitably persist, and those who may embrace Socialism, must be warned that they are not likely to receive "honour among men" in consequence; they are certain to be miscontrued, misrepresented, and reviled, and to be regarded as advocates of dynamite outrages or childish absurdities, even by those who are gradually learning their very doctrines.

Socialism is emphatically a new thing, a thing of the present century—and one of the unforeseen results of the great industrial revolution of the past 150 [y]ears. During this period man's power over the rest of nature has suddenly and largely increased: new means of accumulating wealth and also new means of utilising land and capital have come into being.

9

WHAT SOCIALISM IS (LONDON: FABIAN SOCIETY, 1890), 1–3.

Fabian Society

[From its formation in 1884 until the turn of the century most of the Fabian Society's tracts were published in the name of the Society. In his major study of the Fabians, Edward Pease (1916, 274), having been secretary for twenty-five years, listed the authors who had drafted these pamphlets, including *What Socialism Is*, which was written by George Bernard Shaw in 1890. Although Shaw is widely recognised as one of the most prominent Fabian socialists of the 1880s, advocating a gradual transition to social democracy, he was at the same time impressed by Karl Marx's social and economic theory in *Capital*. Although by 1890 his enthusiasm had begun to wane, the influence remained (Bevir 2011, 152–174).

What Socialism Is (Fabian Society 1890) serves to illustrate how, in discussing socialism in terms of the reduction of inequality, the elimination of poverty, protecting rights, ensuring equality of opportunity and building democratic institutions, there were lingering affinities with Marxism but also significant differences. In the first volume of *Capital*, Marx was clear that the reluctance to regulate was deeply ingrained in the capitalist system. Bourgeois consciousness, he argued, denounces "every conscious attempt to control and regulate the process of production socially, as an inroad upon such sacred things as the rights of property, freedom and the self-determining 'genius' of the individual capitalist" (Marx 1976, 477). The socialists, Shaw argued, were trying to socialise the land and machinery gradually or make this the property of the whole people. There would be no more idle owners and those whose labour made the whole product would benefit from it.

The emphasis on idle owners was part of the theory of rent which was a key characteristic of the work of Shaw and other Fabians (Ricci 1969, 106, 113). Rather than focus on value as had Marx, Shaw saw exploitation in terms of marginal utility. The more workers there were available, the cheaper the capitalists could buy their labour. He saw capital as stored rent (Bevir 2011, 144–145).]

What "Unsocialism" Is.

We English have a habit of speaking of England as if it belonged to us. We are wrong: England is now private property; and if a laboring man out of employment makes so free with "his country" as to lie down for a night's sleep on it without paying its owners for the accommodation, he is imprisoned as a rogue and a vagabond. The price we must pay for our living room rises as the population grows; for the more people there are, the higher they will bid against one another in hiring land in the market for houses and places of business. In London, for instance, the price paid annually to the ground landlords goes up by £304,634 every year, without counting the additional charge for new buildings or repairs and improvements to old ones. After payments of one sort or another to the owners of the whole country have been deducted from the produce of the workers' labor, the balance left for wages is so small, that if every working-class family got an equal share, each share would only come to £75 a year, which (though it would seem a fortune to some poor people) is not enough for a comfortable living, much less for saving. Nevertheless the proprietary classes, without working at all for it, divide among them enough to give over two hundred thousand rich families more than £1,500 a year, and still leave more than £300 a year per family for over a million and a quarter families of moderately well-off people in addition to what they make by their professions and businesses.

The Extreme Cases.

The above figures, bad as they are, only represent averages, and give no idea of the extreme cases of wealth and poverty. Some of our great landowners get upwards of £4,000 a week without ever doing a stroke of work for it; whilst the laborers on their estates, working early and late from the time they are lads until they go into the union as aged and worn-out paupers, get eleven shillings a week. As women get lower wages than men when they work, but receive just as large incomes from property when they are rich and idle, a comparison between the share of our yearly produce that goes to a poor working woman at the East end of London, working sixteen hours a day for a shilling, and the rich, idle lady at the West end, is still more startling. These are facts and figures which no one disputes.

What Comes of Inequality.

If you are a person of common sense and natural feeling, you must have often thought over these terrible inequalities and their cruel injustice. If you are rich, you perhaps think that inequality is a good thing—that it fosters a spirit of emulation, and prevents things from stagnating at a dead level. But if you are poor, you must know well that when inequality is so outrageous as the figures above shew, it fosters nothing but despair, recklessness and drunkenness among the very poor; arrogance and wastefulness among the very rich; meanness, envy and snobbery among the middle classes. Poverty means disease and crime, ugliness and brutality, drink and violence, stunted bodies and unenlightened minds. Riches heaped up in idle hands mean flunkeyism and folly, insolence and servility, bad example, false standards of worth, and the destruction of all incentive to useful work in those who are best able to educate themselves for it. Poverty and riches together mean the perversion of our capital and industry to the production of frippery and luxury whilst the nation is rotting for want of good food, thorough instruction, and wholesome clothes and dwellings for the masses. What we want in order to make true progress is more bakers, more schoolmasters, more wool-weavers and tailors, and more builders: what we get instead is more footmen, more gamekeepers, more jockeys, and more prostitutes. That is what our newspapers call "sound political economy." What do you think of it? Do you intend to do anything to get it remedied?

No Remedy without Political Change.

As things now stand, the produce of industry can be increased in two ways only. The first is to increase the population in order to set more people working; but this of course increases the demand for land to work on, and thus raises rent; so that it is the property-holders and not the workers who are made richer. The second is to get hand work done by machinery, to introduce railways, and to organize labor in factories. But the first cost of machinery, railways and factories has to be paid for out of savings, and not out of the money that people are living on. Now the only people who can spare money to save are those who have more than enough to live on: that is to say, the rich. Consequently the machinery is introduced, and the factories built at the expense of the rich; and as they pay for it, they expect to get all the advantage that comes by using it; so that here again the workers are left as badly off as ever. The worst of it is that when the rich find out how easy it is for them to get still richer by saving, they think it is as easy for everybody as for themselves; and when the worker complains, they say "Why don't you save as we do?" or "How can you expect to be well off if you are not thrifty?" They forget that though you can save plenty out of £18 a week without stinting your family, you cannot save anything out of eighteen shillings without starving them.

The Three Monopolies.

Moreover the propertied classes, by giving their younger sons an expensive education, are able to put them into the learned professions and the higher managerial posts in business, over the heads of the wage-workers, who are too poor to get

CONCEPTS OF POLITICAL CHANGE

more than a very short schooling. So that out of the price paid to them for the use of the land, the propertied classes buy the machinery; and out of the profits of the machinery they buy the education which gives to their working members a monopoly of the highly paid employments; whilst the wage-workers are hopelessly cut out of it all. Here are the figures for the United Kingdom:—

[1]Income of Propertied Classes (10,500,000 persons)	£850,000,000
„ left for Wage-workers (26,500,000 „)	500,000,000
Total National Income ⋯ ⋯	£1,350,000,000

This means that the rich are masters of the wage-workers. The rich alone can afford to go into the House of Commons, or to sit upon the County Councils and Municipal Corporations. Yet the whole country is governed by these bodies. The workman's vote enables him to choose between one rich man and another, but not to fill the Councils and Parliament with men of his own class. Thus the poor keep the rich up; and the rich keep the poor down; and it will always be so whilst the land and the machinery from which the nation's subsistence is produced remains in the hands of a class instead of in the hands of the nation as a whole.

What Socialism Is.

Socialism is a plan for securing equal rights and opportunities for all. The Socialists are trying to have the land and machinery "socialized," or made the property of the whole people, in order to do away with idle owners, and to keep the whole product for those whose labor produces it. The establishment of Socialism, when once the people are resolved upon it, is not so difficult as might be supposed. If a man wishes to work on his own account, the rent of his place of business, and the interest on the capital needed to start him, can be paid to the County Council of his district just as easily as to the private landlord and capitalist. Factories are already largely regulated by public inspectors, and can be conducted by the local authorities just as gas-works, water-works and tramways are now conducted by them in various towns. Railways and mines, instead of being left to private companies, can be carried on by a department under the central government, as the postal and telegraph services are carried on now. The Income Tax collector who to-day calls for a tax of a few pence in the pound on the income of the idle millionaire, can collect a tax of twenty shillings in the pound on every unearned income in the country if the State so orders. Remember that Parliament, with all its faults, has always governed the country in the interest of the class to which the majority of its members belonged. It governed in the interest of the country gentlemen in the old days when they were in a majority in the House of Commons; it has governed in the interest of the capitalists and employers since they won a majority by the Reform Bill of 1832; and it will govern in the interest of the majority of people

116

when the members are selected from the wage-earning class. Inquirers will find that Socialism can be brought about in a perfectly constitutional manner through Democratic institutions, and that none of the practical difficulties which occur to everyone in his first five minutes' consideration of the subject have escaped the attention of those who have worked at it for years. Few now believe Socialism to be impracticable except those with whom the wish is father to the thought.

Note

1 This item is made up of four hundred and eighty-five millions (£485,000,000) which go as Rent and Interest absolutely for nothing, and of three hundred and sixty-five millions (£365,000,000) incomes of professional men and profits of business management. (See Fabian Tract No. 5, "Facts for Socialists.")

10

POSTER FOR *SOCIALISM!:*
THE FIRST OF A COURSE OF
FOUR LECTURES WILL BE GIVEN
IN THE CO-OPERATIVE HALL, HIGH
STREET, ON TUESDAY, NOV. 4, 1890,
BY SIDNEY WEBB, 1890

Sidney Webb

[This poster advertised a short course of lectures on socialism, including the first by Sidney Webb scheduled for 4 November 1890. Although Webb was unable to give the lecture because of illness, the planned event was part of an important development in the early years of the Fabian Society and British socialism. The lecture advertised in the poster (Webb 1890) was intended to contribute to what he described in a letter of 18 October to Beatrice Potter (later Webb) as "a big series" (Mackenzie ed, 2008, 224) in Leicester. Webb's Fabians arranged the event in collaboration with the more radical Socialist League which hired the city's Cooperative Hall.

The event was scheduled to follow on from the Fabians' "Lancashire campaign" of September and October 1890. According to Edward R. Pease (1916, 97), in his history of the early years of the Fabian Society, the Lancashire campaign represented the beginning of a new socialist movement, differing from the revolutionary and destructive types of socialism which had failed to attract support in the industrial districts of England. Funded by a substantial donation to enable the Fabians to spread their message beyond their London base, the campaign involved series of lectures in many northern towns and cities. Each series usually comprised four lectures, sometimes including one on the Eight Hours Bill.

The campaign for the Bill united moderate socialists with some but not all the Marxists of the Socialist League and the Social Democratic Federation. There was, furthermore, initial reluctance among trade unions to support such a radical policy. By 1890, however, members of some sizable unions had begun to pressure their leaders into supporting the campaign (Callaghan 1990, 18–21). The Leicester series adopted the four-lecture pattern of the Lancashire campaign and Webb's was titled "The case for an Eight Hours' Bill". Later in November 1890, in another letter to Potter, Webb expressed disappointment in not having been able to give the lecture in Leicester (Mackenzie ed, 2008, 232).

The Lancashire campaign helped bring about the formation of local Fabian societies. Over the next few years these local groups merged with branches of the Independent Labour Party and eventually helped bring about the formation of the Labour Party. A statutory universal eight hours' day remained elusive.]

11

ON THE IMPORTANCE OF RIGHT METHODS IN TEACHING SOCIALISM: A PAPER READ TO THE MANCHESTER AND DISTRICT FABIAN SOCIETY, FEBRUARY 10th, 1891 (MANCHESTER: R.J. DERFEL, 1891), 1–15.

R.J. Derfel

[Robert Jones Derfel was influential in the movement to nurture socialism in Wales during the nineteenth century, reaching out to the working class in both Welsh and English languages. Much of his work was written from England. Having left Wales in young adulthood to escape poverty and find work, he eventually settled in Manchester where in 1890 he founded the regional and local Fabian Society.

In his youth Derfel had been a devoted Christian. Upon reading the work of Robert Owen, however, he forsook religion. Nevertheless, the prose in which he described this conversion to socialism reflected his religious background (Ward and Wright 2010, 52–54). His socialist thought has subsequently been portrayed as cosmic mooning (Yeo 1977, 14). Coined by E.P. Thompson, this is a term employed to refer to a thinker who enters a new philosophical universe upon coming to a new way of thinking by means of something not unlike a religious conversion.

Although in the paper *On the Importance of Right Methods in Teaching Socialism*, which he wrote and delivered in Manchester in 1891, Derfel mentioned the gospel of socialism, he did not write it in terms which indicate an expectation that socialism will emerge by means of collective cosmic mooning. He was, rather, concerned to prepare his fellow Fabians for the task of educating members of the working class. The previous year leading Fabians had embarked on the Lancashire campaign in which they had taken their message beyond its London base in an attempt to convert northern, Liberal Party-supporting working-class people (Pease 1916, 95–96). In this paper Derfel (1891) was taking an interim step between that campaign and the forthcoming task of the Manchester Fabians to consolidate and build on the success the campaign had achieved.]

If we are true socialists, not in the Harcourtian sense that we are all socialists now, but real, earnest, and thorough socialists, in the full sense and possibility of the word, we must have a desire to do what we can to make socialism successful.

I will take it for granted that our object in forming ourselves into a society, has been a desire to teach and propagate more effectually, individually and collectively, the gospel of love, plenty, justice, and liberty which we call socialism.

Therefore, it seems to me a matter of great importance, at the beginning of our propaganda, to try and ascertain how to do the work best, and fix on the most effective method to accomplish our purpose. In all undertakings the method is of vital importance. A bad method may not only retard, but spoil and destroy a good movement. When we are going on a journey, we are careful to select the right line, and go to the right station to start. In building a house we first make a plan, and build accordingly. As the twig is bent, so the tree will grow, and the bend cannot be taken out without destroying the tree. So it is with movements as well as trees. If we begin the advocacy of socialism in a wrong way, the wrong way will become stereotyped and it will be difficult, if not impossible, to get it changed.

It is a fact, and we cannot emphasise it too much, that it is possible to advocate a cause in such a way as to do the cause more harm than good. A cause may be made ridiculous, and destroyed by an unwise advocate. I have at times heard tories defend their cause in such a way as to make me feel thankful they were not on my side. And I have also heard liberals and radicals speak so unwisely, that I felt at the time a feeling of sorrow and shame because they were on my side. I must also confess that some speeches I have heard, and some articles I have read, on socialism, have caused me to grieve that the cause we love has been, and still is, advocated in such a way. And this led me to think that a few remarks on "right methods in the advocacy of Socialism," might be useful and timely at the commencement of our propaganda in Manchester.

I will not mention names, for measures, not men, must be our motto; but any one who has paid any attention to the socialist movement, must have noticed that there are socialists and socialists. Some delight to call themselves *revolutionary socialists*—not in the sense of evolution and development, but in the sense of violent, and if need be, a bloody overthrow of the present order of things. In the sense of evolution, all socialists are revolutionary, but all are not, I hope, in any other sense. If some socialists did not label themselves revolutionary, we would be justified in calling them by that name from the tenour of their writings and speeches. Their every word smells of sulphur, blood, and fire. In every speech and article they breathe forth threatenings of blood and death. In my opinion this is very unfortunate. It creates alarm in the minds of timid folk, and they have to be reckoned with as well as others. It makes socialism odious and ridiculous in the sight of many who are neither fools nor cowards. Instead of attracting to, it repels people from socialism. It closes the eyes, the ears, and the hearts of many against socialism. And it is full of danger, not only to the cause of socialism, but to the common liberty of the people. While socialists are in a miserable minority, violent speeches and writings of a few socialists merely reminds the people of the three tailors of Tooley-St. and makes them laugh with scorn. But should the advocates of violence ever become numerous enough to be a source of danger to the country, I am fully convinced that coercive laws would be passed, which would make it a matter of difficulty to advocate not only socialism, but any other measure of reform, and that might throw our movement backward for generations to come. Besides, if socialists were numerous and strong enough to change the order of society by means of a war, they would be strong enough to do it without war, and therefore war would be unnecessary. The pen is more powerful than the sword. Reason, argument, and persuasion have done more for man than war ever has done, or can do. What we have to do, is to educate the people till we get the majority on our side. At present the country is not ripe and fit for socialism, and a socialistic state could not succeed till they are. The people of this country have the power in their own hands at the present time, to win everything they want, if they would only use it; and people who will not fight with the ballot box, are not very likely to lose much blood on the field of battle.

There is another class of men who claim to be socialists, and who are generally known as socialists, but who call themselves *anarchists,* and anarchist communist. I would not wish to say one disrespectful word about the anarchists as men. I have no doubt their motives are pure. But I think at the same time they have no right to call themselves socialists, and that they are out of place on a socialist platform. An anarchist is an extreme individualist, and their place is to stand side by side with Auberon Herbert and his party. And those who call themselves anarchists-communists, call themselves by a self-contradictory name. Socialism is a regulated society, the co-operation of all for the benefit of all; anarchism is no government at all, except the will of the individual. Socialism is each for all and all for each—anarchism is each for himself. Anarchism and socialism are the negation of one another. It seems to me that where each would be a law to himself, social order would be impossible. There seems to be no practicability, and therefore no possibility in the idea. But socialism is practical and possible, and therefore it is something we can work for with a hope of realising. At all events, to advocate anarchism on socialist platforms, tends to confuse the public mind as to what socialism is, and therefore it is calculated to do the cause of our principles some harm.

RIGHT METHODS IN TEACHING SOCIALISM

Again, some socialists avail themselves of every opportunity, in company, on platform, and in press, to *disparage the temperance movement,* and jeer at abstainers. I think this is greatly to be deplored. The evils of intemperance are so great and palpable, that it seems to me almost a calamity for any socialist to apologise for it. That temperance would not permanently abolish poverty, I admit. Nothing but socialism, in its ultimate form of communism, can do that. But even under present conditions, if half of the money so injuriously spent in drink, was spent in food, clothing, furniture, books, and other useful things, the demand would so enormously increase, that all available labour could not supply it for a long time to come. But more than all, socialism can never be realised until we have an educated and a sober people. Prosperity for all cannot thrive where intemperance flourishes. If the most perfect system of society possible were established in any state to-morrow, if the drink traffic was allowed within its borders, it would not be long before that state would suffer all the evils that afflict society to-day.

Another matter that is often under the lash is *thrift.* With much that is said on the question of thrift I can agree. I know that those who have nothing, can save nothing. I know that those who receive barely enough to buy food, should not be expected to save, and it would be cruelty to preach thrift to them[.] I know that thrift by itself can never cure the disease of poverty—nothing but socialism can do that. Yet I think it is a mistake on the part of socialists to preach against thrift, because as long as the present system of society lasts, thrift will continue to be a virtue. A thriftless man or woman injure not themselves alone, but also their families, friends, and society. Improvident men and women, instead of being elements of strength, are a burden and a source of weakness to society. Even in a socialistic state, I cannot think that carelessness and wastefulness will ever be held in honour, or that carefulness and foresight will be treated as a crime.

Again, some friends are never tired of *praising the tories, and heaping abuse on the liberals and radicals.* What any socialist can see in toryism to praise, I am at a loss to know. I am not aware that the tories ever initiated any movement for the benefit of the masses; but I do know they have opposed every reform as long as ever they could. What few reforms we have, were got through the labours of liberals and radicals. That they did not do more is the fault of the country as much as the party. I suppose the people of the stone age did what they could, and it is folly to blame them for not making bronze tools. Who would think of abusing those who made tallow candles, for not making gas before it was discovered, or gas makers for not providing electric light before the how to make it was known? To blame the liberals for not passing socialistic measures in the past, is unreasonable. They could not have done it if they had tried. They could not do it to day, for they have not the majority to do it. Till the voters will return a majority of socialists to parliament, socialist measures cannot be passed, and therefore I think it is unwise to abuse the party of progress for not doing the impossible. From the liberals we may expect some help; from the tories nothing but fierce opposition.

If it be unwise to abuse liberals, it must be stupid folly for socialists to abuse one another. I am sorry to see that they do so in certain quarters. We never can hope to see eye to eye on everything, but we can agree to disagree, and each in his own way strive to bring about a better state of society for all.

Abusing employers is also a favourite method of advocating socialism with some speakers and writers, and in my opinion an unwise and an unjust method to pursue. Employers did not make the system and conditions of life more than the workman did; both are slaves of the system. In every business, no doubt there are a few lucky or unlucky masters, who have such a run of success and make money so plentifully, as to place them, apparently, above their surroundings, and enable them to do much as they like. Business, like men and animals, seems to be gregarious. Nothing succeeds like success. To those who have, more is given. And the number of successful ones, in the aggregate, no doubt is great, but they are only a small minority of the whole. For every successful one there are dozens of unsuccessful ones. Many of them fail every day, and make arrangement with their creditors, or pass through the Bankruptcy Court. Many more struggle on through life, working night and day, Sunday and holiday, to try and win success, without avail, living in continual misery till they die, leaving a legacy of difficulties to their relations and friends. My belief is, that no class would be more benefited by a change in the system of society, than the majority of the employers. At all events, no good can be done by abusing them, and railing at them seems to me as wise and useful as railing at frosts, floods, and storms.

Again, I think we shall gain no useful end by assuming an air of *superiority and infallibility* Dogmatism always tends to defeat itself. As a matter of mere policy, it is unwise to underrate our opponents, or to treat them as if they were children, idiots, or knaves. We can be firm in our own opinions without assuming that we have all knowledge, and that others have none. Sweet reasonableness is the best. Full freedom to think and speak, which we claim for ourselves, we must ungrudgingly concede to others, and in this manner we shall promote a feeling of brotherhood in the world, which all who advocate a new system of society ought to do. Here I think a word of caution against over confidence, will not be out of place. Robert Owen was so sanguine of success, that he thought his new moral world would be established in England during the reign of William IV. He lived to see his mistake. Let us profit by his example, and not be too sanguine. Some seem to think the system of society can be changed all at once, and in course of a few years. I wish the thing were possible, but wishing will not make it so. The present system has its roots reaching to the far past. It is strong by the force of heredity, and its defenders are numerous, are in possession and have the command of wealth, education, leisure, the police and military to fight their battles. I fear it will take many generations to realise the views we advocate. In all probability it will be brought about step by step, till the whole programme is won. For some

RIGHT METHODS IN TEACHING SOCIALISM

time, I think, the individual and social systems will exist side by side, with this difference—the social will grow more and more, and the individual will gradually decay and ultimately disappear for ever.

The world moves, and moves forward. It is not conceivable that it can as a whole ever move backward. Men and things move with the world, We are in the stream, and are carried forward with it. It is little we can do to control it. Resist we cannot. As Robert Owen abundantly proved, we are the creatures of circumstances. Even as part of our surroundings the share we have in their control is comparatively small Change and movement seems to be the permanent order of existence. Nature can never stand still. The universe standing still is a thing inconceivable. There is no such a thing as finality in nature. The mighty and infinite forces which give birth to ideas of progress, justice, and brotherhood, will always be behind them until they triumph. And they seem to be altogether independent of us. At all events, there is room to doubt if we are, at best, much more than the proverbial fly on the wheel, vainly boasting how quickly he makes the wheel turn. The tide of socialism is already rising and flowing, and our duty seems to be to guide the swelling waves into safe and beneficial channels. Socialistic legislation has been going on for generations, and is still going on, much of it unconsciously, and it will continue to go on until the socialistic programme has been won all along the line.

But whether the change will come about that way or not, our duty as socialists is to do our utmost to realise our views as quickly and completely as possible. And in order to do so, we must endeavour to present socialism, privately and publicly in its most lovely, reasonable, and attractive aspect. When business men have any goods to sell, they take pains to show them to the best advantage. We ought to do no less with socialism. If we introduce socialism in garments torn in strife and besmeared with blood, and with face begrimed with smoke, she will not be very likely to win the love and admiration of mankind. But introduce her in the robes of peace and plenty, with clean face and smiling lips, showing good will to all, and the public will look at her, and see she is comely. They will listen to her words, and gradually they will learn to love her, and then will accept her as the guiding genius of their lives.

It is no use to ignore facts. Facts are stubborn things, and will insist on being in evidence, whether we will it or not. Closing our eyes on facts will not remove them, and pooh poohing them will not alter their significance. All the misery of the world does not altogether spring from the order of society. Some of it is the direct result of incapacity, stupidity, thriftlessness, and the apathy of the workers themselves. However much we may affect to despise the rich and admire the workers, we may as well at once own to the fact that workers are not all angels. There are many who will insist on being wrong, do what you will for them, and many will fall in spite of every effort to keep them right. Nature, I am afraid, in the future, as in the past, will continue to produce the deaf, blind, and dumb, as well as idiots and imbeciles, and many other kinds, which are and will be a burden on society. Even under a socialistic order of the most perfect kind, it is more than probable that some will grow up wrong, and some of the right ones will go wrong. There will always be work for the schoolmaster, and always subjects to receive the sympathy and help of society at large. At all events, for the present and for a long time to come, I fear there is much work to be done in teaching the workers to understand the doctrines of socialism. Their education has been neglected, and their toil so hard and incessant, that their intellect is deadened, and they fail to realise the truth of the gospel of socialism when first they hear it preached.

But before we can present socialism in its best aspects to the public, we must first of all study the question in all its bearings, so as to have a thorough knowledge of the subject. As far as we can, we must read what the leading socialists have thought and written upon the question. And not read them superficially, but thoroughly, by digesting and assimilating them till they become our own as well as the writer's. When we can, it will be advisable also to read the works of leading opponents, so that we may know all that can be said against socialism, and be ready to answer them. And we shall be all the stronger if we study the history of socialism from the birth of the first idea of it, till the present time, and know all the experiments that have been made to bring it into practice. We cannot know too much of the subject, for the more we know the stronger we shall be. In this, as in everything else, the proverb, "Knowledge is power," holds true.

Here let me say, that I think we ought to teach socialism to the people in the words and language the people understand. I have noticed a tendency and a habit with some socialists, to deal largely in words and phrases borrowed from learned books on political economy. Even the Fabian essays on socialism are spotted with such words. Mrs. Besant writes of the *guerdon* of failure, and the "bitter carking harassment of daily want," &c. Surely the word reward would have been better than guerdon, and distressing quite as expressive as carking. The words *laissez-faire, bourgeois, proletarian,* and others, to many ordinary people are unintelligible, whilst English equivalents for those words are plentiful. Again, there is the word *economy, economic,* and so forth, which is used so frequently by speakers and writers. I fear the word, when used, very often sheds darkness instead of light on the subject treated. I doubt sometimes whether the writers and speakers themselves have any very clear idea of what they mean when they use the word. If they use it in any definite sense, I confess that I often fail to comprehend what that meaning is. As for the generality of people, it is certain the word conveys no clear idea to their minds. The word has so many meanings and shades of meanings, that the use of it without a definition will only convey uncertain ideas[.] When used to denote management, usage, order, method, and so forth, surely these words would convey clearer ideas to the minds of ordinary people than the words economy, economics, &c. If we want to reach the people, we must reach them through words they can understand.

RIGHT METHODS IN TEACHING SOCIALISM

Now, having by study qualified ourselves for the work of teaching our principles, we must proceed to work. But first of all we must look out for opportunities and fields to labour in. These we have in the family, in the work-room, in the club-room, and other places of meeting. In tram and train, on river and road, we can have opportunities for propaganda, In addition to these, we must make use of all political and other organizations, whenever we have a chance to get an audience to hear our views explained. And I think we ought at once to prepare a permanent home for our society. And this home should be open every day in the week, including Sunday, where members can meet at all times, and be sure of genial company. It ought further to have one large room, where meetings and discussions can be carried on. This surely is not more than a society numbering about a hundred members can accomplish. After firmly establishing a central home, we might proceed to found branches all over the district, so as to make ourselves a powerful organization for the spread of socialism.

I see no reason why our movement should not develop into a religion of humanity—a church of man, where every member shall be engaged in the service of man. If Robert Owen, during the time when he was the most popular man in the world, had established permanent organisations to teach and practice his views, the cause of socialism would now be more forward than it is. Let us profit from his omission, and establish meeting places where we can meet, not only men, but women and children also. We must have the women with us, and the children also, so that we may train them in youth in the principles of socialism. We want to catch the state and the press, but we cannot catch either till we catch the people. Once we catch the children, the women, and the men, it will be easy work to catch the press, the ballot box, and the state. And when the state has been captured, the beginning of the end will have commenced.

In order to bring that state of society about, at all events, to begin that state, I think we as a society ought at once to try and do some practical work tending to that end. If we are to be anything more than a mere talking machine, we must initiate some work to attempt at least to show the practicability of our views. Of talking machines there is no end. Church, chapel, secular hall, tory, liberal, and radical clubs, and so far as I can see, socialistic societies are little more than talking machines. I see very little practical work done or attempted to be done by any of them. It was supposed by some at one time that Secularism would show the people how to make the best of this world, but it has long since degenerated into a talking machine against Christianity. It pursues a policy of destruction instead of construction. A better way, I think, would be to build up something better than the churches, and destroy superstition by the superiority of beauty and usefulness of secular work. There is a good deal of common sense in humanity with all its faults, and it can see, when it has a chance, which is the best and most useful. There was no need for gas to go on a lecturing tour against tallow candles. It was enough for gas to show

CONCEPTS OF POLITICAL CHANGE

itself for people to accept it as better than candles. The same thought applies to everything else. In the long run, we may depend upon it, the fittest will survive. Therefore if we desire the speedy triumph of our principles, we ought to do something to give them, at least in part, a tangible form, that men may see the superiority of socialism over the present order of society. To do that, something beside talk is required. We must give our ideas shape by practical experiments. Even under present circumstances, much may be done by co-operation and resolute perseverance[.] Had the money wasted on strikes been employed to found industrial co-operative works, or to provide free homes for the workers, the country would have been ere now spotted with socialistic industries, and the eviction scenes which have been lately witnessed, would have been impossible, as the workers might have been living in their own houses. What practical work we should undertake, it is for the society, and not for me, to decide. But I am fully convinced, if we are to be anything more than a new talking machine, we must at least attempt to accomplish some practical and useful work.

But the work we have to do cannot be accomplished in a day, and we must remember that organizations, press, and platform are only means to an end—the tools and not the work. We must use the tools constantly to keep them bright; and deftly to make them effective. If we purpose to make any impression on the mass of ignorance and indifference around us, we must take pains and use diligence to teach our principles to the people. We must teach them, and not preach at them. People do not like to be preached at, nor to be abused. Abuse the devil, and the saints will fight for him. Men are much like dogs. If you want a dog to follow you, you must teach it to love you, and then it will obey you. If you attempt to drag the dog by the ears against its will, it will resist and bite you. So men. If we want the people to follow us, we must win their love by teaching them. We must open their eyes, their ears, their hearts, and understandings, by reason, argument, and persuasion, and compel them by conviction to accept our doctrines. We must throw ourselves, body and mind into the movement, and show by earnestness and self-sacrificing efforts that we are sincere in our professions. We must have life and enthusiasm in our movement. Lukewarmness and cold indifference will never accomplish anything. We must have the coolness of the Saxon in argument, and the fire of the Celt in oratory, to make the movement successful.

The harvest is great and the workers are few. Let us commence the work without delay[.] Our cause is noble and good, and must ultimately win[.] Let us have confidence in ourselves and in our cause, for it is the cause of man in all that is good and right all the world over[.] There are great and numerous difficulties in the way, but they are things to be overcome. Our enemies are many, and all are well armed and drilled; but our motto is, "Up, comrades, and at them!"

A king of Sparta, 880 years before Christ, in showing his army of 10,000 men, pointing to them, said, "These are the walls of Sparta, and every man is a brick"

128

RIGHT METHODS IN TEACHING SOCIALISM

Our Sparta is socialism, and I hope the Fabian Society will be a wall of living men around it, and that every member of the society will prove himself a brick.

The country is covered by the deadly upas trees of poverty, degradation, and misery; and our mission as socialists is to wind the ropes of reason and arguments around the trunks of these deadly trees, and by a pull, a long pull, and a pull altogether, to uproot them one by one, till the last of them has disappeared for ever.

12

WHAT IS SOCIALISM?: A DISCUSSION BETWEEN MRS. ANNIE BESANT AND MR. W. J. NAIRN (GLASGOW: SDF, 1892), 1–8.

Annie Besant and W.J. Nairn

[In 1892 the pamphlet *What is Socialism?: a Discussion Between Mrs. Annie Besant and Mr W. J. Nairn* reproduced a debate that took place four years earlier in *Justice*: the newspaper of the Social Democratic Federation (SDF), the main Marxist party of the United Kingdom. W.J. Nairn founded the SDF's Glasgow branch, which published the pamphlet. Annie Besant, who had been a member of the Fabian Society since 1885, on its executive the following year, and one of its greatest orators and writers until she resigned in 1890, joined the SDF in 1888, the year of the debate. Their disagreements were mainly over their different interpretations of capital, and the subsequently different ideas about what to do about it. Each claimed to consistent with Marx.

In 1889—thus one year after she had joined the SDF—Besant contributed the chapter on industry to the *Fabian Essays on Socialism*. She had, nevertheless, become frustrated with Fabian gradualism by 1887, participating in the protest movements that led to the deadly police reaction known as Bloody Sunday. Also in 1889 she published nine articles in *Justice* (Mackay, 2009: 340). By the time the debate with Nairn was published as a pamphlet three years later she had left both the Fabians and the SDF.

As her simultaneous involvement with the SDF indicates, Besant was never a conventional Fabian but, rather, on the quasi-Marxist left of the Society. Her later philosophical, scientific and theological work indicates, moreover, that she was not a conventional socialist of any type (Bhattacharya, 2017). In 1888 she not only remarked in her own journal *Our Corner* that the socialist movement was drifting into revolution, but also asked readers to join her in forming a new, humanistic religion (Mackay, 2009: 325). She joined the Theosophical Society the following year, leading her close Fabian colleague George Bernard Shaw allegedly to question her sanity (Mackay, 2009: 348). In November 1890 she severed her connections with the Fabians, as Edward Pease (1916: 98) put it, "suddenly and completely". The debate in this pamphlet (Besant and Nairn, 1892) can thus be interpreted as one between Nairn who believed he was continuing to follow Marx and Besant in whose mind socialism had come to vie with her rapidly-developing religious beliefs.]

To the Editor of "Justice."

Dear Comrade,—Already the spread of Socialism is such that strange doctrines are preached under its name. The other Sunday we had that brave woman, Mrs. Besant, lecturing to us. Amongst other things she said that "Socialists did not intend to abolish capital, and that no intelligent Socialist was in favour of abolishing rent."

What do Socialists mean by capital? I take it this is something like it. A spade is an instrument for aiding production, but is not necessarily capital. If held by an individual or individuals as against society, then and not till then does it become capital. Now as Social-Democrats believe that instruments of this kind held to-day by the few as against the many should in future be held by the whole for the benefit of the whole, it appears to me to be as clear as two and two make four that we are engaged in a crusade in favour of the abolition of capital (1). Mrs. Besant says no, and in that grand maternal dogmatic style of hers informed us that the reason why Socialism was not spreading faster was because some Socialists teach that doctrine through ignorance (2).

Then as to the question of abolishing rent. I read, whenever I go into the hall of the Glasgow Central Branch, that "Rent is Robbery" (3). The duty of Socialists should be to abolish robbery in every shape and form, and if "rent is robbery," Socialists ought to abolish rent; but as Mrs. Besant said "no intelligent Socialist was in favour of abolishing rent," it is possible the members of the Glasgow Branch are not intelligent. Mrs. Besant was asked to give the name of any intelligent French, German or English Socialist (4). The information was not forthcoming. She was also kind enough to inform us that under Socialism rent would be paid for land. She was not clear on this point, but to me it appears that either the land then would be farmed by the few, the many receiving rent, or else the land would be held by all and wrought for the benefit of all. If the land is to be farmed by the few, they paying competition rent to the many, it leaves open the field for the profit-monger and can't be Socialism. If, on the other hand, Mrs. Besant means that the land is to be held by the people and wrought for the benefit of the people—fancy the people paying rent to the people; it looks like taking a shilling out of one pocket and putting it into another. She also informed us that if the land was nationalised the power of capital would go (5). In this connection allow me to say that here Mrs. Besant seemed anxious to abolish capital through nationalising the land, and of course was at variance with her former statement "that Socialists did not want to abolish capital" (6). Now I know if I were to look up some of the back numbers of *Justice* I should find the organ of Social-Democracy teach the very opposite. I know I should find *Justice* characterising Land Nationalisers as middle-class reformers, and doubting whether Land Nationalisation would not do more harm than good.

I write this, first, because Mrs. Besant mentioned that she was a member of the S.D.F., and, secondly, because I and others considered that some of her doctrines were at variance with the teaching of the S.D.F., and, thirdly, that, if Mrs. Besant is right, to give an opportunity of showing that I and others have been wrong.— Yours truly,

WILLIAM NAIRN.

----

(1) Capital is, roughly, wealth used for the purposes of production; all machinery, *e.g.,* is capital. Mr. Nairn's definition of capital is wholly of his own making, and is entirely new to me. As I pointed out to him at Glasgow, the S.D.F. does not ask that capital shall be destroyed, but that it shall be "collective or common property," a very different thing. If Mr. Nairn preached "all food should be destroyed," and then explained that by "food" he only meant nourishment forcibly taken from the weak by the strong, he would at least lay himself open to misconception. The use of an accepted and understood term in an entirely new and personally defined sense, especially when the new definition does not accompany the statement, is likely to lead to misunderstanding.

(2) I did not say that "some Socialists teach that doctrine through ignorance," for I never heard anyone put forward such a doctrine till I listened to Mr. Nairn. I did say that Socialists injured the cause of Socialism if they put themselves forward as its exponents without taking the trouble to acquaint themselves with the meaning of the words used.

(3) Rent is the difference of fertility of different soils, the difference of advantage of different sites. I fail to see how it can be called "robbery." No objection could be made by a Socialist to the phrase, "The exaction of rent by individuals is robbery," but that is a very different thing. The law of rent is one of the strongholds of the Socialist position.

(4) I could not give the name of any intelligent Socialist who was in favour of "abolishing rent," because I know of none.

(5) This is a complete, though doubtless unintentional, mis-statement. What I did say was that such vast accumulations of capital in private hands as we have now could not have been made if the land had been common property. I believe that Land Nationalisation is not practicable by itself, and that the taking of land and capital must proceed at the same time. I never advocate Land Nationalisation by itself, but always point out—as I did in the lecture criticised by Mr. Nairn—that the possession of the means of production is as necessary as the possession of the soil.

(6) This is wholly unintelligible to me, as I have not the smallest anxiety to abolish capital, though I am extremely anxious to bring it under common control. I want to abolish the private capitalist, not the means of production.

WHAT IS SOCIALISM? A DISCUSSION

I do not point out the fallacy underlying the phrase about "the people paying rent to the people," because it is obvious, and your space is valuable.

ANNIE BESANT.

———

Sir,—We Socialists are in the habit of talking about the "Science of Socialism." In the opinion of Mrs. Besant that science can't be very exact when we find her defining capital to be "Roughly wealth used for the purpose of production: all machinery is capital." That definition means this if it means anything, that from the very moment a machine was first used by man there capital was to be found, and so long as machines are or will be used by man there capital will be. Is this the way that Socialists as a rule put it? I think not. In the "Genesis of Capital," p. 6, I find this: "In the work of production under the slave-owning system we see the implements of labour (machines) and the means of consumption, and of enjoyment, but no capital." I would ask Mrs. Besant does she admit that the air we breathe is wealth? does she admit that the air we breathe is a most essential portion of wealth used for the purpose of assisting production? does she call the air we breathe capital, and if not why not? Mrs. Besant says that the S.D.F. asks that capital shall be held as "collective or common property." The S.D.F. does nothing of the kind. What the S.D.F. says is this: "The Land, with all the Mines, Railways and other means of transit to be declared and treated as collective or common property," and again, "The Means of Production, Distribution and Exchange to be declared and treated as collective or common property." The S.D.F. does not say anything about these being capital: Mrs. Besant takes the liberty of saying it for them. I define capital to be, "Wealth, instruments of production, forces or powers, held by the individual or individuals as against the rest of society." I challenge Mrs. Besant to give a better. In the definition of capital which I give, whilst the words may be different, and whilst the definition may or may not be more exact and complete than that given by leading Socialist writers, the idea or ideas conveyed to the reader or enquirer will, I think, be found to be the same. I said in my last letter that a spade was an instrument for aiding production, and only became capital when held by the individual or individuals as against the rest of society. Mrs. Besant says this is new to her. I have already shown, according to the author of "The Genesis of Capital," that instruments for aiding production can be in existence and be used and still no capital. Now to show that it is only when these instruments are held by the few as against the many that they become capital. Quoting "The Genesis of Capital," p. 4, "A negro is a negro, it is only in certain definite social conditions that he becomes a slave. A spinning machine is a spinning machine, it only becomes capital under fixed social conditions." The same argument is used by Karl Marx in "Wage-Labour and Capital." Mrs. Besant says she never heard anybody talk about the abolition of capital until she heard me. Indeed! In "Wage-Labour and Capital," on p. 7, I find this: "Now capital also is a social condition of production. It is a bourgeois condition of production, a condition of the production of a bourgeois society." On p. 8 of the work, "Capital necessarily pre-supposes the existence of a class which possesses nothing but labour-force." On p. 9 (same work), "Capital perishes if it does not exploit labour." Now can Mrs. Besant not see that if we are engaged in the upsetting of this bourgeois society, and if "capital is a bourgeois condition of production," we must of necessity abolish capital? If "capital necessarily pre-supposes the existence of a class which possesses nothing but labour-force," and if we are desirous of bringing about a system of society whereby that class will have something more than their labour-force," can Mrs. Besant again not see that we are engaged in a crusade for the abolition of capital. If we are engaged in assisting to bring about a time when the workers will not be exploited, and if "capital perishes if it does not," can Mrs. Besant not see that under Socialism capital would be no more. I believe Mrs. Besant is right when she says that "Socialists injured the cause of Socialism if they put themselves forward as its exponents without taking the trouble to acquaint themselves with the meaning of the words used." Hence the reason for this letter.

Mrs. Besant still believes that rent could and would be paid under Socialism. I would ask by whom? to whom? I hope Mrs. Besant will answer this, if she can, and not do as she did in her last letter, ignore it.—Yours truly,

WILLIAM NAIRN.

––––––––

Dear Sir,—I have no time, especially at present, for prolonged newspaper controversy, and only answered Mr. Nairn's first and splenetic attack on me lest the ignoring of it should be taken as lack of courtesy. This answer must end the controversy as far as I personally am concerned. The book quoted by Mr. Nairn, "The Genesis of Capital," is unknown to me; and as I have not read the book and Mr. Nairn does not name the author, I am unable to judge of the weight that should be attached to the opinions expressed therein. But leaving this book on one side, the sense in which the word "capital" is used in political economy is best determined by reference to the writings of economists; it will be found that they differ considerably as to its extension, but all include in it machinery and instruments of production. To avoid burdening your pages with quotations I will confine myself to Marx. We may or may not agree with the analysis of capital expressed in his well known formula C eq. c plus v, but he defines his c, or constant capital, as the "part of capital represented by the means of production, by the raw material, auxiliary material, and the instruments of labour." ("Capital," vol. 1, p. 191, Engl. edn.) "Throughout this book, therefore, by constant capital advanced for the production of value, we always mean, unless the context is repugnant thereto, the value of the means of production actually consumed in the process, and that value alone." (p. 195.) "In every case the working-class creates by the surplus-labour of one year the capital destined to employ additional labour in the following year." (vol. II., p. 596). "A part of the functioning constant capital consists of instruments of labour, such as machinery, etc., which are not consumed, and therefore not reproduced, or replaced by new ones of the same kind, until after long periods of time," p. 617. "With the increase of capital, the difference between the capital employed and the capital consumed increases. In other words, there is increase in the value and the material mass of the instruments of labour, such as buildings, machinery, drainpipes, working-cattle, apparatus of every kind that function for a longer or shorter time in processes of production," etc., p. 620. "Constant capital or value of the means of production," p. 625. I might multiply such quotations, but these will suffice to justify my use of the word. I quote Marx, because his authority has weight with many Socialists, although I should think it unwise to use an accepted word in a new sense without careful explanation, in propaganda in a country where Marx is little known, even had he—as he has not—rejected the sense in which it is used by economists. Taking Marx's definition of capital, Mr. Nairn will see why I am in favour of placing it under common control instead of "destroying it."

I used the word "roughly" because of the controversies that have arisen over the extension of the term capital, as over the phrase "means of production." Some restrict them to direct, others extend them to indirect, "instruments of production." Some say that when a man eats a steak he is "consuming capital," others that capital is only "spare subsistence."

I do not call air wealth, because I include exchangeability and production by labour in my definition of wealth. Not including it in wealth, I should not include it in "capital."

But all these matters are mere logomachies; what is important is that we should make our meanings clear, and not lay ourselves open to misunderstanding by careless use of generally accepted words in new senses left unexplained. As to rent, the fallacy I alluded to lay in using the word "people" in two different senses. If rent be paid by "the people" to "the people," what is gained by the transaction? It is paid by "the people" as individuals; it is used by "the people" as a community. Suppose ten persons live in ten houses, the position of some of the houses being more advantageous than those of others; they cannot all live in the more advantageous houses, and those who have them enjoy an advantage from which the others are excluded; this is hardly fair to the excluded ones, who may justly complain that they are shut out from sharing the advantage. Now, suppose the advantage enjoyed by the dwellers in these houses is taken from them in the shape of rent, paid into a fund controlled by the whole ten, and used by them to supply some general want, say to build a wash-house for the use of all; the advantage then has really been communalised, and all have a share in it. If the community broke up into small independent communes, each competitive as regards the rest, but wholly communistic in internal arrangements, rent might disappear within each such commune; but there would be no equality among the communes; some would be better off than others, life would be easy in some, hard in others. I am a collectivist and not a Communist-Anarchist, and am against such an ideal. I hope to see a Socialist nation, throughout whose land equality shall prevail.—Sincerely yours,

ANNIE BESANT.

Part 4

POLITICAL ECONOMY

13

MINERS' EIGHT HOURS' BILL. SPEECH BY J. KEIR HARDIE, MP, IN THE HOUSE OF COMMONS, REPRINTED FROM *THE LABOUR LEADER* (LONDON: JOHN PENNY, 1902).

Keir Hardie

[In July 1903 Keir Hardie's speech in parliament delivered three months earlier in the second reading of the Mines (Eight Hours) Bill, was published in abridged form as *Miners' Eight Hours' Bill* in the Independent Labour Party Platform Series of pamphlets. The speech is further abridged in the present volume, omitting a few sentences which present details of cases offered by Hardie (1902) to support his dismissal of the argument that shorter working hours both increased the risk of injury and produced less in terms of output. The sections of Hardie's speech of 1902 that are presented here focus on his arguments that British coal prices were relatively low in comparison with other European countries, and that the mine owners were selfish, making huge profits, a reduction of which they could easily afford.

The campaign for an eight-hour day had begun towards the end of the 1880s. The activity of the well-organised gas workers was prominent at this early stage. It grew into a wider campaign in the early 1890s, pursued by socialists and a growing number of trade unionists, for an act of parliament to make this limit on daily working hours a legal requirement (Callaghan 1990, 21; Pelling 1976, 97, 103, 119, 124).

The campaign was initially opposed by many trade unionists and also by the quasi-Marxist H.M. Hyndman who led the Social Democratic Federation. Nevertheless, support spread considerably among workers and by the late 1890s the resistance among the union leaders was being overcome (Callaghan 1990, 19–22). Although Hardie's attempt to bring about such legislation for the miners was unsuccessful in 1902, the miners eventually got their eight-hour day in 1908 (McCormick and Williams 1959, 225).]

POLITICAL ECONOMY

THERE are three main lines of objections taken to the Bill. First of all, that it would restrict the output, and so increase the price of coal, and thereby burden industry; second, that it would increase the accident and death rate in connection with the getting of coal; and, third, that there is such a variety of conditions in connection with coal winning—thick seams and thin seams, deep pits and shallow pits, that you cannot apply a sort of cast-iron regulation to all these varying conditions.

I will take the last point first. It is perfectly true that you cannot apply cast-iron regulations to all those various conditions; but no one in his senses proposes to apply cast-iron regulations. What this Bill proposes is that no matter what the conditions may be, eight hours should be the maximum that a workman should be allowed to be employed underground. Make the number of hours as much less as you please; take all the elasticity you want; but this Bill says you shall not be allowed to go beyond these hours. I ask the two hon. members from the North of England who are opposing this Bill, whether or not that is the principle on which their own counties are worked?

*   *   *

I would remind the House that in spite of all the burdens which it has imposed on the coal industry, and in spite of the terrific burden which our system of mineral royalties imposes on coal, our working collier is still the cheapest in Europe, and our selling price of coal is the lowest of any country in Europe. We have to go to America, where wages are very much higher, to find lower prices, but so far as Europe is concerned, our country is still the cheapest. The average selling price last year was 7s. 7d. per ton in Great Britain; in Germany it was 7s. 9½d.; in France 9s. 11¾d.; and in Belgium 9s. 11¼d. Therefore the British coalmaster has the advantage of 2d. per ton over the competitor nearest to him, and 2s. 4d. per ton over the Belgium coalmaster. It lies ill on the lips of colliery owners to come to this House and seek to create a feeling of fear that this Bill is going to injure industry, because it may slightly increase the cost of production. It will be well within the recollection of the House that the Chancellor of the Exchequer twelve months ago proved to demonstration that these same colliery owners had pocketed £34,000,000 sterling over and above their legitimate profits; and that they had imposed a burden, not of 2d. or 3d. per ton, but of from 3s. to 5s. per ton. If men act in that fashion for their own selfish aggrandisement, surely the argument about increasing the cost of production 2d. or 3d. per ton, in order to abtain a public advantage, will not carry much weight with the public outside this House.

One word in regard to the North of England difficulty. I submit that this is not the stage at which to argue it. This is the Second Reading stage. In Committee is the time and place to discuss the application of the measure to the varying conditions of the country, and if it can be shown that a uniform application of the Bill is impossible, or that it would inflict permanent injury on any section of the coal field, I am quite certain that the Federation will not stand in the way of a settlement. I therefore express the hope that whatever diversity of opinion may rise up in the Committee stage, the House will once again pass the second reading of this Bill by a greatly increased majority.

Reprinted from *The Labour Leader* for March 20th, 1902.

18,000 "Platform" leaflets distributed last week. Help us to bring the circulation up to 100,000.

14

THE NEW UNEMPLOYED BILL OF THE LABOUR PARTY (LONDON: INDEPENDENT LABOUR PARTY, c. 1907), 3–15.

J. Ramsay MacDonald

[As a result of the general election in 1906 the Labour Representation Committee (LRC), having been formed six years earlier, returned twenty-nine MPs including Ramsay MacDonald (Morgan 2006, 25–26). Soon after the elections, the LRC became the Labour Party. Before the election the Liberal Party had made a vague commitment to address the plight of the unemployed, but on being returned to government prevaricated rather than fulfil the expectations they had brought about. With support from a significant number of Liberal MPs, senior Labour figures pressed the government to act, thus achieving an early, minor victory which spurred Labour to press for more substantial measures to deal with the unemployment issue. The Liberals stalled once again and so in March 1907 Labour made the unemployed and the aged the main issues of the parliamentary session, introducing the Party's unemployment bill in July and, after a delay, reintroducing it in 1908. MacDonald's pamphlet *The New Unemployed Bill of the Labour Party*, published in late 1907, was part of the Labour campaign on the issue (Brown 1971, 559–602).

In the final three paragraphs of the pamphlet it becomes clear that MacDonald (c. 1907) was not actually writing in his role of Labour Party member but, instead, as a member of the Independent Labour Party (ILP) which was formed in 1893, seven years before the LRC. Many leading ILP members had joined the new party. Although the unemployment bill was unsuccessful, the ILP became an intellectual force within Labour, publishing a stream of pamphlets such as MacDonald's of 1907, agitating for radical policy. What may seem like rivalry between the two parties was actually the ILP intellectuals performing a vital policy-shaping role within Labour.]

INTRODUCTION.

WHO SHOULD BE RESPONSIBLE FOR THE UNEMPLOYED?

We are never without the unemployed now. At a time when we are congratulating ourselves that our national exports have reached a point never before touched, the "Labour Gazette"[1] tells us that 28,914 skilled men, thrifty enough and well paid enough to join a Trade Union, are out of work; and it is surely no exaggeration to assume that the workmen for whom no returns are made can show at least a similar percentage of unemployment. On that basis we reckon that no fewer than half a million workpeople find their labour-power an unsaleable commodity, and, with their dependents, are suffering both the fears and the pangs which want of work brings to wage earners.

Who should be responsible for them? Some people say they should be responsible for themselves. I wish they could be. But the average wage of a British worker is only £45 per annum. The higher grades of the skilled trades are better, some of them reaching £5 to £6 per week, [b]ut the average wage of the poorer paid workers is much less than this low average of £45, women in particular being the worst victims. Now, under such circumstances, the very first duty of a man is to his family. He can save money only by a ruinous sacrifice of life. Accumulating money under such circumstances is being penny wise and pound foolish. It is no more "saving" than it is saving for a man to slowly starve himself to death.

There are thousands of men and women living to-day whose labour is so sweated that their wages are not high enough to replace the wear and tear of life. As a consequence, we have physical deterioration through alcoholism, disease, low vitality, high infantile mortality. The State has a duty to these people. That duty is to tax the wealth which they have created (but which has gone to enrich other people) so that they may be rescued from deterioration and helped during the most trying times of their poverty-stricken lives—*e.g.,* when they are underfed children at school, unemployed adult men and women, aged workers.

SOCIALISM AND UNEMPLOYED SCHEMES.

If this help be given as a mere palliative or as charity, the evil conditions are only perpetuated. Out-door relief for the sweated worker may help him a little, but it perpetuates sweating. So in dealing with the unemployed. Temporary relief is worse than useless, except in special cases. Unemployed schemes must, therefore, be educational; they must be in the form of training, so that surplus labour at one point of the market may be trained to be effective elsewhere, and also so that labour of little use in busy factories may be made useful under less stressful conditions.

We can imagine society divided into three great circles of workers. The inner is composed of the young energetic workmen, keen in eye and quick of hand. In the middle the pace has slackened, unemployment is common, and the numbing shadow of 40 winters is over the people. The outer circle holds the aged and the otherwise least efficient. The stream is across the circles from the centre. Youth gets pushed further and further out. The flare up of energy at the centre goes flickering onwards until the outer borders of death and darkness are reached. Our problem is to organise this drift, to make channels through which it will run, to lead the youth through to independent manhood and the man down to honoured age.

And whilst we are doing this we shall find that our infinite waste resources lie at our hand enabling us to carry out our ideas. It used to be believed that by employing unemployed labour on ordinary work carried on in State workshops, we could establish municipal, national, and finally, international socialism. That, however, cannot be done. We cannot make the unemployed the founders of the Socialist State. Failure would be the result of such an attempt.

But if we begin to organise our waste wealth—our waste national resources as well as our waste labour power—we shall begin a new form of social organisation. We shall utilise what is now useless. Barren fields will become fruitful. Village life will revive. A new mechanism of exchange will be created. Outside this for some time—the length of time will be determined by our intelligence—capitalism will flourish and ripen towards socialism. But it will then be like an island in the midst of a sea slowly washing its coasts away. We make a profound mistake when we assume that labour which is waste or inefficient for capitalist purposes, is waste or inefficient for every other purpose. Let us organise it. Let us fit it into conditions under which it is no longer waste.

This must be the idea directing and inspiring all efforts to deal scientifically with the unemployed. This is the aim towards which the Labour Party's Unemployed Bill is a first substantial step.

THE LABOUR PARTY'S UNEMPLOYED BILL.

CLAUSE 1.

(*1*) *For the purposes of this Act the council of every county and of every county borough shall be the local unemployment authority:*

Provided that the council of a borough or urban district with a population of over twenty thousand shall be the local unemployment authority of that borough or district, and its area, for the purposes of this Act, shall be excluded from the areas of the county.

(*2*) *Local unemployment authorities may act together as joint bodies for the purpose of carrying out the provisions of this Act.*

UNEMPLOYMENT COMMITTEES TO BE GENERAL.

Any scheme that satisfactorily deals with the unemployed must cover the whole country. Urban districts must co-operate with the rural districts in creating schemes of work, and obviously if only certain places are provided with machinery for dealing with unemployment, that is not only unfair to men living in other districts, but it attracts to great unemployment centres men from various parts. As these favoured centres are, moreover, likely to be specially poverty-stricken to begin with, they are made worse and not better by such provisions.

The provision made for dealing with unemployment must be systematic. It must be a regular part of the educational and constructive work of the country, and should be as much a part of our ordinary local government as the provision of schools, public parks, libraries or allotments.

Hence the provisions of this Clause.

CLAUSE 2.

(1) *The council of every borough including a county borough, urban district, and parish, and the overseers in those parishes where there is no council, shall register the unemployed persons of their areas; and shall, when they are not the local unemployment authority, communicate as quickly as possible all information thus obtained to the local unemployment authority of the district.*

(2) *The expenses incurred under this section shall be raised out of rates levied on the respective areas.*

A CENSUS OF UNEMPLOYMENT.

The first essential to the treatment of the unemployed problem is a census of unemployment.

The present means are not adequate. The Board of Trade monthly returns, published in the "Labour Gazette," deal only with Trade Unions, which represent skilled artisans in more regular employment than is the case with the vast masses of unskilled and casual workers.

Mr. J. A. Hobson, commenting upon this says:

> "The returns made by the Trade Unions which only take account of the members who are in actual receipt of 'unemployed benefit,' gravely under-represent the 'unemployment' of Trade Union members. . . . Taking the term 'unemployed' as commonly applied to members of a skilled trade, we must, without doubt, expect to find a larger percentage of 'unemployed' among non-unionists than among union members.

We must, therefore, know where we stand, and to do this, registers for the unemployed must be opened all over the country.

CLAUSE 3.

Where a workman has registered himself as unemployed, it shall be the duty of the local unemployment authority to provide work for him in connection with one or

POLITICAL ECONOMY

other of the schemes hereinafter provided, or otherwise, or failing the provision of
work, to provide maintenance should necessity exist for that person and for those
depending on that person for the necessaries of life: Provided that a refusal on
the part of the unemployed workman to accept reasonable work upon one of these
schemes, or employment upon conditions not lower than those that are standard
to the work in the locality, shall release the local unemployment authority of its
duties under this section.

RIGHT TO WORK.

This Clause recognises the right of the unemployed workman to demand an opportunity to work. If the local authority has been so lax in its duty as to be unable to offer him relief work, it ought to be compelled to keep his body and soul together. When he has fallen to the bottom of the gutter, he can demand this from the Guardians, but when he makes that demand he has become so demoralised that in most instances he is never able to regain self-respect.

We want to keep him from losing his self-respect, and from associating with the demoralising influences which surround a man who has been out of work for a long time. We hope that only under very special circumstances would the maintenance grant be given, but the poor man must be protected against the lazy or unsympathetic Local Authority, and this provision gives him that protection.

This Clause is a Right to Work clause and not a Right to Doles clause.

Therefore, if a man will not work, the local authority may be released from its obligations and he may be dealt with under Clause 7 (3).

A safeguard is necessary, however. We do not recognise the right of any Local Authority to supply labour from its unemployed registers or through its Labour Exchanges at less than the current rates of wages paid in the various trades of the districts. We do not, therefore, propose to recognise the offer of blackleg position as releasing the Local Authorities from their obligations. The London Central Unemployed Labour Exchanges are not much more than bureaux for the supply of blacklegs, and have been condemned by the Labour Party, the Parliamentary Committee of the Trade Union Congress, and the General Federations of Trade Unions, and wherever anti-Labour majorities are found on Local Authorities, there is a real danger that Labour Exchanges will be used in this way. This Clause prevents such a thing.

It should be noted that no attempt has been made to describe the wages to be paid for work either as "standard" or "trade union." Our experience of the administration of a standard wage by the Government is very bad, and we are convinced that any such expression would not protect the workman. On the other hand, if "trade union" is specified, a large part of the work having to be done in districts where there is no trade union, or being of a kind for which no trade union standard has been set, the expression would be absolutely meaningless. The Clause has been so worded, however, as to make it clear to the committees that they must pay a living wage. The most perfect legislation must be supported by intelligent

NEW UNEMPLOYED BILL OF THE LABOUR PARTY

administration, and our friends on local bodies must take upon themselves the responsibility of seeing that the wages paid are adequate.

CLAUSE 4.

It shall be lawful for His Majesty in Council by order to establish a central unemployment committee consisting of not less than two persons nominated by a national body or bodies representative of trade unions, and otherwise of persons representative of the Board of Agriculture, the Board of Trade, the Board of Education, and the Local Government Board, with a secretary appointed by the Local Government Board, for the purpose of

(*a*) *framing schemes for the provision of work for unemployed persons;*
(*b*) *advising the Local Government Board and any of the authorities created by this Act on any matter referred to the Committee by that Board;*
(*c*) *co-ordinating the work of the unemployment committees, and otherwise acting under the provisions of this Act.*

A CENTRAL UNEMPLOYED COMMITTEE.

Our experience of the Unemployed Act of 1905 shows that a special central body is required to see that the Act is actively administered by Local Authorities on the one hand and the Local Government Board on the other; and as other departments are interested in this work, as well as the Local Government Board, we propose that they should be represented on this Committee.

It is also essential that representatives of labour should be on this body.

This Clause is adapted from the Board of Education Act of 1899 (Clause 4).

The Clause will create a committee of representative men who will be in touch with all experiments, and be interested generally in the problem. They will have all germane information at their disposal, and they will consider themselves responsible for the successful working of the Act. They will also be in touch with the departments which could co-operate in providing land and experience required for national schemes of work.

The Committee will issue an annual report.

CLAUSE 5.

(*1*) *With a view to carrying out the provisions of this Act the Local Government Board shall appoint unemployment commissioners to make enquiries necessary for the working of this Act, to inspect and examine work being done under this Act. and otherwise to report to and advise the central unemployment committee.*
(*2*) *There shall be paid out of moneys provided by Parliament to the commissioners so appointed such salaries or remuneration as the Treasury may from time*

POLITICAL ECONOMY

to time determine; and all expenses incurred by those commissioners in the execution of their duties under this Act, to such amount as may be sanctioned by the Treasury, shall be defrayed out of money provided by Parliament.

UNEMPLOYMENT COMMISSIONERS.

This Clause completes the effectiveness of the last one. It gives the Central Unemployment Committee a staff of servants. These Commissioners will come and go, keeping in personal touch with what is being done. They will advise as to general administration as well as to practical details regarding the carrying on of the works.

The Commissioners and the Central Committee together will secure an active and intelligent administration. They will be ears listening to every complaint from the localities. They will fashion a real national policy of education and relief which will completely end the worst fears of unemployment as we know it to-day, and embark the State upon far reaching constructive social activities.

CLAUSE 6.

(*1*) *Every local unemployment authority under this Act shall establish an unemployment committee, constituted in accordance with a scheme made by the authority.*

(2) *Every such scheme shall provide that—*

(*a*) *At least a majority of the committee shall be appointed by the local unemployment authority from their own members;*

(*b*) *The authority may appoint other persons having experience in industrial or agricultural organisation;*

(*c*) *One-fifth of the committee shall be selected from nominations made by registered trade unions or the trades councils in the area;*

(*d*) *The chairman of the committee shall be a member of the local unemployment authority.*

LOCAL COMMITTEES.

I am convinced that it was a great mistake to try and create a separate organisation for dealing with the unemployed. Such an organisation looks important, but in practice it becomes insignificant. Unemployed schemes must become part and parcel of the ordinary duties of the ordinary local administrative bodies. The work must be reported and discussed on these bodies like education or public health, and a member of these bodies must be responsible for answering questions or defending policy. Only in this way can the light of public interest be kept upon this work. The work should therefore be done by a Committee appointed by and responsible to the Borough and County Councils.

But in view of the special nature of the work it is advisable to co-opt upon this committee certain representatives and specialists. The clause provides for this, and in drafting it we have taken as a model the constitution of the old London Technical Education Board which worked under the control of the London County Council. Care is of course taken that organised labour will be represented on these Committees.

CLAUSE 7.

(*1*) *All matters relating to the exercise by a local unemployment authority of their powers and duties under this Act, except the raising of a rate or borrowing money, shall stand referred to the unemployment committee.*

(*2*) *The unemployment committees shall draw up a scheme for providing work for the registered unemployed persons of their area, and such scheme shall, so far as possible, provide for the classification of applicants for work, so that they may be set to work which is suitable to the individual applicant, and so that in all cases of physical and industrial unfitness, special regard shall be given to the ultimate improvement of the applicants.*

(*3*) *When the local unemployment authority are of opinion that unemployment in any case is owing to deliberate and habitual disinclination to work, they may report the case to a court of summary jurisdiction, and the court may issue an order which shall permit the local unemployment authority to enforce control over the person named in the order for a period not exceeding six months, which period must be passed in the performance of reasonable work under the supervision or control of the local unemployment authority.*

(*4*) *The local unemployment authority may assist an unemployed person by aiding the emigration or removal to another area of that person and any of his dependents.*

(*5*) *The local unemployment authority shall not supply workmen to firms of employers or their agents, servants, or representatives during times of trade disputes in which these firms or employers are involved.*

HOW THE COMMITTEES WILL WORK

The second section of this clause clearly lays it down that education and training must be the main idea determining the work to be done by the Unemployment Committees. Distress Committees working under the provisions of the Unemployed Workmen's Act of 1905 found great difficulty in observing this, but unless this is the aim of the committees legislation will not yield the good results which it might.

Hollesley Bay and similar undertakings have on the whole been educational, but their value has been greatly diminished owing to the lack of facilities for small holdings, allotments, and land settlements, caused by our present land monopoly.

POLITICAL ECONOMY

But one of the most interesting experiments in using the Unemployed Act for purposes of training was carried on by the Women's Committee of the Central Unemployed Body which opened workshops for women where sewing was done, and which gave assistance in the shape of payments to women attending classes for the training of charwomen. In the workshops women were taught to make simple garments and, before their time was up, most of them had improved in a most marked way. They became neater in appearance, they took pride in their work, and altogether this experiment, conducted by a Committee which intelligently applied its powers, is one of the most important which the Act of 1905 has made possible.

"HE WHO WILL NOT WORK——."

But the provision in this clause which has given rise to most comment is sub-section 3. However little one may like it, such a provision is necessary in any comprehensive measure like this. Some men are born loafers, more still are made loafers by evil social conditions; but whatever may be his origin, the loafer exists and has to be dealt with. He must not be allowed to damage the claims of the deserving temporarily unemployed. So long as he is mixed up with the unemployed his little ways and escapades will be palmed off, as though he were a typical example of the mass, upon a public only to willing to hear unfavourable things about the poor unfortunate out-of-work. He must be treated separately. He too must be educated. A sentence of six months' work will do him good. He is carefully protected in this Bill against unjust treatment, as is evident if the wording is studied. "Deliberate and habitual disinclination to work" must be proved against him.

By way of appendix I regret that this subsection cannot as yet be applied to men who loaf about preying upon society like slugs on cabbages, but who find themselves well supplied with this world's goods. That may come some day.

CLAUSE 8.

(*1*) *A local unemployment authority shall with due expedition forward to the Local Government Board for consideration the scheme or schemes of the unemployment committee.*

(*2*) *The Local Government Board shall consider the schemes and report upon them to the local unemployment authority, and may advise such modification as they consider necessary.*

(*3*) *The Local Government Board shall decide whether a local scheme shall be wholly or partly paid for from moneys voted by Parliament, or whether it shall be wholly or partly paid for from moneys voted by the local unemployment authority from the funds provided for special or general county, county borough, borough, and urban district purposes.*

Provided that when by a resolution of the local unemployment authority on a report from the unemployment committee the area is declared to

150

be suffering from exceptional unemployment, and the Local Government Board, after inquiry made through the commissioners appointed under this Act fail to prove otherwise, the Local Government Board must sanction a scheme or schemes for a period to be determined upon to be carried out by the local unemployment authority, and paid for from moneys provided by Parliament:

Provided that the Local Government Board may, as a condition of the grant of money, make such regulations as the Board consider necessary for enforcing adherence to the terms of the scheme, including the power of inspection at all times; and

Provided that in no case shall the Local Government Board provide money for assisting emigration.

(4) The cost of emigration and establishment charges, including rent of offices, equipment, wages, and salaries of clerical staff required for carrying out this Act, shall be paid from county, borough, and district funds.

CENTRAL AND LOCAL AUTHORITIES.—FINANCE.

This clause was one of the most difficult to draft in the Bill. In any satisfactory scheme the Local Government Board and the Local Authorities must co-operate, and the greater part of the money required must come from the Exchequer. All should come, some people say, and whilst I agree with that in theory, it appears to be impossible to carry it out at present.

Under the clause as drafted the Local Authority must present a scheme, and when there is no exceptional distress the Local Government Board can decide that the cost of the scheme shall be borne by the rates. This burden cannot be made very heavy, but can just be heavy enough to make local responsibility real and to secure careful administration. At any time, however (although the conditions provided in the next clause may be taken to indicate when) the Local Unemployment Authority may declare that its area is suffering from exceptional distress. The onus of proof that it is not, is then thrown upon the Local Government Board; but when there is exceptional distress *all* the costs of the scheme must be borne by the Exchequer.

These financial provisions must not be regarded as being more than provisional, and after experience the clause will probably be amended so as to carry out the intentions of the Labour Party with greater certainty.

EMIGRATION.

It ought to be noted by the way in which sub-section 4 is drafted, that the Labour Party declares that emigration is no cure for unemployment. Such is the meaning of the provision that no national funds shall be spent on emigrating people. But, on the other hand, there are individual cases benefited by emigration, and if these people are willing to go away and are convinced that they cannot prosper here,

POLITICAL ECONOMY

they may be emigrated from local funds. By putting the burden of doing this on the local rates, wholesale emigration is discouraged and even stopped, but in cases of individual need emigration is still possible.

CLAUSE 9.

(1) The Local Government Board after taking the advice of the central unemployment committee appointed under this Act, shall draw up such a scheme or schemes as shall admit of the employment of unemployed persons on works of national utility; and the Board may at all times and shall during all periods when the Board of Trade returns show that the unemployed persons exceed four per cent. of the employees reported upon as regards the state of the labour market, or when the registers of the registration authorities created by this Act show exceptional distress to exist, carry into execution such scheme or schemes by offering employment to unemployed persons from any local area or areas; and any money required for this purpose shall be paid by the Local Government Board out of moneys provided by Parliament.

(2) Any scheme or schemes under this section may at the discretion of the Local Government Board be carried out in co-operation with a scheme or schemes under the control of a local unemployment authority.

NATIONAL UNDERTAKINGS.

This section is of the greatest importance. There are many undertakings, like afforestation, which can never be put in hand by local authorities—even by County Councils. They are essentially national in their character. The reclamation of the Wash, for instance, should be done by the nation, and the land gained should be the property of the nation. Afforestation in the large scale which is possible if the vast areas are to be utilised in the Highlands, in Yorkshire, and in the Midlands, now handed over to the devastating influences of shooting tenants, or running to waste because it pays no one to cultivate them, can only be undertaken by the nation, and made to yield wealth to the nation. Every waste area should be carefully scrutinised with a view to finding out its capacities; and this would be the duty of a Central Authority, charged with the task of utilising human material when that cannot be profitably utilised by competing employers and by a society organised solely to increase income from property, and not to make life richer for the masses of the people.

The problem of the waste area and the waste labour of the unemployed can only be solved by a Central Committee energetically exercising powers conferred upon it similar to those provided for in this Clause. One of the purposes one had in drafting this Clause was to make the deserts of our country fruitful. The Forestry Department of Germany does it; why, should we not do it in Great Britain, too?

NEW UNEMPLOYED BILL OF THE LABOUR PARTY

CLAUSE 10.

For the purposes of this Act the Local Government Board and any local unemployment authority may provide dwellings, buildings, material, tools, implements, machinery and plant, and acquire land compulsorily, and no additional allowance shall be made on the purchase price or hiring rate on account of the purchase or hiring being compulsory.

DWELLINGS, LAND, Etc.

This Clause gives to the Unemployed Authorities full power to exercise their duties, and prevents their being tied up with red tape. Particularly does it give them power to hold land and to acquire it, in spite of landlord opposition, at its market value, and free of the encumbrance of an extra ten per cent., which Landlord Parliaments have imposed on prices when sales are compulsory.

CLAUSE 11.

The provision of work or assistance or maintenance under this Act shall not disentitle a recipient to be registered or to vote as a parliamentary, county, or parochial elector, or as a burgess.

CITIZENSHIP.

This Clause needs no comment. A Lord Cromer when he becomes unemployed receives £50,000 by way of assistance from the State, but not only is he not disfranchised, but is allowed, in the House of Lords, to exercise as much influence as a man elected by a constituency to the House of Commons. A man who has suffered all the pangs of unemployment is as good and as impartial a judge upon Breakfast Table Taxes and Old Age Pensions as the capitalist employer for whom he made profits, or upon the Land Laws as the Duke of Devonshire whose interests are indisolubly mixed up with the existing evil conditions. There is nothing connected with aid under this Bill which can justify the forfeiture of a man's citizen rights. The men who have suffered shipwreck under the present system have as much right to influence legislation as those who live by piracy on the high seas. One might as well propose to disfranchise the parents of children attending free Council Schools as the recipients of assistance under such an Act as this.

CLAUSE 12.

The Local Government Board shall, after consultation with the central unemployment committee, frame rules for the carrying out of this Act.

POLITICAL ECONOMY

CLAUSE 13.

In the application of this Act to London, the London County Council shall be the local unemployment authority, and the borough councils shall be the registration authorities.

CLAUSE 14.

This Act may be cited as the Unemployed Workmen Act, 1907.

WORK FOR THE UNEMPLOYED!

The Independent Labour Party has been the pioneer of practical proposals for dealing with unemployment. When the other parties looked on in despair whilst willing workmen starved, the Independent Labour Party pointed out not only why unemployment happened, but how it ought to be dealt with immediately. Ours was but a voice in a wilderness. How could men be employed, mused those who did not see Social problems with our eyes, when it did not pay employers to engage them? We first of all succeeded in convincing many who were not prepared to see the whole way to Socialism with us, that that answer was a cowardly shirking of the question. If men starve in a land of plenty, if shoemakers go shoeless at a time when they are told that there is no demand for their labour, it is because the machinery of distribution will not work, and we are bound to improve it.

Meanwhile the people starve. We then had to produce schemes that provided relief for the unemployed. We had to make the unemployed a great political question. We succeeded. A Tory Government gave us the Unemployed Workmen's Act; much against its wish we forced a Liberal Government to provide money to keep the Act going. In a mean pettifogging way it did its best to prevent the money being spent, but again we forced its hand.

Now we have produced our own bill in co-operation with the Labour Party, and the unemployed agitation passes into another stage. Next session the Labour Party has decided this will be its chief bill. The Independent Labour Party should be once more to the front in this agitation. There is no mere tinkering here. Every successful attempt made to fill the mouths of the unemployed and his family not by charity, but by work such as is provided for in this bill, is a stage towards the complete state of the democratic organisation of industry. The solution of the unemployed problem is the beginning of the Socialist state.

Note

1 October, 1907.

15

SOCIALISM AND AGRICULTURE (LONDON: INDEPENDENT LABOUR PARTY, 1908), 3–15.

Richard Higgs

[A consistent demand of the Independent Labour Party since its formation in 1893 until the First World War was that of land reform (Tichelar 1997, 129–130). Richard Higgs (1908) contributed to that tradition with his pamphlet *Socialism and Agriculture*. Although it demonstrates Higgs' considerable knowledge of agricultural methods, issues and problems, as a pamphlet this was a political rather than academic work. As a socialist he argued for the establishment and development of collectivist farming.

For several decades before Higgs wrote the pamphlet agriculture in the United Kingdom had, notwithstanding exceptions in some regions and products, in general undergone a decline in productivity. Wages, conditions and living standards of farm workers remained relatively poor. The reasons for the general decline and for variations around the country were complex. One contributing factor was the tendency of farm owners to cut costs of production rather than risk changing to products that would yield high income but also involve greater costs (Hunt and Pam 2001, 259–265). Higgs was well aware of this factor. The problem was, as he put it in the pamphlet, that of organising the production of agricultural wealth of the best quality, without scarcity or waste, in a way that would produce what he called "the highest type of humanity". Collectivist agriculture was, in his view, the way to resolve that problem.

There was considerable sympathy for various ideas of land reform at the time Higgs wrote his pamphlet. Aware of the potential of such reform policy to gain electoral support, the Liberal Party proposed measures in this field which were mild in comparison with Higgs' collectivist proposals. In 1914 the Labour Party advocated public ownership as a long term aim but its immediate demands were restricted to better productivity, higher wages, the enjoyment of a full life for farm workers and devolution of land ownership and control by means of local government (Tichelar 1997, 128–129). This was not inconsistent with the view on the way to begin to introduce collectivist agriculture suggested by Higgs. The outbreak of war meant that the debate was put aside.]

POLITICAL ECONOMY

PRESENT-DAY FARMING.

In these days people talk freely about Agricultural problems without understanding in the least the greatness of the issues involved or the far-reaching importance of the subject. There is no political or economic subject so much studied and understood in its various parts as is the Agricultural problem, and there is no subject that is so little understood or so little studied in its entirety as that same vast problem.

Agricultural economics is the most difficult branch of social science and the one which offers a greater field for the amusing antics of the faddist, the crank, and the ignoramus than any other. To discuss the question of wages, hours, or conditions of employment in the engineering, textile, or mining trades, it is not necessary to have a close knowledge of the technical working of these industries. To consider intelligently the problem of municipal or national ownership of electrical undertakings, the railways, or steamship lines, it is not necessary to understand all about ohms and volts, etc., to be proficient in the details of the block system, or to understand the science of navigation. But in Agriculture it is different. Agricultural economics can only be studied by those who have a technical knowledge of agricultural life and work, and the variations in that knowledge cause a great bias as to the economic reasonings which are based upon it.

Town people, as a rule, know less about the production of their own food than about almost any other industrial subject. To them agriculture is either merely a constant succession of simple operations of the back garden order, or else a vague unknown problem which is too abstract and complicated for them to trouble about. Agriculture has not so far produced an economist with a real grip of its problems in relation to the problems of the towns, nor has it produced a great idealist. Neither Blatchford, Morris, Bellamy, or any other writer, has yet given to us an ideal of agricultural life in the future, from a Farmer's point of view. All that has been so far offered to the agricultural people has been a life of slavery in the backwoods, whose chief attraction is that greatest discovery of the 20th century, the £150 cottage, without space, without sanitation, and surrounded by a quagmire of mud.

The agricultural economist must understand the work of the farmer in relation to rotations of crops, varieties of soils and their treatment, manures, their composition and uses, agricultural implements and their developments, the various breeds of animals and their peculiarities. He must also know something of the condition of markets and the trend of a variety of trades, as well as the progress of mechanical traction and the problem of the railway rates. This knowledge he must be able to associate with a close acquaintance with village life and the peculiar characteristics of the rural mind, and must co-ordinate this with a knowledge of the development of the modern movement towards higher wages, shorter hours, and better conditions of life for the workers.

SOCIALISM AND AGRICULTURE

This, then, is a brief outline of what agricultural sociology is, and it will be seen to offer an unrivalled field for further study. There being considerable difficulty in presenting so vast a subject in pamphlet form, the following pages are intended to stimulate thought, to raise discussion, and above all, to stir the people to action upon the most vital problem of our time.

The real Agricultural problem is as follows:—

The organisation of the production of Agricultural wealth of the best quality, without scarcity, without waste, and in such a way as to produce the highest type of humanity.

All other problems, such as sizes of farms, systems of tenure, methods of cultivation, etc., are parts of the main question, and should be studied only with that idea in view.

To see how far modern methods of farming fall short of solving the great problem, it is well to briefly look at the Agricultural life of our land to-day. We hear of a "decayed Agriculture," a "ruined industry," an "empty country side," and such things, but the farmer's capital of the United Kingdom, estimated at £6 per acre for the 47,500,000 acres under cultivation is £285,000,000. This is actual working capital, apart from the value of the land, buildings, fences, etc., and capital which is quite capable of being withdrawn and placed in other industries. It is but little short of the combined value of all the gasworks, ironworks, waterworks, and canals in the kingdom.[1]

The same writer states that the total value of the Agricultural lands and the farmhouses, buildings, fences, roads, ditches, etc. (profits under Schedule A of Income Tax, 1902-3, equals £52,000,000 capitalised at 18 years' purchase) amounts to the huge sum of £936,000,000, or nearly the total estimated value of the whole of the railways of the United Kingdom.

The census of 1901 gives us a total of 1,128,604 persons occupied in Agriculture in England and Wales alone, of whom 1,071,040 were males and 57,564 were females. These figures include 12,035 woodmen, and 128,229 non-domestic gardeners, nurserymen, seedsmen and florists; 123,125 being males and 5,140 being females. These persons are of ten years of age and upwards.

The census being taken in the early part of the year, it probably falls far short of the real number of those engaged in Agriculture. This total of 1,071,040 males engaged in agriculture, forestry, and nursery work is nearly one-tenth of the total number of males engaged in all occupations in the least agricultural and most industrial part of our Islands. The total given by the census is 10,156,976.

In addition to the above, it has been estimated that there are 50,000 children regularly engaged in Agricultural work.[2]

Now how are these people treated, and what is the relationship between this huge army of workers and the problem of the towns?

POLITICAL ECONOMY

On referring to Mr. Wilson Fox's report on wages, earnings, and conditions of employment of Agricultural labourers in the United Kingdom, 1905 (c. d. 2376), we find that Agricultural labour is the worst sweated and worst treated of any labour in the Kingdom, and that the Agricultural Labourer is not under the Truck Acts. That his wages, *including the full value of all Truck, estimated not by an outsider or himself, but by his employer,* vary from 8/11 per week in Sligo and 8/9 in Mayo, in Ireland, to 22/2 per week in the County of Durham, or an average of—

18s. 3d. per week for all kinds of English Farm Labourers.
17s. 3d.　　　”　　　”　　　Welsh　　　”
19s. 3d.　　　”　　　”　　　Scottish　　”
10s. 11d.　　　”　　　”　　　Irish　　　”

These figures are for able-bodied male adults; foremen or casual labourers not included.

To show the great poverty of the Agricultural Labourers, it is only necessary to state that amongst the male workhouse inmates over 10 years of age at the census of 1901 there were 9,469 Agricultural Labourers out of a total of 106,863, rather more than one-eleventh of the whole; or, deducting the general labourers and those who occupations are unspecified, there were 37,296 inmates who have a definite trade, more than one quarter of whom were Agricultural Labourers; and this in spite of the fact that Agricultural Labourers are employed at a considerably greater age than are most other workers.[3]

Having now seen that present-day farming is one of the greatest factors in the sweating problem, and noticing by the way that by reason of the varying times and seasons causing a great fluctuation in the numbers of those employed, and, in consequence, aggravating the unemployment problem, we must now see whether present-day farming succeeds in feeding the people and providing them with their other various Agricultural needs.

According to the Official Statistics published by the Board of Agriculture, there were in 1906 510,833 separate holdings from which particulars of crops, stock, and cultivations were gathered. These 510,833 holdings were largely farmed and managed by separate holders, and without any co-ordinated idea as to what kind of crops or how much of each they were severally to produce.

There exist no statistics of any kind showing the needs of the people, and as a result all Agriculture is guess work and haphazard to the last degree. It cannot be too often repeated that farm produce is largely highly perishable and that the greatest of all needs is the need for organisation. Every one is more or less familiar with the huge figures of our imports of food stuff, and it is useless to labour the point that most or all of it could be produced at home. The problem is *how?* Even now, with our limited production, home grown foods often meet a glutted market, and the grower has sent to him a bill of costs, and loses his produce into the bargain.

158

SOCIALISM AND AGRICULTURE

In this connection, it may be mentioned that the constant extension of the operations of the foreign chilled meat companies and their increasing control of British markets is a growing menace to individual producers in our free trade country, and a great factor in depreciating the value of a large part of our Agricultural produce. How far this control of our markets has gone may be gathered by those who have studied the prices of beef in the last few years and seen the large number of retail shops and railway vans devoted to the foreign trade and noted the constant complaint of the graziers in the agricultural papers as to the low price of beef and the unremunerative state of the grazing industry.

Under present conditions of production and distribution foreign produce is sent far inland and home grown stuff is sent to the coast towns, and goods are conveyed from one place to another quite irrespective of anything but the vaguest kind of need for them. It should be perfectly easy to know that a town of a certain size would need certain specified quantities of beef, milk, mutton, pork, poultry, potatoes, vegetables, fruit, and other Agricultural produce; and it should be quite as easy to say that that quantity could be produced on a specified number of acres of agricultural land, and that the remainder, as well as luxuries and local specialities, must be imported from a distance.

Every Poor Law Authority and other big consumers are able to estimate their needs of these things, and it is but a small step from that to estimating the needs of the whole people of a town. But to estimate needs is one thing, to estimate produce is another; and recent legislation, by increasing the number of producers, tends to increase the confusion. While it is fairly easy to estimate the amount of produce of a farm of 500 acres under one management, it is practically impossible to estimate the produce of that farm if cut up into 50 sections of 10 acres each and with 50 different styles of farming.

Modern farming has not succeeded in producing food in a clean, healthy, and wholesome state. The filthy story of private enterprise in Agriculture still awaits a sensational writer to tell. In Agriculture there is a story of uncleanness and horror that by its magnitude and intensity would put even Chicago into the shade.

It would be an easy matter to dwell upon these things and tell of verminous fruit pickers, strawberries littered with manure and sulphured just before picking, dirty fruit baskets, unhealthy and unclean poultry and pigs, tuberculous goats, dirty milk, the evil work of amateur slaughtermen, and such things; but it is of no use while the whole tendency of the times is to produce those conditions which encourage and perpetuate all that is insanitary and unhealthy by the multiplication of farms.

Is efficient inspection of farms and the proper enforcement of the best sanitary conditions a reasonable proposition, I ask?

The plain fact of the matter is that real sanitary inspection is impossible under present conditions; it is too costly for one thing, and if proper sanitary conditions were insisted upon the necessary outlay would be so great that all the smaller men would have to go under. So that the mighty fabric of Small Holdings which is

POLITICAL ECONOMY

being built up with so much labour is really based upon the twin foundation stones of insanitary conditions and sweated labour.

To show that life on Small Holdings is no better but rather worse than life on large farms for the workers, the following evidence from Mr. Wilson Fox's report to the Royal Commission on Agriculture, 1895, may be given. It should be noted that owing to the current prices of Agricultural produce and the keenness of competition the conditions of the life remain practically unchanged to-day.

A farmer of 30 acres says: "I am now working harder than ever I did when I was a labourer, and am earning less." His wife said: "We often have not a penny we can spend; when we were working for wages we had better food than we have now."

One who farmed 47 acres of freehold says: "I brought up a family and nearly worked them to death. They said: 'Father, we are not going to stop here and be worked to death for nothing.' So they went off into shops and left me and the old woman to struggle along. When they were here they got no wages, now they are ladies and gentlemen." Such instances could be multiplied indefinitely.

In order to show that in a free trade country the conditions of life of the Small Holder cannot be other than slavery, it is only necessary to mention that the cost of production of the average crop may be roughly stated as follows:

Labour, including manual and horse, or other power,	75%
Rent, Rates, Taxes, and Insurance, etc.	5%
Manures	15%
Seeds and Sundries	5%
	100

This of course varies very much in various crops and in varied systems, as, for instance, when two crops are grown in one year the rent, etc., is halved, but even on the largest farms, and with the best machinery and organisation, the cost of the average crop in labour is well over 65 per cent. It is easily seen that with the increased capital expenditure on roads, fences, buildings, etc., necessitated by Small Holdings, rents must be higher and labour greater, so that the only possible profit must come from long hours and women and children's labour.

Modern Agriculture under Individualism has failed on every count. It has produced sweating, filth, and scarcity, and it now remains for us to see whether the people should not own and manage their own food supply, and whether by so doing they would better their conditions. They could not well be worse and still let us claim to be a civilised people. The heart of the poverty problem lies in the fact that National and Municipal efforts have not been directed towards the three great needs that Agriculture supplies—food, clothing, and shelter. When the people's food is as well organised and managed as the people's roads, when the crops of wool and flax are as well managed as the Post Office, and when the crops of timber are as well ordered as the people's Navy, we shall then be far on the road towards abolishing poverty.

COLLECTIVIST FARMING.

The principle of Collectivism in agriculture is by no means new or unknown. It is accepted in a great variety of directions throughout our public life, amongst others by the following bodies who own and manage Agricultural land:—

1. The Commissioners of Woods and Forests.
2. The Ecclesiastical Commissioners.
3. The War Office.
4. The Charity Commissioners.
5. Various Agricultural Colleges and Dairy Institutes.
6. The Prison Authorities.
7. The Municipalities.
8. The Poor Law Authorities, Rural and Urban.
9. The Hospital Authorities.
10. Various other bodies, such as the Metropolitan Asylums Board, &c. To these it may be added that Collectivist Farming was strongly recommended by:—

A Departmental Committee of the Board of Agriculture. (See report on British Forestry c.d. 1319.)

This Committee recommended under date Nov. 29th, 1902, "that large state forests be established in such a way as to yield *as large a profit as possible*. Not, it is true, as a means of State revenue, but as a department of Education, although, whatever the motive, the fact remains that Collectivist farming for profit has been thus advocated under a Tory Government.

In this connection it should be especially noted that the report on Forestry above quoted contains the following striking sentence:—"Professional, equally with scientific, witnesses pressed for instruction or demonstration areas, under State or Corporate control, so as to secure that continuity of management without which a sustained annual yield and a maximum return is impossible."

If this is so in Forestry, it applies with a hundredfold greater force in general Agricultural matters, and this weighty pronouncement of experts contains one of the greatest arguments it is possible to bring forward in favour of Collectivist Agriculture. Is not the food of the people of more value than Forests, and are not "continuity of management" and "a maximum return" as necessary when growing fruit trees as they are for the advancement of the science of Forestry?

In this connection it should be remembered that every farm loses a large portion of its *usual maximum productiveness* owing to that lack of "continuity of management" above mentioned. How much it is difficult to say with certainty, but probably more than 10 per cent. of its time is so lost. Changes of tenancy, illness, or

POLITICAL ECONOMY

old age of tenants, and the inexperience of young men, frequently cause farms to "run down" or fall below their usual maximum productiveness. This loss is quite apart from loss of productiveness owing to fluctuations of markets necessitating a change of system and other such causes.

The following instances of the Collectivist principle being successfully applied to Agriculture will show that the industry is well fitted to be developed in that direction.

Glasgow owns 1,700 acres of Agricultural land.

> It raises crops to the value of £5,848 annually.
> It grows oats, potatoes, turnips, cabbages, wheat, and barley; and as much hay as supplies all the wants of the cleansing department stud, as well as those of other departments.
> It has also started sheep farming.

Nottingham farms nearly 1,900 acres.

> It owns 800 cows and other cattle, 150 horses, from 500 to 700 sheep, and 500 pigs. It has a wages bill of £4,500 per annum, and a turnover of £16,000 per annum; and as a result of cleanliness and efficiency, combined with fair wages, it is constantly extending its operations.

Reading farms 870 acres.

> It has about 250 cattle, 65 shire horses, and a herd of pedigree Berkshire pigs. It employs about 80 men in the winter on the farm, and considerably more in the summer; and, in addition, a number of carpenters and wheelwrights and other estate workers. The crops grown are of the best quality, and the financial result is highly satisfactory.

Other instances of successful Municipal farming could easily be given, but these will suffice. Another interesting instance of the possibilities of Collectivist farming is furnished by the Returns published by the Board of Agriculture of the various Agricultural Colleges and Dairy Institutes, etc. (See Annual Report on the Distribution of Grants for Agricultural Education and Research, 1905-6, c.d. 3317.) In a summary of the financial results of these Institutions, we find that out of nine Institutions having a total expenditure of £49,299 for all purposes, including housekeeping and such items, no less a sum than £13,305 was cancelled by receipts from sale of farm produce, or, roughly speaking, more than 25 per cent. of the total expense. These Institutions are run solely for educational purposes and not for profit.

Amongst smaller instances of successful Collectivist Agriculture it would be possible to produce the evidence of a large number of the smaller Rural Workhouses, two of which must be taken as typical. Eastry Union, near Dover, Kent,

SOCIALISM AND AGRICULTURE

has about ten acres of land. It keeps pigs and grows potatoes, cabbages, onions, turnips, lettuces, radishes, tomatoes, etc. Casual labour is used, and tramps are a source of *profit* rather than loss.

An Agricultural paper, under date November 23rd, 1907, gives the following item of news:—

> The farm account in connection with the Carlisle Workhouse, shows a profit on *the last six months* of £156, realised mainly by the sale of vegetables, corn, hay, and pigs. A proportion of the produce is also used in feeding the paupers themselves.

Wherever a few fowls are kept, or a few flowers or vegetables are grown to supply the needs of the inmates of a public institution, there the principle of Collectivist Farming is accepted, and it only needs the development of existing conditions to make a profound change in the whole of the revenue of the country and to turn some of the most expensive branches of the public service into profit makers instead.

Many opportunities present themselves for the further application of the principle, with a view to raising revenue for the people, not the least of these being the utilization of the bye-products of the farm. Amongst these may be mentioned timber and firewood, flints, stones, and brick earth. Direct ownership and management of stones would result, in some districts, in a reduction in the cost of materials for the upkeep of the roads by 20 per cent. and upwards.

The great Agricultural estates of the Commissioners of Woods and Forests and Ecclesiastical Commissioners offer exceptional advantages for effecting an enormous saving to the taxpayer.

These estates comprise, roughly speaking, 350,000 acres. (This acreage of the Crown and Ecclesiastical Commissioners is not published, but was given to the writer by a high official. The figures are not guaranteed, but may be taken as approximately correct.) This land is at present let to tenant farmers, and is situated in various parts of the country. As the occupiers gradually gave up their holdings, the land could be taken over to the public service to produce such things as—

1. Army Horses.
2. Army and navy foodstuffs, such as beef, mutton, pork, veal, potatoes, fruit, tinned and fresh milk, etc.; also hay, straw, corn, and flax for rope making, and many other such things.
3. Timber and firewood of many kinds to be used in the public service.
4. Such things as leather, road metal, wool, building materials, etc., for use in reducing rates and taxes.

Now assuming that the whole of this 350,000 acres was without capital, it would only take an outlay at £6 per acre of £2,100,000, or about equal to two battleships, to bring it to the public use, and this would be a remunerative outlay of the first order, bearing an immediate and direct result to the taxpayer. But many of the farms are even now in the hands of the public, and capitalised by public funds, though devoted to private trading. The remainder would gradually revert to the people, and big economies would result from unified management. It should be noted that these two bodies, the Office of Woods and Forests and the Ecclesiastical Commissioners, have always a staff of trained and experienced men ready to take over the management of the farms as they fall in.

In this connection it should be mentioned that the *house refuse and road sweepings alone* of our big towns provide an immense source of fertility which is now practically wasted. How great that waste is may be shown by the calculation which has been made that the house refuse and road sweepings of London, if placed on the land at the rate of 20 tons per acre, when well rotted every other year, would provide fertility for 116,000 acres, an area more than 1½ times its own size—an undertaking far beyond the power of private enterprise in any form.

The War Department is the owner of various large tracts of land, the acreage of which is not published, at every garrison town, especially at Aldershot and on Salisbury Plain, where the management is understood to be of the usual War Office order. This land, if placed under the excellent management of the Office of Woods and Forests, would prove a most valuable revenue producing asset of the nation. Many of the big hospitals and other semi-public bodies derive a precarious rental or most precarious profit from large farms owned and managed by them. Many benefits would result if, instead of the governors of the hospitals selling their produce in the country and buying it again in the towns, they sent it direct from their own farms; and, with the coming municipalisation of the hospitals, the value of the land would be greatly increased.

The Prison Authorities are easily in a position to do a great deal towards extinguishing the huge sum charged in the National expenditure to Courts of Justice account. All the penal establishments should have workshops and farms under their control, and work in harmony with Local Urban Authorities, who could assist in the provision of fertilising material as before shown, and so tend to become self-supporting.

In the big towns where a lack of Agricultural knowledge in the managing bodies is likely to be an objection to Collectivist farming, the need could be met by either purchasing the goods wanted from farms managed by Rural bodies or else by the engagement of a first-class Agricultural expert, in the same way as is done with success in the engineering, legal, electrical, medical, architectural, and other professions. Finally, every public body should be encouraged to take up a farming department whenever and wherever it would be found convenient and in harmony with its other work; the whole supervised, criticised, and assisted by the Board of Agriculture, in the same way that other departments of public life are under the Board of Trade and the Local Government Board.

Space will not permit of a full discussion of the effect of such a policy as that above outlined upon the problems of unemployment, sweating, housing, etc., in their entirety, but it may be well in passing to glance briefly at these subjects and see whether a Farmer's ideas will not help in their solution. The poverty problem and all that is involved therein is essentially an agricultural problem, because it is in the first place a problem of the provision of Agricultural produce for the people. Practically all the writers on the question of unemployment ignore the fact that, as before shown, agriculture in England and Wales employs nearly one-tenth of the male occupied population and is a seasonable industry of the first importance. It employs under modern conditions of work a very fluctuating number of workers; how great that fluctuation is may be seen when it is stated that on fruit farms the numbers often vary from 150 persons largely working overtime in summer to a dozen or so working short time in winter. While fruit-growing may be taken as an example of extreme fluctuation of labour, it is nevertheless true that even on the quietest and most old fashioned corn and sheep farms there are busy seasons when extra workers are wanted and the ordinary workmen are working overtime. In addition to this, it should be remembered that not only do the seasons cause fluctuation in agricultural work, but the weather in the various seasons acts largely upon unemployment. For instance, a cloudy and dull week in the strawberry districts will cause many to walk the roads looking for a job; a late cold spring will delay farm work; while a "growing" autumn will delay the raising of the potato and mangold crops, with disastrous results to the casual workers employed in that work. Any proposed regulation either of hours, wages, or employment which ignores these vital facts must be doomed more or less to failure. Factories and workshops can be started and stopped practically at will, but farm work depends entirely on the seasons and the weather. The adoption of Municipal and State farming for the purpose of supplying State and Municipal needs would also necessitate workshops in which to work up the produce of the Farms and also to regulate the labour. It should be remembered that there is nothing revolutionary about combining agricultural work with factory work, because many skilled agricultural trades, such as sheep shearing, hop drying, tree pruning, etc., can only be done during a short time of the year, and the workers in those trades have to be engaged in other occupations during the rest of the year. From the Agricultural point of view, such a combination of intelligent and well paid workshop labour with farming would enable much work to be well done in the spring and autumn which is now badly done in the winter, when the land is neither fit for horses or men to be upon it. This regulation of employment by production for public use, instead of for trading purposes, would early tend to absorb the whole of the unemployed at a living wage, and bring the workless man to the source of wealth in a rational and simple manner. It would of course be unable to absorb those who by reason of lack of physical, mental, or moral development were fit subjects for Farm Colonies or some other form of curative agencies for their especial diseases. By this treatment of the problem of unemployment the subsidiary problems of sweating, housing, home work, child labour, etc., would largely cease to trouble society, because State and Municipal farming would regulate the wages of the largest section of the workers in the same way that Individualist farming at present degrades the workers as a whole by setting the standard of wages on the lowest level.

165

POLITICAL ECONOMY

The reform here advocated is the easiest and simplest of all reforms; it needs no great Acts of Parliament, no beating of the great war drum against the hosts of the House of Lords, and it is the one reform that would do more for the people than any other. It needs but a departmental readjustment to decide that public-owned land, which is probably at least one-fifth of all the land under crops, shall be used for National purposes, and gradually as fresh land was needed it could be purchased, and with the purchase would go all the old disputes as to rights of way, game laws, systems of tenure, etc., that have been the battle ground of the interests for centuries.

The Municipalities could easily purchase farming land as needed, and it only needs an effective agitation in the democratic parties to bring this about.

When any considerable portion of the farming land of the country comes under the control of the people, all the whole conditions of dirt, chaos, and waste will disappear; a living wage will be paid; and by the addition of indoor workshops, as already indicated, a regular supply of skilled labour will be available at the varying seasons of the year, and a six days' week and the eight hours' day, even in harvest, will become possible.

The Farming Land is the key to the problem of poverty. It is the great store-house of the national wealth, and the most important question before the democracy is whether it will choose to assert its right to have this real "Bank of England" in its own possession and for its own benefit, or be content to muddle along in the bad old methods of an out of date Individualism.

Agriculture is the cinderella among the industries. In all lands and in all times farm workers have been amongst the lowest in the social scale. English labourers, Scottish "hinds," Continental peasants, the cowboys of the western plains, and the Indian ryots, all alike are ignorant, despised, underpaid, and neglected of men. Agriculture is the universal drudge who feeds, clothes, and houses mankind, and everywhere its workers are below the level of those of the town. But the end of the story is at hand. The Socialist Party is the fairy godmother, and Collectivism is the magic wand which will transform this poor despised slave into the Queen amongst industries. Collectivism will raise agriculture to its true place and make its people take their rightful position as the most honoured amongst craftsmen. Collectivism will promote agricultural science and stimulate the genius of our farmers to produce finer crops and animals than they have yet accomplished, even though Britain is now the Stock Farm of the World. It will destroy all that is little, mean, and ignoble in our country side, and fill the beautiful hills and valleys of our native land with a wealth far surpassing that of Eastern fables. It will reveal to our town bred people their great Agricultural inheritance, and will use the brown earth, the golden glory of the corn, and the myriad tints of our native plants, to paint upon Britannia's Isles the fair picture of a nation's ideals.

Collectivism in Agriculture, by beginning at the elementary needs of man, will cause our social problems to vanish away as the mist of the morning at the rising of the sun of freedom. It will produce a race of men and women who are keen with the intelligence and shrewdness of the towns, and self-reliant and strong as the countrymen, and who are worthy to carry into the new time the best traditions of our national life.

The old story tells us that the first Paradise was an Agricultural one, and the modern science of sociology tells us that the Kingdom of Heaven and the dream of the ages, whose advent is being hailed in every Socialist meeting in the land, must come through the medium of a renewed and glorified Agriculture.

Notes

1 *Riches and Poverty,* by Chiozza Money, pages 57-8.
2 *Child Slaves of Britain,* by R. Sherard, page 17,
3 *Riches and Poverty,* by Chiozza Money, pages 57-8.

Part 5

WAYS OF ORGANISING

16

MANIFESTO OF THE JOINT COMMITTEE OF SOCIALIST BODIES (LONDON: TWENTIETH CENTURY PRESS, 1893), 1–8.

Joint Committee of Socialist Bodies

[The Joint Committee of Socialist Bodies was an initiative of William Morris. Having been an early member of the Marxist Social Democratic Federation (SDF), Morris had left at the end of 1884 to help form the Socialist League. Comprising Marxists and anarchists, the League was always unstable. This eventually brought Morris' departure in 1890 to form the Hammersmith Socialist Society (HSS). Morris maintained the anti-parliamentarism which had brought about his departure from the SDF. His radical, purist stance also meant he was at the opposite end of the socialist spectrum from the Fabians. Hence, his attempt to unite British socialists in the Joint Committee was an optimistic endeavour. Nevertheless, both the Fabians and the SDF agreed to participate in the Committee with the HSS to write the *Manifesto of the Joint Committee of Socialist Bodies* in 1893. The five delegates from each of these organisations included senior figures such as H.H. Hyndman and Harry Quelch of the SDF and George Bernard Shaw, Sidney Webb and Sydney Olivier of the Fabians.

The *Manifesto* starts by conceding that the socialist movement has been hindered by the divisions among its key players. It goes on to focus on the considerable goals on which those players can agree in the struggle against capitalism. The divisions between the Fabians and SDF constituted one difficulty for the Joint Committee (Johnson 2000, 999; Laybourn 1994, 157). Reflecting divisions such as this, there is no discussion in the *Manifesto* of the means or methods to achieve those goals (Joint Committee of Socialist Bodies 1893).

The absence of method, furthermore, meant that although he put his name to it Shaw was sceptical of the Committee and its Manifesto from the beginning (Johnson 2000, 999). Perhaps the most critical problem was, however, the absence of, and failure to work with, the Independent Labour Party (ILP) which had been formed in January 1893. The attitude of the Fabians was

171

particularly unhelpful. For much of 1893 Shaw distrusted the ILP, worrying that its independence would mean the Fabian influence would be lacking. Although Shaw's distrust waned later in the year, by then the Joint Committee had had little impact on the left. Moreover, Webb continued to be less than enthusiastic about working with the ILP (Bevir 2011, 205–212). In 1900 the SDF, Fabians and ILP would all collaborate in the events leading to the formation of the Labour Party; by then, however, the Committee and its manifesto had faded into obscurity.]

There is a growing feeling at the present time that, in view of the increasing number of Socialists in Great Britain, an effort should be made to show that, whatever differences may have arisen between them in the past, all who can fairly be called Socialists are agreed in their main principles of thought and action.

This is the more hopeful since, though much has been made of those differences by the opponents of Socialism, it is safe to say that they have been rather of less than more importance than similar disputes of the early days of great movements which have afterwards become solid and irresistible. There has indeed been constant co-operation in propagandist work between the individual members of different organisations, and occasional co-operation between the organisations in political emergencies; but more than this is now needed if we are to make a serious advance in the work of gathering together and directing the great body of thought and feeling which is setting towards Socialism.

Meanwhile the necessity for the development of a new social order is getting more obvious to all thinking people, and without the growing aspirations towards Socialism the outlook of modern civilisation would be hopeless.

The vigorous propaganda which has been carried on for the last twelve years, and the complete change in the attitude of the working classes and the public generally towards Socialism, could not but attract the notice, and perhaps excite the anxiety, of the politicians of the possessing classes; but they have shown hitherto that they have lacked both the will and the power to do anything effective towards meeting the evils engendered by our present system. In spite of factory acts and factory inspectors, in spite of sanitary legislation and royal commissions, the condition of the working people is, relatively to the increased wealth of the country, worse than it was twenty years ago. Children are still growing up among such surroundings and so insufficiently nourished that health and strength are for them an impossibility; dangerous and unwholesome trades, inflicting hideous diseases on those who work at them, are still carried on by the capitalists with impunity; overcrowding, accompanied by increasing rents, is the rule rather than the exception in all our great cities.

At the same time the great and growing depression in the most vital of industries, agriculture, tends to drive the people more and more from the country into the towns, while it so narrows the field from which healthy and vigorous industrial recruits have been drawn in the past that the physical deterioration of our city population is more severely felt than ever before.

Moreover, the question of the unemployed is more pressing to-day than at any recent period. The incapacity of the capitalist class to handle the machinery of production without injury to the community has been demonstrated afresh by the crisis of 1890, itself following upon a very short period of inflation; since which time every department of trade and industry has suffered from lack of initiative and want of confidence and ability among these "organisers of labour." As a result the numbers of the unemployed have increased rapidly; the prospect of any improvement is still remote; and the stereotyped official assurance that there is no exceptional distress only emphasises the fact that it is prosperity, not distress, which is exceptional. Indeed, the greatest "prosperity" possible under the present system could only lessen the mass of those without occupation, and bring them down to a number manageable by the employers. Meantime small improvements made in deference to the ill-formulated demands of the workers, though for a time they seem almost a social revolution to men ignorant of their own resources and of their capacity for enjoyment, will not really raise the condition of the whole people.

In short, the capitalist system, by which we mean the established plan of farming out our national industries in private property lots, and trusting to the greed of the owners and the competition between them to ensure their productive use, is the only arrangement possible in a society not organised enough to administer its own industry as a national concern. This shiftless method has indeed kept the shop open, so to speak, but at a frightful cost in human degradation, as might have been expected from its basis. All the investigations undertaken with a view to convicting Socialists of exaggeration and one-sidedness in their attacks upon it have shown that the facts are worse than any Socialist dared to surmise, and that half a century of ameliorative regulation by means of factory legislation and the like has failed to weaken the force of former exposures of Capitalism.

Among recent anti-Socialist statisticians Mr. Robert Giffen has been led by his own counterblast to Socialism into the exclamation, "That no one can contemplate the present condition of the masses without desiring something like a revolution for the better." And the facts as to London poverty, laid bare by Mr. Charles Booth, dispose of the possibility of leaving things as they are; although Mr. Booth, who is a Conservative in politics, undertook his great inquiry expressly to confute what he then thought to be Socialist overstatements. The horrible revelations concerning English home life made by the Society for the Prevention of Cruelty to Children have effectually dispelled the illusion that the cruelty and selfishness of the factory and mine have not infected the household, or that society can safely abandon its children to irresponsible private ownership any more than its land and capital.

WAYS OF ORGANISING

Under these circumstances of a continued degradation of the really useful part of the population—a consequence as inherent in the present system of ownership as it was in the system of chattel slavery—the need for a new social order is obvious. Some constructive social theory is asked for and none are offered except the feudal or Tory theory which is incompatible with democracy, the Manchester or Whig theory which has broken down in practice, and the Socialist theory. It is, therefore, opportune to remind the public once more of what Socialism means to those who are working for the transformation of our present unsocialist state into a collectivist republic, and who are entirely free from the illusion that the amelioration or "moralisation" of the conditions of capitalist private property can do away with the necessity for abolishing it. Even those re-adjustments of industry and administration which are Socialist in form will not be permanently useful unless the whole state is merged into an organised commonwealth. Municipalisation, for instance, can only be accepted as Socialism on the condition of its forming a part of national and at last of international Socialism, in which the workers of all nations, while adopting within the borders of their own countries those methods which are rendered necessary by their historic development, can federate upon a common basis of the collective ownership of the great means and instruments of the creation and distribution of wealth, and thus break down national animosities by the solidarity of human interest throughout the civilised world.

On this point all Socialists agree. Our aim, one and all, is to obtain for the whole community complete ownership and control of the means of transport, the means of manufacture, the mines, and the land. Thus we look to put an end for ever to the wage-system, to sweep away all distinctions of class, and eventually to establish national and international communism on a sound basis.

To this end it is imperative on all members of the Socialist party to gather together their forces in order to formulate a definite policy and force on its general acceptance.

But here we must repudiate both the doctrines and tactics of Anarchism. As Socialists we believe that those doctrines and the tactics necessarily resulting from them, though advocated as revolutionary by men who are honest and single-minded, are really reactionary both in theory and practice, and tend to check the advance of our cause. Indeed, so far from hampering the freedom of the individual, as Anarchists hold it will, Socialism will foster that full freedom which Anarchism would inevitably destroy.

As to the means for the attainment of our end, in the first place we Socialists look for our success to the increasing and energetic promulgation of our views amongst the whole people, and next to the capture and transformation of the great social machinery. In any case the people have increasingly at hand the power of dominating and controlling the whole political, and through the political, the social forces of the Empire.

The first step towards transformation and reorganisation must necessarily be in the direction of the limitation of class robbery, and the consequent raising of the standard of life for the individual. In this direction certain measures have been brought within the scope of practical politics; and we name them as having been urged and supported originally and chiefly by Socialists, and advocated by them still, not, as above said, as solutions of social wrongs, but as tending to lessen the evils of the existing *régime*; so that individuals of the useful classes, having more leisure and less anxiety, may be able to turn their attention to the only real remedy for their position of inferiority—to wit, the supplanting of the present state by a society of equality of condition. When this great change is completely carried out the genuine liberty of all will be secured by the free play of social forces with much less coercive interference than the present system entails.

The following are some of the measures spoken of above:—

An Eight Hours Law.
Prohibition of Child Labour for Wages.
Free Maintenance of all Necessitous Children.
Equal Payment of Men and Women for Equal Work.
An Adequate Minimum Wage for all Adults Employed in the Government and Municipal Services, or in any Monopolies, such as Railways, enjoying State Privileges.
Suppression of all Sub-contracting and Sweating.
Universal Suffrage for all Adults, Men and Women Alike.
Public Payment for all Public Service.

The inevitable economic development points to the direct absorption by the State, as an organised democracy, of monopolies which have been granted to, or constituted by, companies, and their immediate conversion into public services. But the railway system is of all the monopolies that which could be most easily and conveniently so converted. It is certain that no attempt to re-organise industry on the land can be successful so long as the railways are in private hands, and excessive rates of carriage are charged. Recent events have hastened on the Socialist solution of this particular question, and the disinclination of boards of directors to adopt improvements which would cheapen freight, prove that in this, as in other cases, English capitalists, far from being enlightened by competition are blinded by it even to their own interests.

In other directions the growth of combination, as with banks, shipping companies, and huge limited liability concerns, organised both for production and distribution, show that the time is ripe for Socialist organisation. The economic development in this direction is already so far advanced that the socialisation of production and distribution on the economic side of things can easily and at once begin, when the people have made up their minds to overthrow privilege and monopoly. In order to effect the change from capitalism to co-operation, from unconscious revolt to conscious re-organisation, it is necessary that we Socialists should constitute ourselves into a distinct political party with definite aims, marching steadily along our own highway without reference to the convenience of political factions.

We have thus stated the main principles and the broad strategy on which, as we believe, all Socialists may combine to act with vigour. The opportunity for deliberate and determined action is now always with us, and local autonomy in all local matters will still leave the fullest outlet for national and international Socialism. We therefore confidently appeal to all Socialists to sink their individual crotchets in a business-like endeavour to realise in our own day that complete communization of industry for which the economic forms are ready and the minds of the people are almost prepared.

ALFRED BEASLEY,
SAMUEL BULLOCK,
J. E. DOBSON,
W. S. DE MATTOS,
W. H. GRANT,
H. M. HYNDMAN,
WILLIAM MORRIS,
SYDNEY OLIVIER,
TOUZEAU PARRIS,
HARRY QUELCH,
H. B. ROGERS,
GEO. BERNARD SHAW,
WILLIE UTLEY,
SIDNEY WEBB,
ERNEST E. WILLIAMS,

The Joint Committee of the Social Democratic Federation, the Fabian Society, and the Hammersmith Socialist Society.

Signed on behalf of the undermentioned bodies:—

H. W. LEE, Secretary Social-Democratic Federation, 337, Strand, W.C.
EDWARD R. PEASE, Secretary Fabian Society, 276, Strand, W.C.
EMERY WALKER, Secretary Hammersmith Socialist Society, Kelmscott House, Hammersmith.

17

WHY WE ARE INDEPENDENT (LONDON: LABOUR REPRESENTATION COMMITTEE, 1903), 1–4.

Labour Representation Committee

[In 1903 the three-year-old Labour Representation Committee (LRC) entered into a secret pact with the Liberal Party but also published the leaflet *Why We Are Independent*. The purpose of the Lib-Lab pact was to avoid competition with one another in a number of parliamentary and local governmental seats. There had already been cooperation between the LRC and the Liberals, with the Liberal Richard Bell being elected on an LRC platform in the parliamentary seat of Derby. This was one of two seats won in 1900, the other being Keir Hardie's victory in Merthyr (Howell 1976, 19–20). By 1903 many in the LRC were already worried about being too close to the Liberals, reflecting suspicion that the LRC would lose its independence and face domination within the pact. The situation was not helped by some Liberals who did, indeed, want their party to be the higher-ranking participant in the relationship. In this atmosphere the pact was made but Hardie, Ramsay MacDonald and other senior figures on the Labour side engineered a strategy in which there could be cooperation with the Liberals as long as this was, or at least appeared to be, from a position of strength on the Labour side (Bealey 1956, 368–369).

Making extensive use of a resolution declared at the Labour conference of 1903 in Newcastle, the *Why We Are Independent* leaflet aimed to reassure LRC supporters that independence would not be abandoned (Labour Representation Committee 1903). The "Newcastle resolution" stated that Labour MPs, candidates and officials should not identify with or promote the interests of the Liberal and Conservative parties or any sections thereof (Bealey 1956, 362–363). This carefully did not rule out cooperation with other parties if this was to promote the interests of Labour rather than either of the two major parties. The LRC tended, accordingly, to construe its strategy involving electoral arrangements as being in the interests of Labour, even when the broader policy to which it contributed also benefited the Liberals. The leaflet serves to illustrate the caution that senior members of the LRC felt compelled to take in conducting its political affairs.]

<u>LABOUR REPRESENTATION COMMITTEE.</u>

A FEDERATION OF
TRADE UNIONS,
TRADES COUNCILS,
THE INDEPENDENT LABOUR PARTY,
AND THE FABIAN SOCIETY.

WHY WE ARE INDEPENDENT.

The Labour Representation Committee has decided that it must be an independent factor in politics, and it has been much criticised in consequence.

Let us quote the famous Newcastle resolution, and then explain why it was passed.

The Newcastle Resolution.

In view of the fact that the L.R.C. is recruiting adherents from all outside political forces, and also, taking into consideration the basis upon which the Committee was inaugurated, this Conference regards it as being absolutely necessary that the members of the E.C., Members of Parliament, and candidates run under the auspices of the Committee, should strictly abstain from identifying themselves with or promoting the interests of any section of the Liberal or Conservative parties, inasmuch as if we are to secure the social and economic requirements of the industrial classes, Labour representatives in and out of Parliament will have to shape their own policy and act upon it regardless of other sections in the political world; and that the E.C. report to the affiliated association or bodies any such official acting contrary to the spirit of the constitution as hereby amended.

Such is the resolution carried at Newcastle, by a vote of 659,000 against one of 154,000. This was the only possible decision, and the reason is apparent to anyone who understands the present position of the Labour movement.

This is a New Movement.

It originated in the desire of the workers for a party that really understands and is prepared to deal with their grievances, and has grown to its present strength by the systematic attacks in the Press and the Law Courts upon combined Labour and its funds. It is the workers' reply to the aggressive action of Federated Masters and Trusts.

But upon this conflict between Capital and Labour neither a Liberal nor a Conservative Ministry can be trusted to stand by the workers. The nation is called upon to settle economic and industrial difficulties for which neither of the old political parties offers any definite or satisfactory solution. Would it not, therefore, be futile to commit this new movement to parties which neither understand nor sympathise with its aims?

Trade Unionism and Party Politics.

Consider also the composition of the Labour Representation Committee. The resolution of the Trades Union Congress which brought the Committee into existence, called for co-operation between the Trade Unionists, the Socialists, and the Co-operators. The movement is, therefore, not merely Trade Unionist, Socialist, or Co-operative, but is one in which these three sections can work side by side for common aims and objects.

Take the case of the Trade Unionists. Does anyone propose that the Trade Union movement should become either Liberal or Conservative? If there be such, he is the greatest enemy that Trade Unionism has.

The most pressing necessity of the moment is an adequate Parliamentary Fund, such as the Labour Representation Committee is now raising. But how can Conservative Trade Unionists be expected to pay the election expenses of Liberal candidates, or Liberal Trade Unionists pay to add to the strength of the Conservative party in the House of Commons?

The thing cannot be done. If it be attempted, the movement will be wrecked, and Labour will have to be content for ever to occupy the position of the hewer of wood and the drawer of water. A Labour party and Labour candidates alone can unite Trade Union votes, and claim a hearty support from funds subscribed by Trade Unions.

Wanted! A United Labour Party.

Once more, consider the workman as an Elector.

Suppose the Committee recognised Liberal or Conservative candidates. When, in former days, candidates appealed for Trade Union support they found that Trade Unions contained both Liberals and Conservatives. The Liberals would not support a Conservative, nor the Conservatives a Liberal. Were this to be continued, it would mean that the present comparative impotence of Labour in Parliament would be perpetuated, and the Labour Representation movement would fail as it did in 1875.

The employing and landlord classes know that so long as the only issues are between Liberals and Conservatives (whether the candidates are Labour or not), Trade Unionist will continue to vote against Trade Unionist, and Co-operator against Co-operator, and there will be no united Labour Party.

WAYS OF ORGANISING

The Wisdom of Independence.

The only way to unite the democracy is to begin afresh, make a new appeal, raise a new issue, declare for a new political combination. That is what was done at Derby and Merthyr, at Clitheroe and Woolwich.

It is only when a Labour candidate runs in accordance with the Newcastle resolution that he can expect to receive a practically united Trade Union and Socialist vote. He will lose the support of the richer people who are not in sympathy with Labour's demands, but, on the other hand, he will secure the votes of thousands of workers.

Woolwich proves that. At Woolwich, **because our candidate was independent,** he united electors who had previously opposed each other, and he won the seat. Woolwich shows the political wisdom of the Newcastle resolution.

WE ARE INDEPENDENT, THEN

Because we must unite the democracy;

Because we must have the support of all sections of the Labour movement;

Because if we are Liberal or Conservative, the Trade Union movement cannot unitedly support us;

Because this policy has already secured the support of about 1,000,000 Trade Unionists.

Because we raise new economic and industrial issues, upon which the old political parties speak with an uncertain and hesitating voice;

Because we must be free in Parliament to lay down our own Labour policy, and adopt the most effective means for vindicating the rights of Labour and improving the social condition of the people.

ISSUED ON BEHALF OF THE COMMITTEE,

April, 1903.   J. RAMSAY MacDONALD, *Secretary*

CONSTITUTION OF THE COMMITTEE.

As Amended at the Newcastle Conference, February, 1903.

I.

The Labour Representation Committee is a Federation of Trade Unions, Trades Councils, the Independent Labour Party, and the Fabian Society. Co-operative Societies are also eligible for membership.

II.—OBJECT.

To secure, by united action, the election to Parliament of candidates promoted, in the first instance, by an Affiliated Society or Societies in the constituency, who undertake to form or join a distinct group in Parliament, with its own whips and its own policy on Labour questions, to abstain strictly from identifying themselves with or promoting the interests of any section of the Liberal or Conservative parties, and not to oppose any other candidate recognised by this Committee. All such candidates shall pledge themselves to accept this Constitution, to abide by the decisions of the Group in carrying out the aims of this Constitution, or resign, and to appear before their constituencies under the title of Labour candidates only.

III.—THE EXECUTIVE.

The Executive shall consist of thirteen members, nine representing the Trade Unions, one the Trades Councils, one the Fabian Society, and two the Independent Labour Party. The members shall be elected by their respective organisations at the Annual Conference.

IV.—DUTIES OF THE EXECUTIVE.

The Executive Committee shall appoint a Chairman, Vice-Chairman, and Treasurer; shall transact the affairs of the Committee, and make proper arrangements for the payment of permanent officers when necessary.

It shall keep in touch with Trade Unions and other organisations, local and National, which are running Labour candidates, and on the approach of a General Election, it shall prepare a list of candidates run in accordance with the Constitution, shall publish this list, and shall recommend these candidates for the support of the working-class electors. Its members shall strictly abstain from identifying themselves with or promoting the interests of any section of the Liberal or Conservative parties.

It shall report to affiliated organisations if the chief officials of any affiliated body publicly oppose the approved candidates of the Committee, or if any member of this Executive, Member of Parliament or candidate, who has been endorsed by the Committee, acts contrary to the spirit of this Constitution.

V.—THE SECRETARY.

The Secretary shall be elected by the Annual Conference. He shall be under the direction of the Executive Committee, who shall have power to suspend or dismiss him for good cause shown, and to appoint a temporary successor to act until the next Conference.

WAYS OF ORGANISING

VI.—AFFILIATION FEES AND DELEGATES.

Every Trades Council shall be entitled to affiliate, and to send one delegate to the Conference on paying £1 per year, and may send one additional delegate for each 10s. paid. Other organisations shall pay 10s. per annum for every 1,000 members or fraction thereof, and may send one delegate for each 1,000 members paid for.

VII.—ANNUAL CONFERENCE.

The Committee shall convene a Conference of its Affiliated Societies in the month of February each year. Notice of all resolutions for the Conference and all amendments to the rules, shall be sent to the Secretary by December 1st, and shall be forthwith forwarded to the affiliated organisations. Notice of amendments shall be sent to the Secretary by January 15th, and shall be printed on the agenda.

18

WHY IS THE L.R.C. INDEPENDENT? (LONDON: LABOUR REPRESENTATION COMMITTEE, c. 1905).

Labour Representation Committee

[As an amended and updated edition of its *Why We Are Independent* of 1903, the leaflet *Why is the L.R.C. Independent?*, published by the Labour Representation Committee (LRC) in late 1905 or the very beginning of 1906, begins with a summary of the resolution passed at the Newcastle conference of 1903, outlining the LRC's independent stance, rather than quoting the resolution as had the earlier leaflet. There is also a little more evidence added with the intention to support that stance. Finally, at the end of the second leaflet (Labour Representation Committee c. 1905) one finds in large letters the statement "Vote for Hardie", indicating preparedness for the forthcoming election campaign of January 1906.

The amended leaflet serves to illustrate the continuing difficulty the LRC faced in working cooperatively with the Liberals, while recognising that in the short term such cooperation would be beneficial. A crucial problem was that clear differences remained in the very nature of the LRC on the one hand and the Liberal Party on the other regarding the trade unions. For many in the LRC it was a matter of identity and group loyalty (Powell 1986, 383). Among the Liberals, on the other hand, many had sympathy for the plight of workers but could only support trade union activity insofar as it worked not only in the interest of the workers involved but also in a perceived common good for the country (Powell 1986, 386).

Notwithstanding the lingering reticence and distrust shared by many in both the LRC and the Liberal Party, the secret pact made with the Liberals in 1903 culminated in a successful general election of January–February 1906 in which the LRC, having taken two seats in 1900, increased its share to twenty-nine. Immediately after the election the LRC transformed itself into the Labour Party and gained another seat (Howell 1980, 19–20).]

THE Labour Representation Committee has decided that it must be an independent factor in politics, and it has been much criticised in consequence.

Let us quote the famous Independence Clause and then explain why it was passed.

The Independence Clause.

To secure, by united action, the election to Parliament of candidates promoted, in the first instance, by an affiliated Society or Societies in the constituency, who undertake to form or join a distinct group in Parliament, with its own whips and its own policy on Labour questions, to abstain strictly from identifying themselves with or promoting the interests of any section of the Liberal or Conservative parties, and not to oppose any other candidate recognised by this Committee. All such Candidates shall pledge themselves to accept this Constitution, to abide by the decisions of the Group in carrying out the aims of this Constitution, and to appear before their constituencies under the title of Labour candidates only.

Such is the resolution carried at Newcastle in 1903, by a vote of 659,000 against one of 154,000, maintained at Bradford in 1904 by 533,000 against 422,000, and at Liverpool in 1905 by 742,000 against 140,000. This was the only possible position for the Labour Party to take up, and the reason is apparent to anyone who understands the present position of the Labour movement.

THIS IS A NEW MOVEMENT.

It originated in the desire of the workers for a party that really understands and is prepared to deal with their grievances, and has grown to its present strength by the systematic attacks in the Press and the Law Courts upon combined Labour and its funds. **It is the Workers' reply to the aggressive action of Federated Masters and Trusts.**

But upon this conflict between Capital and Labour neither a Liberal nor a Conservative Ministry can be trusted to stand by the workers out and out. The nation is called upon to settle economic and industrial difficulties for which neither of the old political parties offer any definite or satisfactory solution. Would it not, therefore, be futile to commit this new movement to parties which neither understand nor sympathise fully with its aims?

TRADE UNIONISM AND PARTY POLITICS.

Consider also the composition of the Labour Representation Committee. The resolution of the Trade Union Congress which brought the Committee into existence, called for co-operation between the Trade Unionists, the Socialists, and the Co-operators. The movement is, therefore, not merely Trade Unionist, Socialist, or Co-operative, but is one in which these three sections can work side by side for common aims and objects.

Take the case of the Trade Unionists. **Does anyone propose that the Trade Union Movement should become either Liberal or Conservative? Whoever does, is the greatest enemy that Trade Unionism has**.

The most pressing necessity of the moment is an adequate Parliamentary Fund, such as the Labour Representation Committee is now raising. But how can Conservative Trade Unionists be expected to pay the election expenses of Liberal candidates, or Liberal Trade Unionists pay to add to the strength of the Conservative party in the House of Commons?

The thing cannot be done. If it be attempted, the movement will be wrecked, and Labour will have to be content for ever to occupy the position of the hewer of wood and the drawer of water. **A Labour Party and Labour Candidates alone can unite Trade Union votes, and claim a hearty support from funds subscribed by Trade Unions**.

WANTED! A UNITED LABOUR PARTY.

Once more, consider the workman as an Elector.

Suppose the Committee recognised Liberal or Conservative candidates. When, in former days, candidates appealed for Trade Union support, they found that Trade Unions contained both Liberals and Conservatives. **The Liberals would not support a Conservative, nor the Conservatives a Liberal**. Were this to be continued, it would mean that the present comparative impotence of Labour in Parliament would be perpetuated, and the Labour Representation movement would fail as it did in 1874.

The employing and landlord classes know that so long as the only issues are between Liberals and Conservatives (whether the candidates are Labour or not), Trade Unionist will continue to vote against Trade Unionist, and Co-operator against Co-operator, and there will be no united Labour party.

THE WISDOM OF INDEPENDENCE.

The only way to unite the democracy is to begin afresh, make a new appeal, raise a new issue, declare for a new political combination. That is what was done at Derby and Merthyr, at Clitheroe and Woolwich, and at Barnard Castle.

It is only when a Labour Candidate runs in accordance with the L.R.C. Constitution that he can expect to receive a practically united Trade Union and Socialist Vote. He will lose the support of the richer people who are not in sympathy with Labour's demands; but, on the other hand, he will secure the votes of thousands of workers.

Woolwich proved that. **At Woolwich, because our Candidate was independent, he united electors** who had previously opposed each other, and he won the seat. Woolwich shows the political wisdom of the L.R.C. policy of independence.

We are Independent, then

BECAUSE

We must unite the democracy;

We must have the support of all sections of the Labour movement;

If we are Liberal or Conservative, the Trade Union movement cannot unitedly support us.

This policy has already secured the support of about 1,000,000 Trade Unionists;

We raise new economic and industrial issues, upon which the old political parties speak with an uncertain and hesitating voice;

We must be free in Parliament to lay down our own Labour policy, and adopt the most effective means for vindicating the rights of Labour and improving the social condition of the people.

Issued on Behalf of the Committee,

J. RAMSAY MacDONALD, *Secretary*

28, Victoria Street, London, S.W.

**VOTE FOR
HARDIE**

19

LABOUR AND POLITICS: WHY TRADE UNIONISTS SHOULD SUPPORT THE LABOUR PARTY (LONDON: LABOUR PARTY, c. 1907).

Labour Party

[Soon after returning twenty-nine of its members to parliament at the 1906 general election, and gaining another seat shortly afterwards, the newly formed Labour Party (c. 1907) produced a campaigning leaflet which aired a note of cautious optimism. The leaflet appealed for British workers to persuade their unions to affiliate to the party, drawing attention to its eventual success in the Taff Vale case and legal victories in two other industrial disputes on the basis of meagre resources. The Taff Vale decision, which meant unions could be held responsible for the actions of their members, was overturned by the Trade Disputed Bill of 1906 (Klarman 1989a, 1533–1535). The other two cases were Denaby & Cadeby Main Collieries Ltd. v. Yorkshire Miners' Association of 1906, which returned a verdict that favoured the Labour-supporting trade unions (Klarman 1989a, 1530–1533), and Steele v. South Wales Miners Federation which, although it found in favour of a Liberal-supporting union, nevertheless demonstrated the potential for success in cooperation between Labour and the trade unions (Pelling 1982, 892–893). The leaflet predicted far greater legislative success if Labour's parliamentary representation could be enhanced.

The Labour Party's optimism would soon be dented. In 1907 Walter Victor Osborne of the Amalgamated Society of Railway Servants union took the party to the High Court. As a Liberal, he sought a declaration that his union was in breach of the law for donating a part of his dues to support another party – Labour. Following the Labour Party's recent legal success, the likelihood of Osborne winning seemed slight. Initially, indeed, his case failed. Nevertheless, the verdict was overturned in the Court of Appeal the following year. Labour and the Trades Union Congress took the case back to the Lords without success, as the final verdict towards the end of 1909 was that the union's support of a political party was *ultra vires* – beyond its legal power (Pelling 1982, 889–890). That verdict was overturned in 1913 by the Trade Union Act which nevertheless allowed members to opt out from paying into

187

a political fund which each union was required to introduce. The leaflet captures a crucial short period in the early development of the Labour Party, its relations with the unions and its funding, before the Osborne decision was made.]

The Late Lord Salisbury, speaking on the Shop Hours' Bill, on February 26th, 1901, said:—

> "This is one of the cases in which the two Houses of Parliament occupy a somewhat unique position. They are asked to legislate as to matters affecting the personal happiness and well being of a very large number of persons—a very large class—to which, with scarcely an exception, the members of the two Houses do not themselves belong. It is, therefore, very difficult for them to know how such a measure would affect the comfort of the class concerned."

The Right Hon. John Morley, M.P., speaking at the Queen's Hall, London, on March 20th, 1905, said:—

> "It is only those who are directly brought into contact with the misery and vicissitudes of the ordinary life of toil, who really know, and we, with all our feelings and sympathies, do not know what we can do. We don't know what the State can do, and it is worth silver and gold—more than silver and gold—that we should have in the House of Commons men who can tell us at first hand how the case stands."

Thus, "Whig and Tory now agree" that if Parliament is to legislate for Labour, Labour must be directly represented in Parliament.

Since 1900 the Labour Representation Committee, now the **"Labour Party"** has been trying to secure this representation.

Was it not time?

Legal decisions were threatening to deprive combined Labour of every right it was supposed to have. The Taff Vale and the South Wales Miners' cases stand out in our history as marks of the time when Trade Unionists refused to enter politics and had not yet formed a Labour Party.

Since then a Party has been formed, nearly a million members belong to it, and public opinion, as reflected in the Law Courts, has begun to do workmen more justice.

The uncertainty in the position of Trade Unions is not the only danger. **Capital is combining more effectively than ever** against the common interest. The American Trust is beginning to flourish on English soil. How can Trade Unions unaided hope for success against such combinations of capital as the following?

J. & P. Coats, Ltd. (Sewing Cotton)	£12,000,000
National Telephone Co., Ltd.	10,500,000
Calico Printers' Association	9,200,000

Fine Cotton Spinners and Doublers	8,750,000
Bleachers' Association, Ltd.	8,250,000
Associated Portland Cement Manufacturers	8,000,000
Vickers, Sons, and Maxim, Ltd.	7,450,000
Guest, Keen and Nettlefold, Ltd.	5,000,000
British Electric Traction Co.	4,940,000
Bradford Dyers' Association	4,500,000
Wall Paper Manufacturers	4,200,000
United Collieries, Ltd.	3,000,000
Yorkshire Woolcombers' Association	3,000,000
British Cotton and Wool Dyers' Association	2,750,000
The Salt Union	2,750,000

So long as it suits these and other combinations to work harmoniously with the Unions there will be peace. But when the interests of labour conflict with the interests of these Trusts there will be war, and victory will favour **the millions of money rather than the rights of men**.

Further, employers are now developing into a system, the black list, which is a wicked method of victimising the obnoxious Trade Unionists; and by other petty methods (such as Sick Clubs that are practically compulsory) they are gaining an increasing power over the liberties of the workman.

Nor are they content with the power which their massed capital gives them. They see with true instinct that it is the law-making authority—Parliament—that holds the key of the position, and so they have their committee in the House of Commons, called the **Employers' Parliamentary Council**. This Council is not a party affair; both parties are represented upon it. It has defined its objects in a privately-circulated statement, from which the following is an extract:—**"To take action with respect to any Bills introduced into either House of Parliament affecting the interests of Trade, of Free Contracts, and of Labour, or with respect to the action of Imperial or local authorities affecting in any way the said interests."**

It showed how effective it was when in spite of a majority of 122 in the last House of Commons, the representatives of this Council on the Grand Committee on Law, killed the Trades Dispute Bill.

They would do the same now, but they have to fight us on the floor of the House of Commons, and not merely in the outer Lobbies, and that makes all the difference.

Over and above special Trade Union grievances, there is a grave social problem which must be solved. One in every three persons over 65 years of age—that is, **one in every two** of the workers—has to **live by charity**. In 1905 **12 workmen were killed** and **over 300 injured each day** in the course of their employment. Many of these **accidents are preventible**.

Every year it is becoming more and more difficult for a workingman to find a **decent house** at a **reasonable rate**. Industry is crippled, and the life of a worker rendered precarious by **extortionate railway charges, mining royalties,** and **land rents**. These questions can only be dealt with properly when there is a body of men in the House of Commons who regard the improvements of the social condition of the masses as the first concern of a Democratic Parliament, and who, irrespective of the convenience of other parties, are determined to force the matter to an issue.

Who else will face these questions?

The miner will not trust his employer to weigh tubs of coal unless a check-weigh-man is there to look after his interest. The textile worker will not trust his employer to pay him his piece wages fairly without a Particulars Clause in a Factory Act. How absurd it is that the men who cannot be trusted in these smaller matters are to be trusted to legislate so as to solve the social problem in its widest significance.

Trades Unionists must not neglect politics.

As an example of what can be done, take the case of the Unemployed Act of 1905. We had then only four Independent Labour Members in the House, but mainly by their action the Unionist Government was forced to carry it into law.

We appealed to you to make that handful of Independent M.P.'s into a crowd. At the last Election you made a beginning and the result is before the country to-day.

The present Liberal Government introduced an unsatisfactory Trades Dispute Bill. The Labour Party carried a satisfactory one.

The Government introduced a weak Workmen's Compensation Bill. The Labour Party carried amendment after amendment strengthening it.

The Feeding of neglected School Children has been talked about for years. Not until there was a Labour Party in Parliament was a Bill dealing with the subject carried.

The condition of Government Workers, the Appointment of Factory Inspectors, and a score of other Labour interests were effectively dealt with within three months of their election by the thirty men, who, as an independent and separately organised Party, represent Labour in Parliament.

You are having more than value for your money.

The Labour Party has not spent more money upon its central organisation during its seven years of existence than would keep a thousand men on strike for a month. And yet at the last General Election the candidates of the Labour Party won some of the most hopeless seats in the country, polled 323,195 votes, and increased the representation of the Party in Parliament from four to thirty.

LABOUR AND POLITICS

Look at these interesting accounts:—

Cost of Defending Trade Unionism in the Law Courts.		Cost of Defending Trade Unionism in Parliament.	
Taff Vale Case	£43,000	Labour Party Affiliations: Fees from beginning (seven years)	£4,316
South Wales Miners' Case	75,000		
Denaby Main Case (at least)	50,000	Parliamentary Fund: Total Expenditure from beginning to December, 1906	10,606
		Estimated Cost of Elections: Fifty Candidates at £1000	50,000
		Total	£64,922
Total	£168,000	Result:	
Result:		**A Labour Party of 30 members, and**	
Trade Unionism		**the most successful Labour session ever**	
undermined.		**known**.	

It is, therefore, **the duty of every Trade Unionist** to see that his Union is affiliated to the Labour Party, to which 180 Trade Unions, with a membership of over **1,000,000** and 80 Trades Councils, have already become affiliated.

20

THE PARTY PLEDGE AND THE OSBORNE JUDGEMENT (MANCHESTER: THE NATIONAL PRESS LTD, 1910), 1–16.

Keir Hardie

[The Amalgamated Society of Railway Servants (ASRS) was deemed liable in 1901 for industrial action damaging to the Taff Vale Railway Company. This set a precedent but also galvanised the trade union movement which put its weight behind the Labour Representation Committee, which became the Labour Party in 1906. In his book *From Serfdom to Socialism* of 1907, having seemingly won a victory in the courts in the shape of reversal the previous year of the Taff Vale ruling, Party leader Keir Hardie (2015, 77–78) expressed optimism regarding the future of the labour movement. That year, however, the movement faced a new challenge. The liberal ASRS member Walter Osborne objected to the party pledge because it in effect committed electoral candidates funded by affiliated unions to join the Parliamentary Labour Party if elected and accept its constitutions and decisions. Osborne took the ASRS to court in 1908, insisting that trade unions acted illegally by such funding. The following year Osborne won the case when the House of Lords, referring to the Trade Union Act of 1875, deemed support of a union for a party *ultra vires* (beyond the law). This set a new precedent (Klarman 1989b, 893; Pelling 1982, 889–890).

Hardie's pamphlet *The Party Pledge and the Osborne Judgement* of 1910 helps illustrate his determination to restore the progress that had inspired his optimism three years earlier. The pamphlet starts with the section of the Labour Party constitution which came to be known as the "pledge". Hardie then offers a detailed account of the close legal argument that was employed to block the attempt to unite the economic and political wings of the Labour movement – party and unions – in parliamentary government. The political nature of the Osborne judgement is in focus in the pamphlet (Hardie 1910).

In 1913 the Trade Union Act reversed the 1909 ruling by the House of Lords. Nevertheless, unions were required to set up a separate fund for such purposes.

PARTY PLEDGE AND THE OSBORNE JUDGEMENT

Each member could, importantly, contract out of paying to the fund if they so desired (Pelling 1982, 890).]

BEFORE going into the legal aspects of the case let me briefly state what is the Constitution of the Labour Party.

THE CONSTITUTION.

"THE LABOUR PARTY is a Federation consisting of Trade Unions, Trades Councils, Socialist Societies, and Local Labour Parties.
Co-operative Societies are also eligible.

OBJECT.

To secure the election of Candidates to Parliament and organise and maintain a Parliamentary Labour Party, with its own whips and policy.

CANDIDATES AND MEMBERS.

(1) Candidates and Members must accept this Constitution; agree to abide by the decisions of the Parliamentary Party in carrying out the aims of this Constitution; appear before their constituencies under the title of Labour Candidates only; abstain strictly from identifying themselves with or promoting the interests of any Parliamentary Party not affiliated, or its Candidates; and they must not oppose any Candidate recognised by the National Executive of the Party.
(2) Candidates must undertake to join the Parliamentary Labour Party, if elected."

These are the parts of the Constitution to which objection is taken, especially the sections headed "Objects" and "Candidates and Members." The Party has 40 M.P.'s in the present Parliament, each of whom is paid an allowance of £200 a year from the Party funds. In the actual working of the Party the method is as follows. Each affiliated organisation decides upon the number of candidates for which it is prepared to make itself responsible, and then proceeds to select the men. The selection is sometimes done by the Executive of the Society, but also, and this I think most frequently, by a ballot vote of the members. When a selection has thus been made the Society forwards the names to the Labour Party Executive, with an undertaking to make itself responsible for the election expenses of its nominees. The nominees are then asked to sign the Party Constitution as an indication of their acceptance of its provisions, and, this done, they are then put upon the Party's list of candidates. When the Labour organisations in a constituency desire to run a candidate they must satisfy the Executive that the political organisation of the place is fairly efficient, and that the candidature will not be a wild cat adventure. When all this has been done a conference must be called of all the working-class organisations in the constituency, which are either actively affiliated to or are eligible to become affiliated to the Labour Party, and this conference, after receiving nominations, may select the candidate. Thus, the whole procedure, from start to finish, is thoroughly democratic. In the House of Commons the members of the Party decide their own policy without interference from the Executive or any outside authority. This is a right which the Parliamentary Party has always claimed, and which has never been seriously challenged. Where a member has a conscientious or other valid objection to supporting a finding of the Party the almost invariable rule has been to allow him freedom of action, both of speech and vote, and this freedom has been frequently claimed and exercised. From this it will be seen that all the talk about the coercion exercised by the Party on its well dragooned Pledge-bound adherents is either due to misunderstanding, as in the case of Lord James, or is the outcome of ignorant, implacable hostility to the Party itself. The so-called "Pledge" refers more, much more, to the action of candidates and others *outside* of Parliament than it does to the action of members within, as an ordinarily careful reading of the Constitution as quoted above will show.

HISTORICAL.

In 1868 the Trade Unions began to consider a levy for running candidates and maintaining M.P.'s. The reason why that was not done before was that the working class had no votes until that year. By 1874 there were quite a number of Labour Candidates in the field, and from then onwards the unions used their funds for political purposes without let or hindrance. The Labour Party was formed in 1899, and took part in the elections of 1900, 1906, and 1910, with the result stated above. In 1907 some Welsh miners raised an action to have it declared that the Parliamentary levy of 1/- a year imposed by the Miners' Federation was illegal. The miners were not then affiliated to the Labour Party but had a Labour representation scheme of their own. The County Court Judge ruled the levy to be legal, and on appeal this decision was upheld by Justices Darling and Phillimore. In 1908 a Mr. Osborne raised an action against the A.S.R.S. on the same issue, complicated somewhat, however, by the fact that certain amendments to the rules of the Society had been carried in what was alleged to be an unconstitutional fashion. Despite this, Mr. Justice Neville decided in favour of the Society, whereupon an appeal was taken to the higher Courts of Appeal, with the result as set forth hereafter. It is worth noting in passing that so long as the funds of the A.S.R.S. were used to finance a Liberal Labour M.P., Mr. Osborne, himself an ardent Liberal, had no concern for the conscience of the Conservative minority. It was only when the Society decided that its candidates and members must belong to the Labour Party that his conscience appears to have become acute. Most of the unions connected with the Labour Party have now been served with injunctions, and the scope of these is being gradually widened so as to prohibit political action of all kinds, national or local, by the unions. Statesmen of all parties and their organs of the Press are all concerned about saving the rights of minorities in the trade unions, and a web of subtleties and legal quibble is being woven round the case to perplex the minds of the voters. The trick will fail.

THE PRESENT POSITION.

I want, at the outset, to set forth the position clearly. The position now is this: that a Trade Union is not free to spend its funds or any part of its funds for political purposes. Now, see what that means. Suppose you had a union every member of which was Conservative, and the members of the union wanted to run a Conservative Labour candidate and pay him from the union funds. Suppose every member in that union was willing to do it. Suppose they were agreed unanimously as to who should be the candidate. The law steps in and says, "No, you must not spend your own money in sending that man to Parliament." If you had a union composed entirely of Liberals the same thing would be true; or if it was composed entirely of Socialists the same thing would be true. The point is this: that, at the present time, suppose a Trade Union is unanimous in its desire to spend a part of its funds for Labour representation, the law says: "We don't allow it." And I am here to say, my constituents, that whether you be Liberal, or Conservative, or Socialist, you must join together to put an end to that state of affairs. It is an interference with your rights as Trade Unionists, and an interference which *you will not long brook.* Talk about the rights of minorities! It is the rights of majorities which have been taken away by the Law Courts.

REASONS FOR THE JUDGMENT.

Now, what is the reason for that judgment? The House of Lords, who gave the final judgment, decided the question of the Osborne levy on two quite separate and distinct grounds. One of these grounds was this: that because the Trades Union Acts do not specially authorise political representation, therefore it must be held to be illegal. That was one reason. Another reason was this: that because a Labour member is paid to go to the House of Commons to represent the interests of the working class, therefore the Labour Party is unconstitutional, and a Trade Union must not support an unconstitutional party. The Law Lords were unanimous in their decision, but arrived at their conclusions for different and widely differing reasons. The great majority held the levy to be illegal because political action is *ultra vires,* that is beyond the scope of the lawful functions of a Trade Union; whilst a small minority held on the other hand that political action by a Trade Union was not *ultra vïres,* and that a levy for this purpose was quite legal, but that the Labour Party was an unconstitutional party, and that, consequently, a levy for the support of such a party was illegal. Lord James, of Hereford, in particular, made it quite clear that his decision rested solely on the fact that the rule of the A.S.R.S. made it obligatory on all their candidates to conform to the Constitution, and accept the whip of the Labour Party.

WAYS OF ORGANISING

I will take the first statement first. It is said that because Labour representation is not specially mentioned in the Trade Union Acts therefore it is illegal. Lord Halsbury in giving judgment in the House of Lords said, referring to the Trade Union Acts, 1871-5:—

> My Lords, the Act is, as it were, the charter of incorporation, and it undoubtedly renders some things lawful, which, but for the enactment, would be unlawful, and with a degree of minuteness gives a specific authority to certain contracts and to certain applications of funds that appear to me to be *absolutely exhaustive*. . . . I therefore content myself by saying that this levy is to my mind manifestly beyond the powers possessed by a Trade Union.

Lord MacNaghton on the same occasion said:—

> There is nothing in any of the Trade Union Acts from which it can be reasonably inferred that Trade Unions, as defined by Parliament, were ever meant to have the power of collecting and administering funds for political purposes . . . I am therefore of opinion that a rule which purports to confer such a power as that now in question on any Trade Union . . . must be *ultra vires* and illegal.

Lord James, of Hereford, took a different view:—

> For instance, I think it may well be in the interests of Trade Unionism and labour that the funds of a Trade Union should be devoted to the payment of the expenses of a Member of Parliament, who should represent such interests. I also concur in the view presented to your lordships by Sir Robert Finlay (for the Society) that Section 16 of the Act of 1876 is not a clause of limitation or exhaustive definition. It seems to me that the legislature only intended to require certain qualifications to exist before an entity could become a Trade Union, but the objects or limits of action of a properly qualified Trade Union are not dealt with by the section. So far I am in agreement with the case presented by the appellants. —(The A.S.R.S.)

Lord Atkinson agreed with Lords Halsbury and MacNaghton, whilst Lord Shaw did not express any decided opinion on the point one way or the other, though his leanings seemed to be towards the view of Lord James. In the Court of Appeal the Master of the Rolls had also declared that:—

> In my opinion it is not competent to a Trade Union either originally to insert in its objects, or by amendment to add to its objects, something so

wholly distinct from the objects contemplated by the Trade Union Acts as a provision to secure Parliamentary representation.

BEFORE 1875.

Lords Justices Fletcher Moulton and Farwell concurred in this. Now I am not a lawyer, and don't propose to discuss the legal aspect of the case. There are, however, one or two statements which run through all the judgment referred to above, and which cannot be allowed to pass without challenge. The first is that a Trade Union has no political powers because these are not "expressly conferred" by the Trade Union Acts, nor can political action be "derived by reasonable or fair implication or deduction" from the statutory powers conferred on Trade Unions, nor can political action be regarded as being "collateral or ancillary" to the powers possessed by a Union. Let us look at each of these statements, and, to do so understandingly, certain facts must be borne in mind. The first is that one hundred years ago a Trade Union was, in the eye of the law, an illegal conspiracy. The theory of the law was that whilst one man might lawfully give up his job in an effort to get better wages, it was illegal for two or more to do so because it then became an illegal conspiracy in restraint of trade. In 1824 an Act was passed to remove this restriction, but the Trade Union itself was still an illegal association with no protection from the law. The officers were liable to be gaoled, liable to be banished. The books of Trade Unions in those days had to be kept buried in the secretary's garden or hidden somewhere out of sight. Away down in Dorsetshire the agricultural labourers formed a Trade Union in 1834 to try and get their wages raised. Their wages were 7s. a week, they wanted them raised to 8s. a week, and they formed a Union for the purpose. The farmers and the landlords summoned the leaders before the law courts, and six of them were sentenced to seven years' penal servitude. The Liberal Government of the day did not think the sentence "excessive" and refused to intervene in the men's behalf. This kind of thing went on until 1871, in which year a Liberal Government was in office, returned by the votes of the newly-enfranchised working-men in the Burghs. The Government was pledged to legalise Trade Unions, and in 1871 passed the Trade Union Acts for that purpose. But, as so often happens with Liberal legislation, what they gave with the one hand they withheld with the other, and the Trade Unions found that they were very little better off. And what happened then? They commenced a big agitation to have the Trade Union Law put right. At the General Election of 1874, 14 Labour candidates went to the poll against Liberal candidates, and one of those 14 stood *for the Merthyr boroughs*. These candidates *were financed by Trade Union money*. The result of the agitation was that the Liberals were defeated and the Tories came in, and the next year the Tory Government passed the Act under which Trade Unions have gone on from then till now. Now, see what that means. The Law Lords say that at the time the Trade Union Act was passed in 1875 political action had not been heard of; and yet I am showing you that the reason why the Act came to be passed was because of the political action of the

Trade Unions, and but for that political action the Act would not have been passed at all. It is therefore monstrous for men sitting in the highest Courts of Appeal to be so *ignorant of the history* of this question as to make statements as absurd as the ones I have quoted.

If political action and Parliamentary representation cannot be fairly deduced from Trade Union work as being "collateral" or "ancillary" thereto, then words have lost their meaning. It is not disputed that the object of Trade Unionism is to enable the working class to take concerted action to improve their condition. By the Common Law of England a strike is illegal; so too is picketting and boycotting. What the Trade Union Acts said was this: that so far as workmen were concerned these acts should no longer be illegal if done in connection with a trade dispute. That was all, and to say that this shut out from the purview of the Trade Union any other legal method of improving the condition of the working class is absurd. If the Unions decide to get an eight hour day by Act of Parliament, instead of by striking, surely it is a fair deduction that if they may spend money on a strike to attain their end they may also spend it in political action. The law did not create Trade Unions; all that it did was to remove certain restrictions on the workings of the Unions. Most of the Law Lords admit this in their judgment, but say all that was legalised was the things then actually being done by the Unions, and that political action was not included in these things. I have shown the absurdity of that contention by a reference to the 1874 election. As a matter of fact I myself, as a lad working in the mines, paid 1s. as a political levy to defray the expenses of the late Alexander MacDonald during his candidature for the Kilmarnock Burghs in 1868. However, the Law Lords have declared the opposite and the only appeal from them is to the House of Commons. Thrice during the past few years the House of Commons has been called in to reverse or modify judgments of the House of Lords; once in the celebrated case of the Free Church of Scotland, next in the Taff Vale case, and last in the case of a friendly society. As it has done before, so must it do again, and restore to the Unions their freedom to apply their funds for political purposes where the members decide in favour of that being done.

AN ILLEGAL CONSPIRACY.

I now come to the second point, viz., that the Labour Party is itself an unconstitutional body. I am specially anxious to bring out the importance of this, because it goes far beyond the question raised by Osborne. His point was that a Trade Union has no power to use its funds for political purposes. In deciding the issue several of the Law Lords went out of their way to say that even though a Trade Union had the power it would still be illegal for it to contribute to the funds of the Labour Party, because the Labour Party is in itself an unconstitutional body. The objection of Lord James, whose broad sympathy with the workers will not be disputed by anyone who knows his record, was much narrower. He held that political action, including representation in Parliament, was clearly within the scope of the powers of a Trade Union, but that, inasmuch as the Labour Party Pledge was unconstitutional, and as the rules of the A.S.R.S. bound all their candidates to accept the Labour Party Constitution, he had no option but to decide against the Union. As this issue has not yet been directly before the Courts we cannot say there has been any direct decision, but the opinions of the judges in the Court of Appeal, and the House of Lords, leave us in no doubt as to what that decision will be when the question does go before them, as go it surely will. When the Osborne judgment has been reversed, and the Unions made free to pay for representatives in Parliament the next move will be to have it declared that they must not pay for Labour members. Nay, it is possible, and not improbable, that action may be taken against Labour M.P.'s for sitting and voting in unconstitutional fashion. As the penalty for each vote is £500 the outlook is cheerful. If my reading of the situation be correct the Labour Party now occupies an almost identical position in the eye of the law with that occupied by the Trade Unions at the beginning of last century.

A MONSTROUS CLAIM.

Before stating what in my opinion should be done to meet this state of affairs let me first show clearly the line taken by the judges. Justice Fletcher Moulton was the first to raise the question in the Court of Appeal. After deciding that Parliamentary representation could not be made an object of a Trade Union, he went on to say:—

> But there is another and more far-reaching objection to the rules of this Society as they stand, according to the contention of the defendants. One has only to look to Rule 13, section 4, to see that the object of the Parliamentary Fund is to procure Members of Parliament who shall be bound to vote in a prescribed manner, and that it is in consideration of their undertaking so to vote that the funds of the Society are to be expended in procuring their election and in supporting them in Parliament. Any such agreement is, in my opinion, void as against public policy . . . The reason why such an agreement would be contrary to public policy is that the position of a representative is that of a man who has accepted a trust towards the public, and that any contract, whether for valuable consideration or otherwise, which binds him to exercise that trust in any other way than as on each occasion he conscientiously feels to be best in the public interest is illegal and void . . . And it is no answer to say that before or at the election he openly avowed his intention to be thus contractively fettered. The majority who elected him may be willing to permit it, but they cannot waive the rights in this respect of the minority.

What that means is this: that it is illegal for working folk to select and pay members of their own class to represent their interests in Parliament, and that it is illegal for a constituency to elect such members. Mr. Justice Fletcher Moulton would not only interfere with the powers of a Trade Union but also with the rights of a constituency. As this is a power which Parliament itself cannot exercise it is not likely that it is going to be admitted in the case of a Law Court. It is one of the most monstrous claims ever put forward from the bench.

After quoting from the rules of the A.S.R.S. the learned judge added, "the conditions of the Labour Party bind members when elected to abide by the decision of the Parliamentary Party in carrying out the *aims of its Constitution,* and the new Clause 7 set out above treats the members of Parliament as responsible to the Society." Both of these were in his opinion illegal, "and to use the funds of any society" for procuring the election of, or for supporting in Parliament, any candidate or member so bound, was also, in his opinion, "illegal." So much for Mr. Justice Fletcher Moulton and his opinions.

Lord Justice Farwell followed on much the same lines. He stated the problem in all its naked boldness, thus: Can Trade Unions:—

> Lawfully apply their funds in promoting the election, paying the election expenses, and providing for the maintenance of a Member of Parliament who is to be bound to vote according to the directions of a body *formed for advancing the interests of a class,* in the present case of workmen, but which might equally well be of employers?

Was not such a purpose "in itself illegal?" And he added:—

> The defendants' scheme is in effect to subsidise candidates, and maintain them if returned to Parliament, for the purpose of *representing exclusively the interests of railway workmen.* In other words, certain constituencies are to be disfranchised by substituting for a member representing them a paid delegate bound to put the interests of those who pay him before all other considerations. But this is so utterly unconstitutional, that no court of law can possibly regard *money subscribed for such a purpose as money subscribed for a lawful purpose.*

Two things should be noted here; working-class representation, according to Mr. Justice Farwell, is in itself illegal, Pledge or no Pledge, and a voluntary organisation, like the I.L.P., is just as much debarred from subscribing to the funds of the Labour Party as is a Trade Union. The "purpose" being unlawful, the money subscribed for that purpose is also unlawful.

IN THE LORDS.

Lord Halsbury, who delivered the leading judgment, whilst not "expressing dissent" from the opinions expressed in the Court of Appeal, did not care to commit himself on the Constitutional point, because it was not an issue in the case before them. Lord MacNaghton followed the example of Lord Halsbury, at the same time administering a quiet snub to the Court of Appeal for having dragged in the Constitutional issue. "I do not think it necessary," he said, "and I doubt whether it is expedient or profitable, to discuss the so-called Constitutional question, which was introduced, rather unfortunately I think, into the case in the Court of Appeal." Lord James, who followed, was very definite on two points. First, he totally disagreed with those who said that it was illegal for a Trade Union to use its funds, or impose a Levy for political purposes. He agreed with the contention that Trade Union Acts were merely descriptive of what a Trade Union was, and that Clause 16 of the Act of 1876 was neither a Clause of "limitation nor exhaustive" of the powers of a Trade Union. But because of "one particular fact existing in the case" he was bound to give his decision against the Society. That "one particular fact" was that the Society compelled all its candidates to accept the Constitution of the Labour Party. He added:—

> I construe this condition as meaning that the member undertakes to forego his own judgment, and to vote in Parliament in accordance with the opinions of some person or persons acting on behalf of the Labour Party. And such vote would have to be given on all matters, including those of a more general character—such as confidence in the Ministry or the policy of a Budget—matters unconnected, directly at least, with the interests of Labour. Therefore, I am of opinion that the application of money to the maintenance of a member, whose action is so regulated, is not within the powers of a Trade Union.

He preferred not to enter into the "very broad Constitutional question raised for the first time in the Court of Appeal," but added that his silence must not be taken to mean agreement with Justices Fletcher Moulton and Farwell. It is quite clear that Lord James's "one particular fact" which caused him to give his decision against the A.S.R.S. is the Labour Party Pledge. It is equally clear that his reading and interpretation of the Pledge is at fault. That I have already dealt with and so need not repeat the argument here. The fact I want borne in mind is that Lord James is the one judge thus far who bases his judgment exclusively on the Pledge, and not upon the Trade Union Acts or the representation of the interests of a class. In fact he expressly stated that he thought it might "well be in the interests of Trade Unionism and Labour that the funds of a Trade Union should be devoted to the payment of the expenses of a Member of Parliament who should represent such interests." Lord Atkinson expressed no opinion on the Constitutional issue. Then followed Lord Shaw. He had not made up his mind whether or not Trade Unions were legally empowered to pay for Labour representation, and therefore he confined himself to the Constitutional aspect of the question, and regretted that the Master of the Rolls in the Appeal Court, and the Law Lords then sitting, had not definitely dealt with and decided the Constitutional issue. On this point the issue was whether the Union funds, assuming Unions had the power to enter

WAYS OF ORGANISING

politics, were not being devoted to an illegal and unconstitutional object when applied to the upkeep of the Labour Party? His own words were:—

> ... I find myself compelled to consider this appeal upon the other ground taken, involving an examination of the conditions which accompany the payment under the Constitution of the Labour Party, viz., the ground that the contributions are to be devoted to the payment of Members of Parliament, who accept the same under obligations inconsistent with our Parliamentary constitution, and contrary to public policy.

He referred to the "fulness and learning" with which the subject had been treated by Lords Justices Fletcher Moulton and Farwell in the Court of Appeal, and argued before the Lords by Mr. Spencer Bower, Osborne's lawyer. Lord Shaw then proceeded to quote from the Constitution of the Party, and described the representation at the Conference, and succeeded in making the astounding deduction that the Trade Councils and local Labour Associations might "swamp" the larger Trade Unions by their votes. The Conference, he presumed, also decided the policy of the Party. Therefore the A.S.R.S. was not seeking for direct representation in Parliament, but the power to contribute to the funds of a party in which the opinions and desires of the A.S.R.S. might be over-ridden by the other affiliated societies. Under the rules of the A.S.R.S. a Member of theirs is "responsible to" and "paid by" the Society, and must at the same time have agreed to abide by the decisions of the Labour Party in "carrying out the aims of the Constitution." That meant, said his lordship, that a Member, even where he thinks the well being of the country and the interests of his constituency will suffer must, "under the terms of his contract," place the decisions of the Labour Party before all these other considerations.

> My Lords, added Lord Shaw, grandiloquently, I do not think that such a subjection is compatible, either with the spirit of our Parliamentary Constitution, or with that independence and freedom which has hitherto been held to lie at the basis of representative government in the United Kingdom.

Now there can be no mistaking his lordship's meaning. What is in his mind is not the fact that Labour Party candidates have to sign the Constitution, but that there is a Constitution, which really means that there is a Labour Party. His whole argument, and the language in which it is couched, puts this beyond doubt. The man who goes to Parliament as a paid representative to serve the interests of the working class by supporting a Labour Party with its own organisation and policy is, in the opinion of his lordship, playing an illegal and unconstitutional part, and the logical outcome of his argument would be, not the abolition of the Pledge, but the abolition of the Constitution and the abandonment of the Party organisation. In no other way could his objection be met. To make the point quite clear I will

PARTY PLEDGE AND THE OSBORNE JUDGEMENT

give one other extract from his argument. He is dealing with men who accept a salary:—

> It is no doubt true that a member, although party to such a contract of subjection, would in point of law enter Parliament a free man, because the law would treat as non-enforceable and void the contract which purported to bind him. And it is no doubt true that—parties remaining outside of and making no appeal to the law—this subjection may arise in practice through the operation upon certain natures of various motives, including notably those of sycophancy or fear. But when the law is appealed to to lend its authority to the recognition and enforcement of a contract to procure subjection of the character described, with the concurrents of money payments, and the sanctions of fines or forfeitures, the law will decline such recognition or enforcement because the contract appealed to is contrary to sound public policy. I should be sorry to think that these considerations are not quite elementary. And they apply with equal force not to Labour organisations alone which operate by administering—under, it may be, careful supervision—the subscriptions of its members, but with even greater force to individual men, or organisations or trusts of men, using capital funds to procure the subjection of Members of Parliament to their commands. In this latter case, indeed, adhesion to the principle is of a value all the greater because its violation might be conducted in secret. It needs little imagination to figure the peril in which Parliamentary Government would stand if, either by the purchase of single votes, or by subsidies for regular support, the public well-being were liable to betrayal at the command and for the advantage of particular individuals or classes.

After quoting a number of authorities, mainly concerned with purity of elections, and consequently without direct bearing on the case, and saying that the payment of a member imposed no taint, provided no conditions were attached to it, he concluded his argument as follows:—

> In brief, my opinion accordingly is: The proposed additional rule of the Society that "all candidates shall sign and respect the conditions of the Labour Party, and be subject to their 'Whip'"; the rule that candidates are to be "responsible to and paid by the Society"; and, in particular, the provision in the constitution of the Labour Party that "candidates and members must accept this Constitution," and agree to abide by the decision of the Parliamentary Party in carrying out the aims of this Constitution, are all fundamentally illegal, because they are in violation of that sound public policy which is essential to the working of representative government. Parliament is summoned by the Sovereign to advise His Majesty freely. By the nature of the case it is implied that coercion, constraint, or a money payment, which is the price of voting at the bidding of others,

destroys or imperils that function of freedom of advice which is fundamental in the very constitution of Parliament. *Inter alia,* the Labour Party Pledge is such a price, with its accompaniments of unconstitutional and illegal constraint or temptation. Further, the pledge is an unconstitutional and unwarrantable interference with the rights of the constituencies of the United Kingdom. The Corrupt Practices Acts, and the proceedings of Parliament before such Acts were passed, were but machinery to make effective the fundamental rule that the electors, in the exercise of their franchise, are to be free from coercion, constraint, or corrupt influence; and it is they, acting through their majority, and not any outside body having money power, that are charged with the election of a representative, and with the judgment on the question of his continuance as such. Still further, in regard to the Member of Parliament himself, he too is to be free; *he is not to be paid mandatory of any man, or organisation of men,* nor is he entitled to bind himself to subordinate his opinions on public questions to others, for wages, or at the peril of pecuniary loss; and any contract of this character would not be recognised by a Court of Law, either for its enforcement or in respect of its breach. Accordingly, as it is put in the words of Lord Justice Fletcher Moulton, "Any other view of the fundamental principles of our law in this respect would, to my mind, leave it open to any body of men of sufficient wealth or influence to acquire contractually the power to exercise that authority to govern the nation which the law compels individuals to surrender only to representatives, that is, to men who accept the obligations and the responsibility of the trust towards the public implied by that position." For these reasons, my Lords, I am of opinion that the appeal should be refused.

The whole argument here again is that a Member of Parliament who accepts payment from "any organisation" is acting illegally; that it is "fundamentally illegal" for a candidate to be "responsible to" and "paid by" his Trade Union. It is also "fundamentally illegal" for a candidate to bind himself to abide by the decisions of his party in "carrying out the aims" of the Party Constitution. In Lord Shaw's mind the Pledge is a mere item in the indictment against the Labour Party. His objection is to the whole thesis upon which the Party is founded. Everyone of its fundamentals is illegal and unconstitutional. Lord James's objection is to the pledge *qua* pledge; the objection of Lord Shaw and of Justices Fletcher Moulton and Farwell goes much deeper, goes in fact right down to the roots of the Party. It is the Party these men are opposed to; get rid of the Pledge to-morrow and their objection remains as strong as before. For the moment they appear to put the stress on the Pledge. It would, however, be but a poor compliment to the ingenuity of our Law Lords to assume that they could not find another equally good reason for condemning the Party even were the Pledge removed. Nor would State payment of members remove their objection. So long as the Labour Party continues to be a working-class organisation the objections to it so forcibly expressed by our highest legal authorities will hold good. Delete everything which they regard as being unconstitutional from the Constitution and then the very form and structure of the Party itself would still imply everything to which objection has been taken. It would still be "a body formed for advancing the interests of a class." No one will dream for a moment of denying that such is the *raison de etre* of the Labour Party, and it is that which constitutes the damning fact in the minds of the Law Lords.

And, now, what is to be done? Are we to abolish the Pledge and eviscerate the Constitution in order to make the Party constitutional? I hope not. I say to all whom it may concern that we have fought for our Labour Party to make it what it is, and we are going to fight to keep our Labour Party what it is—let the opposition be what it may.

A FIGHTING PRECEDENT.

Let us see whether the past has any guidance to offer. If the Labour Party be unconstitutional, so, as I have shown you, was the Trade Union movement a hundred years ago. Our old fighting fathers fought to get their Trade Union movement legalised. They did not change the Constitution of the Unions to suit the convenience of the judges, or to bring their action within the pale of the Constitution. "Change your Constitution," they said, "to suit our Unions." And the Constitution was changed. We shall do the same for our Labour Party—Pledge and all. The issue is the same as it was then, it is only the point of attack that is different. The issue then was whether the working class was to be free to form industrial organisations to protect their interests as a class. The law said no, and laws which had been passed to meet quite other conditions were made to do duty against the Unions. In those days the worker had no vote. Now the emancipation of the working class has advanced a stage. The worker is now an enfranchised citizen and is claiming the right to have a political organisation to protect the interests of his class. And new laws, axioms, and theories designed to put down corruption in the State are being applied to prevent him. As though the Labour Party was on a par with the action of a few unscrupulous knaves, seeking to corrupt the electorate that they might enrich themselves at the expense of the State. Why is the Labour Party illegal? Because it represents the working class, because its members are paid by the working class to go to represent them. Mr. Balfour and others have been pointing out the terrible tyranny of compelling a Trade Unionist who does not believe in the Labour Party to pay for a candidate with whom he does not agree. This is a difficulty which is always bound to exist in every civilised country. They are now offering us payment of members. We shall get payment of members and of official election expenses either this year or, at furthest, next year. When we get payment of members what is going to happen? That the Tory working man and the Liberal working man, and the Tory capitalist and the Liberal capitalist, and the Tory landlord and the Liberal landlord will have to pay taxes to pay the salaries of Socialists like myself. Therefore, they are not getting rid of the dilemma by offering us payment of members; that much is certain. But what about the Party being illegal, because we are pledged to stand by the class to which we belong? "Is there no class legislation in Parliament at the present time? Is the Labour Party the only Party that stands by its own class? When the Budget was being discussed a year ago, what did you see then in the House of Commons? Captain Pretyman, a young able landlord, who is receiving a big income from unearned increment in the value of his land, fought the land clauses of the Budget step by step, and inch by inch. What was he and his fellow-landlords fighting for when opposing the Budget? Was it for the good of their country? Or was it for the *good of their own pockets?* But, then, Captain Pretyman is a patriot when he opposes the Budget: it is only when a working man fights for old age pensions for his own class, fights for an eight hour day for miners, fights for a proper Workmen's Compensation Act, fights for the feeding of hungry school children—it is only when working men do that that they become rebels. When landlords are fighting for their class, when brewers are fighting for their class, when railway directors are fighting for their class, when colliery owners are fighting for their class—and we see these things in the House of Commons every session—that is all right and proper; but when a Labour Party goes there to fight for the rights of the poor, they become rebels. Ah! but, says Sir Rufus Isaacs—speaking, I suppose, for the Government—the Osborne Judgment can never be completely reversed. Neither Sir Rufus Isaacs nor Mr. Arthur James Balfour have the settlement of this question. The last word rests with the Trade Unionists at the ballot-box on the day of the poll. In 1906, Sir Rufus Isaacs' predecessor, Sir John Lawson Walton, speaking for the Government, said: "The Taff Vale decision can never be completely reversed," and he spoke for one hour and thirty minutes in the House of Commons proving to the country that the Taff Vale decision could never be completely overturned. But there were 29 of us sitting there *as a Labour Party* who had drafted our own Bill, and within a fortnight of Sir John Lawson Walton making that speech he got up in his place and accepted our Bill, which completely reversed the Taff Vale judgment.

NO SURRENDER.

And what was done for Taff Vale has got to be done for Osborne. Who are these men that attempt to dictate to us the conditions on which we shall be allowed to have a Labour Party? I do not know how others feel about these things, but when I read the speeches of men like Mr. Balfour, Sir Rufus Isaacs, and others of less account, like some of the young whipper-snappers of both parties, some of whom are themselves paid from their party funds, saying: "Of course we want to see workingmen in Parliament; the working class should have some members there to speak for it," my blood begins to boil. We are not there on the sufferance of either Liberal or Tory, we are not there because landlords and employers of labour or Law Lords love us: we are there because *they can't keep us out.* We are not there as the representatives of some outcast class which requires to have a few men from its own ranks that it may not be altogether overlooked: we are there to represent the nation, for the working class is the nation. Forty members

PARTY PLEDGE AND THE OSBORNE JUDGEMENT

now—yes, and 400 within 20 years from now. They will say that will never be. Look to our own Colonies. Look to Australia, where the Commonwealth to-day has a Labour Ministry. Take the elections just finished in New South Wales. There the Labour Party has come back with an absolute majority. Take what is going on in Germany, where everybody admits that at the next election a majority of the German voters will vote for the Social Democratic Party. Take all these things and you will see why the employers and the landlords, and their servants the lawyers, are trying to make it difficult for us to have a Labour Party. They see the working class rising, they see it emerging, they see it beginning to fill the places which they have hitherto held as a monopoly. Why, every man you send to the House of Commons fills a seat which otherwise would have been filled by one of your masters or one of the idle class who live at your expense, and the more Labour men you send there the *less room there is* for them.—(Loud applause.) And so they think to stop this movement in time before you have crushed them out, because they know, my friends—many of you do not know it, but they know perfectly well—that just as the working class increases its representation in the House of Commons, so will the laws passed there become more and more in favour of the working class. They would like to confine you to industrial action through your Trade Union; they would like to say to you, "the Trade Unions have no right to take part in politics"; they would like to have you where once every five or six years they could starve you into submission to their will. When the strike or the lock-out takes place it is you and your children, remember, who have got to starve and suffer and get into debt. The employer may have to go without a part of his dividend for three months, but he knows perfectly well that after the trouble is over he will be able to recoup himself. And *whilst the strike lasts* he will never miss a meal, he won't require to smoke one cigar less, he won't require to economise even in the matter of his wine bill. His life will go on in all its luxury during the lock-out as it went on before. It is you and those who are near and dear to you who will have to do the suffering. They would like you to confine yourselves to Trades Union action. They know perfectly well that where you can meet them on terms of perfect equality is the floor of the House of Commons. They cannot lock you out there: they cannot starve you there. And, what is more, at the ballot-box you are more than their masters, the reason being that you are many and they are few. And therefore, I say, they want to put all these obstacles in your way. They want to create as much discord as they can in the working-class ranks. They are saying to the Conservative working man, Why should you pay for a Socialist member? They are saying to the Liberal working man, Why should you pay for a Socialist member? And our reply to both is this: It is for the working men who pay to select the candidates, and if you want to select a Tory working man select him; if you want to select a Liberal working man select him; if you want to select a Socialist working man select him—but at any rate insist upon having the power to *select your own men.*

And that is what we are fighting for. It is upon this we are going to make our appeal to the country at this coming election if the matter has not been put right by then. And I know this, that in the old Merthyr Boroughs practically every working man in it, Tory, Liberal, and Socialist, will give his vote in favour of the Osborne Judgment being completely reversed. To change the policy or tactics of the Party now would be fatal. It would be like lowering the flag in the face of the enemy. We have been assailed. Let us fight to keep the ground we have won. If we don't, we shall weaken the morale in our own ranks and encourage the enemy to press us for still further concessions. A few years fighting round this issue will strengthen the *esprit de corp* of the Party, bring all sections closer together, and bring a much needed consolidation to the movement. Therefore, so far as I am concerned, my watchword is No surrender. The Party, Pledge and all, independent, militant, and defiant, must be legalised if it is to continue to be of service to the cause of Democracy.[1]

Note

1 Speech delivered to my constituents at Troedyrhiw on October 15th, 1910.—J. K. H.

Part 6

DEMOCRACY AND THE STATE

21

THE LAW AND TRADE UNION FUNDS. A PLEA FOR "ANTE-TAFF VALE" (LONDON: INDEPENDENT LABOUR PARTY, 1903), 3–15.

J. Ramsay MacDonald

[The word "ante" in the title of Ramsay MacDonald's pamphlet *The Law and Trade Union Funds. A Plea for "Ante-Taff Vale"* of 1903 refers to the legal situation before the House of Lords rejected the decision of the Court of Appeal and reaffirmed the verdict in the Taff Vale case of 1901. The Lords' decision meant that the Amalgamated Society of Railway Servants became liable for tort on the part of members who acted against the Taff Vale Railway Company. This set a precedent for other unions to be treated accordingly. The 1901 verdict differed from those relating to earlier decisions in court which held individuals, who would never be able to afford to pay, liable (Klarman 1989a, 1516–1521).

The Court of Appeal had, MacDonald (1903) stressed in this pamphlet, referred to the Trade Union Bill of 1871 which classified trade unions as clubs which could not be liable in courts of law. As secretary of the newly formed Labour Representation Committee (LRC), MacDonald's aim was to persuade trade unionists and others in the Labour movement not to accept the responsibility bestowed by the 1901 verdict. As he discusses, many had begun to consider futile anything more than trying to limit that responsibility, as the House of Commons was unlikely to repeal the decision. Attempts to limit responsibility would, he insisted, be open to legal interpretation that, in a Parliament dominated by capital, would likely go against the unions. The way forward was, for him, to change public opinion back to that which in 1870 led to pressure on Parliament to consider unions as clubs with voluntary membership, necessary for a just and cohesive society, thus helping bring about the Act of 1871. The LRC would, he predicted, foster the necessary change in public opinion.

Such change would enable the LRC to gain cooperation from the Liberal Party and representation in Parliament. With support from the trade union movement, and with its members in Parliament helped by a pact with the Liberals in 1903, the LRC campaigned for the Taff Vale judgement to be overturned. In 1906 this was achieved through the Trade Disputes Act. The LRC became the Labour Party and MacDonald was elected to Parliament for the first time (Morgan 2006, 21–26). The Trade Disputes Act, 1903, drafted by the labour movement and appended to this pamphlet, is not included here. The note at the beginning of the appendix is included to indicate MacDonald's belief, as discussed in the pamphlet, that the movement's approach needed fundamental revision.]

"Judge-made Law."

When the House of Lords, in July, 1901, reversed the decision of the Court of Appeal and restored the extraordinary decision of Justice Farwell—that trade unions could be sued for the damage done by their agents—trade unionists received the decision with consternation. Some of their leaders told them that they should have expected nothing else—that the House of Lords only declared what was actually the law—that the Ante-Taff Vale position never in reality existed. The contention is absurd. For over twenty-five years every lawyer of any note, every trade union secretary, every politician interested in labour legislation, assumed that no bench of reputable judges could ever give any other decision than that of the Court of Appeal, when it declared that, unions having no legal personality, their funds could not be attacked by injured employers.

And there was good reason for that widespread assumption. During the debate on the second reading of the Trade Union Bill of 1871, the Home Secretary of the day explained that the Government regarded trade unions as clubs, the liabilities of which were "such as courts of law should neither enforce, nor modify, nor annul." Moreover, it was deliberately arranged by the trade union leaders of the time, that the Bill should not make unions legal entities. "The subject," says Mr. Howell,[1] "was mooted in some quarters, and it was discussed with Mr. Bruce [Home Secretary], but neither he nor any of our friends or supporters, in the House or out of it, favoured the insertion in the Act of 1871 of any such powers. It was intentionally omitted from the Bill. . . . I venture to say that no court, however high—not even the House of Lords—can legitimately read into an Act of Parliament anything that was intentionally left out of it."

That that was the case was perfectly well understood, and we find men like Sir Frederick Pollock and Mr. Leonard Courtney commenting, in the Labour Commission Report of 1894, on the *Temperton* v. *Russell* case as follows:—"This case shows that persons injured by the action of trade unions and their agents can only proceed against their agents personally . . . This difficulty is one which illustrates the inconvenience which may be caused by the existence of associations having, as a matter of fact, very real corporate existence and modes of action, but no legal personality corresponding thereto."

Mr. Justice Farwell himself said that "a trade union is neither a corporation, nor an individual, nor a partnership between a number of individuals." In support of

Mr. Howell's contention, quoted above, the Court of Appeal held that "it is incorrect to say that such an entity [a trade union] can be sued unless there is found an express enactment to the contrary. . . In our judgment, for the reasons given above, a trade union cannot be sued, as is now attempted."[2]

When, therefore, the opprobrious description, "judge-made law," is applied to the House of Lords' decision in the Taff Vale case, the description is precisely accurate. By that decision the Law Lords deliberately set aside what Mr. Bruce declared to be the purpose of the Government which was responsible for the Act of 1871, and what had been assumed ever since by the legal and the lay mind alike, to be the law of the land.

Leading up to Taff Vale.

It is important to understand under what circumstances the extraordinary decision was given. It is not just to say that the bench is knowingly prejudiced. There are judges, like Mr. Justice Grantham, who are as incapable of judging in labour cases as a brewer is of giving an impartial decision if allowed to sit on Brewster Sessions. But the blind prejudices of Mr. Justice Grantham must not be taken to indicate the mind of the English bench. The fact is, that English Society has recently been stirred up in opposition to organised Labour. It has heard of the tyranny of trade unionism; it has been told that combinations amongst workpeople are driving trade from the country; it has been taught to regard these combinations as means which lazy and dishonest men have adopted to make their laziness and dishonesty the general rule of work. Unfortunately, our judges live, and move, and have their being in the atmosphere of that Society. They unconsciously respond to its prejudices, and their judgments express its apprehensions. They know nothing of trade unionism from the wage-earner's point of view; they know nothing of the industrial and economic pressure which justifies its action; they know nothing of the internal government which has a very important bearing upon its legal relations. Not half-a-dozen of them know enough about trade unionism to enable them to answer the absurdities of the *Times*' attacks.

Thirty years ago, that was not the case. The Parliament of the time was bombarded by trade union demands. Liberals and Tories alike resisted these demands, and alike showed some willingness to accept them. Outside, a strong Labour movement was gathering like a threatening storm. A Commission had been appointed to enquire into the grievances of the unions, and the result was that the whole country was in possession of a great amount of accurate information regarding the theory and the practice of trade unionism. The Act of 1871, deliberately declining to make trade union funds liable for attachment in consequence of the acts of agents, was passed. The bench and the bar were in touch with the prevailing spirit, and the protection of the funds was accepted as being not only equitable but legal.

DEMOCRACY AND THE STATE

The Labour movement quietened down, split over Liberalism and Toryism, and then ceased to be an independent and active factor in politics. Within the space of six years three Labour members had been elected to Parliament, the Labour Representation League ceased to exist, trade union officials began to associate themselves with ordinary capitalist parties, they fought a man all day over a trade dispute and spoke for him all evening in a political contest. Meanwhile, trade unionism failed to keep in touch with public opinion. Capital seized opportunity after opportunity to gain fresh ground. The bench gradually drifted away from its knowledge of, and sympathy with, the spirit of 1870, and a series of decisions hampering to trade unionism and subversive to the intention of the earlier law-makers began to be delivered. Peaceful picketing was declared to be legal only under such conditions as made it impossible; conspiracy became such a danger-ous factor in trade union action that the planning of a concerted movement against employers was beset by a maze of pitfalls; finally, to cap all the other judgments, the Law Lords decided that a union could be sued with its agents, and its funds made liable for damages.

What is the real explanation of these decisions? They are the reading by Society-minded men of laws passed when the democratic spirit was prevalent. They indicate that the source from which public opinion springs has changed since 1870. The wage-earners made the laws; the capitalists are administering them. The present condition of the Trade Union Law shows the practical impotence of Trade Unionism in the public mind at the present moment. It is not enough for the people to make laws, they must continue to make the public opinion which controls administration.

What Must We Do Now?

The decisions, as has been pointed out, have endangered the liberty of workmen in respect of picketing and conspiracy, and have laid the funds of unions open to the attacks of employers. Everyone recognises that the last change is the most serious, and I propose only to deal with it in this pamphlet. Trade Unionists have been rather slow in moving in the matter, and now that they have moved they do not seem to be quite certain as to their ground.

They are beset with two difficulties. They have not only to protect their union funds, but they have to do it in such a way as will be considered fair and reason-able by Parliament. Let us see what they have proposed hitherto.

Up to the present they have decided to accept the law as interpreted by the Law Lords, and they have not attempted to disclaim trade union liability. They believe that it is now necessary to accept that responsibility, and they are attempting to justify their action on the ground that the interpretation of the law by Mr. Justice Farwell was right, or, at any rate, that the House of Commons will not now agree to anything else. But whilst accepting liability they are anxious to limit it, and after having considered the matter exhaustively, they have discovered that they can limit liability only in one of two ways. In the first place, they may decide that

214

no act done by an agent, except by the precise sanction and authority of the rules of a union, can be made the subject to an action against the union; in the second place, they may decide that only for the acts of the executive can union funds be made responsible.

Before discussing whether union funds should be liable or not, I propose to examine those alternative methods of limiting liability within reasonable bounds.

Liability Limited by Rules.

The draft Bill submitted to the Conference of Trade Unionists, which met at the Holborn Town Hall on the 11th March last, was drafted so that the rules of a union were to be the only sanction for acts which might involve trade union funds. The more this method is examined, the more objectionable it is seen to be. According to this proposal, unions profess to accept liability, but then they say—"We ourselves, meeting in our own assemblies, shall have the right to say for what acts we shall be responsible." No legislature—even if it had a majority of Labour members—could honestly accept such a claim. The rules might be so drafted that no responsibility would really be assumed, and, at any rate, the amount and nature of responsibility would vary between union and union. An engineer would obey one set of rules, a boot and shoe operative another. Judges would not then have to administer the law of the land only, but also rules of unions passed at meetings of the unions themselves. Should such a measure be passed, unions would soon have to submit to the Chief Registrar interfering in the conduct of trade disputes, and determining the conditions under which agents, officers, and executives are appointed; or perhaps they would have to allow the legislature to decide the general provisions of their rules. But such a measure can never pass. It violates the most fundamental principle of sound government, inasmuch as it allows a section of the community to lay down, on its own account, how far it is to obey the law of the land. It is just as though the employers asked that the Factory Acts should declare in general terms the responsibility of the masters to their workpeople, but allow masters' associations to decide how far in each factory that responsibility should be recognised. Legal responsibility, limited by rules voluntarily made by those upon whom the responsibility rests, is a departure which, it is to be hoped, will never be made by the British House of Commons.

Liability for Executive Acts.

When this proposal is abandoned, we have to consider the other of accepting responsibility for all executive acts. This, from a constitutional point of view, is not so objectionable as the former, though it still might mean that the executive would allow agents to act without proper sanction so that the funds might escape liability. Such neglect of duty would, however, soon be the subject of legal decisions, and executives would find that a deliberate inactivity, when activity was their duty, would not in law protect them. This, then, is the more honourable and satisfactory expedient, from the point of view of the House of Commons. It is quite reasonable that liability should be imposed on trade unions only for the acts of duly accredited agents and responsible officials, and if liability had to be accepted, it ought to be on condition that the executive has sanctioned the act or acts for which damages are claimed.

As a matter of fact, however, as soon as this liability is imposed upon trade unions, they have no protection for their funds at all. The subtle law of agency then comes in, and no man can say beforehand who is an agent and who is not, what body—*e.g.,* local strike committee—is in the eyes of the law (or the judges) in the position of an executive, or what may be legally construed in executive orders to be "sanction." So soon as responsibility for executive acts is admitted, the unions will have to go time after time to the Law Courts for definitions as to what an executive act is, and judges whose minds are warped by the common Society thoughts and opinions of the time, will be asked to decide in relation to specific point after specific point what is the scope and nature of trade union responsibility. Instead of putting an end to litigation, the acceptance of responsibility on the part of unions for the acts of their executives will only begin a long chapter of appeals to the Courts to settle questions of agency, and that will happen however clear to the lay mind may be the wording of the Act of Parliament.

This is the dilemma in which the trade union movement finds itself to-day. It desires to accept responsibility, but every attempt to define that responsibility fails to secure the funds against unreasonable encroachments. The unions must, therefore, consider whether they ought to accept responsibility at all.

Society v. Trade Unionism.

Trade Unionists have mistaken the problems ahead of them. The attack from which they are suffering has not arisen from any special blunder they have made or injustice they have done, but from a general opposition to, and suspicion of, Labour organised so as to control the conditions of work. Such conduct as was revealed by evidence given in the *Quinn* v. *Leathem* case was not creditable to the men concerned, but had there been no *Quinn* v. *Leathem,* trade union*ism* would at this stage have been suspected and distrusted. Capital is demanding more freedom to treat labour as it chooses; the man in high places, troubled by the pressing problems of national industry, and having no intelligent appreciation of their nature, takes the superficial view that trade unionism is an anti-social movement, that combinations of workmen are legal entities, and that their funds should be made responsible for acts done as part of the operations of these combinations. Any Bill promoted by trade unionists must face this opposition. And it must not be forgotten that that opposition is concentrated in the social stratum from which the majority on both sides of the House of Commons is drawn.

The consequence of this is, that the House of Commons will allow the unions to accept responsibility, but will not allow them to limit it. It will argue that it is the business of the unions to elect responsible men for agents, and that if other kinds of men are elected the unions ought properly to bear the responsibility. No other course is open to a legislature which is determined to mete out even-handed justice to all classes. So that, whether the unions propose such a Bill as was submitted at the Holborn Town Hall making liability depend on the rules, or such an one as is now drafted making liability depend on the sanction of executives, the House of Commons—and certainly the House of Lords—will decline to assent to the proposal. A Liberal majority might accept either of these Bills for the sake of votes, but the House of Lords would reject either measure—unless it saw that the latter made the position of the unions hopeless by exposing their funds to every attack.

Should Funds be Liable?

The question therefore arises: Can the unions convince public opinion that their nature is such that their funds should not bear liability? Can they, in other words, restore public opinion to the position it occupied in 1870? Is Ante-Taff Vale possible? I answer all these questions in the affirmative.

We must begin by defining once more the nature of trade unions. They are voluntary organisations, their executives are purely administrative bodies, their secretaries are routine officers, they do not constitute a legal personality. Their members are but individuals who have combined to advance their personal interests primarily. They can enforce no contract and no obligation by law, and the property which they can hold legally as a body is the very minimum necessary to enable them to own their own offices. They correspond precisely to the description given them by the Commission of 1867. "Trade unions are essentially clubs and not trading companies . . . . The objects at which they aim, the rights which they claim, and the liabilities which they incur, are, for the most part, it seems to us, such as courts of law should neither enforce nor modify, nor annul. They should rest entirely on consent."

Since that time, trade unions have increased in membership, but an increase in size has no effect at all on the nature of their organisation. They are like a heap of sand—consisting of separate particles—not like a human being, consisting of dependent functions. They have none of the organic characteristics of a State.

Therefore, the individual member acts as an individual, not as an agent. He may be endowed with plenipotentiary powers for a given purpose and as the result of a given decision, and whilst acting under these powers, the men who endowed him with them may be responsible for his conduct, but nobody else except those men can be responsible for him. So soon as the specified act has been done, he lapses back again to the position of an individual member of his club.

The Individual and the Law.

It has been argued against this point of view that it is really a justification for lawlessness on the part of trade unions. Such a conclusion is groundless. The individual is subject to the common law and to the criminal law, and the proper punishment of the individual is a sufficient deterrent from unsocial and illegal conduct. It may be held that membership of a trade union lays one specially open to breaches of the common law during trade disputes, and that therefore trade unions, as clubs, should be placed under special disabilities. One might as well argue that because members of political clubs may be considered more liable to plot and engage in treason, the law of sedition should be applied to such clubs with special severity. The law which the individual, as an ordinary individual, has to obey, is sufficient to control and punish the individual as a member of a club or a trade union. Moreover, as a matter of common knowledge, the conduct of trade unions during the thirty years from 1870 to 1901, when they were supposed to be exempt from corporate liability, was more honourable and more praiseworthy than the actions of Limited Liability Companies and Boards of Directors which were not exempt from such liability. If Society desires to impose the responsibilities of a corporation upon trade unions in order that the action of their members may be more social, Society is making a mistake in its methods. This point was well made by that eminent jurist, Sir Frederick Pollock, when he wrote in his valuable memorandum on "The Law of Trade Combinations," published in the Labour Commission's Report:—"Ultimately, the rights of minorities can be secured only by securing general respect for every citizen's lawful freedom of action and discussion, and this must be the work of enlightened public opinion, and not of legal definitions."[3] On the other hand, the history of Labour combinations amply shows that when the members of unions feel themselves to be unfairly treated by the law, they begin to pursue underhand methods of action, their moral sense of citizenship becomes blunted, and anti-social and illegal conduct is the consequence.

When the trade unionist tries to amend the laws of picketing and conspiracy, he does so because he claims an individual right to do certain things. The first two clauses of the Trade Union Bill are simply claims of individual right, not claims of corporate liberty, and they carry with them only an individual, not a corporate responsibility. So, strictly speaking, the description "Trade Union Bill" is a mistake. It ought to be "Trade Unionists' Bill." It is necessary to make this point, because it is well to emphasise the fact that what alterations in the law the trade unionists demand, are all of the nature of individual right and are based on the assumption that trade unions are simply combinations of individual persons, who claim no special exemptions because they belong to such combinations, and who consequently may justly object to these combinations being regarded as anything more than loose unions of individuals, the claims and liabilities of which are voluntary in their nature, and such as no court of law should enforce, modify, or annul.

Whilst considering this, we must not forget that the funds of trade unions have not been accumulated for fighting purposes only. Trade unions are benefit societies, and though their industrial aspect is the most important, their expenditure in relief to the unemployed and in subsidising the aged, is one of the most striking features of the industrial history of the last half century. And yet the effect of an

Trade Unions in Industry.

Something remains to be said on the industrial functions of the unions. They have been created so as to make effective the desire of the workers to protect themselves against capital, and secure some proportion of the advantages of increased efficiency in wealth producing. They embody the claims of labour to share with capital the function of determining under what conditions wealth is to be produced and distributed in society. The claim commonly made to-day by capital that it, and it alone, has to determine how labour is to be employed, is nothing but impertinent arrogance. The smooth working of industry must always depend upon the mutual goodwill of capital and labour, and between these, the State must endeavour to hold an even balance whilst existing conditions remain. Capital, in pursuit of its own interests, has been held to have the right to ruin people if the ruin be carried on on the lines of proper competition and trade rivalry; and, in a similar way, labour should claim the right to bring what pressure it can to bear upon its rival capital, provided it exercises that right in such a way as to make it clear that it is legitimately pursuing general and not personal ends. The distinction between the case of Allen, who asked for the discharge of Flood because Flood's employment was a menace to the working class, and that of Quinn, who persecuted Leathem vindictively, after Leathem had promised to observe the conditions which the Butchers' Union asked for, is real. Trade unionists have a right to demand full legal liberty to damage employers with whom they cannot agree, provided their disagreement is legitimately on points of industrial interest; and they can justify that claim on the ground that the condition of trading prosperity is a joint agreement, not a one-sided edict. Every day it becomes more and more a question of practical importance, how far the community should step in and create a proper tribunal for adjusting disputes between employers and employed, or decree minimum conditions for labour. But whilst the State hesitates to assume responsibility for this, trade unionists must be exceedingly careful lest the occasional serious disputes which arise owing to the negligence of the State, are settled by crippling the power of labour to offer a serious resistance to the encroachments of capital.

If Corporations, then—

If, however, Parliament insists upon unions being liable as if they were corporations, it must give them the full rights of corporations. They do not want special privileges, and they ought not to accept special disabilities. Those who are so anxious to force a corporate existence upon unions only desire such privileges as are necessary to enable employers to dip their hands into trade union exchequers. The unions, however, have a right to demand that Parliament shall accept the logical results of the Taff Vale decision; and to understand what these results are, one has only to turn to the position of trade unions in New Zealand in the eye of the law. There, the corporate unions are recognised as the only organisations of workpeople, and a workman is practically forced by law to belong to these organisations. There, a court fixes the minimum wages paid in trades. There, the State decides how disputes are to be settled, and enforces its decisions by penalties. I am not sure that it is advisable for us to copy too closely the New Zealand line of evolution, but it will be well for employers to understand what movement they are starting if they insist upon perpetuating the injustice of the Taff Vale decision. If, for the purposes of employers, trade unions are to be considered as though they were corporate bodies, they will have to insist upon corporation being carried so far that they themselves may reap some advantage from it.

The True Policy.

The true trade union policy, however, is to demand a restitution of the conditions accepted in practice before the Taff Vale decision. Whatever concessions are got will only be by instructing public opinion, and public opinion will not regard with favour any proposals for a limited responsibility, whilst, on the other hand, an unlimited responsibility would ruin Labour combinations in a decade. An intelligent defence of the ante-Taff Vale position will lead to a clearer understanding of the nature of trade unionism, and a better appreciation of the civil rights of the trade unionist. It will, moreover, help to restore a healthy and intelligent public opinion on civil and industrial matters, and enlighten the State on its responsibilities as the great arbiter in all disputes between Capital and Labour.

The working classes must boldly face the elements with which they have now to deal. They have sunk themselves socially and politically for the last thirty years. Instead of settling their own policy in the State, instead of taking an independent stand on the great interests of the time, instead of steadily moulding public opinion in accordance with the needs and outlook of an intelligent and self-respecting labouring community, they have been content to allow men of no special knowledge and no close connection with Labour and its problems, to lead them and voice their opinions. The result is that Labour, even when armed with the vote, is in many respects less powerful now than it was before the creation of a democratic franchise. This fundamental fact lies at the root of all these unfortunate decisions which, though not in accordance with law, are in keeping with social prejudice.

The trade unions are now beginning to admit this, and the million workers who have become affiliated to the Labour Representation Committee mark not only a new and powerful political movement, but also a new and powerful intellectual influence upon national opinion. The Labour Representation movement is now the one hope of the country. It will not only lead to the passing of beneficial laws, but will so tone national opinion that judges, when administering the laws, will

THE LAW AND TRADE UNION FUNDS

have no temptation to set aside the intention of Parliament in making them. The Independent Labour movement is the only adequate reply to the challenge thrown down by recent legal decisions.

Notes

1 "Labour Legislation," p. 186.
2 Law Reports, King's Bench Division, 1901. I, pp. 170-177.
3 Page 159.

Appendix.

The Bill as drafted by the Joint Committees (the Parliamentary Committee of the Trade Union Congress, the Federation of Trade Unions, and the Labour Representation Committee) and amended after the Holborn Town Hall Conference. The clauses in italics are the text of the Bill as introduced by Mr. Shackleton; the other two clauses have been disallowed by the Speaker as not coming within the scope of the title of the Bill; if the Bill secured the ante-Taff Vale position the part of Clause 3 and the whole of Clause 4 within brackets would be omitted.

22

THE WOMEN'S SUFFRAGE CONTROVERSY (LONDON: ADULT SUFFRAGE SOCIETY, 1905), 1–4.

Margaret Bondfield

[Well known as the first female cabinet minister, serving as Minister of Labour in Ramsay MacDonald's government from 1929 to 1931, Margaret Bondfield had also been a prominent trade unionist in the late nineteenth century and a campaigner for full adult suffrage in the decade before the First World War. This put her at odds with Independent Labour Party (ILP) members Emmeline and Christabel Pankhurst who restricted their demand to giving women suffrage on the same grounds and to the same extent as that enjoyed by men. Bondfield only objected to this more limited campaign if it sought to preclude the case for full adult suffrage.

The Pankhursts' position was supported by Keir Hardie who had helped found both the ILP in 1893 and the Labour Representation Committee (LRC) in 1900. Nevertheless, some ILP members shared Bondfield's view. When in 1906 the LRC became the Labour Party and he became its leader, Hardie was in the minority and Bondfield in the majority in the new party on the suffrage issue from 1905 to 1908 (Rowan 1982, 77–79).

The position of Bondfield (1905) regarding the suffrage issue reflected her broader views on relations between the feminist and labour movements. For her, the two campaigns should not be conflated. In opposition to the idea that women should become involved in politics specifically in terms of their gender identity, she believed that the best course of action for women was to work within the labour movement to try to achieve collectivist legislation aiming to maximise the welfare of men and women (Harrison 1989, 153). Her leaflet *The Women's Suffrage Controversy* of 1905 was an early contribution presenting this controversial position, written the year before she helped found the Women's Labour League (WLL). Closely aligned to the Labour Party, the WLL officially voiced the policy advocated by Bondfield until the party itself changed its position to wholehearted support for women's suffrage in 1912. Thereafter, under the leadership of Marion Phillips, the WLL and Labour became ever more closely interlinked, the WLL

THE WOMEN'S SUFFRAGE CONTROVERSY

eventually becoming effectively the party's women's section by the end of the First World War (Kingston 1975, 125–127).]

THE Women's Enfranchisement Bill, introduced by Mr. Bamford Slack during last session is, no doubt, an admirable measure from the point of view of the rate-paying spinster, and to it—as such—I offer no opposition.

Working men and women who, like myself, believe in Adult Suffrage, could not consistently object to the efforts of any section of the community to ensure its enfranchisement.

Unfortunately, the middle class advocates of this limited Bill are not content with devoting their time and money to legitimate propaganda, but they have made a determined effort to capture the Labour forces, and it is against this that I, as a woman Trade Unionist, enter my protest.

Those advocates of the limited Bill, who claim the support of Labour, base their claims mainly on two grounds:—

1. That the majority of those enfranchised by the Bill would be working women.
2. That it would remove sex disability.

They further argue in support of their policy:—

1. That in order to secure sex equality in future franchise reforms, it is essential to remove sex disability on the present property franchise.
2. That the root cause of all the economic disabilities under which women suffer is the political disqualification of their sex.

In the first place the limited suffragists have entirely failed to prove their claim that the majority of those enfranchised under the Bill would be working women.

The present electoral qualifications can be roughly summarised under the following heads:—

1. The owners of property.
2. Householders.
3. Occupiers of business premises rented from £10 up.
4. Lodgers who are sole occupiers of a room valued at not less than 4s. per week unfurnished.
5. Service voters, *i.e.,* persons separately occupying a house by virtue of their appointment though not actually paying rent.
6. Graduates of universities possessing Parliamentary representation.

Working women are not property owners, nor are they university graduates, and only a very small proportion would be enfranchised under qualifications 2, 3 and 5. It is upon the fourth qualification mainly that the limited suffragists base their claim.

DEMOCRACY AND THE STATE

Those of us, however, who belong to the workers know that proportionately very few women wage-earners are sole occupants of rooms valued at a rental of 4s. per week unfurnished. For instance, the skilled women workers of Lancashire, who are in the most favourable position economically, usually share a room with a sister or friend if they are unmarried. Recent investigations made in London among educated woman workers bordering on the professional class, such as Civil Service employés, telephone operators, clerks, etc., has proved that very few indeed of these could qualify—mainly owing to the fact that they live at home or share rooms; factory workers, such as jam makers, tea packers, etc., and dressmakers, show a still smaller proportion, while domestic servants and shop assistants are entirely outside the pale. In the latter case, owing to the living-in system and the migratory nature of their employment, even the men are unable to qualify as citizens.

It would be amusing if it were not rather pathetic to think of our enthusiastic young friend, Miss Christabel Pankhurst, quoting the wrongs of the voteless chainmakers of Cradley Heath as an argument in favour of the limited Bill, and at the same time explaining that the majority of those women earn from 5s. to 8s. per week.

It is therefore obvious that this Bill will increase class disabilities without fulfilling its second claim; for there can be no doubt that the Bill as at present drafted will not remove the judge-made law of coverture—*i.e.,* the disability of married women. Even if the Bill were amended on the lines of the Scotch Municipal Franchise Acts, it would only abolish sex disability for elective purposes, and women would still have no part in the administrative work of the nation, while married working women, whether wage-earners or not (such as the members of the Women's Co-operative Guild and similar organisations), having no property apart from their husbands, would still be voteless.

With regard to the contention that the limited Bill is a stepping-stone to sex equality in future electoral reforms, my convinced opinion is that any further strengthening of the propertied base of our electoral system indefinitely postpones the realisation of the democratic ideal of adult suffrage.

Lady Knightley demonstrated this in her speech at York when she said that "extending the franchise to women who paid rates and taxes would remove the need for universal suffrage, which was a real danger"; and Dr. Stanton Coit evidently agreed with her when he said at the Queen's Hall meeting that the limited Bill "would remove the danger that would result from giving illiterate persons the vote."

Those who say that only the people who pay rates and taxes (meaning direct taxation) should be allowed a voice in the government of the country seem to ignore the fact that the burden of indirect taxation presses more heavily, in proportion, on the working classes.

It is, of course, only just that those who pay rates and taxes should have a voice in fixing them, but surely the injustice of compelling those to obey the laws who have no voice in making them is equally apparent.

By an equal expenditure of energy the Labour Party could secure Adult Suffrage, as well as a host of other reforms which are legitimately its business.

If a parallel is needed, one has only to consider the Shop Hours Act, 1904. Its promoters argued that it was the only Bill which had any chance of passing through Parliament, &c.; its most ardent and honest supporters are now finding out that the Act will not secure the reform promised by its promoters, and it has blocked practical legislation indefinitely.

As to the economic disabilities of women in industry, the limited suffragists are surely strangely confusing cause and effect.

They argue "working women are poor because they are disfranchised." But supposing the limited Bill is passed then they would be disfranchised *because they are poor*.

We would point out to our Manchester friends, who seem to think the vote is the panacea for all industrial ills, that women will have to improve their conditions of employment by trade organisation as men have done in the past. Industrial legislation is apt to be inoperative unless backed by a strong organisation of the workers affected.

Miss Eva Gore Booth's now famous pamphlet "To the Working Women of England," in which she demonstrates (to her own satisfaction, at least) that because of their political power "working men eat beef steak and butter, whilst working women live on bread and margarine," has undoubtedly afforded considerable amusement, but it has also its serious aspect. Labour leaders may laugh at its absurdities, but it is difficult to over-estimate the mischievous effect of the distribution of such pernicious literature among the rank and file of women workers at this time when so much depends upon their economic education. It is distressing to find an attempt being made to foster distrust of men of their own class, to create a sex war in industry, and so play into the hands of the employing classes.

The members of the Freedom of Labour Defence, and opponents of special industrial legislation for women, are at least consistent in the arguments they advance in favour of the limited Bill, but it is difficult to understand the position of Mr. Keir Hardie when he states that "there must be many thousands of working women in every big city as well as in the textile districts of England and Scotland who would be qualified under such a measure, but even if this was not the case it appears to me that every woman *because she is a woman* should fight tenaciously for her own sex in the matter."

Surely, not "because she is a woman," but because she is a human being jointly responsible with man for the progress of the human race, should women strive for the recognition by the State of her right to full citizenship.

We have had the curious spectacle of Labour members fighting the battle of propertied women who have enough leisure and money and influence to do their own work.

We witnessed at Liverpool the absurd anomaly of a Socialist Party asking the Labour Party to support a Bill based on property and privilege.

It is encouraging to know that the proposal to back the limited Bill was rejected by 480 votes to 270.

I trust that by voting for the London Trades Council amendment in favour of Adult Suffrage the delegates to the Labour Representation Conference will demonstrate their recognition of the fact that the only reform of our complicated electoral system worth one moment of Labour's political energy is the destruction of its propertied base, the sweeping away of all existing anomalies, the abolition not only of sex but of class disability, and the enfranchisement of all adult men and women.

ISSUED BY
The Adult Suffrage Society.

Office: 122, Gower Street, London, W.C.

Membership.—"Any man or woman who will work for Adult Suffrage, and who is opposed to all property qualification, is eligible for membership of this Society."

Contributions.—"Every member shall contribute to the funds of the Society not less than One Shilling per annum (or 1d. per month) payable in advance."

23

THE CITIZENSHIP OF WOMEN: A PLEA FOR WOMEN'S SUFFRAGE, THIRD EDITION (LONDON: INDEPENDENT LABOUR PARTY, 1906), 5–15.

Keir Hardie

[Keir Hardie was an enthusiastic backer of the campaign by fellow Independent Labour Party (ILP) members Emmeline and Christabel Pankhurst for the extension of the suffrage. In October 1905 he gave his active support when Christabel, who like her mother Emmeline was a member of the Women's Social and Political Union (WSPU), was jailed for her direct action. The Pankhursts did not demand universal adult female suffrage but, rather, women's suffrage to be on the same basis as that of men. The ILP was divided on the issue, with Philip Snowden among those who sided with Hardie (Marcus 1978, 747–748). Hardie's support for the Pankhursts put him at odds with those in the Labour movement, including the Labour Party until 1909, who argued that this resulted in the wealthy continuing to have the vote while still denying it to many working-class men and women. Two years later, Emmeline and Christabel Pankhurst resigned from the ILP under pressure from within the party (Cowman 2002, 130–131, 135–136). Under Christabel's influence the WSPU drifted away from the left to take a more pragmatic approach to supporting electoral candidates. This attracted criticism for what her sister Sylvia Pankhurst described as "Incipient Toryism" (Cowman 2002, 144).

Hardie's pamphlet *The Citizenship of Women: A Plea for Women's Suffrage* helps illustrate the divisions that had begun to emerge on the left regarding the extension of the suffrage. Hardie (1906) expressed his support for a Liberal MP's private member's bill – the Women's Enfranchisement Bill which presented the less extensive demand – on the basis that it would enfranchise far more working-class than middle and upper-class women, and also because a bill for universal adult suffrage would have little chance of success, at least in the short term. The bill did not gain sufficient support in parliament and thus failed in 1907. At the Labour Party conference that year Hardie warned that, rather than obey an

DEMOCRACY AND THE STATE

instruction from the party on the issue of the suffrage, he would resign (Minkin 1978, 6). Nevertheless, by 1912 the party had come to accept the principle of women's, rather than adult suffrage.]

Votes for Women.

IT is not my purpose to write a learned dissertation or even an elaborate essay on the Woman question; this has been done by men and women well qualified for the task, and doubtless will be again. My present object is to re-state in plain and homely language the case for Woman Suffrage. To deal with the Woman question as a whole would involve a long inquiry into the causes responsible for the differences in the status of the sexes, including woman's economic position, the marriage laws, and our social polity. These are all subjects interwoven with the position of women, but they are beyond the scope of my ability, and, for the moment, I leave them aside and confine myself to the one question of their political enfranchisement. I do so mainly because that is a question ripe for settlement by legislation. The other questions hinted at may be left to evolve their own solution as time and chance determine. None of them are within the ken of politics, nor should they be brought into the political arena until women are in a position to influence equally with men the creation of opinion upon them, and, where necessary, the legislation which may be required to assist in solving them. John Stuart Mill declared it to have been one of his earliest, as it remained one of his strongest, convictions, "that the principles which regulate the existing social relations between the two sexes—the legal subordination of one sex to the other—is wrong in itself, and now one of the chief hindrances to human improvement; and that it ought to be replaced by principles of perfect equality admitting no power or privilege on the one side nor disability on the other." I hold it to be true with those who say that the foundation upon which this "perfect equality" is to be reared is the political enfranchisement of women.

In sentiment we have advanced somewhat since 1790, when a learned writer of the period explained that people who should not be included in the county franchise were those who "lie under natural incapacities, and therefore cannot exercise a sound discretion, or (who are) so much under the influence of others that they cannot have a will of their own in the choice of candidates. Of the former description are women, infants, idiots, lunatics, of the latter, persons receiving alms and revenue offices." We do not now speak of women as being in the same category as "idiots" and "lunatics," but for political purposes we treat them as if they were.

No one seeks to deny the existence of differences between the sexes, differences subtle, deep seated, and ineradicable. But these, being admitted, afford no justification for the usurpation by man of the right to say what duties and responsibilities woman may be allowed to undertake, and what must be withheld from her because of her sex. Such a theory can only be upheld on the old

THE CITIZENSHIP OF WOMEN

tradition of the East that woman is one of the lower animals over whom lordly man was given dominion. The harem is the logical outcome of this belief. It is only by removing the disabilities and restraints imposed upon woman, and permitting her to enter freely into competition with man in every sphere of human activity, that her true position and function in the economy of life will ultimately be ascertained. We can at present form no conception of what woman is capable of being or doing. We have no data upon which to base any real conclusions. Nowhere is woman treated as the free and equal companion of man. Amongst coloured peoples living in a state of nature and in a tribal environment which has evolved itself, and wherein custom is the only law, the woman, though far from being the degraded creature which she has so often been pictured by superficial observers, is still her husband's drudge, and frequently a part of his wealth. In the military stage of social evolution, or the age of chivalry, as it has been dubbed by persons of a poetic temperament and a vivid imagination, the woman is pictured as being the weaker and more spiritualized sex, requiring to be protected by her lord, and almost worshipped as a superior creation. "Half angel, half idiot," aptly describes this conception of woman. This is but a preverted way of declaring her inferiority; the homage paid to her is like that we should pay to a child: in no sense is it a recognition of equality; very often it is the exact opposite. In modern life we get back to the savage stage. Woman of the working class is again the drudge who does the menial work. Her husband works for, and is dependent for the opportunity to work upon, a master; his wife works for, and is dependent for her livelihood, upon a husband. That there are varying degrees of this feeling of subjection goes without saying, and I think it could be shown that the position of women, as of most other things, has always been better, more near an equality with man, in Celtic than non-Celtic races or tribes. Thus in Scotland a woman speaks of her husband as her "man," whilst in Staffordshire the term used is nearly always "the master."

The universality of this subjection of woman is assumed by many as an infallible testimony to the truth of the theory that woman must in some way be inferior to man. Were it not so, say these quidnuncs, there would be some exceptions to prove the contrary. They overlook the one obvious explanation which explains everything—Motherhood. In the early days of the race, the days of the huntsman and the warrior, when the spoils of war and the trophies of the chase were the only wealth of nations, child-bearing must have been a serious handicap to the woman: add to this the fact that war meant prisoners, and that from the very first, probably, even when men captured in warfare were killed as an incumbrance, women, for reasons which will be understood without being stated, were spared by their captors, and, coming down to later times, when men captives were made slaves and women-raiding became a favourite pastime, we can see explanation enough of the position which in process of time woman came to occupy, and from which she is only now slowly and toilsomely emerging. Already we see how the intensity of the struggle for political recognition is developing, in individual cases, those qualities of mind and brain

229

which man has been wont to assume as being his special monopoly; and from these cases we may infer how richly endowed the field of human thought will become when enriched by the products of the brains of men and women working together on terms of equality, and free from the debasing and sinister influences which subjection, in any form, imposes alike upon the subdued and the subduer. So true it is that one end of the chain which binds the slave is fastened round the life of his master, that the emancipation of women will also infallibly give freedom to the man.

Curious are the changes which a quarter of a century produces in the political arena. Questions arise, which after being ignored and jeered at, are ultimately brought by the force of agitation within the arena in which the political strife of the day is being waged, and keep gathering in importance until they obscure everything else. They are debated, wrangled over, and made leading issues at General Elections, and even whilst the strife which their coming has caused waxes hot, they begin to move away from sight without having been resolved. Disestablishment and Republicanism are questions which illustrate my meaning here. But so also does Woman Suffrage. In the days of the franchise agitations, the enfranchisement of woman, promoted by Mill and strenuously supported by Fawcett, Dr. Pankhurst, and other leaders of reform, promised to become a question of first political importance, but the passing of the one and then of the other of the friends of the movement, leaving no successors to carry on their tradition, it gradually passed into semi-obscurity. As it is again emerging and showing fresh vitality,[1] it may not be amiss to briefly record its history, particularly as it connects itself with the various Reform Bills.

In the Reform Act of 1832 the word "male" was interpolated before "persons." Never before and never since[2] has the phrase "male persons" appeared in any Statute of the Realm. By this Act, therefore, women were legally disfranchised for the first time in the history of the English constitution. In 1851 Lord Brougham's Act was passed, providing that the word "man" should always include "woman," except where otherwise stated. That seemed to clear the ground, and give women the same legal status as men. But, alas!

In 1867 the Representation of the People Act came before the House. John Stuart Mill's amendment, that it should be made expressly to include women, was defeated, but so also was the amendment that the phrase "male persons" of 1832 should be replaced. The word "man" was used instead. During the discussion the Hon. John Deman, Justice of the Common Pleas, asked the following question:—

> "Why, instead of the words 'male person' of the Act 1832, the word 'man' had been substituted in the present Bill? In the fifth clause he found that after saying that every 'man' should be entitled to be registered, it proceeds to say, 'or a MALE PERSON in any University who has passed any senior middle examination.' In the light of Lord Brougham's Act, if the

THE CITIZENSHIP OF WOMEN

Court of Queen's Bench had to decide to-morrow on the construction of these clauses, they would be constrained to hold that they conferred the suffrage on female persons, as well as on males."

After the Bill became law, it was thought, therefore, that women were entitled to vote, and in Manchester 5,347 women got on the register as voters. In Salford 1,500 (about) were registered, and large numbers in other places. Great uncertainty prevailed as to how to treat them, but most revising barristers threw them out. The Manchester women consolidated their claims, and appealed against the decision, and the case of Chorlton v. Lings was heard in 1868.

The case was tried in the Court of Common Pleas, with Mr. Coleridge, afterwards Lord Coleridge, and the late Dr. Pankhurst representing the women. It was argued that inasmuch as women had in the middle ages been recognised as voters by the State, and as that right had never been expressly taken away, therefore they had a *primâ facie* right to vote. Further, it was contended that under Lord Brougham's Act referred to above, the Franchise Act of 1867 must apply to women, since the term used was "men," and not "male persons," as in the Act of 1832. Despite this pleading, the judges decided that no women had no statutory right to be recognized as citizens, and that until that right was expressly conferred upon them by Act of Parliament, they must remain outside the pale of the franchise.

In 1884 Mr. Gladstone procured the rejection of the amendment to his County Franchise Bill, which would have enfranchised women, by threatening to abandon the Bill if the admendment was carried. In 1899 came the case of Beresford Hope v. Lady Sandhurst, in which it was decided that women were incapacitated from being elected members of a County Council. The case is important from the point of view of the Franchise (Parliamentary) question, because the judges quoted, approved, and confirmed the decision in the case of Chorlton v. Lings. One of the judges, Lord Esher, Master of the Rolls, delivering his judgment, said:

"I take the first proposition to be that laid down by Justice Wills in the case of Chorlton v. Lings. I take it that neither by the common law nor the constitution of this country from the beginning of the common law until now can a woman be entitled to exercise any public function. Justice Wills said so in that case, and a more learned judge never lived. He took notice of the case of the Countess of Pembroke in the County of Westmorland, who was hereditary sheriff, which he says was an exceptional case. The cases of an overseer and a constable were before him, and what I deduce from his judgment is, that for such somewhat obscure offices as these, exercised often in a remote part of the country, where nobody else could have been found who could exercise them, women had been admitted into them, by way of exception, and that, striking out these exceptions, the act of voting in such matters being a public function, *prima facie* and according to the constitutional and common law, a woman cannot exercise it. But that case goes further. It says that

DEMOCRACY AND THE STATE

this being the common law of England, when you have a Statute which deals with the exercise of public functions, unless that Statute expressly gives power to women to exercise them, it is to be taken that the true construction is, that the powers given are confined to men; and that Lord Brougham's Act does not apply."

The judge had in this case to interpret the Muncipal Corporations Act, in which the word "PERSON" is used throughout. In addition, there is an interpretation clause (63rd section) which provides that for all purposes connected with and having reference to the right to vote at municipal elections words in this Act importing the masculine gender include women. It was held that the right to be ELECTED was not conferred by the Act, but only the right to VOTE, the word "person" not being regarded by the judges as including women, Lord Justice Fry going so far as to say:

"I regard the 63rd section as ascertaining both affirmatively and negatively the rights which have been conferred upon women; ascertaining them affirmatively by express statement, and ascertaining them negatively by necessary implication. What is given to them is the right to vote, what is denied by the necessary implication are all the other rights which may be conferred by the Statute. I do not regard the negative implication arising from that section (63rd) as applying to the whole Act, as applying to crimes, or to the obligations on the duties of witnesses or matters of that sort, but I regard it as applying to the RIGHTS granted by that Statute."

In Miss HALL's case, 1900, the right of a woman to become a law agent in Scotland was denied by the judges on the ground that "person" when it is a case of exercising a public function means "MALE PERSON." The judges relied on the case of Chorlton v. Lings as the ground of their decision. Now, in view of these decisions, the situation is quite clear.

A woman, for the purposes of citizenship, has no legal existence in Great Britain, and has to be created before she can be enfranchised. To the uninitiated this may appear absurd and ridiculous, but it is plain unvarnished truth none the less. A woman may be a criminal, a queen, a tax and rate payer and owner of property, but she may not be a citizen of Great Britain and Ireland until a right to become such has been created by Act of Parliament. If only people would bear this fact in mind they would be saved from much error when considering her claims to the franchise.

During the past few sessions of Parliament a measure has been introduced, originally at the instigation of the Independent Labour Party, having this for its object. It is a Bill of one clause, which reads as follows:—

"In all Acts relating to the qualifications and registration of voters or persons entitled or claiming to be registered and to vote in the election of members of Parliament, wherever words occur which import the masculine gender the same shall be held to include women for all purposes

232

THE CITIZENSHIP OF WOMEN

connected with and having reference to the right to be registered as voters and to vote in such election, any law or usage to the contrary notwithstanding."

There are those who see in this innocent-looking measure a sinister attempt to extend and strengthen the property qualification, and by enfranchising propertied women enable these to range themselves on the side of the reactionaries in opposing the enfranchisement of working-class women. Needless to add, a strong section of the Liberal Press adopts and enforces this mis-statement with all the ingenuity which a fertile and untrained imagination can lend to a bad cause. One would have thought the record of the Liberal party in connection with Woman Suffrage would have chastened the ardour of those organs of Liberalism which are opposing this Bill in the interests of "true female suffrage"; but the gift of perspective is rare in politics, and a strict desire for accuracy an inconvenient failing when there are party ends to serve. The late Mr. Gladstone, as already stated, threatened to abandon his Reform Bill in 1884 if the Woman's Enfranchisement Amendment were carried. There have been three Conservative premiers who have publicly committed themselves, in speech at least (none of them have acted), to this reform, which has yet to find the first Liberal premier who will say a word in its favour. (Since the foregoing was written the present Prime Minister has informed a deputation of 400 women that he is in favour of their enfranchisement, but could hold out no hope that the reform would be passed by this Parliament.)

Any one who takes the trouble to read the Bill quoted above will note that it does not propose any franchise qualification, but asks that, whatever the qualification, women shall enjoy the franchise on the same basis as men. It is a Bill which only proposes to do one thing, and that is, to remove the sex disability which debars a woman, because she is a woman, from becoming a voter. If the qualification for men be a property one, it shall be the same for women, no more and no less; and if it be a manhood suffrage, it shall also be a womanhood. A woman may have the brain of a Bacon, the talent of a Shakespeare, the eloquence of a Demosthenes, and the wealth of a Crœsus all combined, but being a woman she may not vote for a member of Parliament, and this Bill proposes to remove the disability which stands in the way of her becoming a citizen; to remove her from the category of "idiots, lunatics, and paupers," and to recognize that, woman though she be, she is a human being who may become a citizen.

And now let us ascertain, if we can, what women would be enfranchised under the terms of the Bill quoted above.

There are four main heads under which the franchise qualifications fall to be grouped—(1) Owners of property; (2) Householders; (3) Lodgers; (4) Service. One set of opponents of the Woman's Enfranchisement Bill say that it would be from classes one and three that the new citizens would be drawn, which, if true, would leave working-class women out in the cold. Few working women own property, and not many earn wages enough to pay the four shillings a week for

DEMOCRACY AND THE STATE

unfurnished apartments, which is necessary to qualify for the lodger franchise. By what has become known as the latchkey decision the appeal court has now held that every male occupant who occupies an unfurnished room, irrespective of the amount paid as rent, and who has the free use of the room, is entitled to go on the voters list as a householder. Rich men, they assert, would be able to put their wives and daughters on as voters and outvoters, which would tend to greatly increase an evil which is already of sufficient magnitude. Fortunately, we have already an index to guide us as to the extent to which this statement is true, even were the worst fears of our opponents to be realized. There are, roughly, 7,000,000 electors in Great Britain, of whom 220,000 are lodger voters. A very large proportion of these are workmen, and it is doubtful whether rich men's sons, qualifying from their fathers' property, account for more than 20,000 of the whole. Even were a like number of daughters to be put upon the voters' roll, they would not, save in those few constituencies where the property vote is already overwhelming, and where, therefore, they could do no harm—save in these few cases, I say, they would not constitute an appreciable fraction of any constituency. As for the out-voters, we may surely anticipate, with some degree of assurance, that the Liberal Government will at least put an end to their existence, and so we need not worry ourselves about them one way or the other. In so far as the service franchise will give women the right to vote, those brought in will be working women, and we may pit these against the daughters of the rich. It will, I think, be conceded that the great bulk of those who will be enfranchised by the Bill will be householders, and here, I repeat, we have reliable data upon which to base our conclusions. Women may not be elected to a town or burgh council, but they may vote in the election of such councils. Owing to a difference of opinion in the ranks of the Independent Labour Party over the Woman's Enfranchisement Bill, it was decided to make a serious effort to obtain from the municipal registers some guidance as to the class of women already registered as municipal voters, and who would be entitled to be placed upon the parliamentary list should the Bill become law. Accordingly, a circular was issued to every branch of the party, some 300 in all, containing the following instructions:—

> "We address to your branch a very urgent request to ascertain from your local voting registers the following particulars:—
>
> "1st—The *total* number of electors in the ward.
> "2nd—Number of women voters.
> "3rd—Number of women voters of the working class.
> "4th—Number of women voters not of the working class.
>
> "It is impossible to lay down a strict definition of the term 'working class,' but for this purpose it will be sufficient to regard as 'working class women' those who work for wages, who are domestically employed, or who are supported by the earnings of wage-earning children."

THE CITIZENSHIP OF WOMEN

The returns to hand are not yet complete, but they comprise fifty towns or parts of towns, and show the following results:—

Total electors on the municipal registers 372,321
Total women voters   59,920
Working women voters, as defined above   49,410
Non-working women voters   10,510
Percentage of working women voters, **82·45**.

As will be seen at a glance, the proportion of women voters on the registers tested for the purposes of the above return—and these were not in any way selected, but were included because they were in the ward or parish within which the branch was situated—is equal to one-sixth of the whole. Assuming, as we may fairly do, that the same proportion obtains for the country as a whole, it would give us 1,250,000 women municipal voters, of whom 82 per cent. are working women, and every one of whom would at once be placed upon the parliamentary register were the Bill now before Parliament to become law.

Here, then, we have it proved beyond cavil or question that whatever the Woman's Enfranchisement Bill might do for propertied women, it would for a certainty and at once put 1,025,000 working women on the parliamentary voters' rolls of Great Britain, and a like proportion in Ireland. The fact speaks for itself. The Woman's Enfranchisement Bill does not concern itself with franchise qualifications; it is for the removal of the sex disqualification only; and yet on the present franchise qualifications and reactionary registration laws it would at once lift 1,250,000 British women from the political sphere to which "idiots, lunatics, and paupers" are consigned, and transform them into free citizens, and open wide the door whereby in the future every man and every woman may march side by side into the full enjoyment of adult suffrage.

Hitherto I have been dealing with those opponents whose objection to the Bill is that it does not go far enough, and who prefer waiting for a measure of adult suffrage under which every man and every woman, married and single alike, shall be enfranchised at one stroke. Now, I have had some experience of politics and of political methods, and I give it as my deliberate opinion that nothing would so much hasten the coming of that much-to-be-desired time as would the passing of the Woman's Enfranchisement Bill. If the workers were prepared to lay every other reform on the shelf, and begin an agitation for adult suffrage, they might, if specially fortunate, be successful in getting it about the year 1929. Manhood suffrage could probably be secured almost at once and for the asking; but the complete enfranchisement of all men and all women at once would be resisted bitterly by all parties. And the main difficulty in the way would be the enfranchisement of all women, married and living with their husbands, as well as single. The leap from what is now to what this proposes is too great for the mind of the British elector to grasp, and not by any means the least of the opposition would come from the working classes. Reformers gain nothing by shutting their eyes to facts which stare up at them from every part. I speak what most people know to be true when I say that the chief obstacle to reform of any kind in England is the conservative, plodding, timid mind of the average man. Hence the reason why all our reforms have come to us, not leaping and bounding, but slowly and hesitatingly. Even the franchise, such as it is, has been dribbled out to us in almost homœopathic doses. This difficulty applies to women's enfranchisement in a special degree. The male man, even he of the working class, will not lightly or all at once part with the authority which has so long been his, and admit the wife of his bosom to a political equality with himself. But once women are admitted to citizenship and some women become voters, the male mind will insensibly accustom itself to the idea of woman citizenship, and the way be thus prepared for adult suffrage complete and unrestricted by sex, poverty or marriage.

To those who are opposed on principle to women having the vote at all I have little to say. These I find it easier to pity than to reason with. But when they foresee the deluge following upon the enfranchisement of women I refer them to the Colonies. There women are citizens and voters, but they have not because of that ceased to be wives—even housewives, or mothers. Their outlook on life has been a little broadened by the possession of the vote which, willy nilly, forces them to interest themselves somewhat in political and social questions. They are thus in a fair way to become better companions to their husbands, and—and I say this with deep conviction—better mothers. Women whose circle of interests is circumscribed by her pots, pans, and scrubbing brushes, varied by an occasional gossip with a neighbour or quarrel with her husband, can never, however affectionate, be other than a curb upon the opening, eagerly questioning intelligence of her children. Broaden the outlook of the mother, and you open a new world for childhood to grow in, and bind many a wild, wayward youth to his home-life who is now driven out into the hard world for lack of that sympathetic, intelligent companionship which an educated and enlightened mother can alone supply. Colonial statesmen and social reformers all admit that woman's influence in the sphere of politics has been healthy and quickening, and, as it has been there, so undoubtedly would it be here.

The "half angel, half idiot," period is over in the woman's world. She is fighting her way into every sphere of human activity. Her labour is coming into competition with that of man in nearly every department of industry. The women's trade union movement is growing by leaps and bounds. In the learned professions she is forcing herself to the front by sheer determination and force of intellect in a way that will not be denied. Sooner or later men will be compelled to treat with her and recognise her as a co-worker, and they could not begin better than by admitting her right to be a co-voter. Those who prate so glibly of adult suffrage might surely learn something of men's opinion of women by taking note of the way in which lawyers and doctors are resisting her encroachments upon their preserves. A woman may be Queen of England, but she may not enter the profession from which Lord Chancellors are drawn.

The enfranchisement of women is not a party question. Its supporters and opponents are distributed over all parties. The measure is again coming well within the

THE CITIZENSHIP OF WOMEN

sphere of practical politics, and it is for women to see that it is kept there until a settlement is reached. If they will, as I think they should, make it not a test but *the* test question at elections, and resolutely refuse to work for or in any way countenance any candidate who is not whole-heartedly with them, they will, if not in this Parliament, then certainly in the next, secure the passage of a measure through the House of Commons at least which will place them on terms of political equality with men. If this comes as part of a measure for giving complete adult suffrage, well and good; but political equality they should insist upon, whatever the conditions of that equality may be.

Disraeli, speaking on this question in the House of Commons, said:

> "I say that in a country governed by a woman—where you allow women to form part of the other estate of the realm—peeresses in their own right, for example—where you allow a woman not only to hold land, but to be a lady of the manor and hold legal courts—where a woman by law may be a churchwarden and overseer of the poor—I do not see, where she has so much to do with the State and Church, on what reasons, if you come to right, she has not a right to vote."

And with these words I conclude.

J. KEIR HARDIE.

Notes

1 On Friday, May 12th, 1905, when the Woman's Enfranchisement Bill was down for second reading, there were 300 women in the lobbies canvassing for the Bill, and when it was talked out, these marched out and organized a meeting in the open air. The opposition to the Bill came from both sides of the House in about equal proportions.
2 Whilst these sheets are being revised a Bill comes to me, introduced by W. R. Cremer, M.P., and others, which proposes to confer the vote upon every "man" and "male person" of full age.

Part 7

THE NEW RELIGION AND THE OLD

24

A SOCIALIST'S VIEW OF RELIGION AND THE CHURCHES (LONDON: CLARION, 1896), 1–16.

Tom Mann

[Having been a member of the Social Democratic Federation (SDF) in the 1880s, Tom Mann was nevertheless uncomfortable with the quasi-Marxism upon which its leaders, especially H.M. Hyndman, insisted. The SDF line, not always followed by its members, discouraged self-organisation of the workers in their unions, thus opposing something of which Mann was a strong supporter (Callaghan 1990, 18–22, 45–47). In the early years of the decade that followed, Mann was enthusiastic in support of the new unionism, which sought to extend trade union organisation beyond the skilled workers. This, he believed, would serve an educational purpose, encouraging workers to become involved in the control of their lives (Callaghan 1990, 51–52). The formation of the Independent Labour Party (ILP) in 1893 gave Mann the opportunity to become active in a party far more suited than the SDF to his beliefs and inclinations. He indeed went on to serve as the ILP's general secretary for a period in the mid-1890s.

Mann's distaste for firm control on the part of leaders was not restricted to politics and industrial relations; it also extended to religion. He saw the value of religion to the socialist cause and his prominence in the ILP enabled him to promote active Christianity such as his own in the 1890s. There were close ties between the ILP and the Labour Church movement and Mann served an important linking role (Bevir 2011, 288–289). It was from this perspective that he wrote the pamphlet *A Socialist's View of Religion and the Churches* in 1896. In the pamphlet Mann (1896) criticised contemporary, organised Christianity for hypocrisy and its clergy for lack of courage. The established church ignored poverty. This was because it was closely knitted into the existing, grossly materialistic system. As such, the established church and its clergy did not adequately fulfil its professed purpose of providing moral and spiritual guidance for humanity. If the church did not change, Mann predicted, ordinary people would reinvigorate religion for themselves.]

THE NEW RELIGION AND THE OLD

I MAKE no apology for writing this chapter upon Preachers and Churches. In our day every institution is open to criticism, and rightly and necessarily so; and although—if this should meet the eyes of preachers—many of them will doubtless consider it presumption on my part to attempt even to deal with such a subject, let it be so. We live in England, and not in Russia—plutocratic England, it is true, but with Democracy getting a good grip. And if by writing this I simply lay myself open to criticism, it may still be the case that I shall have served some small purpose by helping to make clear what it is we object to in orthodox preachers, with their orthodox doctrines and congregations. It cannot be that I am wholly correct—it may be I am very wrong; but feeling strongly upon the subject, and often indulging on Labour platforms in sentiments identical with those I have here given expression to, I now venture (upon invitation) to place before another audience the views I hold, as well as those I condemn.

At the outset, I desire to say that I am fully alive to the fact that there are

CLERGYMEN, MINISTERS, SUNDAY-SCHOOL AND BIBLE-CLASS TEACHERS,

who cannot be covered by the general terms of censure I have made use of in what follows. I am happy in possessing the close friendship of not a few who, I am quite sure, are not merely as devoted as any men and women on earth to the cause of truth and righteousness, but strive continuously to make right-doing prevail in every sphere of life. But it is just these who, more than others, feel and know what a terrible responsibility rests upon preachers and teachers as a whole; and who also know, to their sorrow, how shamefully deficient the Churches are in supplying the much-needed correction, and stimulus, and light.

The Churches set up a claim to be the moral and spiritual guides of humanity, to whom all men should look for guidance as to their conduct in this life, and qualifications for life hereafter. The question I propose to examine is: Do they fulfil these functions?

In a complex society like ours, where the average person, on reaching girlhood or boyhood, must perforce begin work of some kind to obtain a maintenance, a very large share of one's time, thought, and energy must of necessity, under present conditions, be devoted to the mere work of obtaining a living. Indeed, it is the paramount question, by the side of which all others fall into comparative insignificance. Consequently, if guidance is needed anywhere, it is in connection with the means whereby a livelihood is to be obtained. The virtues—including honesty, sobriety, and obedience to superiors—are all emphasized in the Sunday schools, Bible classes, and churches; exactly how to apply them being, of course, too great a task.

A GENERAL CONDEMNATION OF "SIN,"

and urgent advice to "flee from the wrath to come," and find salvation by reliance upon the sacrifice in the crucifixion of Jesus, sums up the teaching of the average

SOCIALIST'S VIEW OF RELIGION

school, church, and chapel. Where does this land a man? Judging by a lengthened experience, I unhesitatingly declare that I find that the average church or chapel goer, who is influenced primarily by what he obtains from its functions, becomes a narrow, saving, squeezing creature, taking little or no part in the vigorous life of the community, but very commonly becoming, by his isolated action, a source of weakness in any real democratic movement. If he takes part in municipal or political life, he usually does so on the flimsiest party lines. He generally attributes the cause of the poverty of the poor to their utter degradation, caused by their dissolute habits, brought about by their unchecked evil tendencies, the human heart being desperately wicked and deceitful above all things. Very rarely is he connected with a trade union. As a rule, he is most loyal to the injunction, "Servants, obey your masters," and will side with his kindred "brethren" to blackleg against his fellows.

The tricks of trade he necessarily becomes familiar with; and, like a business man, he not only indulges in them, but becomes an expert thereat. He will attend a prayer-meeting and bless God for the good things of life, and pray for the salvation of the poor sinners in the slums, and will take, as evidences of God's blessing in return, the possession of a few more shares that will pay ten per cent.; and if fifteen per cent.—why, the more cause for thankfulness, of course! Let none tell me I am concocting a case; such men can be counted by thousands. And why? Because that upon which they have been fed is devoid of real vitalising force. Instead of giving moral discernment to enable a man to understand how, where, and when moral or, if you will, religious principles should be applied, the preachers land him in a complete fog. Beholding those who are held in high esteem in the Churches, that they include the bankers and stock-jobbers, and the company promoters and capitalists and landlords, he follows them rather than the simple carpenter's Son. Between such select and exalted personages and mere Labour agitators, trade unionists, Socialists, &c., there is, as surely there ought to be, he concludes, a great gulf.

The Church is in a helpless backwash having lost the true courage, mental and moral vigour, power of discernment, and hence capacity, to apply what humanity now demands. The parsons, clergymen, and ministers are, for the most part, a feeble folk, who, daring not to lead, are therefore bound to follow.

Other men labour, and in the course of years the Church slowly is dragged along; for the pioneers of righteousness we must look elsewhere than to so-called Christians. The man who is truly religious wants no driving to do his duty. He does not try to make all manner of excuses for the exploiters of the industrious community, and pile up the trifling misdeeds of an unfairly handicapped proletariat.

A TRULY RELIGIOUS BODY OF MEN,

whose religion enabled them to understand between right-doing and wrong-doing, and furnished them with the requisite courage to face all foes, would never be content with the sunny complacency of the average parson in the midst of the life-destroying conditions of our industrial centres.

Shame, say I, and a thousand times shame, upon so feeble a religion as that which can tolerate the awful social life which exists in London at this very time. There are not less than four hundred thousand persons in London alone in a state of semi or actual starvation. There are among these at least a hundred thousand adult males out of work; tens of thousands of women, having no one to rely upon to support them, but in multitudes of instances being responsible for children (or aged or crippled relatives) in addition to themselves, who, over and over again in the course of a year, are deprived of the means of obtaining a livelihood; tens of thousands of children setting off to the Board schools every morning with less than a tenth part of that which is necessary for physical sustenance. Scores of miles of streets, with wretched dens in the background, furnish enormous rents— to whom? To the men of the world? No; to the rich members of your congregations, the great subscribers of your salaries O preachers! who turn up at your church or chapel service and follow you in praying, "Thy kingdom come; Thy will be done, as in heaven, so upon the earth." Can they, do you think, believe that there is anything in heaven corresponding to the wretched slum-dwellers of Whitechapel or Spitalfields? Are there any in heaven corresponding to these Christian rent-takers, who wax fat at the expense of the downtrodden? What are you ministers and plutocratic members of the rich churches and chapels doing to make earth like heaven? Why, it would need an entire change in the basis of society, and the means whereby incomes are obtained. Are these religious plutocrats and preachers trying to change the basis of society, so that better conditions shall prevail? Assuredly not. On the contrary, they are determined opponents of those who do try to make such changes.

The fact is, preachers and congregation are bound hard and fast in a system that is grossly materialistic, utterly soulless in good, and without a single noble aspiration. The Hobbs and Co. Liberator phenomenon indicates how completely swamped is the average Nonconformist soul. Not only did it make haste to get rich, but by the most damnable means that the most cunning Jews and Gentiles combined could devise. Morality! Religion! Where is the religion or the morality in taking ten per cent. usury? Yet who among the orthodox in faith and practice objects to ten or more per cent.? Honesty! Righteousness! Who that believes in the doctrines of Jesus can uphold an industrial system whose very basis from top to toe is ten per cent.?

"THE MAN THAT WILL NOT WORK, NEITHER SHALL HE EAT,"

is an apostolic injunction; but how many ministers or members of our swell churches and chapels believe it? "Yes, but even Hobbs and Wright worked," some will say. Ah, so they did; as did also Mr. Charles Peace of burglar notoriety—the latter with less scoundrelism than the former.

The average preacher or church-goer does distinctly believe, not only that it is right to eat without working, but to get fed, clothed, housed, insured, and buried into the bargain. Who among them condemns as a religious duty the taking of interest and rent? And if these are defended, and I can get sufficient interest or rent to keep me and mine without working, what religious principle comes in after that to say I must work? Or, am I to work like the Yankee millionaire—on six days a week endeavouring to amass the biggest fortune on record, entirely irrespective of how many will be ruined; and on Sunday attending church, receiving the blessing of the minister, and helping to carry the collecting-plate to show how godly I am? If ever Deity was insulted, it is by these devourers of widows' houses, who receive direct sanction and approval from orthodox exponents of orthodox religion. Let none rise to say, "Oh, but we would never endorse the enormities of the Liberator Company." If not, where, then, would you stop? The whole shoal of interest-takers and stockbroking gamblers are specimens of the same type in embryo. Not so successful as the millionaire, perhaps—why? Because they lacked opportunity. Never had the brains to scheme like the others, and the courage to come down a resounding crash at the end. Why? Because they hadn't had time to go far enough. The difference isn't in kind; it is only in degree. As in the time of Nahum, so now, to describe London we must indeed say, "Woe to the bloody city! it is full of lies and robbery."

I do not state or imply that all this is done hypocritically; what I do say is "that the truth is not in them." Christians need to be "born again." Orthodox religion is acquiescing in an irreligious condition of Society. Christianity is made part and parcel of the national commercialism, and wholly subservient to the individualistic acquisitiveness of the age. The Fatherhood of God and Brotherhood of Man have come to be mere threadbare phrases when used by an ordinary religionist. Church or chapel is regularly attended, not indeed to obtain guidance out of the industrial and social wilderness, but to maintain tradition and keep up appearances. Some Christians positively believe, doubtless, that religion consists in church-going, hymn-singing, and muttering over the words found in the Prayer Book, or offered up by the minister; failing to realise that these are but the means to an end. If they are used as the end itself, then indeed does moral darkness assert itself.

It does appear to be the case that with industrial England, as with pastoral Israel, in the time of Amos, the outward ritual is made the chief concern. At that time the Mosaic ritual was jealously attended to, but the message was:

"I HATE, I DESPISE YOUR FEAST-DAYS,

and I will not smell in your solemn assemblies. Though ye offer Me burnt offerings, I will not accept them; neither will I regard the peace-offerings of your fat beasts. Take thou away from Me the noise of thy songs; for I will not hear the melody of thy viols. But let justice run down as waters, and righteousness as a mighty stream" (Amos v. 21-24). This is a sweeping condemnation of fashionable church-going whilst the state of Society is unsound. See verse 11 of the same chapter: "Forasmuch therefore as your treading is upon the poor, and ye take from him burdens of wheat: ye have built houses," &c.

Now, it was not the custom even in brutal Israel for one man to literally knock another down in order to take his wheat from him. There were more refined methods of exploitation then as now—though, doubtless, modern civilisation even in Christian England, could give the old Jews many points, and beat them at legalised robbery; and it is this legal robbery that is here condemned as much as any other kind.

But nothing puts the case more clearly than the condemnation by Jesus of the orthodox professors of religion of His time (see St. Matt. xxiii. 13, 14)—

"But woe unto you, scribes and Pharisees, hypocrites! for ye shut up the kingdom of heaven against men: for ye neither go in yourselves, neither suffer ye them that are entering to go in. Woe unto you, scribes and Pharisees, hypocrites! for ye devour widows' houses, and for a pretence make long prayers: therefore ye shall receive the greater damnation."

No language could be stronger, and yet this was directed against the respectably religious of that day. These Pharisees have their exact counterpart to-day in England.

I know the risk I run by any attempt to deal with the subject of future salvation. But with a keen remembrance of the influence orthodoxy exercised over me—of the years of unrest, of the flimsiness and mimicry, with its pretences of solemnity and make-believe solidity,—I feel bound to deal with the subject. I know many young men who have striven hard to find "salvation"; and with blind guides to lead them, many years were spent in finding what ought to have been reached in a few months. The talk about the one thing needful under orthodoxy (it will be noted that I continually guard myself by referring to "orthodoxy") means nothing more than fixing attention upon Jesus as the Saviour, He having been sacrificed to reconcile mankind to the Father. I make no comment upon this doctrinal point. What I want to expose is the demoralising effect produced by the individual being taught that salvation for him consists in reflecting upon and believing in his acceptance with God, because of Christ's sacrifice, irrespective of the life he leads. "No one says this," some will cry. Yes; but, indeed,

IT IS SAID AND TAUGHT IN NINETEEN CHURCHES OUT OF TWENTY,

and the effect is to cause the individual to think of himself or herself, and to value, out of all proper proportion, his or her own personal salvation. Selfishness begins this, and with selfishness it usually ends. Whilst one can admire the energy put forth and the trouble taken in the voluntary street-corner preachers and singers, one can only pity those who speak, as well as those who may in any way be influenced by what is said. A million times over is the same story told—personal salvation by faith in Christ. It seems to me it would be a truly religious act if all such received a severe castigation for wasting so much time trying to assuage the sorrows primarily brought about by a vicious industrial system, instead of boldly tackling that industrial system itself.

SOCIALIST'S VIEW OF RELIGION

Salvation surely consists in living in accordance with Divine harmony,—in loving order and living it,—in hating disorder here on earth, and striving might and main to remove it so that earth may be more like heaven. Oh, the unworthiness of followers of Jesus being primarily concerned about their poor little souls! He that seeks to save his soul on these lines will lose it; but he that will lose his own life by working for the salvation of the community—all such must be saved. Up! off your knees, young men! Let us have more effort directed to the removal of evil! Don't go continually begging of God to do that which you ought to do! This world is wrong, and wants righting, and you and I are responsible for doing our share towards righting it. What horrible villainy have you been guilty of, that half your time needs be taken up in praying for forgiveness? The man that loves righteousness will seek to live righteously, and all such are already saved. His duty is to be at work removing the cause of wrong-doing.

A little less time spent at orthodox mission meetings, and more time spent in helping on effective industrial organisation, to ensure right-doing in the business of life, is sadly needed just now. This orthodox mission work is exactly what our exploiting plutocrats rejoice in. It is so gracious of them to give an occasional ten pounds to keep a mission going, that they may with reasonable safety exploit an additional twenty from their employés, and still receive the praise and blessings of the faithful.

"Go to now, ye rich men, weep and howl for your miseries that shall come upon you. Your riches are corrupted and your garments are moth-eaten. Your gold and silver is cankered; and the rust of them shall be a witness against you, and shall eat your flesh as it were fire. Ye have heaped treasure together for the last days. Behold the hire of the labourers who have reaped down your fields, which is of you kept back by fraud, crieth: and the cries of them which have reaped are entered into the ears of the Lord of sabaoth" (St. James v. 1-4).

What have our

LANDED ARISTOCRATS AND CAPITALISTIC PLUTOCRATS

who go to church and chapel regularly, to say to St. James? Dare they claim to be better than those whom James condemned? If so, in what way? And if not, are they not condemned by the book in which they pretend to believe? Not that I am affirming that every rich man is necessarily a candidate for hell. What I do contend is that, be we rich or poor, if our mental and moral standard is such that we continue to support the present hellish system,—which the ordinary capitalist upholds, and is sanctioned in upholding by the average Church,—then we are violating every genuinely religious principle.

I am not condemning religion, but the lack of it. Religion to me consists of those ethical principles that serve as a guide in all matters of conduct—social, political, and industrial alike; and the essence of the whole thing is this: the choice between a life whose actuating motive shall be self, either in acquiring wealth, renown, prestige, or power, and a life which shall have primary regard for the well-being of the community as a whole. To do this is to engage in making it possible for "His kingdom to obtain on earth as in heaven." If I am asked, "Do I think that all that is necessary is a perfected industrial machinery on Socialistic lines?" I say emphatically, "No! I don't think that is all."

I do distinctly believe in the necessity for Socialism out and out, and that it is my duty to work for its realisation. But I know also that something more than good machinery is necessary, if really good results are to be obtained. I desire to see every person fired with a holy enthusiasm to put a stop to wrong-doing. Before this is possible, individuals must submit themselves to much and severe discipline. The baser sides of our nature must be beaten down that the higher and nobler side may develop. Regard for the brethren (brethren meaning all) must be the mainspring of our action; the development of the highest possible qualities in ourselves is undoubtedly a religious duty, but for this chief reason—that we may be of the greater service.

"He that would be greatest among you, let him be servant of all."

This to me is the ideal test and standard. As Jesus was the servant of mankind, so I, as a follower of Jesus, must learn to be of use. The irreligious man is not the only deliberate maker of mischief, but equally so the indolent and useless man. Swedenborg has well said—

"All religion has relation to life, and the life of religion is to do good." Further: "Heaven consists of those of all nations who love God supremely, and their neighbours as themselves. Hell is the assembly of the selfish—of all who love themselves supremely and gratify their lusts at any cost to others."

The astounding anomaly of our time is the complete separation of religious principles from every-day industrial life. Spiritual pastors teach the young to regard God as the common Father; and when the young become of age to reflect upon the shameful inequalities created and maintained by our social system, they are discouraged by their elders from trying to alter it, and are treated as agitators and destroyers of the peace.

Honesty demands a frank statement that the so-called religious of our time are

AFRAID TO APPLY THE PRINCIPLES OF JESUS.

They make a pretence of championing His cause; but in reality the Socialist agitator and the Trade Union organiser is doing far more than the preachers and the Christians, the Missionary Societies and the Bible Societies to make Christ's gospel prevail. The Churches are afraid of Socialism. Why? Because the wealthy in their congregations are anti-Socialists. If any say this is not so, then it will not be difficult to give an effectual reply by quoting instances where the minister has seen the light and dared to proclaim the truth, and where the men who "have great possessions" (relatively) have very soon taken their departure. I have heard of complaints from one or two such ministers that they not only lost the employer class by their boldness, but that they did not succeed in securing the adhesion of any counteracting proportion among the workers. There is less to be surprised at in this than some seem to think. The Churches having gone astray worse than lost sheep, are not likely very easily to win back Democracy. Whether they will ever do it or not is an open question.

The clergyman is undoubtedly at a serious discount as an adviser. "Serve him right," say I. Nor will he ever redeem his position except by honest effort on behalf of Democracy. Not that Democracy will suffer materially if this is not done. The greatest trouble is past. Democracy is learning how to provide for itself, and never was the Democracy so truly religious as now. And it is gradually getting more so. This religious evolution will increase as the bad environment is altered on one side, and the ethical gospel is lifted up and followed truthfully on the other.

I know that many preachers contend that industrial and economic matters are nothing to them; theirs is a religious work, and men must be left to themselves to find out how to apply religious truths. "If they were to take sides, it would mean the break-up of the Church," and so on. To endorse a religion apart from principles that are to guide our every-day behaviour is monstrous. If one's religion does not compel one to take sides in favour of a righteous basis of society, the sooner it ceases to encumber the earth the better for all concerned. A minister who can't find time to make up his mind as to the direction in which he should travel on industrial and economic matters, will probably not find time to be of any practical use to the world, nor yet to the denomination to which he may belong. I am fully aware of the fact that by

DECLARING IN FAVOUR OF SOCIALISM,

many who might have been disposed to consider the possibility of some mild action favourable to Democracy, now stand off. To such let me say: I have purposely avowed myself a Socialist here, so that those who read this may know what to expect from those on whose behalf I can speak. We do not want, and will not have a parson's patronage, or goody-goody advice. If there is to be a *rapprochement* it can only be by the parson getting off his high horse, stopping his goody-ism, and meeting men and women frankly as such. If he doesn't, he'll get left high and dry for a certainty.

I am not here demanding that every parson who is to be of use shall be an out-and-out Socialist right off. I am telling him that we workmen who happen to be Socialists are adding largely to our numbers every month, that the whole trend of modern effort in our Trade Unions, Co-operative Societies, Town and County Councils, and Parliament is distinctly socialistic, and if parsons and ministers want to stop it, they had better refurbish their weapons. I can easily understand that some genuine men among the clergy will be disquieted by wondering whether the Socialists are coming round their way for a general sharing-out arrangement, and so they are slow to make a move. Such is the enlightenment that exists in these quarters! Let me hasten to reassure all such that if they are able to subscribe to the following very mild statement of John Ruskin, they need not be seriously alarmed:—

"So far am I from invalidating the security of property, that the whole gist of my contention will be found to aim at an extension in its range, and whereas it has long been known and declared that the poor have no right to the property of the rich, I wish it also to be known and declared that the rich have no right to the property of the poor" ("*Unto this Last*").

That surely should be a self-evident proposition to the mind of a moralist, but it goes rather a long way, as it would mean nothing less than a righteous distribution of wealth. It is to be hoped that no preacher will ask what business is this to him. Surely "Thou shalt not steal" is emphatic enough, and when we add Carlyle's trifle to it, "Thou shalt not be stolen from," it gains a little in clearness. The Church will doubtless concern itself in a few generations to come about such an elementary subject as the enforcement of honesty. We workmen contend that honesty of distribution should become a fact. Forty-nine-fiftieths of present-day poverty, and the bulk of the crime and villainy that now disgrace our country, would disappear, if the Society thieves were to disappear.

But timid Christians and their preachers are likely to reply that, "to bring about such a change is impossible; human nature won't admit of it." If not, what becomes of the Lord's Prayer: "Thy kingdom come . . . as in heaven so upon the earth"?

IF THIS IS A PIOUS FRAUD,

please be frank enough to say so. Some of us, when we say the Lord's Prayer, do indeed mean it, amongst whom I am glad to be one. I am not willing to be included with those cowards who say it is impossible of realisation. Whatever is right we are bound to work for, even if its fruit is in the dim and distant future. We believe that the Lord's Prayer is not only realisable, but we are of those disciples who will make it so. This done, the question of a "living wage" will be settled.

As yet in this Christian land we haven't been able to establish a living wage, even when it means nothing more than a sufficiency of material necessities to maintain life. Many in connection with the Churches have recently said that a living wage is impossible, *i.e.,* that it is impossible in this "religious" country to see that each of God's children, our own brothers and sisters, shall be as well fed as a horse. Let Carlyle again be heard:—

"There is not a horse in England, able and willing to work, but has due food and lodging, and goes about sleek-coated, satisfied in heart. And you say, 'It is impossible.' Brothers, I answer, if for you it be impossible, what is to become of you? It is impossible for us to believe it to be impossible. The human brain, looking at these sleek English horses, refuses to believe in such impossibility for Englishmen. Do you depart quickly; clear the ways soon, lest worse befall. We for our share do purpose, with full view of the enormous difficulty, with total disbelief in the impossibility, to endeavour while life is in us, and to die endeavouring, we and our sons, till we attain it, or have all died and ended!" ("*Past and Present*").

This is the correct spirit in which the modern crusade against our social villainies is to be conducted. It is especially the work of the Church to set the pace. It ought, but we don't expect it will; and yet, I feel sure that those young men and women who are certain to be touched by the devotion and fervour of our modern crusaders, will not require much converting to our side. They are too noble to remain in the ranks of the inactive and selfish. They, too, will come forth to join in the noble work of social reconstruction. We have a glorious and an inspiriting work in hand—nothing less than the purifying of the industrial and social life of our country and the making of true individuality. For, let it be clearly understood, we Labour men are thoroughly in favour of the highest possible development of each individual. We seek no dead level of uniformity, and never did. Our ideal is: "From each according to his capacity, to each according to his needs." We can't reach that right off; but when we have done so, we shall not be "far from the kingdom."

To engage in this work is to be occupied in the noblest work the earth affords; to do it well, we want not only men and women of good intention—the Churches have these now—we shall want men and women of sound sense who will understand the science of industrial economics, as well as of the highest standard of ethics. To mean well is one thing, to be able to do well is a better thing, and we cannot do well except by accident, unless we know something of the laws that underlie and control the forces with which we shall have to deal. By way of indicating what we hope to reach, it may prevent fear and trembling if I say it is neither more nor less than that set forth by

JOHN STUART MILL,

in his "Autobiography," where he says:—

"The Social Problem of the future we considered to be, how to unite the greatest individual liberty of action with a common ownership in the raw material of the globe, and an equal participation for all in the benefits of combined labour."

Nothing very awful in that surely, and yet there is sufficient to revolutionise modern Society! What does a really religious man care how far it goes? To him the one important question is, "Is it right?" Does duty demand that he shall endorse it and work for its realisation? To me all other duties sink into comparative insignificance. I will yield to none if I know it in facing the straight path, and honestly endeavouring to walk in it, and therefore I dare not take my eyes off this big problem.

Much has already been done in removing barriers. The work of the Trade Unionists for the last sixty years has borne good fruit. In the early years of the present century, Capital had complete sway. Unrestricted industrial competition was the accepted gospel universally applied in Great Britain. In Parliament the landed aristocracy had complete power. In industrial life, the then infantile but now powerful plutocracy had undisputed control. The law was against combination, consequently there were few Trade Unions. Neither was there anything in the nature of Factory Acts. And what was the result? Our industrial history of that period is the blackest page in England's life. Not only men, but women and children had to work fifteen to sixteen hours a day. Children, too, of six, even five years of age, were called to the mills at five o'clock in the morning; if they were a minute late, an overseer with a slave-driver's lash stood there to thrash them and the girls and women like dogs. Some power of revolt existed, and this country owes more than it thinks to the revolutionary course of the early Trade Unionists. We still have England's industrial prestige maintained by child labour at ten and eleven years of age.

In thousands of instances the standard of life is such that when a man is in full work, so little does he earn that the wife and mother must not only get up herself at five o'clock in the morning, but must also wake her children, and

TAKE THE INFANT OUT INTO THE RAW
WINTRY AIR

to leave it with some nurse, while she, the mother, must go to the mill, reaching there at six, to take her stand by the men, work all day, and return home at night to commence house duties, and this because the family would starve if she did not. Oh, Church people! if ever a crusade were needed it is here in England now. The honour of our country is left with us to guard. For humanity's sake, let us see to it that we wipe out these accursed blood-red stains.

There is much to be proud of in Britain's history, but whilst such conditions remain we cannot wait to comment upon the work done in face of so much waiting to be done? Who shall do it? Every man and every woman is expected to contribute a share. The social salvation of the entire community is the religious duty in which you preachers and people are called upon to engage.

Oh! rich women of the Churches, have you no social and political duty? You, who spend so much on your own persons, have you no care for the body of Society? And you women of the middle classes, who have a great power, will you not use that power to wipe out these stains on our national and Christian character? If you take up a determined stand in connection with the Churches, they will be compelled to become active. The work will be done with or without you, but quicker with you than without you.

> Women! who shall one day bear
> Sons to breathe New England air,
> If you hear without a blush
> Deeds to make the roused blood rush
> Like red lava through your veins,
> For your sisters now in chains,
> Answer! are ye fit to be
> Mothers of the brave and free?

To the women already in the Socialist movement, I can say with full assurance that you are stimulating and ennobling the men, as well as doing your own share of ardent advocacy of sound principles. These few remaining years of the nineteenth century shall yet see great and glorious changes made in the removal of the causes that produce poverty, and therefore crime and suffering. To help in this work should be our greatest desire and chief delight, and the success of this work will mean: International solidarity, and world-wide fraternisation.

25

THE NEW RELIGION, 2ND EDITION (LONDON: CLARION, 1897), 1–12.

Robert Blatchford

[Robert Blatchford's Clarion movement, with its newspapers, pamphlets and bicycling excursions into the countryside to spread the socialist word in the late nineteenth century, was always most active and influential in the north of England. In his pamphlet *The New Religion*, published in 1892 and then again five years later, he argued that the success of socialism in the north was achieved not through formal plans for the politics and economics of a new state, but instead by an ethical movement for a new life. This, he stressed, was tantamount to a new religion (Blatchford 1897).

Blatchford was a supporter of the Labour Church movement formed by the Unitarian minister John Trevor, who held its first meeting in Manchester. Blatchford addressed the second meeting and the movement soon spread around Lancashire and Yorkshire and eventually around the country (Bevir 2011, 278–297).

Blatchford had been involved with the Marxist Social Democratic Federation but, since 1893, had been associated with the Independent Labour Party. He suggested in the pamphlet that, unlike in London, Marx was less relevant to socialism in the north than the ethical works of writers including John Ruskin and Thomas Carlyle.

Although Blatchford focused on the north, the idea of a new religion was popular among socialists throughout Britain in the 1880s and 1890s (Yeo 1977). In the second edition of *The New Religion*, reprinted here, Blatchford was unable to resist the opportunity to mention the contribution of his *The Clarion* newspaper in this new religion, stressing its circulation of almost 50,000. Even as the edition went to press, however, changes were beginning to emerge in British politics, economics and political philosophy which were inconducive to the success of a religious formulation of socialism. Business was organised on a larger scale, politics was beginning to be seen as a function of the state to control society, and an ethos of distribution and consumption was beginning to dominate culture (Yeo 1977, 46).]

THE NEW RELIGION

IT would be easier to say what the great masses of our workers need than what they desire. Many of them would ask for more wages, many for shorter hours of work, not a few for better racing "tips," or more beer.

Go amongst the masses of the poor in our crowded Lancashire and Yorkshire towns, and ask them what they wish for. The men will say "a living wage," or "an eight hours' day;" the wives, poor drudges, will tell wistfully of how their work is never done, of the struggle they have to make both ends meet. A little more money, a little more ease, a little more pleasure of their hard and jaded lives— these things they desire, and would be unreasonably grateful for. But speaking of the northern workers in the mass, I cannot, of my own knowledge, report the existence of any earnest and efficient desire for the attainment by all of the best that human life can yield. The more prosperous workers are without heed; the more penurious are without hope. In both cases the fact is due less to lack of noble impulse or of native sense than to lack of knowledge. Show the more successful workers the truth about our social system, and they are just enough and generous enough, ay, and wise enough, to wish to right it. Show the crushed and miserable poor that their suffering and debasement are not inevitable; show them that they have just claims to a better life, and sure means for its attainment, and they will prove that they possess the courage and the intelligence to fight and win.

Half a century ago Carlyle described most vividly and truly the state of mind of the northern working masses:—

"Thus these poor Manchester manual workers mean only, by fair day's wages for fair day's work, certain coins of money adequate to keep them living—in return for their work, such modicum of food, clothes, and fuel as will enable them to continue their work itself! They as yet clamour for no more; the rest, still inarticulate, cannot shape itself into a demand at all, and only lies in them as a dumb wish; perhaps only, still more inarticulate, as a dumb, altogether unconscious want."

Ten years ago, perhaps five years ago, that passage was still literally true of all the masses. To-day it is true of the majority. But there are signs of change.

There is now, in the North of England, a party of progress; and, which is of more value and significance than the existence of any party, there is, blazing or smouldering amongst our densely-populated districts, a new enthusiasm; almost a new religion.

The party, indeed, can hardly claim the name of party yet. It is scattered, it is badly organised, it consists of many and somewhat incongruous elements; resembling more a number of isolated clans in revolt than a unanimous people banded for revolution. Its rise has been sudden, its growth rapid: so rapid indeed has been its growth, and so completely has it severed itself from all established political, religious, economic, and social ideas and methods, that as yet its significance has not been realised nor its principles understood by Aristocracy, Plutocracy, or

THE NEW RELIGION AND THE OLD

Democracy, by Church, or Press, or Parliament. To the misgovernors and misleaders of the people the new Labour Party is an insignificant mob of ignorant men, led by a few self-seeking demagogues; to the Tories it is a mere effervescence of malcontent Radicals and windy Socialists; to the Liberals it is a "Tory dodge." To those who are in the party, and have helped to make it, it is a vast and increasing army of educated, alert, and resolute reformers, who can neither be intimidated, nor cajoled, nor bribed to turn aside from the task they have undertaken—the task of securing to the British people the possession, control, and enjoyment of their own country and their own lives.

Ten years ago there were not five hundred Socialists in Manchester. Now there must be thirty thousand. Two years ago Socialism was despised and rejected of men. Now it is on all lips and pens. It is written about, argued about, spoken about, and preached about. It is the foremost topic of discussion the country through. It is even recognised and sometimes acknowledged by its opponents as a thing not wholly dependent upon madness or dishonesty for its inculcation, nor upon bombs and bludgeons for its accomplishment. It has passed through the stages of contempt and vilification, and has entered the stage of discussion. It has a literature of its own, and a Press of its own. The *Clarion,* which is the first Socialist paper that ever paid its way in this country, has a circulation of nearly 50,000.

So much for the New Party: now of the new religion. Whence came it? What is it? If you asked a London Socialist for the origin of the new movement he would refer you to Karl Marx and other German Socialists. But so far as our northern people are concerned I am convinced that beyond the mere outline of State Socialism Karl Marx and his countrymen have had but little influence. No; the new movement here; the new religion, which is Socialism, and something more than Socialism, is more largely the result of the labours of Darwin, Carlyle, Ruskin, Dickens, Thoreau, and Walt Whitman.

It is from these men that the North has caught the message of love and justice, of liberty and peace, of culture and simplicity, and of holiness and beauty of life. This new religion which is rousing and revivifying the North is something much higher and much greater than a wage question, an hours' question, or a franchise question, based though it be upon those things; it is something more than a mere system of scientific government, something more than an economic theory, something more even than political or industrial liberty, though it embraces all these. It is a religion of manhood and womanhood, of sweetness and of light. As John Trevor said in the *Labour Prophet:* "It has not been to a new economic theory merely that these converts have been introduced. It has been to a new life. Their eyes shine with the gladness of a new birth."

For this we are indebted to the idol-breaking of Carlyle, to the ideal-making of Ruskin, and to the trumpet-tongued proclamation by the titanic Whitman of the great message of true Democracy and the brave and sweet comradeship of the natural life—of the stainless, virile, thorough human life, lived out boldly and frankly in the open air and under the eyes of God.

Now I see the secret of the making of the best persons.
It is to grow in the open air and to eat and sleep with the earth.

To love each other as brothers and sisters, and to love the earth as the mother of us all, that is part of our new religion. Our new religion tears the old dogmas to tatters, hurls the old Baals in the dust, declares much of that which the economists call "wealth" to be the same thing that Ruskin calls "illth." Our new religion turns its back upon religious symbolisms and ceremonies and display, and teaches us that love and mercy and art are the highest forms of worship. Our new religion claims man back to freedom from commercial and industrial vassalage; tells him that he is as much a piece of Nature as the birds of the air or the lilies of the field; that he, no more than they, can be healthy or fair, nor in anywise complete without fresh air, and pure water, and sunshine, and peace; tells him that since he above all his kindred of earth and sea is endowed with spirit, so must that spirit be nourished and kept sweet by spiritual sustenance and spiritual effort, else will it inevitably become corrupt and breed disease, contagion: death.

Our new religion tells him that the body must be nourished that the soul may thrive, and that nothing which is got at the soul's expense is cheap, nor anything which is needful for the glory and uplifting of the soul dear:—

> "All parts away for the progress of souls, all religion, all solid things, arts, governments—all that was or is apparent upon this globe or any globe falls into niches and corners before the procession of souls along the grand roads of the universe."

There is no way for the body to be healthy, no room for the soul to breathe and expand, in the slums, in the factories, in the markets and exchanges, the drinking kens and casinos, the political clubs and bethels of our great industrial towns. Therefore the great industrial towns and the competitive-commercial system which produced them are anathema to us, and our religion bans them.

We all know the institutions and the ideals upon which Carlyle and Ruskin and Dickens and Thackeray poured out the vials of their irony and scorn. We all know the great Westminster windmill, where ignorant educated men grind wind with which to fill the bellies of the hapless workers. We all know how those illustrious legislators, when the people ask for bread, spend months and even years in debating as to whether or not it would be rash to offer them a stone. We all know the ragged Falstaffian army of the Press, "without drill, uniform, captaincy, or billet; with huge *over*-proportion of drummers; you would say, a regiment gone wholly to the drum, with hardly a sound musket in it." We all know the champion ineptitude, the adroitest of all political mountebanks at swallowing words and juggling figures, the "poor forked radish" who is raised upon the bucklers by the proverbial twenty-seven millions, as "the triumphant outcome of English history, and fittest man to rule over us." We all know Bobus of Houndsditch, Plugson of Undershot, and Messrs. Bounderly, Gradgrind, Podsnap and Co. We know these men, and the things they profess, and call by the names of "political economy," "practical common-sense," and "religion."

We will have no more of these Dead Sea apes nor of their heroes, nor of their creeds, nor of their aspirations. Never surely since the world went round has it harboured a race of such mean, vulgar, and impossible little infidelities as the British Snobocracy with their gospel of "enlightened selfishness."

A whole nation ordered, or rather disordered, on the supposition that if every man were free to rob and injure every other, universal peace and prosperity would be the natural outcome! A class of useless and idle superior persons consuming and wasting the wealth produced by the toilers, and calmly assuring those toilers that the more wealth is wasted the more employment will it find the poor in producing still more! A Press, ruled less by its editors than its advertisement canvassers, prating of military glory, with half the Crimean veterans in the workhouse! A Church preaching serenely of the religion of Jesus Christ, and voting in almost solid phalanx against every attempt at the practical realisation of Christ's doctrines! A populace singing "Britons never, never, never shall be slaves," yet not so much as daring to put their thoughts into words for fear lest they should lose their work! A great nation of shopkeepers who think God only good for one day in the seven; who attach a "property qualification" to all offices where brains and probity are most needed; who describe adulteration as "another form of competition;" who brazenly pretend that greed, vulgarity, injustice, and the degradation and disfigurement of the country and the people must be maintained for fear art and enterprise and literature and heroism should become extinct! These things we know well, and despise most utterly.

Well do we know the hero beloved of Brixton and Whalley Range Respectability, the "successful" man, the man who "rose from the people by his own efforts," the man who "got on." The New Party will have none of him. The New Party scoffs at and derides the cult of gig-respectability and successful calico-sizing; will pay no honour to selfishness, howsoever successful. Will dignify no self-made men; will erect no statues to Hudson, or Arkwright, or Jay Gould, or Masham. Will rather honour the giver than the getter, rather love the man-helper than the self-helper; will put the names of John Ruskin, Thomas Carlyle, Walt Whitman, and Erasmus Darwin above those of all the money-spinners, fame-winners, blood-shedders, and self-makers that ever encumbered the earth.

The New Party will not aspire to the huckster's heaven of financial success, nor deliver up its soul to escape the huckster's hell of financial failure. The New Party knows that "money never yet paid one man for service to another." It will not value love, duty, or devotion in stolen doubloons like a buccaneer, nor in scalps like a Choctaw Indian. It will spurn self-interest and crown self-sacrifice. It will ask not what a man has got, but what he has given. It will not be led by the Bishop of Manchester to give a judge a large salary for fear he should betray his trust for bribes. It will not reward its Rorke's Drift heroes by a present of a pair of regulation trousers. It will not be imbecile enough to suppose that Miltons, Stephensons, Turners, Harveys, Herschells, Darwins, Ruskins, and Florence Nightingales are to be bought in the market at current rates, and that when the supply falls below the demand, nothing is necessary but to bid higher. It will regard a man's talent as it regards the earth and sea, as the gift of God, to be used by all for the good of all. It will answer the mere commercial hero's demand for more wages: "Strong men and clever men were not sent here to enslave and plunder their weaker fellow-creatures, but to *serve* them. It is the duty of the young to wait upon the old, of the hale to nurse the sick, of the chaste to succour the frail. It is the general's prerogative to go first into danger, the captain's to be the last to leave the sinking ship. The proudest motto the proudest man can take is *Ich Dien,* 'I *serve.*'"

Contrast the new religion with the old. The old religion obeys half the command: "Thou shalt love the Lord thy God with all thy heart, and thy neighbour as thyself." It stops short before it comes to its neighbour. The new religion begins at its neighbour, though it does not necessarily end there. In place of Anglicism with its gentility, Romanism with its pomp and circumstance, and Calvinism with its fire and brimstone, it gives us a charity which "beareth all things, believeth all things, hopeth all things" of *men,* and endureth all things *for* men. It give us a charity as broad, as sweet, as merciful as Whitman's "profound lesson of reception, nor preference, nor denial," whereby "the black with his woolly head, the felon, the diseased, the illiterate person are not denied . . . none but are accepted, none but shall be dear." It gives us a hope which will not be satisfied with a "gentleman God," nor daunted by the terrors of a whitewashed devil and a burnt-out hell. It tells us that while a single English child is hungry or ignorant, a single English woman disgraced and cast out as unclean, a single Englishman denied the work he asks for, or deprived of the light he needs, or the love he desires, or the honour he deserves, there shall be no money for the conversion of the heathen abroad, nor the decoration of cathedrals at home. It tells us, in the words of Ruskin, "Whether there be one God or three, no God or ten thousand, children should be fed, and their bodies should be kept clean." It tells us, in the words of Christ, "Inasmuch as ye have not done it unto one of the least of these, ye have not done it unto Me." It will hearken to no platitudes about holiness from priests who do not pay trade-union prices:—

> "While women are weeping and children starving; while industrious men and women are herding like beasts in filthy and fever-haunted hovels, to build art-galleries and churches, town-halls and colleges, is like putting on a muslin shirt over a filthy skin, a diamond crown upon a leprous head.
>
> "The religion and the culture which demand riches and blazonry while vice and misery are at their side are like painted harlots, hiding their debaucheries with rouge, and their shame with satin and spices.
>
> "The cant and affectation of piety and culture which lisp sentiment and chant hymns in drawing-rooms and chapels while flesh and blood are perishing in the streets, and while the souls of our sisters creep shuddering to hell—this religion and this culture, these maudlin, sickening

THE NEW RELIGION AND THE OLD

things, with their poems and sonatas, their chants and benedictions, are things false and vain and nothing else but *lies*."

There can be no true culture, there can be no true art, there can be no true progress, there can be no true religion without sincerity. I have seen in Manchester a noble picture of Greek women at the fountain, hung up to instil into the minds of the citizens of that sordid, sooty, vulgar, and hideous town a love of beauty, and outside the art gallery I have seen a grey-headed old English woman staggering along, bent double under a sack of cinders.

When the Ship Canal, through mismanagement, was in financial straits, the Manchester city fathers advanced a loan of some two millions—of the ratepayers' money—because the "honour of the city was involved." Two or three years before that, when attention was called to the fact that the Manchester slums were the largest, the foulest, and the most deadly in all England, those same city fathers were afraid to incur the expense of demolishing and rebuilding them. There was much talk then of the burdens of the ratepayers, but not one word about the honour of the city. The honour of the city, it seems, is not concerned with the lives of its people.

Manchester is called a great city. It has a great population, a costly and hideous town-hall, a high death-rate, and a lord mayor. But in the eyes of the New Party Manchester is in nowise great.

A great city is that which has the greatest men and women.
If it be a few ragged huts, it is still the greatest city in the whole world.
The place where a great city stands is not the place of stretched wharves, docks, manufactures, deposits of produce merely.
Nor the place of ceaseless salutes of new-comers, or the anchor-lifters of the departing.
Nor the place of the tallest and costliest buildings, or shops selling goods from the rest of the earth.
Nor the place of the best libraries and schools, nor the place where money is plentiest.
Nor the place of the most numerous population.
Where the city stands with the brawniest breed of orators and bards.
Where the city stands that is beloved by these, and loves them in return, and understands them.
Where no monuments exist to heroes but in the common words and deeds.
Where thrift is in its place, and prudence is in its place.
Where the men and women think lightly of the laws.
Where the slave ceases, and the master of slaves ceases.
Where the populace rise at once against the never-ending audacity of elected persons.
Where fierce men and women pour forth as the sea to the whistle of death pours its sweeping and unrippled waves.

THE NEW RELIGION

Where outside authority enters always after the precedence of inside authority.

Where the citizen is always the head and ideal, and president, mayor, governor, and what not are agents for pay.

Where children are taught to be lords to themselves, and to depend on themselves.

Where equanimity is illustrated in affairs.

Where speculations on the soul are encouraged.

Where women walk in public processions in the streets the same as the men.

Where they enter the public assembly, and take places the same as the men.

Where the city of the faithfulest friends stands.

Where the city of the cleanliness of the sexes stands.

Where the city of the healthiest fathers stands.

Where the city of the best-bodied mothers stands.

There the great city stands.

And Manchester does not stand there, nor does any city in all England, for great cities we have none.

A gulf parts the masses from the classes. This gulf is the gulf of ignorance, and only knowledge can bridge it. It is astounding, the utter ignorance of the lives of the poor, the complete misapprehension of their conditions, their trials, their hopes, and their ideals, which the rich manifest in their words and deeds. For some years past I have been engaged in helping to make and to preach our new religion. Yet, not long ago, a well-meaning clergyman, of Liberal views, who had just read one of my books, came to see me, and asked, "Who is it you are writing for? What is it you complain of? Are you thinking of the residuum—the submerged tenth?"

This from a Manchester clergyman, a man professing great interest in the workers, a man who sat at the time he spoke within a stone's-throw of the Manchester slums.

He thought the workers, except the idle and incapable, were pretty well off, and that poverty would cure itself. He held the notion, common to his class, that the question is simply one of wages. He thought the colliers and the cotton operatives had a good deal to be thankful for. Have they not a living wage?

Yes, they have a living wage. But have we forgotten the long and deadly struggles they were forced to undertake to keep that wage? and is there nothing to be given to the workers but *wages*?

Even if we accept wages as the one thing needful; even if we go as far as the man in "Our Mutual Friend," and consider the labour question simply as "a question of so many pounds of beef and so many pints of porter," can we say that the masses have as much beef and porter as they need?

What of the wages of the tailors, the shirtmakers, the matchmakers, the dockers, the sailors, the railway men, the farm-labourers, the lead-workers, the

THE NEW RELIGION AND THE OLD

slipper-makers, the shop-assistants, the domestic servants, the canal-boat workers, the chain and nail makers, the old soldiers, the match-hawkers, the feather-dressers, the silk-dyers, the artificial flower makers, the fishermen, the costers, the news-boys? What of *all* the workers' *wives?*

But wages are not all. We have to ask how hard and how long these people work; we have to ask what their homes are like, what health they enjoy, how much rest and culture, and fresh air, and wholesome recreation they obtain.

And we find that their homes are dismal and mean, that their labour is long and hard, that they have scarcely any fresh air, or sweet rest, or pure amusements.

And we find that the death-rates are terribly high, that the duration of life is short, that the bill of health is bad. In one district of Manchester a committee of ladies found that 60 per cent. of the population were sick. In some of the slum districts, Dr. Thresh found death-rates of 75 and 90 in the thousand, as against rates of 9 and 16 in the suburbs. In some of the London "model" blocks, Mr. Williams says the death-rate is over 40 and the density over 3,000 to the acre.

Consider again the dangers, the hardships, and the sickness incidental to the work of the sailors, the fishermen, the colliers, the chemical workers, match-makers. Go amongst the cotton operatives and *see* how factory work in factory towns deteriorates the people mentally and physically.

No; it is not of the submerged tenth we are thinking only. It is of the English people. Over all is the shadow of fear—the fear of failure and the workhouse. But I could not in a volume so much as enumerate all the evils of our present English civilisation. There is a whole library of blue-books filled with the statistics and the evidence of the hardships and labours and sufferings of those who create the wealth of this rich miserable country. Not the least of the wrongs of the poor is one of which blue-books take no cognisance, the denial to the best brain and bone and sinew of the nation of the respect due to all men by virtue of their manhood. Our workers are honoured and loved too little; they are governed, and patronised, and lectured overmuch.

What, then, do we demand? We demand that national co-operation shall displace individual competition; we demand to this end the nationalisation of the land and all the instruments of production and of distribution. We demand that our industry be organised, and that production be for use and not for sale.

We demand that our agricultural resources be developed because agriculture is more pleasant and more healthy than manufactures, because in an agricultural nation the towns would be cleaner and handsomer and more wholesome, and because the destruction of our agriculture renders us dependent upon foreign countries for our food, and so exposes us to certain defeat and ruin in case of war.

At present the people of the North have not only ceased to possess their own country, they have ceased to know it. They never see England. They see only brick walls, chimneys, smoke, and cinder-heaps. They are unable to so much as conceive the fairness and sweetness of England. They are strangers and aliens in their own land.

THE NEW RELIGION

We say, then, give the English people their own country. But we do not stop there. We demand that they shall not only be made the free possessors of their own country, but also of their own earnings, of their own lives, of their own bodies and their own souls.

We regard work as a means and not as an end: men should work to live, they should not live to work. We demand for the people as much leisure, as full and sweet and noble a life as the world can give. We want labour to have its own; not merely the price of its sweat, but its due meed of love and honour. In our eyes the lifeboat-man is a hero, and the African machine-gun soldier "opening up new markets" is a brigand and assassin. In our eyes the skilled craftsman or farmer is a man of learning, and the Greek-crammed pedant is a dunce. In our eyes an apple orchard is more beautiful and precious than a ducal palace. In our eyes the worth of a nation depends on the worthiness of its people's lives, and not upon the balance at the national bank. We want a religion of justice and charity and love. We do not want pious cant on Sundays and chicanery and lust all the rest of the week. We want a God who is fit for business, and a business that is worthy of God. We want the code of private honour and the bonds of domestic love carried into all our public affairs. We want a realisation, in fact, of the brotherhood we hear so much about in theory. Because we know the meaning of heredity and environment, because we believe that men are what their surroundings make them, we want justice for all, love for all, mercy for all.

We are the party of humanity. Our religion is the religion of humanity. "The black with his woolly head, the felon, the diseased, the illiterate are not denied." The thief on the Cross, the Magdalen at the well are our brother and our sister; bone of our bone, flesh of our flesh. If you persecute these, if you insult them, if you rob them, you rob and persecute and insult us. Without the love, and the counsel, and the aid of our fellow-creatures, the best of us were savages—little more than brutes. What we are they made us, what we know they taught us, what we have they gave us; we are theirs, and they are ours, and for them we will speak and write, with all the power God gave us.

For me, I am of the people, and I know them. I know them to be capable of the best. I speak for them in the words of Milton—

> "Lords and Commons of England, consider what nation it is whereof ye are, and whereof ye are the governors; a nation not slow and dull, but of a quick, ingenious, and piercing spirit; acute to invent, subtle and sinewy to discourse, not beneath the reach of any point, the highest that human capacity can soar to."

I speak for them in the words of Christ—

> "Inasmuch as ye have not done it unto one of the least of these, ye have not done it unto Me."

THE NEW RELIGION AND THE OLD

I speak for them of my own knowledge, for the brave and clever and good people who have been so kind, and so faithful, and so affectionate to me; and I say that they are so capable and so worthy that the greatest men and noblest women of our time are only indications of the height which the masses may reach and surpass.

Just as by cultivation the acrid wild crab has been developed into the beautiful and luscious apple, may the unripe, ill-fed, neglected wild fruits of the fields and slums be developed into pure and noble and beautiful men and women.

And the means to this end are justice and freedom, and peace and culture, and love and honour from man to man.

Some day, near or far, "the slave shall cease, and the master of slaves shall cease," the hideous mirk and squalor of our modern cities shall be swept away, and in the flower-starred meadows, under the sweet blue northern sky, the men and the maids of merrie England shall dance and sing, and "think lightly of the laws."

God bless them, say I, these our children. We shall rest none the less peacefully under their glancing feet because we have helped to make them happy.

ROBERT BLATCHFORD.

Part 8

GENDER, SEXUALITY AND FAMILY RELATIONS

26

WOMEN AND THE FACTORY ACTS[1]
(LONDON: FABIAN SOCIETY, 1896),
3–15.

Beatrice Webb

[As a social reformer and prominent Fabian socialist, Beatrice Webb made the case in her pamphlet *Women and the Factory Acts* of 1896 for protective legislation exclusively on behalf of women. Such legislation would regulate the working hours and conditions of women in factories. Her case included carefully-crafted responses, supported by characteristically detailed research, to arguments that such legislation and regulation would be detrimental to the cause of women at work (Webb, B. 1896).

Contributing to a debate in the late nineteenth century among campaigners for women's political and social rights, Webb was uninterested in arguments for women's suffrage, which she actively opposed in 1889 by signing the Appeal Against Female Suffrage. The decade of slow progress which followed led her to declare to Millicent Fawcett – president of the National Union of Women's Suffrage Society (NUWSS) – that although she had opposed the abstract right to vote there was now a distinct possibility of gaining social improvements which would make having the vote worthwhile (Caine 1982, 33–35). Having in the 1890s become a socialist after reading and listening to Sidney Webb (who she married in 1892), Beatrice was convinced liberals had overestimated the adequacy of political reform. Capitalism had brought about social problems resolvable only by fundamental transformation of the socio-economic system. Individualism therefore needed to give way to the greater good of society. It was from this position that she demanded protective legislation for women in the form of factory regulation.

In her pamphlet Webb (styling herself Mrs Sidney Webb) challenged the view of Fawcett and other middle-class activists who demanded suffrage but opposed protective legislation. These activists argued that the legislation and regulation would be detrimental to the cause of women to be treated as equals and thus block their professional independence (Livesey 2004). The Women's Trade Union League (WTUL), by way of contrast, argued for such legislation. Webb was thus closer to the WTUL than the middle-class activism of the NUWSS (Caine 1982, 39; Livesey 2004, 239). In her view, protective legislation would provide women with the foundation on which trade union organisation could bring them further gains.]

THE discussions on the Factory Act of 1895[2] raised once more all the old arguments about Factory legislation, but with a significant new cleavage. This time legal regulation was demanded, not only by all the organizations of working women whose labor was affected,[3] but also by, practically, all those actively engaged in Factory Act administration. The four women Factory Inspectors unanimously confirmed the opinion of their male colleagues. Of all the classes[4] having any practical experience of Factory legislation, only one—that of the employers—was ranged against the Bill, and that not unanimously. But the employers had the powerful aid of most of the able and devoted ladies who have usually led the cause of women's enfranchisement, and whose strong theoretic objection to Factory legislation caused many of the most important clauses in the Bill to be rejected.

The ladies who resist further legal regulation of women's labor usually declare that their objection is to special legislation applying only to women. They regard it as unfair, they say, that women's power to compete in the labor market should be "hampered" by any regulation from which men are free. Any such restriction, they assert, results in the lowering of women's wages, and in diminishing the aggregate demand for women's work. I shall, later on, have something to say about this assumed competition between men and women. But it is curious that we seldom find these objectors to unequal laws coming forward to support even those regulations which apply equally to men and to women. Nearly all the clauses of the 1895 Bill, for instance, and nearly all the amendments proposed to it, applied to men and women alike. The sanitary provisions; the regulations about fire-escapes; the pre-eminently important clause making the giver-out of work responsible for the places where his work is done; the power to regulate unhealthy trades or processes: all these made no distinction between the sexes. Yet the ladies who declared that they objected only to inequality of legislation, gave no effective aid to the impartial sections of the Bill. If we believe that legal regulation of the hours and conditions of labor is found, in practice, to promote the economic independence and positively to add to the industrial efficiency of the workers concerned, why should we not help women workers in unregulated trades to gain this superior economic position, even if Parliament persists in denying it to the men? It is clear that there lurks behind the objection of inequality an inveterate scepticism as to the positive advantages of Factory legislation. Indeed, the most energetic and prominent opponents of women's Factory Acts openly avow as much. Mrs. Henry Fawcett and Miss Ada Heather-Bigg, for instance, usually speak of legal regulation as something which, whether for men or for women, decreases personal freedom, diminishes productive capacity, and handicaps the worker in the struggle for existence. I need not recall how firmly and conscientiously this view was held by men like Nassau Senior and John Bright in the generation gone by. To-day there are evidently many ladies of education and position superstitiously clinging to the same belief. Therefore before discussing whether any particular Factory Act is good for women or not, we had better make up our minds on the general question. Does State regulation of the hours and conditions of labor increase or decrease the economic independence and industrial efficiency of the workers concerned?

Now those who object to further Factory legislation are right in asserting that the issue cannot be decided by harrowing accounts of factory tyranny, or particular cases of cruelty or hardship. I shall not trouble you with the long list of calamities in the unregulated trades, on which the official report of the Chief Inspector of Factories lays so much stress—the constitutions ruined by long hours in dressmakers' workrooms or insanitary laundries, the undermining of family life by the degradation of the home into a workshop, the diseases and deaths caused by white lead and lucifer matches. And, I hope, no one in the discussion will think it any argument against Factory Acts that some poor widow might find it more difficult to get bread for her starving children if she were forbidden to work at the white lead factory; that some sick man's daughter would not be allowed to earn the doctor's fee by taking extra work home after her factory day; or that some struggling laundress might find it impossible to make a living if she could not employ her girls for unlimited hours. Either way there must be hard cases, and individual grievances. The question is whether, taking the whole population and all considerations into account, the evils will be greater under regulation or under free competition.

Let us concede to the opponents of Factory legislation that we must do nothing to impair or limit the growing sense of personal responsibility in women; that we must seek, in every way, to increase their economic independence, and their efficiency as workers and citizens, not less than as wives and mothers; and that the best and only real means of attaining these ends is the safeguarding and promoting of women's freedom. The only question at issue is how best to obtain this freedom. When we are concerned with the propertied classes—when, for instance, it is sought to open up to women higher education or the learned professions—it is easy to see that freedom is secured by abolishing restrictions. But when we come to the relations between capital and labor an entirely new set of considerations come into play. In the life of the wage-earning class, absence of regulation does not mean personal freedom. Fifty years' experience shows that Factory legislation, far from diminishing individual liberty, greatly increases the personal freedom of the workers who are subject to it. Everyone knows that the Lancashire woman weaver, whose hours of labor and conditions of work are rigidly fixed by law, enjoys, for this very reason, more personal liberty than the unregulated laundry-woman in Notting Hill. She is not only a more efficient producer, and more capable of associating with her fellows in Trade Unions, Friendly Societies, and Co-operative Stores, but an enormously more independent and self-reliant citizen. It is the law, in fact, which is the mother of freedom.[5]

GENDER, SEXUALITY AND FAMILY RELATIONS

To understand the position fully we must realize how our long series of Factory Acts, Truck Acts, Mines Regulation Acts, and Shop Hours Acts, have come into existence.[6] All these are based upon a fundamental economic fact which has slowly forced itself into the minds of economists and social reformers—the essential and permanent inequality between the individual wage-earner and the capitalist employer. When the conditions of the workman's life are settled, without any collective regulation, by absolutely free contract between man and man, the workman's freedom is entirely delusive. Where he bargains, he bargains at a hopeless disadvantage; and on many of the points most vital to his health, efficiency, and personal comfort, he is unable to bargain at all.

Let us see how this comes about. I will not, to prove my point, take a time of bad trade, when five workmen are competing for one situation: I will assume that the whole labor market is in a state of perfect equilibrium; that there is only one workman wanting work, and only one situation vacant. Now, watch the process of bargaining between the employer and the workman. If the capitalist refuses to accept the workman's terms, he will, no doubt, suffer some inconvenience as an employer. To fulfil his orders he will have to "speed up" some of his machinery, or insist on his workpeople working longer hours. Failing these expedients he may have to delay the delivery of his goods, and may even find his profits, at the end of the year, fractionally less than before. But, meanwhile, he goes on eating and drinking, his wife and family go on living, just as before. His physical comfort is not affected: he can afford to wait until the laborer comes back in a humbler frame of mind. And that is just what the laborer must presently do. For he, meanwhile, has lost his day. His very subsistence depends on his promptly coming to an agreement. If he stands out, he has no money to meet his weekly rent, or to buy food for his family. If he is obstinate, consumption of his little hoard, or the pawning of his furniture, may put off the catastrophe; but sooner or later slow starvation forces him to come to terms. This is no real freedom of contract. The alternative on one side is inconvenience; on the other it is starvation. I need not remind you that the fallacy of free and equal contract between capital and labor has been long since given up by the economists. If you read, for instance, our foremost economist, Professor Marshall, he will tell you that the employer is a combination in himself, with whom the individual wage-earner is seriously at a disadvantage.[7] No competent authority would now deny that unfettered individual bargaining between capitalist and workman inevitably tends to result, not in the highest wage that the industry can afford, but in the lowest on which the workman and his family can subsist.

Here, then, we have the first justification for something more than unfettered bargaining between man and man. But this is not all. We often forget that the contract between employer and workman is to the employer simply a question of the number of shillings to be paid at the end of the week. To the workman it is much more than that. The wage-earner does not, like the shopkeeper, merely sell a piece of goods which is carried away. It is his whole life which, for the stated term, he places at the disposal of his employer. What hours he shall work, when and where he shall get his meals, the sanitary conditions of his employment, the safety of the machinery, the atmosphere and temperature to which he is subjected, the fatigue or strains which he endures, the risks of accident or disease which he has to incur: all these are involved in the workman's contract and not in his employer's. Yet about the majority of these vital conditions he cannot bargain at all. Imagine a weaver, before accepting employment in a Lancashire cotton mill, examining the quantity of steam in the shed, the strength of the shuttle-guards, and the soundness of the belts of the shafting; an engineer prying into the security of the hoists and cranes, or the safety of the lathes and steam hammers among which he must move; a dressmaker's assistant computing the cubic space which will be her share of the workroom, criticising the ventilation, warmth and lighting, or examining the decency of the sanitary accommodation; think of the woman who wants a job at the white lead works, testing the poisonous influence in the particular process employed, and reckoning, in terms of shillings and pence, the exact degree of injury to her health which she is consenting to incur. No sensible person can really assert that the individual operative seeking a job has either the knowledge or the opportunity to ascertain what the conditions are, or to determine what they should be, even if he could bargain about them at all. On these matters, at any rate, there can be no question of free contract. We may, indeed, leave them to be determined by the employer himself: that is to say, by the competition between employers as to who can most reduce the expenses of production. What this means, we know from the ghastly experience of the early factory system; when whole generations of our factory hands were stunted and maimed, diseased and demoralized, hurried into early graves by the progressive degeneration of conditions imposed on even the best employers by the reckless competition of the worst.[8] The only alternative to this disastrous reliance on a delusive freedom is the settlement, by expert advice, of standard conditions of health, safety, and convenience, to which all employers, good and bad alike, are compelled by law to conform.

We see, therefore, that many of the most vital conditions of employment cannot be made subjects of bargain at all, whilst, even about wages, unfettered freedom of individual bargaining places the operative at a serious disadvantage. But there is one important matter which stands midway between the two. In manual work it is seldom that an individual can bargain as to when he shall begin or leave off work. In the most typical processes of modern industry, individual choice as to the length of the working day is absolutely impossible. The most philanthropic or easy-going builder or manufacturer could not possibly make separate arrangements with each of his workpeople as to the times at which they should come and go, the particular intervals for meals, or what days they should take as holidays. Directly we get machinery and division of labor—directly we have more than one person working at the production of an article, all the persons concerned are compelled, by the very nature of their occupation, to work in concert. This means that there must be one uniform rule for the whole establishment. Every workman must come when the bell rings, and stay as long as the works are open; individual choice there can be none. The hours at which the bell shall ring must either be left to the autocratic decision of the employer, or else settled by collective regulation to which every workman is compelled to conform.

We can now understand why it is that the representative wage-earner declares, to the astonishment of the professional man or the journalist, that a rule fixing his hours of labor, or defining conditions of sanitation or safety, is not a restriction on his personal liberty. The workman knows by experience that there is no question of his ever settling these matters for himself. There are only two alternatives to their decision by the employer. One is their settlement by a conference between the representatives of the employers and the representatives of the organized workmen; both sides, of course, acting through their expert salaried officials. This is the method of collective bargaining—in short, Trade Unionism. The other method is the settlement by the whole community of questions which affect the health and industrial efficiency of the race. Then we get expert investigation as to the proper conditions, which are enforced by laws binding on all. This is the method of Factory legislation.

No greater mistake can be made in comparing these two methods than to assume that Trade Unionism sacrifices the imaginary personal liberty of the individual workman to make his own bargain any less than Factory legislation. Take, for instance, the Oldham weaver. Here we see both methods at work. The rate of wages is determined entirely by Trade Unionism; the hours of labor and sanitary conditions are fixed by law. But there is no more individual choice in the one than in the other. I do not hesitate to say, indeed, that an employer or a weaver would find it easier and less costly to defy the Factory Inspector and work overtime, than to defy the Trade Union official and evade the Piecework List of Prices. Or, take the Northumberland coal-miner. He, for particular reasons, objects to have his hours fixed by law. But we need be under no delusion as to his views on "personal liberty." If any inhabitant of a Northumberland village offered to hew coal below the rate fixed by the Trade Union for the whole county, or if he proposed to work two shifts instead of one, the whole village would rise against him, and he would find it absolutely impossible to descend the mine, or to get work anywhere in the county. It is not my business to-day either to defend or to criticise Trade Union action. But we cannot understand this question without fully realizing that Trade Unionism, in substituting for the despotism of the employer or the individual choice of the workman a general rule binding on all concerned, is just as much founded on the subordination of the individual whim to the deliberate decision of the majority as any law can be. If I had the time I could show you, by elaborate technical arguments, how the one method of over-riding the individual will is best for certain matters, and the other method more expedient in regard to other matters. Rates of wages, for instance, are best settled by collective bargaining; and sanitation, safety, and the prevention of overwork by fixed hours of labor are best secured by legal enactment.

But this question of the relative advantages of legislative regulation and Trade Unionism has unhappily no bearing on the women employed in the sweated industries. Before we can have Trade Union regulation we must build up strong

Trade Unions; and the unfortunate women workers whose overtime it was proposed to curtail, and whose health and vigor it was proposed to improve, by Mr. Asquith's Bill of 1895, are without any effective organization. The Lancashire women weavers and card-room hands were in the same predicament before the Factory Acts. It was only when they were saved from the unhealthy conditions and excessive hours of the cotton mills of that time that they began to combine in Trade Unions, to join Friendly Societies, and to form Co-operative Stores. This, too, is the constant experience of the men's trades. Where effective Trade Unions have grown up, legal protection of one kind or another has led the way.[9] And it is easy to see why this is so. Before wage-earners can exercise the intelligence, the deliberation, and the self-denial that are necessary for Trade Unionism, they must enjoy a certain standard of physical health, a certain surplus of energy, and a reasonable amount of leisure. It is cruel mockery to preach Trade Unionism, and Trade Unionism alone, to the sempstress sewing day and night in her garret for a bare subsistence; to the laundrywoman standing at the tub eighteen hours at a stretch; or to the woman whose health is undermined with "Wrist-drop," "Potter's-rot," or "Phossy-jaw." If we are really in earnest in wanting Trade Unions for women, the way is unmistakable. If we wish to see the capacity for organization, the self-reliance, and the personal independence of the Lancashire cotton weaver spread to other trades, we must give the women workers in these trades the same legal fixing of hours, the same effective prohibition of overtime, the same legal security against accident and disease, the same legal standard of sanitation and health as is now enjoyed by the women in the Lancashire cotton mills.

So much for the general theory of Factory legislation. We have still to deal with the special arguments directed against those clauses of the 1895 Bill which sought to restrict the overtime worked by women in the sweated trades. If, however, we have fully realized the advantages, both direct and indirect, which the workers obtain from the legal regulation of their labor, we shall regard with a good deal of suspicion any special arguments alleged in opposition to any particular Factory Acts. The student of past Factory agitations sees the same old bogeys come up again and again. Among these bogeys the commonest and most obstructive has always been that of foreign competition, that is to say, the risk that the regulated workers will be supplanted by "free labor"—whether of other countries or of other classes at home. At every step forward in legal regulation the miner and the textile worker have been solemnly warned that the result of any raising of their standard of sanitation, safety, education or leisure would be the transference of British capital to China or Peru. And to my mind it is only another form of the same fallacy when capitalists' wives and daughters seek to alarm working women by prophesying, as the result of further Factory legislation, the dismissal of women and girls from employment, and their replacement by men. The opposition to Factory legislation never comes from workers who have any practical experience of it. Every existing organization of working women in the kingdom has declared itself in favor of Factory legislation. Unfortunately, working women have less power to obtain legislation than middle-class women have to obstruct it.

GENDER, SEXUALITY AND FAMILY RELATIONS

Unfortunately, too, not a few middle-class women have allowed their democratic sympathies and Collectivist principles to be overborne by this fear of handicapping women in their struggle for employment. Let us, therefore, consider, as seriously as we can, this terror lest the capitalist employing women and girls at from five to twelve shillings a week, should, on the passage of a new Factory Act, replace them by men at twenty or thirty shillings.

First let us realize the exact amount of the inequality between the sexes in our Factory Acts. All the regulations with respect to safety, sanitation, employers' liability, and age apply to men and women alike. The only restriction of any importance in our Labor Code which bears unequally on men and women is that relating to the hours of labor.[10] Up to now there has been sufficient influence among the employers, and sufficient prejudice and misunderstanding among legislators, to prevent them expressly legislating, in so many words, about the hours of labor of adult men. That better counsels are now prevailing is shown by the fact that Parliament in 1892 gave power to the Board of Trade to prevent excessive hours of work among railway servants, and that the Home Secretary has now a similar power in respect of any kind of manual labor which is injurious to health or dangerous to life and limb. I need hardly say that I am heartily in favor of regulating, by law, the hours of adult men, wherever and whenever possible.[11] But although the prejudice is breaking down, it is not likely that the men in the great staple industries will be able to secure for themselves the same legal limitation of hours and prohibition of overtime that the women in the textile manufactures have enjoyed for nearly forty years. And thus it comes about that some of the most practical proposals for raising the condition of the women in the sweated trades must take the form of regulations applying to women only.

It is frequently asserted as self-evident that any special limitation of women's labor must militate against their employment. If employers are not allowed to make their women work overtime, or during the night, they will, it is said, inevitably prefer to have men. Thus, it is urged, any extension of Factory legislation to trades at present unregulated must diminish the demand for women's labor. But this conclusion, which seems so obvious, really rests on a series of assumptions which are not borne out by facts.

The first assumption is, that in British industry to-day, men and women are actively competing for the same employment. I doubt whether any one here has any conception of the infinitesimal extent to which this is true. We are so accustomed, in the middle-class, to see men and women engaged in identical work, as teachers, journalists, authors, painters, sculptors, comedians, singers, musicians, medical practitioners, clerks, or what not, that we almost inevitably assume the same state of things to exist in manual labor and manufacturing industry. But this is very far from being the case. To begin with, in over nine-tenths of the industrial field there is no such thing as competition between men and women: the men do one thing, and the women do another. There is no more chance of our having our houses built by women than of our getting our floors scrubbed by men. And even in those industries which employ both men and women, we find them sharply

274

divided in different departments, working at different processes, and performing different operations. In the tailoring trade, for instance, it is often assumed that men and women are competitors. But in a detailed investigation of that trade I discovered that men were working at entirely separate branches to those pursued by the women. And when my husband, as an economist, lately tried to demonstrate the oft-repeated statement that women are paid at a lower rate than men, he found it very difficult to discover any trade whatever in which men and women did the same work.[12] As a matter of fact, the employment of men or women in any particular industry is almost always determined by the character of the process. In many cases the physical strength or endurance required, or the exposure involved, puts the work absolutely out of the power of the average woman. No law has hindered employers from engaging women as blacksmiths, steel-smelters, masons, or omnibus-drivers. The great mass of extractive, constructive, and transport industries must always fall to men. On the other hand, the women of the wage-earning class have hitherto been distinguished by certain qualities not possessed by the average working man. For good or for evil they eat little, despise tobacco, and seldom get drunk; they rarely strike or disobey orders; and they are in many other ways easier for an employer to deal with. Hence, where women can really perform a given task with anything like the efficiency of a man, they have, owing to their lower standard of expenditure, a far better chance than the man of getting work. The men, in short, enjoy what may be called a "rent" of superior strength and endurance; the women, on their side, in this preference for certain employments, what may be called a "rent" of abstemiousness.

I do not wish to imply that there are absolutely no cases in British industry in which men and women are really competing with each other. It is, I believe, easy to pick out an instance here and there in which it might be prophesied that the removal of an existing legal restriction might, in the first instance, lead to some women being taken on in place of men. In the book and printing trade of London, for instance, it has been said that if women were allowed by law to work all through the night, a certain number of exceptionally strong women might oust some men in book-folding and even in compositors' work.[13] We must not overlook these cases; but we must learn to view them in their proper proportion to the whole field of industry. It would clearly be a calamity to the cause of women's advancement if we were to sacrifice the personal liberty and economic independence of three or four millions of wage-earning women in order to enable a few hundreds or a few thousands to supplant men in certain minor spheres of industry.[14]

The second assumption is, that in the few cases in which men and women may be supposed really to compete with each other for employment, the effect of any regulation of women's hours is pure loss to them, and wholly in favor of their assumed competitors who are unrestricted. This, I believe, is simply a delusion. Any investigator of women's work knows full well that what most handicaps women is their general deficiency in industrial capacity and technical skill. Where the average woman fails is in being too much of an amateur at her work, and too little of a professional. Doubtless it may be said that the men are to blame here: it

GENDER, SEXUALITY AND FAMILY RELATIONS

is they who induce women to marry, and thus divert their attention from professional life. But though we cannot cut at the root of this, by insisting, as I once heard it gravely suggested, on "three generations of unmarried women," we can do a great deal to encourage the growth of professional spirit and professional capacity among women workers, if we take care to develop our industrial organization along the proper lines. The first necessity is the exclusion of illegitimate competitors. The real enemies of the working woman are not the men, who always insist on higher wages, but the "amateurs" of her own sex. So long as there are women, married or unmarried, eager and able to take work home, and do it in the intervals of another profession, domestic service, we shall never disentangle ourselves from that vicious circle in which low wages lead to bad work, and bad work compels low wages. The one practical remedy for this disastrous competition is the extension of Factory legislation, with its strict limitation of women's hours, to all manufacturing work wherever carried on.[15] It is no mere coincidence that the only great industry in which women get the same wages as men—Lancashire cotton weaving—is the one in which precise legal regulation of women's hours has involved the absolute exclusion of the casual amateur. No woman will be taken on at a cotton mill unless she is prepared to work the full factory hours, to come regularly every day, and put her whole energy into her task. In a Lancashire village a woman must decide whether she will earn her maintenance by working in the mill or by tending the home: there is no "betwixt and between." The result is a class of women wage-earners who are capable of working side by side with men at identical tasks; who can earn as high wages as their male competitors; who display the same economic independence and professional spirit as the men; and who are, in fact, in technical skill and industrial capacity, far in advance of any other class of women workers in the kingdom.[16] If we want to bring the women wage-earners all over England up to the level of the Lancashire cotton weavers, we must subject them to the same conditions of exclusively professional work.

There is another way in which the extension of the Factory Acts to the unregulated trades is certain to advance women's industrial position. We have said that the choice of men or women as workers is really determined by the nature of the industrial process. Now these processes are constantly changing; new inventions bring in new methods of work, and often new kinds of machinery. This usually means an entire revolution in the character of the labor required. What to-day needs the physical strength or the life-long apprenticeship of the skilled handicraftsman may, to-morrow, by a new machine, or the use of motive power, be suddenly brought within the capacity of the nimble fingers of a girl from the Board School. It is in this substitution of one process for another that we discover the real competition between different classes or different sexes in industry. The tailoring trade, for instance, once carried on exclusively by skilled handicraftsmen, is now rapidly slipping out of their hands. But it is not the woman free to work all the night in her garret who is ousting the male operative. What is happening is that the individual tailor, man or woman, is being superseded by the great clothing factories established at Leeds,[17] or elsewhere, where highly-paid skilled

276

WOMEN AND THE FACTORY ACTS

designers prepare work for the costly "cutting-out" guillotines, and hundreds of women guide the pieces through self-acting sewing and button-holing machines, to be finally pressed by steam power into the "smart new suit" of the City clerk.

Now this evolution of industry leads inevitably to an increased demand for women's labor. Immediately we substitute the factory, with its use of steam power, and production on a large scale, for the sweater's den or the domestic workshop, we get that division of labor and application of machinery which is directly favorable to the employment of women. It is to "the factory system, and the consequent growth of the ready-made trade," declares Miss Collet, that must "be traced the great increase in the number of girls employed in the tailoring trade."[18] The same change is going on in other occupations. Miss Collet notices that the employment of female labor has specially increased in the great industry of boot and shoe making.[19] But, as in the analogous case of the tailoring trade, the increase has not been in the number of the unregulated women workers in the sweaters' dens. Formerly we had a man working in his own room, and employing his wife and daughter to help him at all hours. Some people might have argued that anything which struck at the root of this system would deprive women of employment. As a matter of fact, the result has been, by division of labor in the rapidly growing great boot factories, to substitute for these few hundreds of unpaid assistants, many thousands of independent and regularly employed women operatives. For we must remember that when these changes take place, they take place on a large scale. Whilst the Society for Promoting the Employment of Women is proud to secure new openings for a few scores or a few hundreds, the industrial evolution which I have described has been silently absorbing, in one trade or another, hundreds of thousands of women of all classes. It is therefore infinitely more important for the friends of women's employment to enquire how an extension of the Factory Acts would influence our progress towards the factory system, than how it would affect, say, the few hundred women who might be engaged in night-work book-folding.

If there is one result more clearly proved by experience than another, it is that the legal fixing of definite hours of labor, the requirement of a high standard of sanitation, and the prohibition of overtime, all favor production on a large scale. It has been the employers' constant complaint against the Factory Acts that they inevitably tend to squeeze out the "little master." The evidence taken by the House of Lords' Committee on Sweating conclusively proved that any effective application of factory regulations to the workplaces of East London and the Black Country would quickly lead to the substitution of large factories. Factory legislation is, therefore, strenuously resisted by the "little masters," who carry on their workshops in the back slums; by the Jewish and other sub-contractors who make a living by organizing helpless labor; and by all who cherish a sentimental yearning for domestic industries. But this sentiment must not blind us to the arithmetical fact that it is the factory system which provides the great market for women's labor. Those well-meaning ladies who, by resisting the extension of Factory legislation, are keeping alive the domestic workshop and the sweaters' den, are thus positively curtailing the sphere of women's employment. The "freedom" of the poor widow to work, in her own bedroom, "all the hours that God made"; and the wife's privilege to supplement a drunken husband's wages by doing work at her own fireside, are, in sober truth, being purchased at the price of the exclusion from regular factory employment of thousands of "independent women."

We can now sum up the whole argument. The case for Factory legislation does not rest on harrowing tales of exceptional tyranny, though plenty of these can be furnished in support of it. It is based on the broad facts of the capitalist system, and the inevitable results of the Industrial Revolution.[20] A whole century of experience proves that where the conditions of the wage-earner's life are left to be settled by "free competition" and individual bargaining between master and man, the worker's "freedom" is delusive. Where he bargains, he bargains at a serious disadvantage, and on many of the points most vital to himself and to the community he cannot bargain at all. The common middle-class objection to Factory legislation—that it interferes with the individual liberty of the operative—springs from ignorance of the economic position of the wage-earner. Far from diminishing personal freedom, Factory legislation positively increases the individual liberty and economic independence of the workers subject to it. No one who knows what life is among the people in Lancashire textile villages on the one hand, and among the East End or Black Country unregulated trades on the other, can ever doubt this.

All these general considerations apply more forcibly to women wage-earners than to men. Women are far more helpless in the labor market, and much less able to enforce their own common rule by Trade Unionism. The only chance of getting Trade Unions among women workers lies through the Factory Acts. We have before us nearly forty years' actual experience of the precise limitation of hours and the absolute prohibition of overtime for women workers in the cotton manufacture; and they teach us nothing that justifies us in refusing to extend the like protection to the women slaving for irregular and excessive hours in laundries, dressmakers' workrooms, and all the thousand and one trades in which women's hours of work are practically unlimited.

Finally, we have seen that the fear of women's exclusion from industrial employment is wholly unfounded. The uniform effect of Factory legislation in the past has been, by encouraging machinery, division of labor, and production on a large scale, to increase the employment of women, and largely to raise their status in the labor market. At this very moment the neglect to apply the Factory Acts effectively to the domestic workshop is positively restricting the demand for women workers in the clothing trades. And what is even more important, we see that it is only by strict regulation of the conditions of women's employment that we can hope for any general rise in the level of their industrial efficiency. The real enemy of the woman worker is not the skilled male operative, but the unskilled and half-hearted female "amateur" who simultaneously blacklegs both the workshop and the home. The legal regulation of women's labor is required to protect the independent professional woman worker against these enemies of her own sex. Without this regulation it is futile to talk to her of the equality of men and women. With this regulation, experience teaches us that women can work their way in certain occupations to a man's skill, a man's wages, and a man's sense of personal dignity and independence.

Notes

1 Reproduced, with some additions, from papers read at the Nottingham Conference of the National Union of Women Workers (October, 1895), and the Fabian Society (January, 1896).
2 Factory and Workshop Act, 1895 (58 and 59 Vict. ch. 37).
3 Petitions were sent in, and meetings held in support of the Bill by, I believe, all the Trade Unions of Women, as well as by the Women's Co-operative Guild, which is mainly composed of women textile workers, whose hours of labor have, for nearly forty years, been rigidly fixed by law.
4 See the *Report of the Chief Inspector of Factories* for 1894, C. 7745, price 5s. 3d.; also the *Opinions on Overtime,* published by the Women's Trade Union League (Club Union Buildings, Clerkenwell Road, London). The evidence before the Royal Commission on Labor was decidedly in favor of an extension of, and the more rigid enforcement of Factory legislation: see, in particular, the Minority Report (published separately, price 2d., by the Manchester Labor Press, Tib Street, Manchester).
5 This was pointed out by the Duke of Argyll, in the final chapter of his *Reign of Law,* which deals with Factory legislation.
6 See W. C. Taylor, *The Modern Factory System*; Von Plener's *English Factory Legislation*; and Miss Victorine Jeans' *Factory Act Legislation.*
7 See, for instance, the *Elements of the Economics of Industry* [1892], p. 382.
8 Some account of this development is given in the first chapter of my *Co-operative Movement in Great Britain.* See also Engels' *Condition of the English Working Classes in 1844,* or Arnold Toynbee's *The Industrial Revolution.*
9 For proof of this see *The History of Trade Unionism,* by Sidney and Beatrice Webb, particularly the first chapter.
10 *The Law relating to Factories and Workshops,* by May Abraham and A. Llewelyn Davies (Eyre and Spottiswoode, 1896, 5/-), contains a convenient summary of all the Acts. With regard to hours, the main provisions are as follows: Textile factories employing women or children, may work only between 6 a.m. and 6 p.m. (or 7 a.m. and 7 p.m.), only 56½ hours net per week, and overtime is absolutely prohibited. In non-textile factories and in ordinary workshops, women may be worked 60 hours per week, overtime is (usually) permitted under certain conditions, and the day's work may (except on Saturdays) range over a period from 6 a.m. to 8 p.m., or, if no children or young persons are employed, even from 6 a.m. to 10 p.m. This absence of a precisely determined legal working-day makes it practically impossible to enforce the law. In "domestic workshops" there is no restriction on women's hours, and in laundries the only limit is a general one of sixty hours per week (or fourteen in any one day), without regulation of the hours of beginning or ending, or of meal-times. This is quite illusory.
11 See Fabian Tract, No. 48, *Eight Hours by Law: a Practicable Solution.*
12 "The Alleged Difference between the Wages of Men and Women," *Economic Journal,* December, 1891; see, on the general question, *Economic Studies,* by Professor W. Smart, and the valuable report by Miss Clara Collet, on the *Statistics of Employment of Women and Girls,* published by the Labor Department of the Board of Trade (C—7564), price 8d.
13 With regard to the employment of women as compositors, an article by Amy Linnett, in the *Economic Review* for January, 1892, should be referred to.

GENDER, SEXUALITY AND FAMILY RELATIONS

14 Looked at from the point of view of the whole community, and not merely from that of one sex, it would, of course, be a matter for further consideration whether, and in what directions, it is socially desirable that men should be replaced by women as industrial operatives. Throughout this paper I have abstained from discussing this consideration.

15 See Fabian Tract, No. 50, *Sweating: its Cause and Remedy*.

16 See the introduction, by Mr. A. J. Mundella, to Von Plener's *English Factory Legislation*.

17 See "Women's Work in Leeds," by Miss Clara Collet (*Economic Journal,* September, 1891, pp. 467–72).

18 *Statistics of Employment of Women and Girls,* C—7564, p. 11.

19 *Ibid,* p. 73.

20 See Fabian Tract No. 23, *The Case for an Eight Hours Bill.*

27

SOCIALISM AND THE FAMILY (LONDON: A.C. FIFIELD, 1906), 43–60.

H.G. Wells

[In 1903 the former liberal H.G. Wells accepted the nomination for his membership of the Fabian Society by leading members Bernard Shaw and Graham Wallas. Wells soon became an internal critic of the Society, challenging rather than simply accepting some of its key ideas. He argued that the Fabians should be transformed into a mass membership society rather than an exclusive one for the middle-class intelligentsia. The Society sought to meet his criticism with plans for literature aimed at a broader readership (Partington 2008, 522–526). Nevertheless, the uneasy relationship continued. In his novel *In the Days of the Comet* of 1906, the vapours of a passing comet transformed attitudes, leading to the transformation of a world riven by hostilities into one of peace and cooperation, including free love, rather than jealousy. Because of Wells' membership, the Fabians were portrayed in the press and the Church as a promiscuous society advocating free love and no moral restrictions on sexual activity. Some leading Fabians, especially Beatrice and Sidney Webb, worried that this might harm the reputation of the Society.

Largely in response, Webb published his short book *Socialism and the Family* that year (Partington 2008, 526–527). In the second chapter, reprinted here, Wells (1906) distinguishes socialism from idealist visions found in anarchism, communism and other early radical ideas. While conceding that early socialist thought may sometimes have presented such ideas, he argued that for the past quarter of a century socialism had in the main become a doctrine proposing possible social change. He mentions the Fabian Society as an organisation in which one would be unlikely to find the less realistic ideas.

Socialism, Wells argued, advocates neither the lack of any legal or moral regulation of sexual activity nor a reactionary society in which traditional values are maintained by keeping the masses ignorant. Instead, socialism denied there should be property in human beings. People needed to be liberated, in particular women and children in the patriarchal family. Neglect was sometimes unintentional, especially in social conditions and circumstances of poverty. Children should be the concern of the state which would serve as over-parent to eliminate maltreatment or neglect. Wells proposed payment of women for the upbringing of their children. This he discussed in greater detail in his pamphlet *Will Socialism Destroy the Home?* (reprinted in the present volume) the following year. Wells was by this time becoming disillusioned with the Fabian Society. He resigned in 1908 (Toye 2008, 157). Thereafter, for many years he resumed his portrayal of himself as a liberal.]

II

I DO not think that the general reader at all appreciates the steady development of Socialist thought during the past two decades. Directly one comes into close contact with contemporary Socialists one discovers in all sorts of ways the evidence of the synthetic work that has been and still is in process, the clearing and growth of guiding ideas, the qualification of primitive statements, the consideration, the adaptation to meet this or that adequate criticism. A quarter of a century ago Socialism was still to a very large extent a doctrine of negative, a passionate criticism and denial of the theories that sustained and excused the injustices of contemporary life, a repudiation of social and economic methods then held to be indispensable and in the very nature of things. Its positive proposals were as sketchy as they were enthusiastic, sketchy and, it must be confessed, fluctuating. One needs to turn back to the files of its every-day publications to realize the progress that has been made, the secular emergence of a consistent and continually more nearly complete and directive scheme of social reconstruction from the chaotic propositions and hopes and denials of the earlier time. In no direction is this more evident than in the steady clearing of the Socialistic attitude towards marriage and the family; in the disentanglement of Socialism from much idealist and irrelevant matter with which it was once closely associated and encumbered, in the orderly incorporation of conceptions that at one time seemed not only outside of, but hostile to, Socialist ways of thinking. . . .

Nothing could have brought out this more clearly than the comical attempt made recently by the *Daily Express* to suggest that Mr. Keir Hardie and the party he leads was mysteriously involved with my unfortunate self in teaching Free Love to respectable working men. When my heat and indignation had presently a little subsided, I found myself asking how it came about, that any one could bring together such discrepant things as the orderly proposals of Socialism as they shape themselves in the projects of Mr. Keir Hardie, let us say, and the doctrine of sexual go-as-you-please. And so inquiring, my mind drifted back to the days—it is a hazy period to me—when Godwin and Mary Wollstonecraft were alive, when Shelley explained his views to Harriet. These people were in a sort of way Socialists; Palaeo-Socialists. They professed also very distinctly that uncovenanted freedom of action in sexual matters which is, I suppose, Free Love. Indeed, so near are we to these old confusions that there is still, I find, one Palaeo-Socialist surviving—Mr. Belfort Bax. In that large undifferentiated past, all sorts of ideas,

282

as yet too ill defined to eliminate one another, socialist ideas, communist ideas, anarchist ideas, Rousseauism, seethed together and seemed akin. In a sense they were akin in that they were the condemnation of the existing order, the outcome of the destructive criticism of this of its aspects or that. They were all *breccia*. But in all else, directly they began to find definite statement, they were flatly contradictory one with another. Or at least they stood upon different levels of assumption and application.

The formulæ of Anarchism and Socialism are, no doubt, almost diametrically opposed; Anarchism denies government, Socialism would concentrate all controls in the State, yet it is after all possible in different relations and different aspects to entertain the two. When one comes to dreams, when one tries to imagine one's finest sort of people, one must surely imagine them too fine for control and prohibitions, doing right by a sort of inner impulse, "above the Law." One's dreamland perfection is Anarchy—just as no one would imagine a policeman (or for the matter of that a drain-pipe) in Heaven. But come down to earth, to men the descendants of apes, to men competing to live, and passionately jealous and energetic, and for the highways and market-places of life at any rate, one asks for law and convention. In Heaven or any Perfection there will be no Socialism, just as there will be no Bimetallism; there is the sphere of communism, anarchism, universal love and universal service. It is in the workaday world of limited and egotistical souls that Socialism has its place. All men who dream at all of noble things are Anarchists in their dreams, and half at least of the people who are much in love, I suppose, want to be this much Anarchistic that they do not want to feel under a law or compulsion one with another. They may want to possess, they may want to be wholly possessed, but they do not want a law court or public opinion to protect that possession as a "right."

But it's still not clearly recognized how distinct are the spheres of Anarchism and Socialism. The last instance of this confusion that has seriously affected the common idea of the Socialist was as recent as the late Mr. Grant Allen. He was not, I think, even in his time a very representative Socialist, but certainly he did present, as if it were a counsel of perfection for this harsh and grimy world, something very like reckless abandonment to the passion or mood of the moment. I doubt if he would have found a dozen supporters in the Fabian Society in his own time. I should think his teaching would have appealed far more powerfully to extreme individualists of the type of Mr. Auberon Herbert. However that may be, I do not think there is at present among English and American Socialists any representative figure at all counselling Free Love. The modern tendency is all towards an amount of control over the function of reproduction, if anything, in excess of that exercised by the State and public usage to-day. Let me make a brief comparison of existing conditions with what I believe to be the ideals of most of my fellow Socialists in this matter, and the reader can then judge for himself between the two systems of intervention.

GENDER, SEXUALITY AND FAMILY RELATIONS

And first let me run over the outline of the thing we are most likely to forget and have wrong in such a discussion, the thing directly under our noses, the thing that is. People have an odd way of assuming in such a comparison that we are living under an obligation to conform to the moral code of the Christian church at the present time. As a matter of fact we are living in an epoch of extraordinary freedom in sexual matters, mitigated only by certain economic imperatives. Anti-socialist writers have a way of pretending that Socialists want to make Free Love possible, while in reality Free Love is open to any solvent person to-day. People who do not want to marry are as free as air to come together and part again as they choose, there is no law to prevent them, the State takes it out of their children with a certain mild malignancy—that is all. Married people are equally free, saving certain limited proprietary claims upon one another, claims that can always be met by the payment of damages. The restraints are purely restraints of opinion, that would be as powerful tomorrow if legal marriage was altogether abolished. There was a time, no doubt, when there were actual legal punishments for unchastity in women, but that time has gone, it might seem, for ever. Our State retains only, from an age that held mercantile methods in less honour, a certain habit of persecuting women who sell themselves by retail for money, but this is done in the name of public order and not on account of the act. Such a woman must exact cash payments, she cannot recover debts, she is placed at a ridiculous disadvantage towards her landlord (which makes accommodating her peculiarly lucrative), and she is exposed to various inconveniences of street regulation and status that must ultimately corrupt any police force in the world—for all that she seems to continue in the land with a certain air of prosperity. Beyond that our control between man and woman is nil. Our society to-day has in fact no complete system of sexual morals at all. It has the remains of a system.

It has the remains of a monogamic patriarchal system, in which a responsible man owned nearly absolutely wife and offspring. All its laws and sentiments alike are derived from the reduction and qualification of that.

These are not the pretensions indeed of the present system such as it is, but they are the facts. And even the present disorder, one gathers, is unstable. One hears on every hand of its further decadence. From Father Vaughan to President Roosevelt, and volleying from the whole bench of bishops, comes the witness to that. Not only the old breaches grow wider and more frequent, but in the very penetralia of the family the decay goes on. The birth-rate falls—and falls. The family fails more and more in its essential object. This is a process absolutely independent of any Socialist propaganda; it is part of the normal development of the existing social and economic system. It makes for sterilization, for furtive wantonness and dishonour. The existing system produces no remedies at all. Prominent people break out ever and again into vehement scoldings of this phenomenon; the newspapers and magazines re-echo "Race Suicide," but there is no sign whatever in the statistical curves of the smallest decimal per cent. of response to these exhortations.

Our existing sexual order is a system in decay. What are the alternatives to its steady process of collapse? That is the question we have to ask ourselves. To heap

284

SOCIALISM AND THE FAMILY

foul abuse, as many quite honest but terror-stricken people seem disposed to do, on any one who attempts to discuss any alternative, is simply to accelerate this process. To me it seems there are three main directions along which things may go in the future, and between which rational men have to choose.

The first is to regard the present process as inevitable and moving towards the elimination of weak and gentle types, to clear one's mind of the prejudices of one's time, and to contemplate a disintegration of all the realities of the family into an epoch of Free Love, mitigated by mercantile necessities and a few transparent hypocrisies. Rich men will be free to live lives of irresponsible polygamy; poor men will do what they can; women's life will be adventurous, the population will decline in numbers and perhaps in quality. (To guard against that mischievous quoter who lies in wait for all Socialist writers, let me say at once that this state of affairs is anti-socialist, is, I believe, socially destructive, and does not commend itself to me at all.)

The second direction is towards reaction, an attempt to return to the simple old conceptions of our past, to the patriarchal family, that is to say, of the middle ages. This I take to be the conception of such a Liberal as Mr. G. K. Chesterton, or such a Conservative as Lord Hugh Cecil, and to be also as much idea as one can find underlying most tirades against modern morals. The rights of the parent will be insisted on and restored, and the parent means pretty distinctly the father. Subject to the influence of a powerful and well-organized Church, a rejuvenescent Church, he is to resume that control over wife and children of which the modern State has partially deprived him. The development of secular education is to be arrested, particular stress is to be laid upon the wickedness of any intervention with natural reproductive processes, the spread of knowledge in certain directions is to be made criminal, and early marriages are to be encouraged. . . . I do not by any means regard this as an impossible programme; I believe that in many directions it is quite a practicable one; it is in harmony with great masses of feeling in the country, and with many natural instincts. It would not of course affect the educated wealthy and leisurely upper class in the community, who would be able and intelligent enough to impose their own private glosses upon its teaching, but it would "moralize" the general population, and reduce them to a state of prolific squalor. Its realization would be, I believe, almost inevitably accompanied by a decline in sanitation, and a correlated rise in birth-rate and death-rate, for life would be cheap, and drainpipes and antiseptics dear, and it is quite conceivable that after some stresses, a very nearly stable social equilibrium would be attained. After all it is this simple sort of life, without drains and without education, with child labour (in the open air for the most part until the eighteenth century—though that is a detail) and a consequent straightforward desire for remunerative children that has been the normal life of humanity for many thousands of years. We might not succeed in getting back to a landed peasantry, we might find large masses of the population would hang up obstinately in industrial towns—towns that in their simple naturalness of congestion might come to resemble the Chinese pattern pretty closely; but I have no doubt we could move far in that direction with very little difficulty indeed.

285

GENDER, SEXUALITY AND FAMILY RELATIONS

The third direction is towards the developing conceptions of Socialism. And it must be confessed at once that these, as they emerge steadily and methodically from mere generalities and confusions, do present themselves as being in many aspects, novel and untried. They are as untested, and in many respects as alarming, as steam traction or iron shipping were in 1830. They display, clearly and unambiguously, principles already timidly admitted in practice and sentiment to-day, but as yet admitted only confusedly and amidst a cloud of contradictions. Essentially the Socialist position is a denial of property in human beings; not only must land and the means of production be liberated from the multitude of little monarchs among whom they are distributed, to the general injury and inconvenience, but women and children, just as much as men and things, must cease to be owned. Socialism indeed proposes to abolish altogether the patriarchal family amidst whose disintegrating ruins we live, and to raise women to an equal citizenship with men. It proposes to give a man no more property in a woman than a woman has in a man. To stupid people who cannot see the difference between a woman and a thing, the abolition of the private ownership of women takes the form of having "wives in common," and suggests the Corroboree. It is obviously nothing of the sort. It is the recognition in theory of what in many classes is already the fact,—the practical equality of men and women in a civilized state. It is quite compatible with a marriage contract of far greater stringency than that recognized throughout Christendom to-day.

Now what sort of contract will the Socialist state require for marriage? Here again there are perfectly clear and simple principles. Socialism states definitely what almost everybody recognizes nowadays with greater or less clearness, and that is the concern of the State for children. The children people bring into the world can be no more their private concern entirely, than the disease germs they disseminate or the noises a man makes in a thin-floored flat. Socialism says boldly the State is the Over-Parent, the Outer-Parent. People rear children for the State and the future; if they do that well, they do the whole world a service, and deserve payment just as much as if they built a bridge or raised a crop of wheat; if they do it unpropitiously and ill, they have done the world an injury. Socialism denies altogether the right of any one to beget children carelessly and promiscuously, and for the prevention of disease and evil births alike, the Socialist is prepared for an insistence upon intelligence and self-restraint quite beyond the current practice. At present we deal with all that sort of thing as an infringement of private proprietary rights; the Socialist holds it is the world that is injured.

It follows that motherhood, which we still in a muddle-headed way seem to regard as partly self-indulgence and partly a service paid to a man by a woman, is regarded by the Socialists as a benefit to society, a public duty done. It may be in many cases a duty full of pride and happiness—that is beside the mark. The State will pay for children born legitimately in the marriage it will sanction. A woman with healthy and successful offspring will draw a wage for each one of them from the State, so long as they go on well. It will be her wage. Under the State she will control her child's upbringing. How far her husband will share in the power of direction is a matter of detail upon which opinion may vary—and does vary widely among Socialists. I suppose for the most part they incline to the conception of a joint control. So the monstrous injustice of the present time which makes a mother dependent upon the economic accidents of her man, which plunges the best of wives and the most admirable of children into abject poverty if he happens to die, which visits his sins of waste and carelessness upon them far more than upon himself, will disappear. So too the still more monstrous absurdity of women discharging their supreme social function, bearing and rearing children in their spare time, as it were, while they "earn their living" by contributing some half mechanical element to some trivial industrial product, will disappear.

That is the gist of the Socialist attitude towards marriage; the repudiation of private ownership of women and children, and the payment of mothers. Partially but already very extensively, socialistic ideas have spread through the whole body of our community; they are the saving element in what would otherwise be a moral catastrophe now, and the Socialist simply puts with precise definition the conclusions to which all but foolish, ignorant, base or careless people are moving—albeit some are moving thither with averted faces. Already we have the large, still incomplete edifice of free education, and a great mass of legislation against child labour; we have free baths, free playgrounds, free libraries,—more and more people are coming to admit the social necessity of saving our children from the private enterprise of the milkman who does not sterilize his cans, from the private enterprise of the schoolmaster who cannot teach, from the private enterprise of the employer who takes them on at small wages at thirteen or fourteen to turn them back on our hands as ignorant hooligans and social wastrels at eighteen or twenty. . . . But the straightforward payment to the mother still remains to be brought within the sphere of practical application. To that we shall come.

28

WILL SOCIALISM DESTROY THE HOME? (LONDON: INDEPENDENT LABOUR PARTY, c. 1907), 1–14.

H.G. Wells

[As was the case in his book *Socialism and the Family* (an extract from which is in the present volume) the previous year, H.G. Wells' pamphlet *Will Socialism Destroy the Home?* of 1907 proposed the payment of women for the upbringing of their children. The pamphlet took up some of the brief and indirect comments of the book regarding the punitive means to discourage ill-treatment, conscious or otherwise, of children. The aim was to foster a society in which there would be no unhealthy, unfit, poorly-nurtured and uneducated citizens. Wells (c. 1907), without using the term, was thus contributing to the discipline of eugenics.

In the late nineteenth and early twentieth century, thus before the rise of fascism in Europe revealed its implications and possible consequences, many prominent British socialists had shown interest in and enthusiasm for eugenics. Their emphasis on nurture and the social and environmental shaping of human nature tended to distinguish socialist and liberal interpretations of eugenics from those on the right who claimed that races had in-born qualities that can be improved if fully developed. Nevertheless, socialist eugenicists were later, in some cases mistakenly, assumed to believe in such in-born qualities that can be retrieved and developed by means of active breeding (Freeden 1979, 645–646). Although this was not the same as a far-right belief in national, racial in-born qualities, the latter belief and that of the socialist eugenicists were sometimes portrayed as bearing affinities with one another.

The question of active breeding has been seen in terms of positive rather than negative eugenics. Positive eugenicists believed that the nurturing or development could be induced by human intervention. Those on the negative wing, whose eugenics was limited to the prevention of perceived weaknesses, included Wells (Paul 1984, 586). In *Will Socialism Destroy the Home?* he does not use the term eugenics. He mentions sterilisation as a possible measure, but mainly advocates the taking of children away from families if necessary and, as he had discussed in *Socialism and the Family*, paying responsible mothers to bring up their children.

WILL SOCIALISM DESTROY THE HOME?

He specifically disassociates himself from social experimentation to positively induce human improvement.]

PEOPLE are told that Socialism will destroy the home, will substitute a sort of human stud-farm for that warm and intimate nest of human life, will bring up our children in incubators and crèches, and—institutions generally.

It isn't so.

Before we state what modern Socialists do desire in these matters, it may be well to consider something of the present reality of the home people are so concerned about.

The reader must not idealise. He must not shut his eyes to facts; dream of a beautiful world of beautiful homes, orderly, virtuous, each a little human fastness, each with its porch and creeper, each with its books and harmonium, its hymn-singing on Sunday night, its dear mother who makes such wonderful cakes, its strong and happy father—and then say, "These wicked Socialists want to destroy all this." Because, in the first place, such homes are being destroyed and made impossible now by the very causes against which Socialism fights, and because in this world at the present time very few homes are at all like this ideal. In reality, every poor home is haunted by the spectre of irregular employment and undermined by untrustworthy insurance; it must shelter in insanitary dwellings, and its children eat adulterated food because none other can be got. And that, I am sorry to say, it is only too easy to prove—and prove by documentary evidence.

Here are some realities.

These entries that follow come from the recently-published Edinburgh Charity Organisation Society's report upon the homes of about fourteen hundred school children, that is to say, about eight hundred British homes. Remember, they are *sample homes*. They are little worse and little better than the bulk of very poor people's homes in Scotland and England at the present time. I am just going to copy down—not a selection, mind, but a series of consecutive entries taken haphazard from this implacable list. I thrust my fingers among the pages, and come upon numbers 191 and 192, etc. Here they are, one after the other, just as they come:—

191. A widow and child lodging with a married son. Three grown-up people and three children occupy one room and bed-closet. The widow leads a wandering life, and is intemperate. The house is thoroughly bad and insanitary. The child is pallid and delicate-looking, and receives little attention, for the mother is usually out working. He plays in the streets. Five children are dead. Boy has glands and is flea-bitten. Evidence from Police, School Officer, and Employer.

182. A miserable home. Father dead. Mother and eldest son careless and indifferent. Of the five children, the two eldest are grown up. The elder girl is working, and she is of a better type, and might do well under

better circumstances; she looks overworked. The mother is supposed to char; she gets parish relief, and one child earns out of school hours. Four children are dead. The children at school are dirty and ragged. The mother could work if she did not drink. The children at school get free dinners and clothing, and the family is favourably reported on by the Church. The second child impetigo; neck glands; body dirty; the third, glands, dirty, and flea-bitten. Housing: Six in two small rooms. Evidence from Parish Sister, Parish Council, School Charity, Police, Teacher, Children's Employment, and School Officer.

193. A widow, apparently respectable and well-doing, but may drink. She must in any case have a struggle to maintain her family, though she has much help from Parish, Church, etc. She works out. The children at school are fed, and altogether a large amount of charity must be received, as two churches have interested themselves in the matter. Three children dead. Housing: three in two tiny rooms. Evidence from Church, Parish Council, School Charity, Police, Parish Sister, Teacher, Insurance, and Factor.

194. The father drinks and, to a certain extent, the mother; but the home is tidy and clean, and the rent is regularly paid. Indeed, there is no sign of poverty. There is a daughter who has got into trouble. Only two children out of nine are alive. The father comes from the country and seems intelligent enough, but he appears to have degenerated. They go to a mission, it is believed for what they can get from it. Housing: four in two rooms. Evidence from Club, Church, Factor, and Police.

195. The husband is intemperate. The mother is quiet, but it is feared that she drinks also. She seems to have lost control of her little boy of seven. The parents married very young, and the first child was born before the marriage. The man's work is not regular, and probably things are not improving with him. Still, the house is fairly comfortable and they pay club money regularly and have a good police report. One child has died. Housing: five in two rooms. Evidence from Parish Sister, Police, Club, Employer, Schoolmistress,

196. A filthy dirty house. The most elementary notions of cleanliness seem disregarded. The father's earnings are not large, and the house is insanitary, but more might be made of things if there were sobriety and thrift. There does not, however, appear to be *great* drunkenness, and five small children must be difficult to bring up on the money coming in. There are two women in the house. The eldest child dirty and flea-bitten. Housing: seven in two rooms. Evidence from Police, Club, Employer, Schoolmistress, and School Officer.

197. The parents are thoroughly drunken and dissolute. They have sunk almost to the lowest depths of social degradation. There is no furniture in the house, and the five children are neglected and starved. One boy earns a trifle out of school hours. All accounts agree as to the character of the father and mother, though they have not been in the hands

of the police. Second child has rickets, bronchitis, slight glands, and is bow-legged. Two children have died. Housing: seven in two rooms. Evidence from Police, Parish Sister, and Schoolmistress.

198. This house is fairly comfortable, and there is no evidence of drink, but the surroundings have a bad and depressing effect on the parents. The children are sent to school very untidy and dirty, and are certainly underfed. The father's wages are very small, and only one boy is working; there are six altogether. The mother chars occasionally. Food and clothing is given to school children. The man is in a saving club. The eldest child flea-bitten; body unwashed. The second, glands, flea-bitten, and dirty; cretinoid; much undergrown. Two have died. Housing: seven in two rooms. Evidence from School Charity, Factor, Police, and Schoolmistress.

199. The house was fairly comfortable and the man appeared to be intelligent and the wife hard-working, but the police reports are very bad; there are several convictions against the former. He has consequently been idle, and the burden of the family has rested on the wife. There are six children; two of them are working and earn a little, but a large amount of charity from school, church, and private generosity keeps the family going. The children are fearfully verminous. There is a suggestion that some baby-farming is done, so many are about. Eldest child anæmic; glands; head badly crusted; lice very bad. Second child numerous glands, head covered with crusts, lice very bad. Four have died. Housing: eight in two rooms. Evidence from Police, Teacher, Church, Parish Sister, and Factor.

200. The home is wretched and practically without furniture. The parents were married at ages 17 and 18. One child died, and their mode of life has been reckless, if not worse. The present means of subsistence cannot be ascertained, as the man is idle; however, he recently joined the Salvation Army and signed the pledge. The child at school is helped with food and clothes. The girl very badly bitten; lice and fleas; hair-nits. Housing: four in one room. Evidence from Church, School Charity, Co-operative, Employer, Parish Sister, Police, and Schoolmistress.

Total of children still living—39.
Total of children dead—27.

Need I go on? They are all after this fashion; eight hundred of them.

Turn from the congested town to the wholesome, simple country; here is the sort of home you have going on. This passage is a cutting from the *Daily News* of January 1st, 1907, and its assertions have never been contradicted:

"Our attention has been called to a sordid Herefordshire tragedy recently revealed at an inquest on a child aged one year and nine months, who died in Weobly Workhouse of pneumonia. She entered the institution emaciated to half the proper weight of her age and with a broken arm—till then undiscovered—that the doctors found to be of about three weeks' standing. Her mother was shown to be in an advanced state of consumption; one child had died at the age of seven months, and seven now remain. The father, whose work consists in tending eighty-nine head of cattle and ten pigs, is in receipt of eleven shillings a week, three pints of skim milk a day, and a cottage that has been condemned by the sanitary inspector and described as having no bedroom windows.

"We are not surprised to learn that the coroner, before taking the verdict, asked the house-surgeon who gave evidence whether he could say that death 'was accelerated by anything.' Our wonder is that the reply was in the negative. The cottage is in the possession of the farmer who employs the man, but his landlord is said to be liable for repairs. That landlord is a clergyman of the Church of England, a J.P., a preserver of game, and owner of three or four thousand acres of land."

Here, again, is the *Times,* by no means a Socialist organ:

Houses unfit for human habitation, rooms destitute of light and ventilation, overcrowding in rural cottages, contaminated water supplies, accumulations of every description of filth and refuse, a total absence of drainage, a reign of unbelieveable dirt in milk-shops and slaughter houses, a total neglect of bye-laws, and an inadequate supervision by officials who are frequently incompetent; such, in a general way, is the picture that is commonly presented—in the reports of inquiries in certain rural districts made by medical officers of the Local Government Board."

And even of such homes as this there is an insufficiency. In 1891–95 more than a quarter of the deaths in London occurred in workhouses and other charitable institutions.[1]

Now suppose the modern Socialist did want to destroy the home; suppose that some Socialists have in the past really wanted to do so, remember that that is the reality they wanted to destroy.

But does the modern Socialist want to destroy the home?

Rather, I hold, he wants to save it from a destruction that is even now going on, to—I won't say restore it, because I have very grave doubts if the world has ever yet held a high percentage of good homes—but raise it to the level of its better realisations of happiness and security.

The reader must get quite out of his head the idea that the present system maintains the home and social purity.

In London, at the present time, there are thousands of prostitutes; in Paris, in Berlin, in every great city of Europe or America, thousands; in the whole of Christendom there cannot be less than a million of these ultimate instances of our civilisation. They are the logical extremity of a civilisation based on cash payments. Each of these women represents a smashed and ruined home and wasted possibilities of honour, service and love—each is so much sheer waste. For the food they consume, their clothing, their lodging, they render back nothing to the community as a whole, and only a gross, dishonouring satisfaction to their casual employers. And don't imagine they are inferior women, that there has been any selection of the unfit in their sterilisation; they are, one may see for oneself, well above the average in physical vigour, in spirit and beauty. Few of them have come freely to their trade, the most unnatural in the world; few of them have anything but shame and loathing for their life; and most of them must needs face their calling fortified by drink and drugs. For virtuous people do not begin to understand the things they endure. But it *pays* to be a prostitute, it does not pay to be a mother and a home-maker, and the gist of the present system of individual property is that a thing *must pay* to exist. . . .

So much for one aspect of our present system of a "world of homes."

Consider, next, the great army of employed men and women, shop assistants, clerks, and so forth, living-in; milliners, typists, teachers, servants who have practically no prospect whatever of marrying and experiencing those domestic blisses the Socialist is supposed to want to rob them of. They are involuntary monks and nuns, celebate not from any high or religious motive, but through economic hardship. Consider all the amount of pent-up thwarted or perverted emotional possibility implied. . . .

We have glanced at the reality of the family among the poor; what is it among the rich? Does the wealthy mother of the upper middle class or upper class really sit among her teeming children, teaching them in an atmosphere of love and domestic exaltation?

As a matter of fact, she is a conspicuously devoted woman if she gives them an hour a day of her time; the rest of the time they spend with nurse or governess, and when they are ten or eleven off they go to board at the preparatory school. Whenever I read some particularly scathing denunciation of Socialists as home-destroyers, as people who want to snatch the tender child from the weeping mother to immure it in some terrible wholesale institution, I am apt to walk out into my garden, from which three boarding-schools for little children of the prosperous classes are visible, and rub my eyes and renew that sight and marvel at my kind. . . .

Consider now, with these things in mind, the real drift of the Socialist proposals, and compare its tendency with these contemporary conditions.

Socialism regards parentage under proper safeguards and good auspices as "not only a duty but a service" to the State; that is to say, it proposes to pay for good parentage—in other words, to *endow the home*. Socialism comes not to destroy, but to save.

And how will the endowment be done?

Very probably it will be found that the most convenient and best method of doing this will be to make a payment to the parents for their children; to assist

GENDER, SEXUALITY AND FAMILY RELATIONS

them, not as a charity, but as a right, to maintain their homes. So long as a child is kept clean in a tolerable home, in good health, well-taught and properly clad its parents are doing their first and most valuable social duty. At present if the father gets out of work we make the mother, however clean and virtuous and good a mother she may be, suffer all the miseries of want and failure. Socialism will not tolerate that. Frankly, Socialism will say to the sound, mothering women, "Not type-writing, nor shirt-sewing, nor charing is your business—these children are. Neglect them, ill-treat them, prove incompetent, and we shall take them away from you, and do what we can for them; love them, serve them, and, through them, the State, and you will serve yourself. You are doing something that enriches the State and it shall not impoverish you."

Is that destroying the home? Is it not rather the rescue of the home from destruction?

Certain restrictions, it is true, upon our present way of doing things would follow almost necessarily from the adoption of these methods.

It is manifest that no intelligent State would endow the homes of hopelessly diseased parents, of imbecile fathers or mothers, of obstinately criminal persons or people incapable of education. *It is evident, too, that the State would not tolerate chance fatherhood, that it would insist very emphatically upon marriage and the purity of the home, much more emphatically than we do now*. That follows necessarily. There is no more foolish lie conceivable than that modern Socialism countenances "free love." But since there are no sound and convincing arguments against the modern Socialist position in this matter its opponents must needs fall back upon lies or hold their peace.

So far, Socialism goes towards regenerating the family and sustaining the home. But let there be no ambiguity on one point. It will be manifest that while it would reinvigorate and confirm the home, it does quite decidedly tend to destroy what was once the most typical form of the family throughout the world—that is to say, the family which is in effect the private property of the father, the patriarchal family. The tradition of the family in which we are still living, we must remember, has developed from a barbaric state in which man owned the wife and child as completely as he owned horse or hut. He was its irresponsible owner. Socialism seeks to make him and his wife its jointly responsible heads. Until quite recently the husband might beat his wife and put all sorts of physical constraint upon her; he might starve her or turn her out of doors; her property was his; her earnings were his; her children were his. Under certain circumstances it was generally recognised he might kill her!

To-day we live in a world that has faltered from the rigours of this position, but which still clings to its sentimental consequences. The wife nowadays is a sort of pampered and protected half-property. If she leaves her husband for another man, it is regarded not as a public offence on her part, but as a sort of mitigated theft on the part of the latter, entitling the former to damages. The society in which we live does not punish her for immorality, it simply makes her paramour "pay" for upsetting her husband's affairs. Politically a woman doesn't exist; the husband is supposed to see to all that. But, on the other hand, he mustn't drive her by physical force, but only by the moral pressure of disagreeable behaviour. Nor has he the same large powers of violence over her children that once he had. He may beat— within limits. He may dictate their education, so far as his religious eccentricities go, and be generous or meagre with the supplies. He may use his "authority" as a vague power far on into their adult life, if he is a forcible character. But he must not kill or sell or torture.

The Socialist would end that old predominance altogether. The family under Socialism would cease to be a possible tyranny. The woman, the Socialist declares, must be as important and responsible a citizen in the State as the man. She must cease to be in any sense or degree private property. The man must desist from tyrannising in the nursery and do his proper work in the world. So far, therefore, as the family is a name for a private property in a group of related human beings vesting in one of them, the Head of the Family, Socialism repudiates it altogether as unjust and uncivilised; but so far as the family is a grouping of children with their parents, in love and respect and mutual help, with the support and consent and approval of the whole community, with the man as he naturally tends to be, the guide and supporter and helper and the woman playing her natural part as mother and teacher, Socialism advocates it, would make it for the first time, so far as a very large moiety of our population is concerned, a possible and efficient thing.

Note

1 "Studies Scientific and Social," vol. ii., ch. xxiv., by Dr. Alfred Russel Wallace. (Macmillan and Co., 1900).

29

SOCIALISM AND THE HOME (LONDON: INDEPENDENT LABOUR PARTY, c. 1909), 1–11.

Katharine Bruce Glasier

[Katherine Bruce Glasier's pamphlet *Socialism and the Home* of 1909 was a response to liberal and conservative arguments that socialism would destroy the home by introducing maintenance of children by the state. Glasier (1909) argued that most socialists would oppose such maintenance unless made absolutely necessary by the poverty which capitalism brought to society. The critics of socialism usually benefitted from capitalism and Glasier singled out Lord Balfour of Burleigh as a key figure in the anti-socialist campaign. This indicates the context in which she wrote the pamphlet. In 1905 the British Constitutional Association was formed with the aim of bringing together libertarian liberals and conservatives who opposed state intervention in the economy and society and who sought to promote personal liberty and responsibility. Parents, the Association insisted, were responsible for their children, meaning compulsory education and school meals funded by rates or taxes should be resisted (Greenleaf 1983, 281–284).

Glasier mentioned that there were both men and women who voiced the argument that socialism would destroy the home. This was more than a casual remark. Indeed, the argument was presented by liberal and conservative women organised in the Women's Unionist and Tariff Reform Association (Thackeray 2010, 831). Another noticeable feature of Glasier's pamphlet is her presentation of socialism in religious terms. She was, both as Glasier and before marriage as Katharine Conway, one of a number of prominent British socialists of the period, including Robert Blatchford and Tom Mann in their different ways, who perceived socialism as a form of religion (Yeo 1977).]

THE irony of history can hardly have asserted itself more strongly than when, in this country, in Britain, the propertied enemies of Socialism sought to rouse the prejudices of the common people against the Socialist ideal by raising the cry of "Socialism against the Home."

What is the Meaning of the Word Home.

To begin with, let it be clearly recognised that the word "home" is essentially the possession of the common people. "Home, Sweet Home," in spite of the fact that its tune was born in Sicily, is more truly the English people's national anthem to-day than any "God Save the King"; while the wealthy family that possesses many dwelling-places may be and practically often is, as "homeless" as the family that possesses no dwelling-place at all.

"Home," or "hame"—the word assuredly represents one of the most power-ful emotions (if it be not the most powerful)—of the English-speaking race to-day. And it is this "home" that Lord Balfour of Burleigh and his anything-but-merry men would persuade the English peoples that Socialism seeks to destroy!

Incidentally here it is interesting to note that when the enemy is talking with rich men, it is "property" that Socialism is said to assail; with the worker it is his "home."

But what do we, and the enemy alike, mean by "home"?

The word has not yet found its place in scientific sociology, though I am hope-ful that Socialist economists may soon succeed in enthroning it there. It is not so old a word as its common use might suggest. When carefully studied I believe it will be recognised as representing the race's aspiration rather than its com-plete experience—its goal rather than its origin. For by "home" in the abstract, I am convinced that the common people of England to-day mean the influence alike upon the individual and the community of the family, of the relationship of father, mother, and child to each other, with all the various outbranchings of that relationship—*when the family has been founded on a love marriage, and been supported and sustained throughout its upgrowing by the mutual service and goodwill of its various members.*

The Love Marriage the Foundation of the Home.

At the end of his second chapter on *The Origin of the Family,* Frederick Engels shows most powerfully how, with the gradual uprising of the common people in the Western races (especially in the Protestant countries, where in large measure the evil influences of an effete Roman civilisation were thrown off together with the power of the Roman Catholic Church), the love-match was at long last proclaimed as a human right—a right for the woman as well as for the man.

At any rate, it cannot be denied (and herein lies the justification of my defini-tion), that the English-speaking peoples who to-day attach a practically religious devotion to the thought of "home," are the same people who for centuries have upheld, both by ideal and practice, this same right of free or natural selection, or the love-marriage. To-day, so strong a power does the word "home" exercise over the ordinary English imagination, that the scientific historian who ventures to trace the origins of the human family—who dares to speak of such bygone things as "group-marriage," polygamy, polyandry, or the dread facts of adultery and prostitution which still betray the home ideal in our midst, is apt to find himself to his bewilderment treated as an unbeliever in the home, and an enemy of the human race.

Of course, this super-sensitive attitude may also be born of conscious hypocrisy. The diseased conditions of the "home," at both ends of the social scale, under capitalism, as I shall show later, are becoming patent. The people who uphold capitalism, while professing to believe in the "home," are therefore in the position which Carlyle describes in his essay on Martin Luther. They only "believe they believe." For them, then, welcome the Iconoclast! But the great mass of the people are, I maintain, perfectly sincere in their attitude, and as wise as they are sincere.

The Love-Marriage an English Institution.

In England, among the common people, even "contract" marriages, the marriages arranged by the families or parents of the bride and bridegroom, which still prevail in France, and to a lesser extent in Germany, have slowly but surely had to give way before the assertion of the human right of freedom in the selection of a life-mate. Considerations of rank and property in questions of marriage (though they still under evil economic conditions obtain, and to the extent that they obtain destroy the ideal of the home) are yet frankly recognised as immoral considerations.

It is the rich and powerful in England who have largely failed to win this right—whose marriages are still governed by reasons of state, family or "cash." Kings and dukes, queens and duchesses may have palaces and domains. It is the workers who have homes. For once—perhaps it has always been so down in the depths of things—the best gift of all has come to the poor people first. And again I repeat, it is this "home" which our enemies say that Socialism has come to destroy! It is the purpose of this pamphlet to maintain on the contrary that it is precisely this "home" that Socialism has come to establish for all classes, for all races, and for all time, as the only finally perfect cradle of the human race. It is precisely this home influence, the law of love as it is learned in and through the home, that Socialism has come, not to destroy, but to fulfil.

Personally, also, although this is outside my subject I would like to express my belief that this ideal of home is also the Christian ideal. But the Church, whether it be Catholic or Protestant, that for centuries has stooped to sanctify "contract" marriages, whether between royal personages, American heiresses and decayed dukes, or French peasants—the Church that has given its blessing alike to war, with its attendant militarism in times of peace, to competition, and to the unearned riches and undeserved poverty of capitalism, has failed to stand for the social conditions in which alone the ideal "home" can flourish throughout society.

That it does so stand will, I believe, be recognised, and at no distant date, as the supreme glory of Socialism.

Conditions that Destroy the Home.

But let us examine these conditions that destroy the home a little more closely.

Contract Marriages. No student of sociology can deny that contract marriages have so failed to satisfy the human heart, that whether in ancient Rome or modern France the tendency has been to associate them with illicit "love" unions, more or less condoned by public opinion to the degradation of all concerned and the ruin of the "home" ideal.

War. Under this heading, account must not only be taken of the young men and fathers cut off in their prime, of burning homesteads and women and children starving in the midst of blackened and bloodstained wastes. There is the "might of been" of all the destructive energy.

What might not the £250,000,000 squandered in the recent South African war have done for the building up of the homes of Britain, if the money had been collectively spent as Socialists desired it should be for the rehousing in garden suburbs of the workers who inhabit the congested, unhealthy, aye, and rack-rented areas of our industrial towns to-day. At the very time we fought the Boer War, there were more men, women, and children in London alone, dying down in one roomed dwellings, than there were white people of all nationalities in South Africa. To this "might have been" must be added the constant burden in times of peace of unproductive armies and the moral pollution of the national life that seems indissolubly connected with the unnatural conditions of "Barracks."

Competition. What does competition in the industrial field mean when applied to the home life of the competitors.

"I know I am a wolf to my fellow-men," said a shopkeeper to me once. "But it is the little wolves at home that sanctify it."

To take a more subtle example. The Glasgow Corporation some fifteen years ago, sought to bring together the machinery of one of their model wash-houses and some unemployed charwomen, and to start taking in at a very cheap rate the washing of the tenement "homes" in some of Glasgow's poorest districts. In ten days the proprietors of the Steam Laundries of Glasgow obtained an interdict from the Local Government Board against such unchartered Municipal Trading. They feared for their laundry profits. The danger was of the remotest kind, but the fear prevailed. In other words the proprietors were alarmed for their own homes' comforts, and had little opportunity, certainly no inducement under the present system to take thought for the comfort of the tenement dwellers. I can even imagine some philosophical Anti-Municipal Trader arguing that it would destroy the sacredness of the tenement home to take the washing out of it!

But to-day, under competition, not only are homes thus mutually destructive. What is worse, the different members of a home are often pitted against one another. Women notoriously undersell men's labour. Children are used to lower the wages of both father and mother. The unmarried woman robs a wife of her husband's chance of employment. Worst of all the woman denied the opportunity of honest work and wage may turn prostitute and threaten the home life of the nation at its root.

Capitalism with its Unearned Riches and Underserved Poverty.

By capitalism is meant the industrial system that is built upon private property in land, railways, mines, factories and other instruments of production. Roughly speaking, in Great Britain the private owners or monopolists represent less than one-fifth of the community. The remaining four-fifths have no right to work except they can persuade some one of the monopolist class to employ them. At once, then, it is manifest that the nation that allows such a monopoly has given away its power to secure a father's right to work for his family, and with that right all that the home stands for. Under capitalism there are always thousands of fathers out of work with the consequent "breaking up" of the home.

Further, of those who are in work: so far from a father's hard and honest effort to-day securing his home in comfort, it is just those who endure the most laborious, often the most dangerous and repulsive, toil, who are the lowest paid—as for example the chemical labourers, with their 2/6 a day; night soil men at 18/- a week, etc., etc.—while a Duke of Westminster gets 30/- a minute without working at all.

It is just the Unearned Incomes, the result of Monopoly, which are the big ones.

But masters only employ workers when they can sell what they produce. Thus the labour of the country follows the money in people's pockets.

The sweated sempstress on 1/- a day, with rent, profit and interest working in the prices of all she buys, can only command 4 pennyworth of labour for all her day's needs!

The Duke can command 30/- worth a minute.

Thus the workers cannot work for the necessities of workers—they must toil for the luxuries of shirkers.

Finally, useful workers are unemployed because the poor have been made too poor to buy and the rich too rich to spend!

The Palace and the Hovel. Lastly, the palace not only produces the hovel by its constant misdirection of labour to ennervating luxuries which was needed for the production of the material necessities of a healthy home life for, it may be, hundreds of families. But excessive wealth and excessive poverty alike tend to destroy the home spirit by closing up all practical opportunities of mutual aid between father, mother, and child. As a result, the duke's son borrows on the reversion of his father's inheritance—the docker's son has to let the old man go to the House.

Conditions that would secure the Home.

It is an incontestable fact that in Britain to-day the vast majority of Socialists have become Socialists *because* they believe in the home. They recognise in Socialism the only system of society that can be trusted, not only to preserve and redeem such home-life as we have already won as a race from its imminent danger of destruction under capitalism, but also to extend and to develop the influence of the home to the uttermost, and to secure its foundations in society as it has never yet been secured—by making all "homes" mutually helpful instead of mutually destructive, as they are to-day.

Let us once more briefly examine our Socialist ideal. Socialists desire that society, or the collective action of the people, should provide for every girl as for every boy the highest possible education that society knows how to give—including the supreme education that comes with the knowledge that "to come of age" means to enter into full citizenship, and the necessity, as well as the opportunity, of work or social service. Socialists claim that society must secure the right to work under healthy conditions, with an abundant wage to every full-grown unmarried woman equally with every full-grown unmarried man.

In all probability under Socialism, as in the village community of an old order, the wages and status of a married man will be higher than those of an unmarried man, but details of that kind can safely be left to the future to decide. Socialists to-day claim for society a complete control over the industry of the country in order that the highest possible supply of every family's need of food, clothing, and shelter may be provided, that the first object of industry should be the supply of the material necessities of home life.

Socialists therefore desire to set every woman, as well as every man, free from oppressive economic considerations in choosing a life-mate: that is, they desire to universalise the conditions of natural selection, and the opportunity of maintaining in comfort the family that springs from such a selection—in short, of the "home." Finally, as Engels points out, Socialism seeks to remove every economic consideration that now practically forces women to submit to their degradation at the hands of men, or *vice-versä,* and with that degradation to the desecration of everything for which the home stands.

Socialism and the Influence of the Home.

But it is when we pass from the consideration of the relations between husband and wife to those of father, mother, and child that our Socialist position as champion of the "home" becomes impregnable.

Let those who raise the cry "Socialism against the home" ask themselves where the Socialists have been to school for their ideal of a social system founded on mutual aid. Where did they obtain even the thought of human brotherhood? More than all—and here let some few unthinking Socialists pause and consider—where are they to obtain the motive forces for the building of the Co-operative

GENDER, SEXUALITY AND FAMILY RELATIONS

Commonwealth they desire save in those emotions which have had their origin in family life at its highest?

"All higher emotions of our life rise from it, the love that gathers man and woman into one organism," writes H. Fielding Hall, in his latest book on Burmah, *The Inward Light*. But that one organism needs to fulfil its function in the work of the bearing and rearing of its children before that truth becomes fully manifest in the race.

Those who are familiar with the biological writings of the brothers Reclus and of Kropotkin, gathered into a wonderfully suggestive form by Drummond in his *Ascent of Man*, will recognise the force of the argument that it has been the helplessness of little children more than any other influence that has led us up as a human race to the possibilities of the Socialist State.

From the plant world, with its flower and fruit triumphs, born of the struggle for the life of others, through the invertebrates to the birds with their wondrous nests, lined on occasion with down torn from the breast of mother and father alike, the same principle of progress is manifest.

Coming to the mammals, the very name suggests that the upward growth is in line with the closeness of the relation between mother and child. Higher qualities constantly manifest themselves in proportion to the need of protection in the offspring.

It is true (and what answer here have the opponents of women suffrage?) that among the mammals motherhood came into the world long before fatherhood; but all along the line there are evidences that the capacity of any given species to survive in the jungle has been in striking relation to the development of the male parent's sense of duty towards the mate and her young, and, it may be added, of his duty towards his fellow mates.

But whither is my argument tending? To the suggestion that the children have been humanity's best teachers—that the struggle to provide them with what they need for life has been the school in which fathers and mothers have discovered the necessity of the Socialist state.

Baby ape attains his maturity in a few short months.

Baby man, when father and mother love has had the *economic power to fulfil itself,* has been declared "an infant" during twenty-one years of life. Hitherto that full right of protection and sustenance of their young has only belonged to the upper and middle classes, and this, as has been shown, has often been greatly hindered of its ennobling influence by the evil foundation of the home in a loveless marriage, and the lack of mutual service engendered by luxury and privilege.

Socialism now steps forward to demand a like opportunity of complete sustenance and preparation, both of body and mind, for life in the twentieth century of their sons and daughters for *every* parent. To prove that this is possible by principles of mutual aid, collectively applied to industry, and only so possible, is the chief work of Socialists to-day. The best method of proof is perhaps to analyse an abundant standard of home comfort. William Morris, for instance, practically assured himself that for every family in the land what John Ruskin called "the

SOCIALISM AND THE HOME

pound a day standard of comfort when cultured men and women have the spending of the pound" was well within the reach of modern collective industry in Great Britain, and that with considerably less than an eight hours day for the strong men from 21 to 55: Useful work replacing useless toil.

State Maintenance of the Children not a Socialist Ideal, but an evil necessity born of Capitalism.

"But," I hear the anti-Socialists cry in chorus, "you Socialists are everywhere demanding the maintenance of the children by the State!"

To that, I have only to reply that such a demand is necessary to-day, because in tens of thousands of instances capitalism has destroyed the home. Socialists recognise if the homeless children of our land are ever to become capable of home-building in the future, those who *have* known what the joy of home-life means, must feed and educate them. Wherever the home fails, then for the sake of the homes of the future the Socialists say that the State must step in as foster parent.

But—and let Socialists never forget this—State interference with the results of capitalist individualism, although absolutely necessary to-day, is not only not Socialism, it is often not even in line with our Socialist ideal. In no respect is this distinction more necessary than in the much-abused cry, "State Maintenance of Children."

Under this head it must be confessed that Socialism has suffered much at the hands of a few desperately clever people—for the most part childless men and women—who simply don't know what they are talking about. They have been too rude to us others to make it necessary for me to mince words in the matter. For their sakes, and for the sakes of those whom their detached sentences may have misled, I venture to assert, without fear of contradiction from any happy father and mother in the land, that State maintenance of children, as opposed to their home maintenance, is alien to the whole history, hope, and spirit of Socialism.

For see to what a monstrous supposition the stray supporters of universal State maintenance of children as a Socialist ideal would fondly lead us. They suggest that the delight of fathers and mothers in their children, and their solicitude for their well-being will grow less strong when love-matches are the rule, when women are educated as well as men, and the children born are "wanted," and not "regrettable accidents!" To those who have any experience of the home-life which has grown out of such conditions, either in our own day or any other, the suggestion is simply ludicrous. Never, I venture to assert, in the history of the human race has the sense of possession in, or better, of responsibility for their children attained to a fiercer heat of emotion than among those fully-developed, hard-working fathers and mothers in our midst whose parenthood has been of free choice, conscious, and deliberate. Furthermore (and that is the climax of my argument), it is this very force, this new heat of emotion that is making the hideous uncertainties of a competitive state of society simply an intolerable torture.

303

GENDER, SEXUALITY AND FAMILY RELATIONS

The race has evolved its highest type of fatherhood and motherhood, and as yet has made no provision for the satisfaction of its soul.

Family Love the Motive Power of Socialism.

The anæmic children of the degraded father and mother of the slum may be able to endure the appallingly stupid and brutally unnecessary, as well as unjust, poverty of to-day.

Here and there a poor "breastless mother"—surely the most pathetic figure of all the ages—the upgrown child-worker who was herself robbed by capitalism in her own day of her mother's care and tenderness, and now knows not what the mingled joy and care of motherhood means—no, not even so much as the beasts of the field or the dog that licks her poor work-hardened hand—she, I repeat, may perchance rejoice in the thought of complete State maintenance for her unwelcomed children. The same may be true of the up-grown neglected son, turned father, who was him-self left to cry himself sick, uncleansed in his cradle, and only knew of a father to fear his reproach. He may be able to tolerate a system of society which has failed to secure the father's right to work with a wage sufficient to maintain his family. Aye, and the children of the rich idlers whose marriages were "arranged," children who were abandoned to the care of hirelings while their father and mother "amused" themselves as they pleased—they, too, in their turn may be deaf to the thought of other fathers' and mothers' agony, whose bairnies cry for bread.

But by the men and women who have known even in least measure in their childhood what "home" means, and growing up have been free to choose in their turn the life-partners who should set still other hearth fires glowing for the upbuilding of the race—by these men and women, capitalism is every day being judged by its fruits, by its effect upon the "home" life of the land, and is every day being more certainly condemned.

Such men and women compare capitalism with feudalism: and they see that evil as was the power of the baron over the serf, yet in the village community it was ordained "that so soon as a man should come of age and take to himself a wife there should be assigned unto him the piece of land on which he might build his house, make him his garden, and sink him his well—that his right should be secured unto him to go out into the wilds to hunt game and get timber for his fire, and to graze his cattle on the common lands."

A husband, then, by his strong right arm, an' he had the will, had power to "bind the house." What a sorry wretch is the unemployed man or the sweated worker of to-day beside that villager!

Such men and women compare capitalism with chattel slavery, and they find that in its worst days chattel slavery never separated mother and babe, or worked the children so that they failed of growth, or left either father, mother, or child to die of hunger and cold in a filthy slum.

Yes—I repeat it; the home-lovers and the home-makers (and thanks be, they are the vast majority of the people in Great Britain) to-day are condemning capitalism.

State Maintenance of Mothers not a Socialist Demand.

I am sorry that in conclusion it is necessary to have to deal seriously with the suggestion that "State maintenance of mothers" is also part of our Socialist ideal.

As a plaster over the running sores of capitalist society, some such temporary arrangement is to-day, I grant, being steadily forced upon us. The unemployed man under our present system of "palliatives" for root evils has actually been brought to the discovery that his wife and children will profit by his desertion of them: for then, at least, the "guardians" will be compelled to relieve their necessities. But such a "State maintenance of mothers" is only another instance of State interference with the results of capitalist individualism. It is in no sense representative of Socialism. The contention of a few Socialist idealists that "under Socialism" as in "the Kingdom of Heaven" the perfected man will be content to work for the community while the community provides for his wife and children may be true enough. But that has nothing to do with a present-day demand for "State maintenance of mothers" as part of our Socialist programme.

On the contrary, with the "Daisy Lord" tragedy fresh in our thoughts, Socialists, who more than any other political party recognise the necessity of social conscience, are everywhere pressing that the State should use its undoubted powers of suggestion by legislation in order to produce an increased sense of moral responsibility on the part of men that should make such tragedies impossible. In Australia and Finland, where women have the vote and the Socialist Labour parties are powerful, stringent paternity laws are already in force, and an unmarried mother can sue the father of her child for aliment six months before its birth.

All over Britain to-day the Socialist propagandists of the Independent Labour Party are asking their vast audiences to plump for a father's right to work for a wage sufficient to keep his family, be it large or small, just as our well paid civil servants have it to-day. There is not the least doubt about the response. Such demand as there may be in society for a "State maintenance of mothers" that leaves the fathers out of count is born either of the diseased conditions of present-day society, or of the sheerly individualist "revolt" stage of our women's battle for freedom.

Surely the slightest study of the conditions of health in the home go to prove that where either a woman or a man desire to be "absolutely independent" of her or his mate, there a marriage ought never to have been at all, or most assuredly, not parenthood. It cannot be said too often—if we cannot presuppose a co-operative commonwealth in the home, then never shall we be able to achieve a co-operative commonwealth in the nation.

But, I aver, with the experience of "home" of the common people, expressed in the world's noblest song and story down through the ages to bear me witness, that we can so presuppose it. How long, long ago is it since the words, "Like as a father pitieth his children," rang out their music for the comforting of a captive race?

To-day tens of thousands of the best and bravest men and women in our land are living in and by that very commonwealth of the home. They know in what they have believed; and from that knowledge it is my earnest belief that the wisdom and power is fast gathering which will build up the Socialist State—in which not only will war between the differing nations and classes of mankind have come to an end, but even the suggestion of a war between the sexes will be impossible.

On the vast field of the delightful wealth possible to homes-that-are-mutually-helpful, as compared with the mean and sordid poverty, and far meaner and more sordid riches of homes-that-are-mutually-destructive, I cannot enter here. My subject has been that of the relation between the two abstract thoughts of Socialism and the home. I have sought to prove that the realisation of the last is bound up with the realisation of the first. From the "home" has come, and is ever coming, the inspiration of Socialism. In Socialism will be found the full salvation of the home.

KATHARINE BRUCE GLASIER.

30

THE NEW CHILDREN'S CHARTER
(LONDON: INDEPENDENT LABOUR
PARTY AND FABIAN SOCIETY, 1912),
3, 6–20.

C.M. Lloyd

[Less well-known today than many of the authors featuring in the present volume, C.M. Lloyd (Mostyn Lloyd) was highly respected in the early twentieth century for his social research into living conditions, especially for the National Committee for the Prevention of Destitution. A barrister and lecturer in social administration at the London School of Economics, Lloyd was a member of both the Fabian Society and the Independent Labour Party. His position on the welfare of children was in line with that of Ramsay MacDonald and Labour Party policy.

Notwithstanding the growing influence of the new liberal idea that welfare was needed to enable individuals to flourish, the Liberal governments of the early twentieth century maintained the traditional liberal policy of keeping taxation as low as possible. Moreover, in 1908, facing strong opposition by a Conservative Party claiming to be able to raise money more easily, if taxation was necessary, at the top of the Liberal agenda were responses to two prominent issues: the increasing pressure to introduce state pensions and the increased German expenditure on armaments (Gilbert 1976, 1059–1061). That was the year in which the Children and Young Person's Act, known as the Children's Charter, was passed. MacDonald and the Labour Party opposed both the Liberal position, which simply responded to problems as they arose, and ameliorative measures such as that of the Marxist Social Democratic Federation which proposed maintenance of children by the state. The aim, for MacDonald, was to foster a morally active citizenry which respected the autonomy of children. This, he believed, would help buttress the working-class family rather than replace it with the state (Stewart 1993, 105–117).

In line with the views expressed by MacDonald, Lloyd, in *The New Children's Charter* published in 1912, criticised the Charter introduced four years earlier for simply introducing punitive measures for parents and other adults for neglect and exploitation and placing troublesome children in workhouses. Such solutions should not, he insisted, really be referred to in terms of a charter at all. Instead legislation should be put in place to ensure children enjoyed their rights to be decently born, nurtured and educated. His pamphlet outlined a range of social measures which such legislation should introduce and concluded with six points which should form a New Children's Charter to serve this purpose (Lloyd 1912). The text of the pamphlet presented here is slightly abridged, omitting some detail near the beginning.]

BERNARD SHAW once said, **"There ought to be no such thing as a rich child or poor child—only a happy child."** To-day we are bombarded with reports, statistics, speeches, books, detailing the poverty of hundreds of thousands of our children. A great host of officials and volunteers is daily engaged in investigating, classifying, and providing public meals for "necessitous" children. Medical inspection in 1911 showed that literally millions of elementary scholars were suffering in a more or less serious degree from diseases of the eye, ear, throat, skin, lungs, etc.—a great proportion of these cases being due simply to poverty. There are many thousands of working-class children who have no playground but the gutter, who have never seen the country or the sea, whose "homes" are but squalid dens of misery or of vice. In the streets of all our great towns, or in the garrets of sweated workers, there are countless child labourers, robbed of sleep, play, and education, to produce profits for a greedy commercial age. And under the Poor Law, in the general workhouses or other institutions, or on outdoor relief (this last too often a starvation pittance), we have in England and Wales alone some quarter of a million children—not merely *poor* but *pauper* children.

The result of this chronic lack of food goes far beyond mere temporary suffering. **"Defective nutrition,"** says Sir George Newman, Chief Medical Officer of the Board of Education, **"stands in the forefront as the most important of all physical defects from which school children suffer."** And it has permanent mental and moral effects of the most disastrous kind. Dr. A. S. Arkle, of Liverpool, reporting on the children in the elementary schools there, noted, among the characters produced by starvation, on the one hand "a sort of acute precocious cleverness" typical of a "class from which the pilferers and small thieves come," and on the other hand, "creatures much more like automata," children in a sort of dreaming condition, "only able to respond to some very definite stimulus." Everyone who knows the inside of a "poor" school will recognise these types—the all too common products of hunger.

DISEASE.

As regards disease, Sir George Newman observes,[1] "speaking generally, it may be said that out of 6,000,000 children registered on the books of the Public Elementary Schools of England and Wales, about 10 per cent. suffer from a serious defect in vision, from 3 to 5 per cent. suffer from defective hearing, 1 to 3 per cent. have suppurating ears, 6 to 8 per cent. have adenoids or enlarged tonsils of sufficient degree to obstruct the nose or throat, and thus to require surgical treatment, about 40 per cent. suffer from extensive and injurious decay of the teeth, about 30 to 40 per cent. have unclean heads or bodies, about 1 per cent. suffer from ringworm, 1 per cent. from tuberculosis in readily recognisable form, from 1 to 2 per cent. are afflicted with heart disease, and a considerable percentage of children are suffering from a greater or less degree of malnutrition. **It cannot be doubted that in the aggregate this formidable category of disease and defect means a serious amount of suffering, incapacity, and inefficiency, which at least must greatly limit the opportunity and diminish the capacity of the child to receive and profit by the education which the State provides, and must involve a continual increase in the national burden of sickness and disablement.**"

In many areas the percentages of diseased children are appallingly high, and in some—and those often the worst—no proper measures are taken to remedy the defects revealed by the official medical inspection. In the County Borough of Croydon, which is not usually considered a poverty-stricken district, out of 4,355 children examined in 1911, no less than 3,857, or 88 per cent., were found to be suffering from defects. In Bristol the percentage of defective children was 59 per cent., in the county of Northumberland 64 per cent. In the county of Staffordshire 24 per cent. of the boys and 55.8 per cent. of the girls examined had verminous or unclean heads or bodies, while in Warrington no less than 68.7 per cent. of the girls were found to have verminous heads. In Cheltenham, of 2,589 children inspected, 1,065 had defects of the nose or throat, adenoids, etc., and in Exeter the Medical Officer estimated that 6,000 out of the 7,500 elementary scholars in the city required dental treatment!

CHILD LABOUR.

In the dark days of the early nineteenth century vast numbers of tiny children were being ground in the industrial machine, sold for 1d. in the market place as weekly slaves, carried off to the mills by cartloads, or performing the work of horses in the coal mines. Since then the public conscience has become more tender, and it is customary to talk as though all child labour were a thing of the past. Many sweeping reforms have been carried, it is true; yet much remains to be done.

In the mills of Yorkshire and Lancashire there are **over 30,000 children between the ages of 12 and 14 working as half-timers**—rising often at 5 o'clock in the morning, to begin work at 6 or 6.30, and then attending school in the afternoon, or going to school in the morning and working in the mill from 1 o'clock to 5 or 6—at a wage which averages about 2s. 6d. for a 26 or 27 hour week.

Outside the textile areas, where the half-time system does not prevail, vast numbers of school children are employed before and after school hours (and sometimes when they are supposed to be at school) in shops, or as messengers or errand boys and girls, as golf caddies and farm labourers, in domestic drudgery, or in street trading. The Parliamentary Committee of 1903 reported that in England alone (apart from half-timers) there were **200,000 children thus employed as wage-earners, 1,120 of them between the ages of 6 and 7; 4,211 between 7 and 8; 11,207 between 8 and 9; and 22,131 between 9 and 10**.

In 1908, Miss Adler, of the London County Council, and Mrs. Hylton Dale, made an enquiry into wage-earning children at a boys' school in Hoxton, and a girls' school in Bermondsey. They found "15 per cent. of the boys were wage-earners. They were employed as errand boys to take out bottles, parcels, or papers, at a tea shop, at a coal shop, at an upholsterer's, at a barber's. As street sellers they sold laces, salt, pot-herbs, vegetables, blacking." One "picked over green stuff" for a greengrocer; one ran errands for a maker of doll's arms; one looked after a crippled boy; one helped at a whelk and mussel stall; one made capsules; one cardboard boxes; one sticks; whilst one covered steels. At the girls' school some ran errands, some minded neighbours' babies, some sold vegetables in the streets, or helped at coster stalls, some played with neighbours' children, some sold alone in the streets, which is "illegal." And in 1912, we read in a report of the Secretary for Education in Leeds of numbers of appalling cases of boy labour—cases which are unhappily not confined to Leeds—such as that of van-boys, aged 14, employed from 8 a.m. to 10 p.m., with no half-holiday; billiard markers, aged 14, employed from 9.30 a.m. to 11 p.m.; errand boys, aged 13, employed from 8.30 a.m. to 9 p.m. (and 11 p.m. on Saturdays); and newspaper shop boys, aged 16, employed from 4 a.m. to 4 p.m.

By what right are all these thousands of children robbed of their childhood, of play, of rest, of physical and mental and often of moral development? By what right do we allow—nay, encourage—boys and girls of 10 to "contribute to the family income"? Is it "good for them"? If so, why do not rich parents dispense with their nurses and governesses and hire their children out to deliver milk or sell evening papers in the streets? Let us get rid of cant, and face the fact that for every one of the "successful business men" whom we hear of as having started life at 8 years old on 6d. a week, we have thousands of workmen whose health has been ruined and their whole development arrested by the overwork of their early years.

POVERTY AND KNOWLEDGE.

One of the most significant signs of the times is the change which, slowly as yet, but surely, is coming over public opinion in regard to what constitutes "education" for the working-class. The old idea that boys and girls ought not to be educated above their station, that there was an element of the miraculous in a carpenter who studied philosophy, and something positively indecent in a house-maid who wanted to play the piano, still struggles hard. But the demand of the people for knowledge and beauty is growing apace, and it is the feeling behind that demand which adds bitterness to the struggle in thousands of homes for bread and health for the children. The poor are as well aware as the rich that "knowledge is power," and they are aware also that knowledge, if it does not mean happiness, at least means the opportunity of a deeper and richer life. They will refuse to be persuaded that a cinematograph show and a halfpenny illustrated paper are all that they require in the way of drama, literature and art. They recognise that they have not had all the education they can profit by at the age of 14 (or 13 if—oh! irony of it—they have been clever or punctual enough to exempt themselves by then). They will even refuse—and rightly refuse—an improved "technical education," which implies that a workman's ideal is to be merely a skilled workman, and that a knowledge of anything beyond his trade is waste. At the present time the vast majority of the children of the nation are denied the opportunities of a liberal education, of realising the best that is in them. Large numbers, through the hunger and disease bred of poverty, through the strain of early and late hours in the streets and the shops and the mills, are deprived even of the chance of making the best of such education as is provided for them. And the ignorance which is produced by hunger and disease and overwork, will in its turn condemn them to more hunger and disease and overwork; for out of their ranks will come the inefficients of industry, the victims of "blind alley" jobs, the juvenile criminals, the sweated workers, the inmates of our workhouses and infirmaries and asylums.

CHILDREN UNDER THE POOR LAW.

There are **under the Poor Law Authorities of the United Kingdom about 300,000 children,** the great bulk of them being between the ages of 5 and 16, and the rest infants under 5. These child paupers are dealt with in various ways by the Guardians. A large number of them are maintained in the general wards of the mixed Workhouse, subject to all the demoralisation that life in such an atmosphere is bound to produce. Public opinion has declared itself strongly against such a method of treatment, and the Local Government Boards of England, Scotland, and Ireland, have for some years been urging the removal of children from the Workhouses and Poorhouses. Despite this, however, there were on January 1st, 1912, in England and Wales, **no less than 8,600 children over 3 years of age still in the General Workhouse wards,** and some Boards of Guardians are either taking no notice of remonstrances, or openly defying the Local Government Board. The number represents, it is true, a decrease during the last three years; for when the Poor Law Commission reported, there were approximately 10,500. Mr. John Burns has described himself as "rapidly accelerating the removal of children from the workhouses," but his satisfaction at such a rate of reduction will hardly be shared by any but the very meanest of the ratepayers.[2]

About 18,000 children are "boarded out," not always under proper conditions. In one Cambridgeshire Union, for instance, the sum paid to the foster parents for a boarded-out child is, or was until recently, 2s. 6d. a week. According to the accepted standard, the minimum on which it is possible to maintain physical efficiency for a child must be put at 2s. 3d. per week for food alone. On that basis there is 3d. left for those foster parents to pay for clothing and other expenses connected with the child! The third method of maintaining pauper children is in separate institutions—Cottage or Scattered Homes. These are far preferable to the workhouse, and some of them are well equipped and comfortable; but they have their own disadvantages.[3]

But it is when we turn to the **Outdoor Relief children,** numbering nearly 200,000, that we find things at their worst. Tens of thousands of these, in the words of the Minority Report, are **"chronically underfed, insufficiently clothed, badly housed, and, in literally thousands of cases, actually being brought up at the public expense in drunken and dissolute homes."** Many Poor Law Authorities are giving utterly inadequate doles of relief for their outdoor children—often as little as 1s. 6d. or 1s. per week. In one benevolent Union, Hertford, the scale of out-relief, we learn from its Rules, is *"ninepence and five pounds of flour for each child not able to support himself or herself."* It is not surprising to find that in London and many other towns there are numbers of pauper children, who, being unable to get sufficient food from what is allowed them out of the Poor rate, are given dinners at school out of the Education rate. Thus do ingenious ratepayers rob Peter to pay Paul!

But over and above the misery and disease which afflicts so great a proportion of the Poor Law children, there is the additional fact of their dishonour. Pauperism is a disgrace. It is the merest hypocrisy to pretend otherwise. The fact that a pauper may be fairly nourished and clothed does not remove the degradation of his pauperism, any more than to pamper a slave removes the essential degradation of slavery. No rich man would tolerate the thought of his child being brought up in a workhouse or a pauper school. Why should we tolerate it for a poor man's child?

THE NEW CHILDREN'S CHARTER.

Such a condition of things, then, is one which no nation that values its existence can afford to ignore. The sluggish public conscience must be pricked. We must shake that complacency with which we regard such niggardly measures as the Children Act of 1908. It may be desirable to increase the punishment for parental neglect, to urge children into the workhouse, to keep them from the blighting influence of the tobacconist and the publican; but it requires a vivid imagination to hail such a catalogue of pains and penalties as the Children's Charter! The new Children's Charter which we put forward demands *that every child shall have the right to be decently born, decently nurtured, and decently educated,* that we shall set up a standard of food, of health, of leisure, and of education, below which no child shall sink.

How is it to be done? The task is not a difficult one from the administrative standpoint. The machinery is ready to our hand, as the Minority Report of the Poor Law Commission has already shown.

(1)—ABOLITION OF THE POOR LAW.

The first step must be the removal of all children out of the Poor Law. The Guardians in England and Wales and Ireland, and the Parish Councillors in Scotland, have proved themselves, as the Minority Commissioners reported, "inherently unfitted, by the very nature of their functions, to have the charge of the children for whom the State assumes the responsibility of a whole or partial maintenance." The high rate of infantile mortality among the destitute, the numbers of children in the general mixed Workhouses, the scandalous condition of the outdoor relief children, the educational defects of even the best administered of the institutional Schools and Homes, the unavoidable stigma of pauperism, the general wastefulness and overlapping, all these and many other inherent evils are an overwhelming condemnation of the Poor Law system. We demand, therefore, that **the whole of the public provision for birth and infancy should be transferred from the Poor Law to the local Health Authorities, and the whole of the public provision for children of school age to the local Education Authorities,** which have already, as the Minority Report reminds us, "in their directors of education and their extensive staff of teachers, their residential and their day feeding schools, their arrangements for medical inspection and treatment, their School Attendance Officers and Children's Care Committees, the machinery requisite for searching out every child destitute of the necessaries of life."

(2)—PROVISION FOR BIRTH AND INFANCY.

The great evils which threaten the children of the people at birth and during their earliest years are malnutrition and the overwork of the mothers. Many mothers can neither feed their babies themselves, owing to their own physical weakness, nor get pure milk for the bottle. Many infants, too, are sacrificed to the ignorance of their mothers, an ignorance born of the miserable conditions of life prevailing among whole sections of the working class. A vast amount of mortality and disease, again, is caused by the necessity that drives tens of thousands of unhappy women to drudging in the home or going out to work up to a few days before and immediately after their confinement. To combat these evils must be the work of the Public Health Authorities. **Every local Authority must make adequate provision for the infants in its area, by maternity hospitals or midwives in the home, by ensuring a supply of pure milk (as is done at Liverpool, Glasgow, Finsbury, Battersea, etc.), by means of Baby Clinics and Schools for Mothers,[4] by giving advice and instruction through its Medical Officers and staff of Health Visitors, and where necessary, by the granting of a sufficient allowance to keep mothers from going out to work just before and just after their confinement**. The need for some measure of endowment of motherhood has been recognised by the Maternity benefit included in the National Insurance Act. But this benefit is by no means adequate, and its scope must be greatly enlarged if every child is to have the right to be well born.

Indeed, it will be necessary to look beyond the few weeks of confinement, and make such provision as will enable thousands of widows and deserted wives with young children dependent on them, to keep out of the industrial market altogether. The grant of an adequate allowance, as suggested by the Minority Report, to such mothers of young families, on condition of their exchanging industrial employment for the care of their children at home, would be an enormous boon to thousands of neglected children.

(3)—SCHOOL FEEDING.

The principle that the community is responsible for safeguarding the school children from hunger, without the stigma of pauperism, has already been placed on the Statute Book in a rather half-hearted way by the Education (Provision of Meals) Act, 1906, and, as regards Scotland, in a more unqualified fashion by the Education (Scotland) Act, 1908, which *compels* a School Board to provide, not only food, but clothing, where necessary.

The scope of this Act of 1906 is narrow, and its administration very imperfect. It only empowers the local Education Authority to give meals, if they choose to do so, and many authorities, in their short-sighted anxiety to save the rates, have not adopted it.

It must be made compulsory. Moreover, it does not allow the provision of meals during school holidays, with the lamentable results that are only too apparent. It is imperative that **the meals should be provided irrespective of school days**. As regards the administration of the Act, we must see that every authority in the service of the meals comes at least up to Bradford's standard of efficiency and decency. It is important that **the educational value of the common meal should not be lost sight of**. Finally, there is the big question to be settled, whether the school dinner is to remain, as at present, a temporary palliative of destitution, or whether it is to hold a permanent place in the curriculum. The "selection" and feeding of "necessitous children" to-day is very unsatisfactory, and there is much to be said for the establishment of school dinners for all. The argument that such a provision would impair "family life" and the integrity of the home is absurd. The homes of the aristocracy have not been destroyed by the absence of their children at Eton or Harrow for three-quarters of the year. Why should the home life of the working class be impaired by their children eating their dinner with their school mates instead of with their mothers? It is true, as Miss MacMillan says, that "the advent of Socialism, of even a rudimentary order, must surely depend to some extent on the development of social feeling. That enlargement of the emotional life and imagination, which also makes possible a system of practical brotherhood (the giving and taking of service on equal terms, the concern and interest once confined to small family groups, radiating in widening circles. . . .), must depend not alone on a theory of life, but on constantly recurring occasions for the deepening and vivifying of mutual interest in larger groups and associations of persons, and above all on new opportunities offered early in life for the social education of future citizens. The school meal offers such opportunities. The children who dine together come into new relations with one another. They come also into new relations with their teachers at table." But those opportunities are certainly not offered by a system of hastily cramming hundreds of ravenous children, selected

THE NEW CHILDREN'S CHARTER

on the basis of their parents' destitution, with bowls of indifferent soup, amid a scene of mess and uproar!

(4)—THE CHILDREN'S HEALTH.

The responsibility for the health of the school child, again, must rest mainly on the Education Authority. There are three necessary lines of action. We must have (1) a completely organised system of medical treatment, (2) healthy home conditions, (3) healthy conditions in the school (including more open-air schools for delicate and ailing children).

SCHOOL CLINICS.

The only sound method of medical treatment is the School Clinic. In London and other places the arrangements made by the Education Authority with the hospitals for treatment of the elementary school children have proved very unsatisfactory. In many districts—in fact, in the majority—nothing has been done at all in the way of treatment, except that the school medical officer advises the parents to take the child to a doctor and have it attended to. A great many parents doubtless do all they can, but many are neglectful, or unable through stress of poverty or otherwise to get the necessary treatment.[5]

It is now becoming more and more widely recognised that Bradford was right when it started its Clinic in 1908, and thus provided the model for scores of other towns, which during the last year or two have awakened to their responsibilities.

What are the advantages of the Clinic? It is a part of the school system, under the control of the Education Authority, uniting in its work school doctors and nurses and dentists, teachers and Care Committees. It is able to give that detailed patient treatment for certain ailments which the hospitals generally cannot give. It provides, as no other method can, for the careful "following up" of cases (*e.g.,* breathing exercises, etc., after operations for adenoids). It is, by its very nature, the most completely "preventive" agency for dealing with disease in the school.

The expense is small. At Deptford, where Miss Margaret MacMillan and her friends have done such magnificent work, about 7,000 children were treated in twelve months, and the cost worked out at less than 3s. per head, as against 5s. 5d. paid by the L.C.C. under its contract with the Hospitals. It is safe to say that every shilling expended on the health of the child will mean the saving of a pound in years to come. For, as Sir George Newman says, "many of the diseases and physical disabilities of the adolescent and the adult spring directly out of the ailments of childhood. . . . As a general proposition it may be said that a State cannot effectually insure itself against physical disease unless it begins with its children." Nowhere can we find a better proof that prevention is cheaper than cure! Nor will the value of the Clinic be confined simply to its hospital work. It can encourage and teach many mothers (it is an astonishing error to suppose that the Clinic, to use

315

the cant phrase, "impairs parental responsibility"); it can bring much happiness and knowledge as well as healing to the children. "The School Health Centre," says Miss MacMillan, "is an extension of the Home Nursery—no more and no less. As the school family is immense, however, and as its needs are various, the head of the School Nursery Clinic must be a doctor, and his assistant must be a trained hospital nurse (without ceasing to be a home nurse first and foremost). The school is not home. No, and yet it must supply something that will be found one day in every home. It must be built to supplement the poor shelters of to-day. . . . Bradford has a large and well appointed Clinic with a staff of three doctors, two nurses, and a dentist. The rooms—thirteen in number—are, or were, in the basement floor of the old Education Committee Office. There is a large waiting room, a nursery (where children can be attended to by the School Nurse), three doctor's rooms, a Röntgen Ray room (where children often sleep comfortably throughout the whole treatment), two dentistries, and two very pleasant rooms where eyes, ears, etc., are examined. The whole has a very homely, cheery look, which is not at all like the atmosphere of the hospitals. The clinic has no associations of mystery, of dread, or even of pain. The children come and go happily, and—most noteworthy of all— many parents come here long before their children are really ill. This is held as the crowning glory of the place. It is claimed that thousands of mothers begin to learn the real meaning of *prevention*." Such a Clinic will be no mere palliative; it will play a prominent part among our municipal institutions. Of course, as poverty and its evil consequences are reduced, the work of the Clinic will necessarily contract. If, in years to come, the Clinic closes its doors because health reigns supreme in the school, a great victory will have been achieved. But our present task is to see that every local Education Authority has its own School Clinic.

HEALTHY HOMES.

Much of the good that is done in the Clinic or in school is unhappily undone in the child's home. Tens of thousands of families are living in foul slums, where cleanliness and light and good air are often a sheer impossibility. Damp, darkness, overcrowding,[6] and vermin, are all making the fight against disease more difficult and more costly. The slum landlord draws his rent, the poor suffer, and the public pays. The housing question is, of course, outside our province here; but it is a vital matter for the health of the children—the school children as well as the babies. **The Children's Charter will not be complete till the nation has ensured through Parliament and the local Authorities that every family has a healthy home**.

OPEN-AIR SCHOOLS.

The movement for Open-air Schools originated in 1904 at Charlottenburg, in Germany. Thence it has spread to England, and these schools have been established by a few Education Authorities, such as London, Bradford, Sheffield, Halifax, Norwich, Carlisle, Barnsley. At Charlottenburg the first year's working showed

THE NEW CHILDREN'S CHARTER

that, as regards the physical condition of the children, about 28 per cent. were cured and 40 per cent. greatly improved after three months. Educationally, it was found that, far from falling behind in their work, the children had kept pace with the ordinary school, and even beaten it as far as mental alertness, general intelligence, and initiative were concerned. Finally, from the point of view of discipline, the moral behaviour of the children had improved to a remarkable extent, owing to the manner in which they had been taught to observe the rules and regulations and perform the daily work of the little community of which they formed a part.

It is estimated that from 3 to 5 per cent. of all the school children in large towns are in such a condition, that, though able to attend school, they are not able to benefit properly by the instruction. Amongst these are many so-called "backward" children. These are not backward because of defective intelligence, but rather because of impaired vitality, due to defective frame, improper feeding, and unfavourable surroundings.

The lesson to be learned from this whole movement is the enormous value of healthy surroundings, not only to the weakly but to the normal child. For, as a great authority on this subject (Dr. Frederick Rose) has said, "the Open-air School contains all the possibilities which may be realised in some future day in the ideal school—open school buildings in rural surroundings, provided with the simplest but best hygienic and educational apparatus, small classes, short lessons, and the instruction brought into touch with actual conditions to such an extent that the children are interested in their work, and regard it as a pleasant occupation, and not as anything distasteful." If we had such an appreciation of the importance of environment as Plato showed 2,300 years ago, when he urged that the youth of the nation should "dwell in a land of health, amid fair sights and sounds, where beauty, that is born of fair works, will come upon their senses like a breeze, and insensibly draw the mind even in childhood into a love of the highest things," we should make short work of the thousands of schools buried in the fetid backways of our crowded cities. Doubtless we cannot yet bring that to pass. But we should do something towards it **if every citizen made it his business to see that where his local Education Authority was building a new school, that school should be built only on a fair and open site**.

(5)—THE ABOLITION OF CHILD LABOUR.

If we are to secure for our children a happy childhood, in which rest, recreation, and school all have their proper part, we shall find there is no room for "employment out of school hours." That shameful thing, "the wage-earning child," must be abolished, whether his "wages" are gained in a cotton mill, in a shop, or in the streets. **The half-time system must be done away with, despite the opposition from the textile areas, and street trading must be prohibited for boys up to 17 and for girls up to 18,** in accordance with the recommendations of the Departmental Committee. For those two reforms Acts of Parliament are needed, especially since the local Authorities show a scandalous laxity in using the powers which they possess to regulate child labour. The Employment of Children Act, 1903, gives a local Authority the power, if it chooses, to prohibit absolutely all labour of children under 14 years, and to fix any age between 11 and 16, below which street trading is illegal. Yet there are over 26,000 children under 14 *actually licensed as street traders* in England and Wales, and a great army of lads working the clock round on vans, in shops, billiard saloons, etc., to whom the local Authority shuts its eyes!

(6)—EDUCATIONAL REFORMS.

What is the minimum of education in the narrower sense that we must claim as the right of every child? At present it stands for the vast majority at nine years of pretty strenuous schooling. During these years—from 5 to 14—the attempt is made to impart a good deal more information than most of the scholars can assimilate in the time, while a good deal that ought to be taught is left out. But the demand is growing steadily for the **raising of the school age to 15 or 16, and it is certain that such a step is vitally necessary for the progress of the nation**. The objection that a poor man cannot afford to keep his children at school after 14 must be met in general by the ensuring of decent wages to every father of a family, and, in cases of particular hardship, by some form of maintenance grant from the Education Authority. In any event, it is a discreditable thing that the governing classes, who would be scandalised at the idea of being supported by their own sons and daughters at the age of 14, should proclaim it as a duty in the working class.

This is not the place to discuss reforms within the school itself. Suffice it to say that there is urgent need of changes in the curriculum, of reductions in the size of classes, and so on. But the worker's education ought not to stop even at 15. **A national system of Continuation Classes** is wanted—not night schools for young people wearied with a long day's labour, but day classes organised in such a way that the boys and girls shall divide their time equally between their industrial employment and their education—a half-time system, in fact, as suggested by the Minority Report, the young person under 18 being employed for twenty-four hours a week, and attending for another twenty-four hours at a Trade School or Continuation Class. Last, but not least, **the number of scholarships which will enable children to pass from the elementary to the secondary schools, and to the University, must be largely increased**. A democracy that denies "higher education" to five-sixths of its citizens is not only robbing the people of their birthright, but is preparing confusion and disaster for itself.

THE NEW CHARTER OF THE CHILDREN.

Here, then, are the six points of our Charter:—

(1) The removal of all children from the Poor Law.
(2) The securing through the Public Health Authorities of a fitting nurture for all infants under school age.

THE NEW CHILDREN'S CHARTER

(3) The securing through the Education Authorities of adequate food for all children of school age.

(4) The prevention and cure of disease in the school children by the Education Authorities by means of School Clinics, Open-Air Schools, etc.

(5) The prevention of child labour by amendment of the Factory Acts, prohibition of Street Trading, etc.

(6) The better education of the children by the raising of the school age, the establishment of day Continuation Classes, and the increase of facilities for Higher Education.

Notes

1 Annual Report of the Chief Medical Officer of the Board of Education for 1910. (Cd. 5925) p. 256.

2 In Ireland the figures are still worse. Last year there were actually 5,213 healthy children under 15 in the general workhouses, as against 2,623 boarded out and in certified schools.

3 See Minority Report of Poor Law Commission. Ch. IV.

4 Among the municipalities which run such institutions themselves, are Birmingham, Cardiff, Derby, Dundee, Glasgow, Sheffield, Lincoln. A number of others support voluntary institutions.

5 The reports of School Medical Officers show this only too clearly. Thus, to take one instance out of many, the Medical Officer for Northampton says,—"the attitude of parents towards this trouble (teeth), seems to be one of complete apathy and ignorance. . . . . . Very little good accrued from reporting ear troubles to parents, and the results of neglect were often serious in these cases, sometimes ending in death."

6 Dr. Leslie Mackenzie, reporting in 1907 on the Physical Condition of Children attending the Board Schools of Glasgow, showed that out of a total of 72,857 children, 5,922 or 8.1% were living in "one-roomed houses," and that the boys from these single rooms were on an average 11.7 lbs. lighter and 4.7 inches shorter than those from four-roomed houses, while the girls were 14 lbs. lighter and 5·3 inches shorter.

319

Part 9

WAR, PEACE AND INTERNATIONALISM

31

HANDS ACROSS THE SEA: LABOUR'S PLEAS FOR INTERNATIONAL PEACE (MANCHESTER: THE NATIONAL LABOUR PRESS, c. 1910), 1–16.

G.H. Perris

[Prominent in the British peace movement, G.H. Perris was one of the founding members of the National Peace Congress in 1904. As a Radical Liberal, he began to perceive his party's foreign policy as a betrayal of liberalism. In 1907 he joined with socialists including Henry Noel Brailsford in opposing the policy of entente with Russia which his party in government had adopted in response to the growing strength and foreign policy goals of Germany (Weinroth 1970, 666). The following year, the Liberal government's foreign policy and plans for rearmament led him to resign and join the Labour Party. Of particular concern was the government's argument that Germany needed to be opposed as a threat to peace (Gomme 2003, 19).

Perris' socialism in his pamphlet *Hands Across the Sea* of 1910 was of a radical nature, criticising the economics at the heart of capitalist society. For Perris (c. 1910), imperialism was a shibboleth for what in effect was the reactionary alliance of money power and class power. Hundreds of millions of pounds were wasted on armaments that rapidly became obsolete in an age of rapid technological advancement. More than a million men were needlessly kept in uniform, ready for war or unrest in the Empire. To pay for this military strength wages were depressed, education underfunded, and social reform stifled. He detected signs that the workers of Europe, long nurtured into servility by means of superstition and the ignorance it begat, had begun to stir, entering into a campaign of revolt. The Social Democratic Party in Germany had begun to expose the irrationality and self-interest that were leading their country into a war with the United Kingdom. It was time for the British Labour Party to act likewise and, as part of the worldwide socialist movement, promote a humane cosmopolitanism.

Perris' position changed in 1914. German aggression led him reluctantly to support the British war effort. As he had come to see the situation, the Kaiser and

WAR, PEACE AND INTERNATIONALISM

the German governing class would need to be removed from power before there could be any hope for his desired new world order.]

THE POWER OF THE PAST.

The whole life of the Western world is poisoned by a hideous contradiction. On the one hand, we see a number of peoples, in their domestic affairs, orderly, economical, good-humoured, and, as we say, "civilised," meaning that they have begun to understand the civil or civic virtues. They have set up systems of Government and law which, generally speaking, they can improve when they wish; and, naturally, trusting these Governments and laws to secure their rights, they have gradually dismantled their ancient fortresses, abandoned the practice of carrying arms, and employ police forces of only trivial strength. Moreover, the character, the interests, and the manner of life of these peoples— English and German, French and American, and the rest—become more and more similar. Trade, travel, and intellectual intercourse bring them constantly closer together. They copy each other's institutions; and, to strengthen their common interests, they have built up a series of common institutions—International Unions to govern postal, railway, and telegraphic communications; Conferences and Conventions to regulate affairs both of property (such as copyright) and labour; international law-courts (at the Hague and elsewhere) supported by a network of Arbitration and other treaties; a sort of World-Duma, in the periodical Peace Conferences at the Hague; all kinds of unofficial congresses; and last, but not least, the growing international organisation of the Labour and Socialist movements. That is one picture: national peace and the beginning of a union of nations; in a rudimentary form, the United States of Europe is an accomplished fact.

Now look on the other picture. In the remainder of their State relations, these same united peoples present a deplorable spectacle not only of disunion, but of bitter mutual suspicion, and even hostility. So little can they trust their common business institutions that millions of their people submit to barracks slavery from fear of foreign attack; and they spend the greater part of their public revenues in maintaining vast armies and navies against each other. We often scoff at the German Emperor's assumption of divine right, and his bombast about the "military virtues"; but when he declares that on "armaments alone" depend the security and prestige of the nation, he is only preaching the savage and stupid doctrine which all Europe, Great Britain included, practises. And practises, mark you, not only under despotism, but under universal or nearly universal suffrage. Thus, for every penny and every moment we give to the affairs of peace, we give a pound and an hour to the machinery of war. Yet we wonder that scares bring us every now and then to the verge of a suicidal conflict; we wonder that poverty still shames our democratic professions, and that reforms are neglected.

Such is the great anomoly of twentieth-century life, the dire disease from which the European body-politic is suffering in every part. Let us realise and remember from the outset that this disgusting and monstrous growth is maintained not by the Emperors and Kings, the soldiers and sailors, the great contractors and money-lenders, who batten upon it, but by the millions of working men and women of Europe, who could abolish it in twelve months if they really wished to do so.

THE IMPERIAL GORGE.

But great social evils can only be abolished when they are fully understood. We must come to close grips with the enemy, and learn the strength and weakness of his defences. Where, then, lies the strength of Militarism, with its poisonous fruit of barracks servitude and perpetually increasing waste on fortresses and ironclads? In the first place, of course, it is rooted in history. Europe has only half emerged from feudalism. The Continental idea of an army we hardly realise in England, where we have not been seriously threatened with invasion for centuries. But consider the case of India, for which we are responsible, and where we keep a large army because we cannot trust the people; or, better, that of Germany, where the army is commonly regarded as the only means by which a number of powerless little principalities could have been welded into a great united State. It is always easier to see the mote in the other fellow's eye than the beam in our own; we can easily see that, with half as large a standing army and no navy at all, Germany would be safe from attack, and that her greatness really lies in her schools, laboratories, workshops, and town-halls. But we have our own form of the common disease, and it is as hateful as any.

History, with us, even now when we dream of German spies, chiefly means the Empire. When British aristocrats, landlords, and capitalists began to meet with severe checks at home, they turned, by time-honoured precedent, to the outer ends of the earth to find more easily exploited estates. Hence our sword-made Empire (as distinguished from the Colonies made by emigrant workmen). These estates, spread over a large part of the globe, had to be "defended," and this was and is given as the chief purpose of the army and navy. Thirty years ago when the cost was only about a third of what it is now, the burden caused a good deal of grumbling, perhaps more than it does to-day. Fourteen years ago, I pointed out that the Estimates for 1897 represented an annual expenditure equal to two-thirds of the cost of the Crimean War, five times as much as the whole public expenditure on education, or six times as much as the whole cost of the London hospitals and charities. And this useless sacrifice has been nearly doubled in the interval.

This expenditure was commended in two ways. In the first place it was said that "trade follows the flag," and that, as the Empire was perpetually expanding, the army and navy must be enlarged in proportion, to protect the claims we were "pegging out for posterity." The area and population of the Empire did, in fact, increase by about one-half between 1883 and 1898, and our armaments in like proportion. But during that period our export trade was practically stationary, and to this day it is true that our trade with foreign countries, despite their tariffs, is three times as large as our trade with British possessions. So that trade very decidedly failed to "follow the flag."

THE BUBBLE BURSTS.

The pill of military and naval expenditure was then coated with the sickly mixture of national vanity, base self-interest, and maudlin sentiment, which its apostles called Imperialism. Financiers, speculators, politicians sang the praises of Mr. Rhodes and Mr. Chamberlain. Lord Rosebery prated about "efficiency," while British credit, labour, life, and treasure were poured out in mad enterprises in Africa and Asia. Everywhere we got ourselves hated; we were simultaneously embroiled on the four Continents. Good institutions were starved, and bad gorged; the Parliamentary machine was strained; Pro-Consuls pranced, and it seemed that Rudyard would never cease from Kipling; social reform was blocked; the gambling and filibustering spirit lorded it over humane and peaceful interests. Yet what a glittering and successful business the Imperialist movement seemed only a dozen years ago.

Then suddenly the bubble burst. Like a lightning flash the Jameson Raid illuminated the whole field of Imperial expansion, revealing a mixture of arrogance and pusillanimity, of greed and incompetence, such as few Englishmen had suspected to exist under the British flag. The Boer War, with its multitudinous scandals, the suppression of the republics, and the establishment of yellow labour, followed. These, and such as these, were the purposes for which we were keeping 200,000 men in South Africa, 437,000 regulars, yeomanry, militia, and volunteers at home, 100,000 British regulars in India and Egypt, in addition to 200,000 native Indian and 17,000 Egyptian troops, and 60,000 Colonials—a total of over a million men—a navy equal to its three strongest rivals, and, behind both, hundreds of thousands of workers in the armament trades. The mafficking was over. The "white man's burden" was seen to be largely the burden of the prodigal son. Repentance was all the deeper because there was no fatted calf to make it easy. Imperialism was revealed as meaning that we must allow Armenians to be massacred and our own poor to die of starvation, in order that we might be free to serve with our blood and our money the bond-holders of Egypt and the magnates of the Rand. Once this historical fact was discovered by the man-in-the-street, there was an abrupt end of the business of Imperial expansion. The game was up. England had awakened from a twenty years' nightmare.

The Empire thus reached its limit. Imperialism, driven underground, has since made ineffectual reappearances in the guise of "Tariff Reform," and in a furtive agitation for Conscription. But the spirit of Rhodes and Chamberlain is dead; and, with it, the reasons they alleged for great armaments have disappeared. Yet the armaments go on increasing. Why?

THE OLD MAN OF THE SEA.

Let us, for a clearer reply, turn to the case of the Navy. And here the outstanding facts are these:—

(1) That, while we maintain, in time of peace, the largest army in the world, except Russia's, and the costliest, we also claim the right to have a navy as strong as any two others. In reality, at any time these last twenty years we have had not merely a Two-Power but a Three-Power standard of naval force.

(2) We are no stronger relatively than we were thirty years ago; but we are now spending on the fleet the frightful sum of 40½ million pounds a year, the hard result of British skill and toil, where we were then spending only 10½ millions for the same result.

(3) Whereas we plead foreign rivalry, it is, in fact, we ourselves who provoked and led the way in this competition.

It is instructive to glance back over the process. There is no blinking the fact—we are a panicky people. There have been three great modern alarms: (1) the "Three Panics" which Cobden scathingly exposed; (2) the scare of 1884, created by Mr. Stead, Mr. Arnold Forster, and Lord Charles Beresford, and the period of great naval programmes to which it led, ending in the scrap-heap of 1905; and (3) the "Dreadnought" period which Mr. Blatchford and Mr. M'Kenna have peopled with phantoms of a German invasion. Noble statesmen at the head of the Admiralty—Lord George Hamilton, Lord Goschen, Lord Spencer, Lord Selborne, Lord Cawdor, Lord Tweedmouth—were always going to make one more final effort; and their colleagues at the Treasury were always ready with groans and crocodile tears at the thought of the tyranny of this "Old Man of the Sea." Goschen was the great plunger of his day. In the five years, 1895 to 1900, he brought our naval charges up from £19½ to £31½ millions a year. He once pretended to dismiss Lord Charles Beresford as an "irresponsible person." But the "talking sailor's" caustic reply was that "the Government has done everything, or nearly everything, that I have wanted them to do for years past." No less telling was the Admiral's story of a certain First Lord who declared one day that "if he had a couple of millions for the navy he would not know what to do with it, but shortlyafterwards came down to the House and said that if he did not have six millions we should lose the Empire."

That was the spirit of the game before the advent of the Labour Party, and while we were building, not against Germany, but against France and Russia. Lord Selborne brought the Estimates up to £37 millions (without naval works) in 1904, although the Russian fleet had been destroyed and the Anglo-French Agreement concluded. And then came another great crash, almost comparable with the anti-Imperialist reaction after the Boer War.

WAR, PEACE AND INTERNATIONALISM

LORD FISHER'S GREAT "SCRAP."

This commenced with an official confession, not in so many words, but in terribly pointed form, of the monstrous folly of the policy of the preceding two decades. Beside the obvious commonsense reasons, there are these two political and technical reasons for keeping armaments at the lowest possible point: (*a*) That the aspect of world-politics is perpetually changing; a distribution of strength that may seem wise to-day may therefore be made foolish to-morrow by some change of policy, some new combination, the emergence of some new problem, or the disappearance of some old one; (*b*) that invention is perpetually changing, and not seldom revolutionising, the machinery of war, as of peace; by overbuilding, therefore, we are either presenting the world with new designs and unnecessarily aggravating the cost of our own "insurance premiums," or we are piling up old types of ships and guns which invention may any day make obsolete.

These were the two branches of the startling confession appended by the Admiralty to the Navy Estimates of 1904–5. In the first place, the old strategy of Imperial defence, which required us to keep fleets in all the seven seas to guard our possessions and trade routes, was frankly abandoned. Schemes of naval works in distant stations were torn up. In future, the fleet was to be concentrated in home and near waters, trusting in the main to cruiser squadrons for work in foreign seas. Thus, the North and South-East American stations of 17 vessels were abolished, an Atlantic fleet of eight battleships withdrawn from the Mediterranean being established instead. Concentration was the note; and it was thought that our better relations with France and the disasters to Russia would react in favour of substantial retrenchment. So it might have been, if concentration had not been so conducted as to mean an imminent menace against Germany. In the second place, and this was the more startling thing, a new and shorter estimate of the effective life of warships was adopted, which condemned most of the vessels recently built as worthless. In twenty years we had spent about £450,000,000 in the vain effort to establish a maritime despotism. We had not fought a single considerable naval battle in that period; yet the greater part of this sum—which would have sufficed to establish old age pensions and industrial insurance in perpetuity without further charge—was now represented only by scrap iron. The whole classes of "protected" and "unprotected" cruisers were condemned as practically useless except for "police" purposes, a verdict affecting 115 vessels which had cost between £35 and £40 millions. Of these, 34 vessels were only five years old. The 38 cruisers of Lord George Hamilton's 1890 programme and all of the same type for which Lord Goschen and Lord Selborne were afterwards responsible, were dismissed to the scrap-heap. But no one proposed to impeach these lordly wastrels.

DREADNOUGHTS: THE SCIENCE OF WASTE.

You may suppose that such a lesson as this could not soon or easily be forgotten. If so, you do not realise what it is to live under a tradition that we must give

328

everything the Admiralty asks for. The mass of toilers who do not read Parliamentary reports or State papers never heard of Lord Fisher's great "scrap," or never understood it. The "governing classes" understand it—otherwise. For them it was really the preparation for a new start, a Spring cleaning of the Whitehall Casino in readiness for a new gambling season. The sacrifice of old ships should have resulted in a large economy. The memorandum announcing it stated that £4½ millions a year would suffice for their replacement. Yet the next vote for new building was £11½ millions. For several years, however, public opinion was mollified with small economies on the total Votes.

Then there appeared the new portent: On October 2, 1905, the Dreadnought was laid down, to be finished in December, 1906. At a stroke the competition of navies was lifted to a yet higher and costlier plane; large classes of ironclads and cruisers recently built were again rendered practically obsolete. A few months before, most of them had been officially given an effective life of from 15 to 22 years. What this new scrap-heap represents in cash—otherwise, in lost labour—it is hardly possible to say, perhaps £70 or £80 millions. The sequel is fresh in all our memories. Dreadnoughts have developed into Super-Dreadnoughts. Twenty of these monsters have been built or laid down at a cost of nearly £50 millions sterling. Now the aeroplane threatens to revolutionise warfare; and experts are talking of an altogether new type of warship, driven by gas or oil fuel with internal combustion engines, which will abolish the existing type of vessel.

Such is the punishment to which science dooms human folly. Invention and large-scale production govern the making of the machinery of manslaughter, as well as of useful commodities. But with what a different result! It is an automatic multiplication of evil. Every step in the increase of armaments is bad in itself, but it is worse in leading to a new stage of still greater waste and provocation. Yet all the forces of Governmental power, professional interest, and fashion go to stimulate the process. We badly want a nationalisation of the large productive industries, so that they may be managed not competitively for the benefit of a few magnates, but co-operatively for the benefit of the whole nation. What a satire it is on our claim to be an enlightened people that the only great manufacturing business we entrust to the State is the one which is a perfect embodiment of the worst human passions, and the most elaborate system of organised waste ever conceived by the wit of man!

"DOG DAY MADNESS."

Again I ask, why do we lie content under this burden? There were reasons for armaments in the past which have long disappeared. The day of warfare is passing, despite our piling-up of arms. I have said that the British Empire has reached its limit. The earth is, indeed, plotted out. I do not mean to say that there will be no more changes of possession; but, with the complete partition of Africa and the recent Asiatic agreements, the great territorial claims may be said to be all staked out.

WAR, PEACE AND INTERNATIONALISM

At the same time, the two Alliances which ten years ago embraced the Great Powers of Europe have been extended by a series of Ententes, and connected by a number of cross-agreements, so that there is a kind of equilibrium which everyone is afraid of disturbing. War there may be, but war in the manner of Napoleon, or even of Bismarck, is to-day impossible, because no human brain could command operations on the scale involved by any conflict between such State combinations, and because rulers, as well as parliaments and people, now see and admit that, as between any of the great European Powers to-day, war would mean economic ruin for the victor as well as the vanquished, for capitalist as well as labourer. The Tsar Nicholas and King Edward were neither of them what we should call eminent economists. But when the Polish banker, De Bloch, wrote his huge book to prove that a European war would mean bankruptcy for both combatants, the Tsar understood enough of it to call the first Hague Conference; and when Mr. Norman Angell published last year his excellent little volume "Europe's Optical Illusion"—to prove that, owing to the complexity of international credit, it is an utter impossibility for one nation to benefit economically by the conquest of another—he found the Palace already converted. This idea, that an Anglo-German war, for instance, "would from the point of view of both nations be Dog Day Madness, seemed" (Lord Esher tells us) "to be quite a familiar one to the King. To whichever victory might fall it would be disastrous to both nations. That was the idea which one could hear from him almost every day."

I cite this royal opinion, attested by an eminent representative of our military forces, just because it is the opinion, not of any mere economist or humanitarian or idealist of any kind, but of an ordinary shrewd business man. Consider for a moment what it means. Everybody admits the ruinous nature of the race of armaments—Lord Salisbury spoke of it almost as strongly as Mr. Gladstone, Mr. Balfour as Sir Henry Campbell Bannerman. The Tsar in his famous rescript of 1898 spoke words of eternal truth, whatever his motives or his after-actions may have been:—

> The financial charges consequent on increasing armaments strike at public prosperity at its very source. The intellectual and physical strength of the nations, labour and capital, are for the major part diverted from their natural application and unproductively expended. Hundreds of millions are devoted to acquiring terrible engines of destruction which, though to-day regarded as the last word of science, are destined to-morrow to lose all value in consequence of some fresh discovery in the same field. National culture, economic progress, and the production of wealth are either paralysed or checked in their development.
>
> Moreover, in proportion as the armaments of each Power increase, so do they less and less fulfil their object. The economic crises due in great part to the system of excessive armaments, and the continual danger which lies in this massing of war material, are transforming the armed peace of our days into a crushing burden which the peoples have more

and more difficulty in bearing. It appears evident, then, that if this state of things were prolonged, it would inevitably lead to the very cataclysm which it is desired to avert, and the horrors of which make every thinking being shudder in advance.

This, I say, is not contested. But militarists are naturally fatalists, and most of them, those who are sincere, justify a process admittedly ruinous by the belief that the desperate conflict they expect will come sooner than bankruptcy, perhaps very soon. Singular as it may seem, the last thing they take into account is the technique of modern warfare, the mass of factors—numbers of men involved, immense growth both of offensive and defensive power, greater industrial and financial disturbance—which make the warfare of the past seem, in comparison, mere child's play. It is not only that they ignore the positive forces which are gradually making warfare impossible—the growing practice of arbitration and mediation, the international interests of finance, and the rising power of Labour. They have never grasped or tried to grasp this lesson of modern science—that profitable warfare as between great modern States is a simple impossibility. Anti-Militarists are sometimes charged with inconsistency in saying that excessive armaments aggravate the danger of war, and at the same time that war between the Great Powers is becoming impossible. There is no inconsistency. The threat implied in the British "two-Power" standard against Germany, to say nothing of certain speeches and newspaper articles, unquestionably adds to the danger that the guns may suddenly go off, as it were, by themselves. On the other hand, a war such as in the old days gave one side supremacy or material advantage is to-day impossible. But a war that would mean complete national ruin on both sides is only too possible. This is the great fact King Edward saw; and what he and Lord Esher could understand is not beyond the intelligence of Premiers and Chancellors, or even of the lower mortals who pass our Navy Estimates. Let it be once understood that the purpose, as well as the process, of competitive armaments is ruin and "Dog Day Madness," and an agreement to stop the competition will soon be reached.

VESTED INTERESTS OF MILITARISM.

Two obstacles still stand in the way of this great international advance—Self-Interest and Superstition; and these two anti-social forces unite, among the mass of men who constitute the armies and navies of Europe and their supply trades, in a superstition of self-interest. The contractor's or financier's point of view is easily understood. He is simply out for immediate profits. But the simple soldier or sailor has no real interest in the maintenance of great armaments. He falls into the ways of thought of his officers, very much as, in the old days, domestic servants were marched to the church of their masters, in order that they might be reminded how good it is to be content with the place it has pleased Providence to give you. Tommy Atkins belongs to the working classes, and his real interests are all with them. He only gets into the army, in nine cases out of ten, because employment is bad when it happens to him to be cast upon the world, or because he has had to begin life without learning a trade. The system of capitalist industry cannot be worked without a surplus of out-o'-works; but these must live, and many of them do so by taking the King's shilling. Let a rational system of industry be established: men will still desire to defend their fatherland, but none will want to go to the recruiting sergeant for employment.

As things stand, however, it is important to realise how large a part of our adult male population is touched by this class or professional view of the question which it is the interest of militarists to cultivate.

The strength of the armed forces of the Empire in time of peace may be summarised approximately thus:—

In Great Britain:
Regulars ··· ··· ··· ··· ··· ···	135,000
Army Reserve ··· ··· ··· ··· ···	140,000
Special Reserve ··· ··· ··· ··· ···	80,000
Territorials ··· ··· ··· ··· ··· ···	300,000

In the Colonies:
British Regulars ··· ··· ··· ··· ···	45,000
Colonial Militia, etc. ··· ··· ···	100,000

In India:
British Regulars ··· ··· ··· ··· ···	76,000
Native Troops ··· ··· ··· ··· ···	165,000
	1,041,000

This, as I have said, is the largest peace establishment in the world, with the exception of the Russian army, which is of about the same size. Those of Germany and France number only about 650,000 men. Of the million of our soldiery, 776,000 are Britishers, 665,000 being located at home, and the remainder exiled mainly in tropical or sub-tropical lands. To this 776,000, we must add 185,000 men of the Fleet and the Naval Reserve. And behind this force of 961,000 able-bodied and middle-aged Englishmen, there lie two bodies, also of adult men, most skilled and able-bodied, whose numbers can be only approximately determined— (1) Those engaged in the arsenals and dockyards, and the numerous armament trades, and (2) Pensioners, small and large, possibly 100,000 of them, since their cost on the Estimates is about £2½ millions a year.

The probability is, then, that at least 1,500,000 adult able-bodied men—or one in six of the "occupied" adult males of the United Kingdom—share, to some extent, in the £65,000,000 a year which we spend on the twin "defence" services. Thus, even when we remember that many of these, like the "Terriers" and Reservists, get a mere allowance, while a large part of the regular army is paid for by

332

India, it will still be seen that we have here the most widely ramified of all our vested interests, a fearful drag upon reproductive industry, and an influence which must often diverge from the straight line of democratic advance. The big prizes, of course, all go to a small class of financiers and industrial magnates, who, in order to keep the game going, exert a thoroughly pernicious influence on Parliament and middle-class opinion. The higher officer ranks of the army and navy are an aristocratic preserve, and are highly organised for the advancement of their professional interests. This alliance of money power and class power, whose shibboleth and trademark is "Imperialism," includes the most determinedly reactionary elements in British society.

"NO MORE OF THIS FOOLERY!"

In a moment of inspiration, addressing a gathering of journalists in 1909, Lord Rosebery spoke of the extraordinary and ominous condition of Europe, of the contradiction between "an absolute absence of any questions which ordinarily lead to war," and universal and overpowering preparations for war. He added these, for him, remarkable words: "When I see this bursting out of navies everywhere; when I see one country alone asking for 25 millions of extra taxation for warlike preparation; when I see the absolutely unprecedented sacrifices which are asked from us on the same ground, I do begin to feel uneasy at the outcome of it all, and wonder where it will stop, or if it is going to bring back Europe into a state of barbarism, or whether it will *cause a catastrophe in which the working men of the world will say: 'We will have no more of this madness, this foolery, which is grinding us to powder.'* " Well, there are signs at last that the workers of Europe are rising in serious revolt against an oppression from which they all suffer. But why has the revolt been so long delayed? It is the old story—Superstition is the handmaid of Selfishness. Ignorance is the strongest of the chains that bind the mass of men to their servile lot.

The "Anglo-German peril" is the latest invention of the war-mongers; and I am bold enough to believe that it will be the last obsession of its kind. I say not "German," but "Anglo-German," because, if the mania existed only on one side, it would soon die out. But, in Germany and England alike, there are a few firebrands and a good many fools; and the shrieks of one and the howls of the other reverberate across the North Sea in endless echoes. There is guilt on both sides; but I fear by far the greater share is ours. At any rate, it is our business to deal with our own shortcomings; a long series of Social-Democratic successes shows that the Germans are dealing very effectively with theirs. In the first place, then, we have to realise that such panics as that of the Spring of 1909 are a disgrace to any strong and truth-regarding people. It was disgraceful in its Fleet Street origin, and in its end at St. Stephen's and in Whitehall. It was disgraceful in that Ministers gave countenance to a campaign of insolent mendacity by making what have turned out to be baseless charges against a neighbouring State—charges repeatedly exposed, yet never apologised for or withdrawn. It was disgraceful because a Government pledged to peace and economy capitulated to a brazen clamour of naval contractors, half-pay officers, and addle-pated journalists challenging them to add another-sixteen millions sterling to the waste on Dreadnoughts. It was disgraceful in its tone of bold and reckless provocation. Every man in his senses knows that a war between this country and Germany would destroy both lands, and might set half Europe ablaze. It would cost hundreds of thousands of lives, and would triple or quadruple the national debt. Before it was over it might bring upon us invasion or famine. If not a shot were fired, and only the trade between the two countries were arrested, many industries and businesses would be stopped, and a frightful economic crisis produced. Yet the militarists in Parliament, as well as in the Press, played with these risks as boys play with fireworks. There is no more urgent task for the Labour Party of the future than to deal straightly with these anarchists. It is peculiarly the task of Labour, for their object is the destruction of everything a Labour Party must stand for. Better poverty, war, any form of anarchy than social reform—such is the motto of the new Jingoism. It is the motto of M. Stolypin, the Russian Premier of the "bloody necktie"; and wherever reformers are weak-kneed it will triumph by sheer impudence. There is no way of dealing with this kind of Jingoism except to grapple with it firmly, and not to leave go till the lie is choked in its throat.

GERMANY AND "MARITIME DESPOTISM."

But, when we have made an end of vulgar panics, there is still a substantial problem of statecraft before the two countries ere a firm peace can be established which will enable them both to put their wealth to better uses. Smugness is a peculiarly Anglo-Saxon vice. We are always absolutely sure about the purity of our national motives—even when we know that national policy is run by a governing class which regards its own interests first, and those of the mass of the nation afterwards. We talk of our Navy very much as the Kaiser talks (though we smile then) about his army. We are quite sure it is for defence only, and that it is a thoroughly democratic affair. In this virtuous spirit all parties do homage to what is still called the Two Power Standard, though, in fact, it is and has for twenty years been a Three Power Standard; and in this same virtuous spirit the Admiralty refuses to give up the right of capturing or destroying private property in naval war, to say nothing of minor proceedings of the same kind, such as blockade, inspection, and prize-money. This is our side of the case.

Now look for a moment at the other fellow's side. I will try to summarise it with the aid of a recent article by Professor Lujo Brentano, the eminent German economist, Free Trader, and Liberal. Professor Brentano keenly desires an Anglo-German understanding; but he sees in the joint rule of commerce destruction and "two keels to one" nothing less than the assertion of a "maritime despotism." The very reasons pleaded for the size of the British Navy are pleaded for a large German Navy. Germany fears, or pretends to fear, invasion, just as we do; she also has colonies, and, above all, an immense and growing maritime commerce, to defend. She fears Jingo reactionists in England, just as ignorant Englishmen fear the Kaiser and his General Staff. But there are these two radical differences:

(1) Germany has never proposed in case of war to attack our private commerce; whereas, "it is part of England's policy to employ her superior naval forces in destroying, at the first blow, the trade of any country with which she may come in conflict, securing by this means not only her despotic overlordship of the seas, but her own commercial supremacy." (2) Germany's fleet, much as its growth has alarmed us, is less than half as strong as ours. Now, if there is anything more certain than another in the international sphere it is this, that no people 60 millions strong, with blood like ours, will ever rest content under the threat of an armed host twice as large as its own, and still wielding the generally-abandoned weapon of commerce destruction.

That is the other fellow's side of the picture; and I confess it seems to me about as good as ours. It is the view of the whole outer world. France took it, and built ships against us, until we made her our partner in the rivalries of Europe. The United States do not say they are building against us; but their great fleet is directed against us as much as against France, Germany, or Japan. We have throughout led the shipbuilding competition, with our claim to twice the naval strength of any other State. The whole competition, the squandering of hundreds of millions of hard-earned wealth, with its resultant depression of wages and starving of education and social reform, result, therefore, from what a not unfriendly observer like Professor Brentano calls "England's maritime despotism." There is no longer a single military despotism of Europe; and the time has come when there cannot be any longer a single naval despotism. We have recognised that fact, at last, so far as the Pacific is concerned, by leaving Japan in possession. We have got to recognise it in the North Atlantic. If this were an age of piracy, England would have a right, by her insular position, to a rather larger police force than Germany. But two keels to one goes far beyond any rational claim, and commerce destruction cannot be justified as a method of defence at all.

THE WEAKNESS OF FORCE.

Well, with all its faults, this is not an age of piracy. I have been content thus far to deal with the Philistine and Jingo on what they would call "ordinary, common-sense, business grounds." But, if intelligent foresight and idealism have largely deserted our middle and upper classes, they more and more influence the world of Labour; and I should disappoint my readers as well as myself if I did not conclude on a higher and firmer note than that of "ordinary business." In their better moments, even our present rulers catch glimpses of a power superior to the doom of a ceaseless rivalry in waste and provocation. Mr. Haldane, speaking as Lord Rector to the students of Edinburgh University on January 10th, 1907, uttered some fine words about this superior power. The foundations of public policy were not sure, he said, unless they were such that all the world could be legitimately asked to accept them as foundations.

It was not brute force, but moral power, that commanded predominance in the world. Armaments, of course, told; but even the most powerfully armed nation could not in these days hold its own without a certain measure of assent from those around, and perhaps the time was near when armaments would count for so much less than was the case to-day that they would tend to diminish and ultimately become extinct. What could most help and give free scope to this tendency was the genuine acceptance by the nations of a common purpose of deliverance from the burden, a purpose which the necessities of their citizens would surely bring, however slowly, into operation. It was not, therefore, after brute power that a nation could in these days safely set itself to strive. Leadership among the peoples of the earth depended upon the possession of a deeper insight.

THE NEW INTERNATIONALISM.

Mr. Balfour, who followed Mr. Haldane, described his speech as "a great discourse, an earnest, eloquent appeal, the result of ripe experience and strenuous mediation, which must heighten the sense of the responsibilities life bore for every one." For a moment these two great political-machine men got above themselves, above their daily occupations, above the crowd of professional idlers who make their regular environment, above the "evil communications which corrupt good manners." Let us pardon them much for that illuminated moment in which they saw that "It is not after brute power a nation can in these days safely set itself to strive." Other and greater voices, like that of the Grand Old Man of Russia, Tolstoy, ring out the same message in still more commanding tones. Moral influence, the influence of single men or of many men peacefully combined, counts for more and more in the world, brute strength for less and less. There is a splendid passage, full of the vigour and daring of a New World, in the greatest of American writers, Ralph Waldo Emerson, which I never get tired of quoting:—

> If you have a nation of men who have risen to that height of moral cultivation that they will not declare war or carry arms, for they have not so much madness left in their brains, you have a nation of lovers, of benefactors, of true, great, and able men. Let me know more of that nation; I shall not find them defenceless, with idle hands springing at their sides. I shall find them men of love, honour, and truth; men of immense industry; men whose influence is felt to the end of the earth; men whose very look and voice carry the sentence of honour and shame; and all forces yield to their energy and persuasion. Whenever we see the doctrine of peace embraced by a nation, we may be assured it will not be one that invites injury; but one, on the contrary, which has a friend in the bottom of the heart of every man, even of the violent and the base; one against which no weapon can prosper; one which is looked upon as the asylum of the human race and has the blessings of mankind.

But this humane cosmopolitan spirit is no longer a vague aspiration of middle-class poets, unsupported by the forces that govern the daily lives of average men. It is the highest expression of the most important of our common needs. Professional men, capitalists, scientists, administrators, reformers, and the representatives of labour, all of these, in their various spheres, demand international union. In the last ten years England has been driven out of her "splendid isolation." National sovereignty is not what it was, and never again can be absolute. We submit silently to judgments of the Hague Tribunal, even in large and ancient disputes like that of the Newfoundland fisheries, and arbitrate over affairs of "honour and vital interest" like the Dogger Bank outrage. The legislation of one country is quickly copied by others. International combines in industry and commerce are the order of the day. Education and cheap travel are rapidly creating ties of understanding and friendly feeling even between peoples supposed to be hostile. We sometimes say "Organise the world!" as though it were a task to be begun. But the political and economic organisation of the world is going on through a thousand channels every day; and they are blind who do not see that this is the supreme reality of the next generation.

THE POWER OF THE FUTURE.

The Trade Union and Socialist movements were not the first to realise the need of an international basis; but, having reached maturity in the leading Western lands, they now realise that need in its purest and strongest form. Capital is an international force, and must be grappled with internationally. No land is so small but it may provide blacklegs to break a strike of dockers or puddlers. Wages, like prices, tend to reach an international level, falling or rising in one country as they fall or rise in others. The great trade crises flow over the whole Western world, and resistance at one point helps resistance at another. Based upon these material interests, every hand-touch of Labour over the frontiers or across the seas creates a new consciousness of the value of solidarity. Ideals and methods become, in ever larger measure, common to the working masses in all lands. Their great leaders stand for much more than national aims; Englishmen get to know and applaud the Frenchman Jaurés, the German Bernstein, the Belgian Vandervelde, and give their platforms to spokesmen of downtrodden Russia and hungering India. A machinery of international Trade Unionism is created. The International Socialist Bureau in Brussels is a nerve-centre of the next vast development of democracy; the annual congresses it organises are pioneers of the Parliament of Man.

If, then, we ask the missionaries of the Independent Labour Party to give special prominence in their coming meetings to the idea of permanent peace and disarmament. It is with the confidence of something more than an ideal. We are part of a world-wide movement against obsolete forms of servitude, savagery, and waste that have been too long allowed to block the road of human advance. The best of the civilisation of to-day is on our side, and the power of tomorrow is ours. Greedy contractors, silly scare-mongers, and their official friends, whether in Germany or in England, are not checked by warlike preparations on the other side—quite the reverse. Each country must get rid of its own parasites. The democratic parties in each land must cut the claws of the enemies of the people. That is the work of National Defence to which we are called, the only road to a real national security, the only true patriotism.

There is a mediæval legend of a terrible dragon which ravaged a fertile countryside in nightly forays. At last, the secret was given away by a young woman who had been living for years in the dragon's cave, in hideous slavery it was supposed, really as the dragon's wife. It was but a pantomine dragon after all, rigged up by an ingenious robber, and made real only by the superstitious fears of his victims. To-day the ancient dragon, War, is found out. To deal the last blow, and then to enter into possession of the people's stolen heritage: such is the programme of the New International, in whose ranks the British proletariat will claim not the least powerful and honourable place.

32

A LABOUR CASE AGAINST CONSCRIPTION (MANCHESTER: NATIONAL LABOUR PRESS, c. 1913), 3–14.

Harry Dubery

[Harry Dubery was a prominent trade unionist, holding high office in the postal workers' union. Also an active member of the Independent Labour Party (ILP), he stressed in his pamphlet *A Labour Case Against Conscription* of 1913 that conscription primarily affected working men. The National Service League was funded by the wealthy in British society to appeal to the worker to defend his liberty, honour and country, when in fact the capitalists and landlords of the industrial system were presently doing him more harm than would foreign invaders. The point, for Dubery (c. 1913), was that all modern wars were rooted in greed and by the class interests of those who stood to gain financially. The ILP had, Dubery suggested, for many years championed the cause of international peace and brotherhood. He was, indeed, contributing to the ILP campaign.

Internationalism had been a major principle of the ILP since the 1890s. Senior ILP members Keir Hardie, Ramsay MacDonald, John Bruce Glasier and Philip Snowden were also prominent in the Labour Party. Dubery's role in the trade union movement, from which the Labour Party was inseparable, is significant. Hardie, MacDonald, Glasier and Snowden sought to cement an alliance between the ILP and the trade unions in the face of opposition from the left of the ILP.

Internationalism was the crucial factor. The interest of the parliamentary committee of the Trades Union Congress in foreign policy and international relations was patchy and generally lukewarm in the years before the outbreak of the First World War (Pelling 1976: 147–8). Nevertheless, Hardie, MacDonald, Snowden and Glasier sought to show that trade unionism was important to the international socialist movement, thus neutralizing the hostility of ILP radicals to the alliance (McNeilly, 2009).]

THE question of compulsory military service has long ceased to be a matter for abstract discussion. There is, at the present moment, an active campaign in

WAR, PEACE AND INTERNATIONALISM

operation to force on the adult male population of the United Kingdom, some form of conscription. Direct and indirect influences are at work; churches, chapels, day schools, Sunday schools, with their Scouts and Boys' Brigades, are being steadily utilised for the propagation of this idea.

Whenever a great military commander, such as the late Viscount Wolseley, dies, the opportunity is seized for a magnificent display of the forces of the Empire.

The Music Hall, the Cinema Theatres, a powerful Press, the death of a King, the crowning of his successor, the development of aerial flight, no means and no incidents are too small or too great for the purpose in hand, and it has now become imperative that the point of view of those who labour with hand and brain should be clearly and unmistakably stated on this all-important question.

It is a matter that primarily affects working men. It is their sons who will enter the conscript army, their daughters who will marry those who have passed through it, their labour power that must produce the additional wealth to meet the cost, their rights of combination that will suffer should the army be ordered to take the place of strikers—a thing which happened in France in 1910—their liberty and independence that will be curtailed in the name of obedience and discipline, and their skill and craftsmanship that may be irretrievably injured by army training during the formative years of life.

The demand for compulsory military service has been co-ordinated. An organisation with vast ramifications, apparently unlimited funds, a wealth of literature, and a horde of speakers, is doing its insidious work. The National Service League is its name, and it came into existence originally to demand the following:—

1. *A strong Navy,* at least equal in strength to the combined forces of any two Powers—equal not merely in actual numbers, but having regard to the duties which the vast extent of our Empire and our sea-borne commerce lay upon our fleets.
2. *A highly-trained, long-service Army* for garrison and police duties in India and elsewhere.
3. *An immense reserve of men*—a *Pan-Britannic Militia*—consisting of all able-bodied white men throughout the Empire. The Militia would be essentially intended for home defence in whatever part of the Empire it happened to be raised, the Australian Militia for Australian defence, the Canadian for Canada, etc. It would *never* be called on for garrison duty away from home, but it would form a reserve of men who would be *called upon* to fill up the casualties in the ranks of the foreign service army in time of war, and would reinforce it to any extent in a big war.

As far as details are concerned, the National Service League are prepared to be very accommodating. In their journal of November, 1903, the scheme advocated was merely for two months in a camp of exercise, and 14 days in each of three subsequent years. In a letter to the Press, signed by Lord Roberts and four vice-presidents, April 3rd, 1907, the League asked for six months' training for the Territorial Force, and that it should be made compulsory for all able-bodied males of the military age. Later in the same year, three or four months' training was demanded. Recently the demand has been made for four months' training for infantry, and an additional two months for other arms. A fortnight's camp training for three subsequent years, with liability to be called out for home defence up to the age of 30.

The great point is to add "the principle of compulsion," but directly it is suggested that compulsion means conscription, the reply comes, "No, we do not mean that," only "compulsory volunteering" or "universal compulsory service." The details do not matter, the principle of compulsion matters; this has been clearly indicated by Lord Roberts, who said in a footnote to *Fallacies and Facts*:—

> "I am glad to have this opportunity to explain that *the National Service League has no special predilection for this partcular period*. The League's desire is to see the principle of universal service for home defence accepted, as it seems to its members that, if this great principle once gains the consent of the majority of our countrymen, there will then be no difficulty in adjusting the details of the scheme which will be necessary to reduce theory into practice."

It is impossible now for the League ever to argue that the scheme is for home defence only; on October 22nd, 1912, at the Free Trade Hall, Manchester, Lord Roberts said:—

> "Germany strikes when Germany's hour has struck. That is the time-honoured policy of her Foreign Office. That was the policy relentlessly pursued by Bismarck and Moltke in 1866 and 1870; it has been her policy, decade by decade, since that date; it is her policy at the present hour. *And, gentlemen, it is an excellent policy. It is, or should be, the policy of every nation prepared to play a great part in history.*"
>
> Next, Lord Roberts definitely demands in the same speech an army "strong enough also to make our strength felt on the mainland of Europe should we ever appear there as the armed ally of another Power, as we were on the verge of doing last autumn."
>
> Thirdly, he asks, "What is my plan?" It is as follows: "Arm and quit yourselves as men, for the time of your ordeal is at hand."

The National Service League therefore demands, first, compulsory service, then that the details as to length of training are to be afterwards adjusted, and also that the conscript army should be utilised for the aggressive policy pursued relentlessly by Bismark and Moltke.

341

One would imagine from the arguments that the United Kingdom spent practically nothing on armaments, whereas, as a matter of fact, the bulk of our taxation is for that purpose as is shown by the following:—

FOR WAR:—

	£
National Debt	26,209,000
Army	27,860,000
Navy	44,085,000
	£98,154,000

FOR ALL OTHER PURPOSES:—

	£
Old Age Pensions	12,200,000
Education	18,729,000
Insurance and Labour Exchanges	2,845,000
Payments to Local Taxation	9,584,000
Road Improvement Fund	1,225,000
Other Civil Services	20,339,000
	£64,922,000

The figures for 1913 show an increase of £10,000,000 on the above, but the proportion for war is still maintained.

How we compare in this respect with other countries is also of moment:—

Country.	Population.		Armaments. (£ millions.)
Great Britain	45,650,000	....	73
France	39,400,000	....	56
German Empire	65,000,000	....	68
Austria-Hungary	49,400,000	....	21
Russia	164,000,000	....	61
Italy	34,800,000	....	23
Spain	19,580,000	....	10

It will thus be seen that in this appalling expenditure on death-dealing appliances the United Kingdom leads the world, and although the figures have increased since that return was taken, the lead by this country is still maintained. The growth of this expenditure is one that should indeed stagger humanity. Up to 1885 the average cost of the Navy was 10½ millions yearly; that of the Army had risen from 13½ millions in 1874 to 18½ millions in 1885, so that in the latter year the cost of both services was 29 millions. In 1894–5, when the Conservatives came into power, the Navy estimates were £17,416,000, and the Army £17,770,000, or £35,186,000. The Governments of two successive Tory Ministries managed nearly to double these amounts, and when the Liberals came into power in 1905 the Army estimates were £29,225,000, and the Navy £36,830,000, or £66,055,000 in all. For 1910–11 the Navy estimates were £40,603,700, and the Army £27,700,000. For the year 1913 the Army estimates are nearly £28,000,000, while the Navy will cost £46,309,300.

It is imperative at the outset that the exponents of compulsory military training should be met on their own ground, and that, apart from the exceedingly important side issues, it should be demonstrated that for Britain "bound in with the eternal seas" a very large army must, in the very nature of things, be entirely unnecessary.

Our actual peace footing according to *Whitaker's Almanack* is as follows:—
Britain's Army under arms in one year:—

	1913
Militia (Channel Islands)	3,113
Yeomanry and Territorials	268,414
Regular Army (exclusive of the Indian Army)	167,354
Total ...	438,881

There is also a reserve immediately available of 137,682, and a special reserve of 62,000, making a total, exclusive of those doing service in the colonies, of nearly 600,000 men that could be under arms in a very few days. The peace footing of France is about 537,000, and of Germany 600,000.

These figures are given because they have a direct bearing on the arguments that follow. The conscriptionist scare reappears at definite intervals, and the last one culminated prior to 1903, the Government of the day appointing an inquiry into the whole question. The report of the Norfolk Commission was the result, and it is to the evidence given before that body that one must turn to find the necessary arguments to refute entirely the statements that conscription is a necessary evil if Britain is to be adequately protected from invasion.

Conscriptionists argue as if the regular army in England were non-existent, yet it was stated before that Commission that as long as there are 120,000 men— Three Army Corps—in the country, there is no fear of invasion. This was admitted by Lord Roberts before the Norfolk Commission, as follows:—

Sir Coleridge Grove: You do not consider that an attempt at invasion is likely if we have three Army Corps at home?

Lord Roberts: I do not think so. (1016–1017.)

The late Lord Wolseley, giving evidence before the same tribunal, said, "I do not think it worth while to contemplate any condition of our sending 120,000 men abroad from these shores so long as there is the remotest possibility, or probability, of an invasion."

Lord Roberts says invasion is not likely while we have 120,000 men at home; the late Lord Wolseley cannot imagine us sending them away while there is a remote possibility of trouble, and our peace footing gives us an available army of over half a million.

No real impression of the actual position of home defence, however, can be gathered unless the Navy is also taken into consideration. There is an overwhelming concensus of opinion that these islands must primarily depend upon the Navy for their defence.

The naval experts have never asked for conscription nor have they ever believed in the serious possibility of invasion. Perhaps the most ridiculous proposition ever put forward in the House of Lords was that Germany could, if she felt so disposed, mobilise, entirely unknown and unsuspected by Great Britain, an army of 150,000, with the necessary munitions of war, obtain ships to convey them to some quiet spot on the English coast, and that one fine day we should find the country already in the possession of the Germans. Such an army would require 500,000 tons of war materials, and although there may be places on the east or south coast where a landing could be made, yet in such a case the enemy would have to transfer all his men, guns, horses, waggons, ammunition, and stores into open boats. At Clacton in 1904 it took two days to land only 10,000 under the most favourable conditions. With this fact before one, the possibility of landing 150,000 men with 500,000 tons of equipment, with the British Army knowing nothing about it, and the Navy equally ignorant, becomes so utterly absurd a proposition as to warrant immediate dismissal from our minds.

At the present moment we have 86 per cent. of our total battleship strength concentrated in home waters, and the invasion cranks should know that in these days of foreign spies, wireless telegraphy, and an unending volume of shipping passing through the North Sea and the English Channel, lengthy notice would most certainly be given; three weeks to six months, according to the experts.

The invading army, even if it escaped a blockade in its own ports, would so far "cover the sea," as to fall an easy prey to our Navy.

Faced with this indisputable fact, the conscriptionists fall back on the possible annihiliation of the Navy. No mere defeat would suffice, for all the while a few ships could be got together, those, operating in combination with destroyers and submarines, would be sufficient to destroy the greater part of the enemy's transports; but the fleet destroyed, then the enemy could pour in troops. But would he?

"If our fleet were defeated," said General Turner, before the above-mentioned Commission, "and our sea ways barred to us, we must yield to hunger."

If we had eight millions trained to arms they would be useless. "With the loss of our sea-command, it would be unnecessary for our enemies to land a single soldier on our coast; to do so would be a wanton waste of human life, for starvation would compel us to sue for peace." (Col. O'Callaghan-Westrop. Report of Norfolk Commission.)

Arguments from Switzerland or any other Continental country fail before the logic of the above facts, and the advocacy of conscription in view of them renders the advocates suspect.

It is part of their presumption that the whole of the population of these islands are equally keen on defending its shores, and would equally suffer presuming an invasion was successful. Lord Roberts addresses his message "To the Nation," "to all patriotic men within the Empire," "to the young men of every rank and social status, of every trade, profession, and calling of every kind." They, in a word, "who now are England." "Is it possible that you can shirk the issue or fail to respond to your country's summons, to the memories of the past, to the hopes of the future."

He finishes his Manchester speech of 1912 by saying, "Men are necessary—men of spirit, men of energy, loving their country. . . . I say to you, therefore, demand the right to defend your country, your own honour as Britons, and your liberties as citizens of this Empire."

We would that those who expound such grandiloquent sentiments would take cognisance of certain facts which must have come under their notice.

How many would be accepted did they respond, in a moment of enthusiasm, to such a call?

When the Director-General of the Army Medical Service published the recruiting statistics for 1900, it was seen that out of 84,402 candidates examined, 23,745, or over 28 per cent., had been rejected as being physically unfit.

General Sir Frederick Maurice showed that large numbers, even greater than those rejected by the recruiting agencies, were subsequently discharged by the regimental medical officers. His alarming statement came, in effect, to this, that 60 per cent. of the men offering themselves are physically unfit to serve as soldiers. Cannot our conscriptionists inquire into the reason for this? Such an inquiry would arm them with facts regarding slum conditions, long hours of labour, wretchedly sordid and filthy surroundings, bad and insufficient food, vitiated atmospheres, problems of unemployment, horrible diseases, high mortality rates among both children and adults, and all the loathsome conditions that make up the modern industrial conditions from the workers' standpoint.

Did they study these facts, it might dawn on them that there are certain important preliminary social problems to be dealt with before such ideals as "a nation in arms" becomes even remotely possible.

Apart from the purely sentimental standpoint, how much real appeal can there be to the ordinary working man on the lines of defending or preserving one's home and land from foreign foes? The great fact has emerged from the careful studies of sociologists, that the enormous annual income of the United Kingdom is so badly distributed that, with an aggregate income of nearly two thousand million per year, 30 per cent. live in the grip of perpetual poverty.

To at least that 30 per cent., the demand to enter a national army could only be received with derision. What have they to defend? Under what European conqueror could their condition be worsened? The inhabitants of Alsace-Lorraine are certainly in no worse condition from the economic standpoint because they are now governed from Berlin instead of from Paris.

There are 700,000 deaths per annum in the United Kingdom. Over 600,000 of those that die leave nothing that can be declared as property for the purpose of the Inland Revenue Officials. What of the homes, the furniture of the poor—the 30 per cent. in the perpetual grip of the direst poverty?

The inheritors of the property of the 3,900 who died leaving nearly £200,000,000, the 87 who died leaving £500,000 each, and the 8 who died leaving £3,000,000 each—these might be keen on a conscript army, although it is doubtful whether they would be found in the ranks. We are told, too, that out of an acreage of 77,000,000 in the United Kingdom 40,426,900 acres are owned by 2,500 persons. Hardly more than one million people hold land, and the great majority possess but the tiniest strip; 40,000,000 are proletarians, disinherited, landless, and conquest would at most mean perhaps a change of landlords.

The penultimate census disclosed the fact that in England and Wales there existed in 1901, 3,286,526 tenements of less than five rooms, of which 251,667 had but one room, 650,000 but two rooms, and 779,992 but three rooms. There are some 6,400,000 houses in England and Wales not assessed to the Inhabited House Duty because the rent is less than ten shillings per week. There is an average of five and one-fifth persons to each house.

The working man is hardly likely to consider seriously the question of home defence until he can be shown just how far he is likely to be injured by foreign invasion. Appeals to him to defend his liberty, his honour, his country, must be preceded by proof that the industrial system leaves him at present either liberty, honour, or a country to defend.

If this country were invaded and overrun by a foreign power, the conquerors would be a clever crowd indeed if they could skin the British worker cleaner than the capitalists and landlords skin him at the present moment.

Faced with this line of argument, it is not unusual for the conscriptionists to state that compulsory military service would have a direct bearing even on these problems. In a letter widely circulated by them in 1909 the last argument used was, "We leave it to the nation to judge whether the additional sum is a high price to pay for. . . . the spell of open-air life and for the general improvement in mental, moral, and physical well-being."

Lord Roberts, in a speech at Manchester in 1906, said "The moral training which men would receive from subjection to judicious discipline, and the habits of self-restraint and method they would acquire, would greatly increase their industrial efficiency, and lead to a recognition of a higher standard of behaviour." Apart from the question as to what would be a higher standard of behaviour on the part of the working man engaged in industry, in the opinion of Lord Roberts, it is necessary to deal specifically with the statement constantly reiterated that army training necessarily leads to improvement in morals and discipline. Those who make the statement never produce the slightest evidence in its support, and for the individual desirous of obtaining satisfactory data, the only course open is to see what has been the result of conscription on the working man in those countries where for many years past, the ideals of those who advocate it, have been fully realised. Here the weight of evidence is all against them; with complete unanimity, from every section of the community, from intellectuals, humanitarians, leaders of religious thought, editors of national newspapers, leading statesmen, and working-class representatives, comes utter condemnation of conscription precisely because the moral effects are so injurious.

M. Drumont, Editor of the *Libre Parole,* a leader of the French Nationalist Party, says, "Compulsory military service, far from being a school of morals, is a school of drunkenness, idleness, and debauchery."

Père Forbes, a well-known preacher in the Catholic Church, stated: "The family in France gives to the army a young man clean in mind and body; the army gives back that same young man steeped to the very lips in debauchery, suffering from disease and degrading vices."

M. Anatole France says: "The barracks are an abomination, the most hideous invention of modern civilisation."

The difficulty is to know what to select from the enormous mass of condemnatory opinions in existence, and although the above are typical, they could be supplemented by many others. The medical testimony is equally damning, not only with regard to the diseases contracted, but also because of those other cases, of which there are large numbers, where soldiers, genuinely ill, but accused of malingering, are left to die. The French Radical papers teem with instances of soldiers who pay with their lives for the officers' prejudice against all who go to the doctor.

In Germany, Bebel used once a year to speak at great length in the Reichstag on nothing else but the cases of immorality which had come under his notice.

One extraordinary proof of the effect of army morals and discipline on the conscripts, is the high rate of suicide. The comparative position is as follows:—

	Rate of Suicide.
Austrian Army...	1 in 887
German do	1 in 1,881
Italian do	1 in 2,570
French do	1 in 3,570
British do	1 in 4,762

Among the remainder of the population of the United Kingdom the rate of suicide is only half that of the army.

Discipline and Obedience. Lord Hugh Cecil stated in a lecture on "Liberty and Authority," delivered at Edinburgh in 1909, "If by discipline is meant self-discipline, that certainly is a most precious quality. But is it the case that soldiers are preeminent in self-discipline? I confess I have never been able to notice that the soldiers are superior in self-control and self-discipline to the civilians. Discipline, then, in the military sense means something different. It means, I apprehend, obedience—what is called in military language—Subordination.

"Obedience is in truth a non-moral habit. It may make for good, but it may also make for evil."

We would remind the advocates of army discipline that "Peace hath her victories not less renowned than war," and infinitely more productive. The discipline of "steady, patient toil," "of the daily round, the common task," is no less effective, nor is the courage required on the industrial field less than that required for the battlefield.

The reported accidents under the Factory and Workshop Acts, in an average year give the gruesome total of over 1,047 persons killed, and 92,600 wounded, in the industrial campaign. Nearly another hundred succumb to poison or anthrax, and almost a thousand others are poisoned but do not die. Over a thousand more are killed in mines and quarries, and another 5,000 injured. Another 500 are done to death on the railways, and fifteen thousand are injured there. If it is risk to life and limb that is to be made an inducement, men may as well remain at their present occupations.

Incidentally, it has been argued that an armed nation would help to solve the problem of unemployment. The answer to this is, first, that unemployment is as serious a problem among the armed nations of Europe as it is in the United Kingdom, and then that the annual expenditure in Europe on armaments amounts to the colossal sum of over £400,000,000. If this money was spent in peaceful pursuits, then, indeed, would the problem of unemployment be advantageously affected. It is clear that money spent on armaments means the withdrawal of good labour from productive to non-productive functions, with the immediate lessening of the actual output of real wealth, and is necessarily accompanied, too, by such serious side issues as the reduction of the real home life of the nation to the extent that time has to be given to army training, and, also, as in France, to an increase in women and child labour in the fields, someone having to take the place of those torn from industry.

"Let us," said a National Service League orator in a recent debate, "see in every nation a potential enemy, and as no man can live unto himself, let us realise that every nation is a complete unit, and that therefore every class, trade, and profession must stand together"; less and less, as a matter of fact, is such a statement true as the years roll on. Every nation, through international trade and commerce, becomes interwoven with every other nation; for the clothes we wear, the food we eat, the raw materials that we use in industry, we become more and more dependent upon people of every race, creed, and colour, and they on us.

When Germany and France suggest higher taxation to increase armaments, the value of gilt-edged securities the world over is adversely affected. When there is a financial crisis in Berlin, unemployment is caused in England. Every great modern war has cost both the victorious and the vanquished dear. All modern wars are caused by sectional greed and by class interests, by those within each nation who stand to gain financially. This fact becomes more and more apparent as time passes, and as a result, an ever-increasing number of the workers of the world are refusing to submit themselves to be the tools of those animated by greed of gold and lust of conquest.

348

The Independent Labour Party has for many years championed the cause of international peace. In October of 1910 it organised a national campaign against the increasingly heavy burden of armaments. Over two hundred and fifty meetings were held, and were addressed by Labour M.P.s and others. The following resolution was moved at each meeting:—

> That this meeting, believing that militarism and war are subversive of civilisation and national well-being, protests strongly against the heavy and growing burden of armaments which arrest social reform and endanger international solidarity, goodwill, and peace. It further affirms that militarism, whilst profitable to certain financial interests, imposes a blood-tax on labour, and threatens to inflict on Great Britain the evils of compulsory military service. The meeting, therefore, declares that disputes between nations should be settled not by brute force, but by reason and arbitration, and urges the workers of this country to take organised action with their fellow-workers in Germany and other lands in defeating the purposes of scaremongers and war-makers and in bringing about the federation of the European States, thus leading to ultimate disarmament and advancing the cause of social justice and international peace.

The appeal is made to all who have the good of the world at heart who believe in international brotherhood, to aid in the endeavour to hasten the time "when Europe will beat her spears into pruning hooks, forget the arts of war, and sing the songs of peace."

33

THE ORIGINS OF THE GREAT WAR (LONDON: UNION OF DEMOCRATIC CONTROL, 1914), 3–17.

Henry Noel Brailsford

[In his pamphlet *The Origins of the Great War*, published by the Union of Democratic Control (UDC) in the early months of the First World War, Henry Noel Brailsford (1914) stressed that the causes of the conflict were economic. He also made the case for British withdrawal from the war. The UDC was founded in August 1914 by Ramsay MacDonald of both the Independent Labour Party (ILP) and Labour Party along with several prominent Liberals as an organisation both demanding the end of secretive diplomacy and seeking to empower citizens to have greater control of foreign policy. The inaugural meeting was attended by Liberal Radicals and ILP members, the latter including Brailsford (Leventhal 1985, 131–132).

Brailsford wrote from his distinctive cosmopolitan perspective, combining the influence of the Enlightenment ideas of Condorcet, the proto-anarchism of Godwin, Marxism, democratic socialism and even radical liberalism (Lamb 2010; 2017). Brailsford had joined the ILP in 1907 as the party best-suited to his internationalism (Leventhal 1985, 95–96). For him, the origins of the war had been German and Russian rivalry for control over Eastern Europe or, as he put it "hegemony of the Near East". Entanglement in this struggle for a European balance of power in the early twentieth century had brought Britain into a war in which it had no real purpose or concern. The British alliance with Russia involved supporting a country which, if victorious, would bring about a situation in that part of Europe at least as bad as that which would result from German victory. Whatever settlement might be worked out at the end of hostilities, what he called "the armed peace" would bring many years of anger and waste, leading eventually to another war of revenge. *The Origins of the Great War* is one of the most sophisticated arguments against the war emanating from the British left. An interesting feature of the pamphlet is Brailsford's analysis of the pro-war stance of the German Social Democratic Party.]

For Englishmen this war is primarily a struggle between Germany and France. For the Germans it is emphatically a Russo-German war. It was our secret naval commitment to France, and our fatal entanglement through ten years in the struggle for a European balance of power, which sent our fleets to sea. It is our sympathy with France which makes the one human link that binds us to the Triple Entente. We have dramatised the struggle (and this clearly was for Sir Edward Grey the dominant consideration) as an attempt to crush France. German thinking followed other lines. Alike for the deputies in the Reichstag and for the mob in the streets of Berlin, the enemy is Russia. It is true, indeed, that if the war should end in the defeat of the Triple Entente, some part of the consequences of defeat would be borne by France. It is clear that German statesmen hoped to acquire some part at least of her extensive and valuable colonial possessions, and on her no doubt would have fallen the financial brunt of the war. She would have paid in money and in colonies for her imprudence in allying herself to Russia. But in spite of this, her place in Germany's imagination was secondary. Her army must indeed be broken before Russia could be dealt with. That was a fatality, a detail in the mechanics of the problem which affected its central political purpose hardly more than the resistance of the Belgians. The politics which made the war, and the sentiment which supported it, had reference exclusively to Russia. Read the speech by which the Chancellor induced the Reichstag to vote the war-credit without a dissentient voice; the only mention of France in it is a reply to the French accusation that German troops had violated the French frontier. The illuminating White Paper (Denkschrift) in which the history of the outbreak of the war is set out from the German official standpoint, contains hardly so much as an incidental reference to France. More significant still is the speech in which Dr. Haase, on behalf of the Social Democrats in the Reichstag, while repudiating the diplomacy which made the war, accepted on behalf of his comrades the duty of patriotic defence. He, too, made no reference to France. "For our people," he declared, "and for the future of its liberties, much, if not everything, depends on a victory over Russian despotism, stained, as it is, with the blood of its noblest subjects." It is for us in this country of the first importance to follow the direction of German thought. If we are to understand why the war was made at all, if we are to grasp the reasons which will make it on the German side an obstinate and determined struggle, if we are to think out with any hope of success the problem of shortening it, we must realise that it was the fear of Russia which drove German diplomacy into a preventive war, and in the end mobilised even the Social Democrats behind German diplomacy. To the diplomatists and the statesmen the issue was from the first not merely whether Austria or Russia should exert a hegemony in the Balkans, but also whether Russia, using Servia as her vanguard, should succeed in breaking up the Austrian Empire. It is not merely a tie of sentiment or kinship which unites Germany to Austria. Austria is the flying buttress of her own Imperial fabric. Cut the buttress and the fabric itself will fall. To the masses of the German people the fate of Servia and even of Bosnia was a matter of profound indifference. A month before the war broke out, three Germans in four would probably have said that not all the Serbs in Christendom were worth the bones of one Pomeranian

351

grenadier. But the Russian mobilisation and the outbreak of war made even for the German masses a supreme and only too intelligible issue.[1] There is rooted deep in the memory of the German people a recollection of the exploits of the Cossacks during the Seven Years' War. The simplest peasant of the Eastern marches has his traditions of devastated fields, and ruined villages. He knows, moreover, that the intervening generations which have transformed the West have left the Russian steppes still barbarous. Even for the Social Democrat the repugnant thought that he was marching out to shoot down his French and Belgian comrades was overborne by the imperious necessity of arming to defend his soil against the millions which the Russian Tsar had mobilised.

The Military Rivalry.

The broad fact about the general war of 1914 is that it is the postponed sequel of the Balkan war of 1912. We all congratulated each other that Sir Edward Grey's diplomacy and the Conference of London had enabled the Eastern peoples to settle the Eastern question without involving the Great Powers in war. The armaments of the Great Powers betrayed their belief that a war averted is only a war postponed. For two years this chaotic struggle, which came in the end with such vertiginous speed, had cast its shadow before it. The first move in the last round of the war of armaments was the direct consequence of the creation of the Balkan League. In justifying the last increase of the peace-effectives of its army the German Government pointed to the new fact of the entry on the European scene of these young and victorious Balkan armies, and spoke bluntly of a possible struggle between the Slav and Teuton worlds. The Balkan League of 1912, formed under Russian guidance, was, in fact, an alliance directed as much against Austria as against Turkey. There followed the reply of France and Russia, the return in the one to Three Years' Service and in the other the imprudently-advertised schemes of military reorganisation, with its vast naval expenditure, its new strategic railways near the German frontier, its rearmament of the artillery, and its gigantic increase in the standing "peace" army. Russia (so an official memorandum declared) would henceforth be able to assume in case of need not merely a defensive, but an offensive strategy.[2] The early months of this year witnessed the outbreak of a military panic in the German press. The fear inspired by the growth of the Tsar's armies was beginning to tell on German nerves, and a pamphlet to which the German Crown Prince contributed an approving note, predicted that the Slav world would have completed its armaments by the year 1916, and would then attempt to deal the death-blow to the German peoples. If Germany has by her own act made the general war in 1914, it is chiefly because her military caste was convinced that it would sooner or later have to meet a Russian challenge.

The Servian Menace.

The German White Paper explains the political issue which was the obverse of this military rivalry. For a generation we in this country have thought of the Eastern question as an issue between Turkey and the Christian races of the Balkans. With the destruction of the Ottoman Empire in Europe the Eastern question became primarily an Austrian question. Russia and Austria, up to the eve of the Young Turkish revolution had been content to divide the hegemony of the Near East. They worked in close association; they presided jointly over the Macedonian reforms; they even recognised a certain division of spheres of influence. Austria was allowed by Russia to exert a predominant pressure upon Servia, while Russia was the leading partner in all that concerned Bulgaria. It was never, at the best, an easy arrangement to maintain. Austria was always detested in Belgrade, and the dominant political party in Servia, the Radicals, were vehemently Russophile. With the murder of King Alexander, and the coming of King Peter, the moral influence of Russia in Servia became supreme, but the little kingdom remained none the less within the Austrian sphere, until the Bosnian crisis shattered the whole conception of an Austro-Russian *condominium* in the Balkans. From the autumn of 1909 onwards, Servia became as absolutely and almost as openly the protégé of Russia, and the tool of Russian policy, as Montenegro had been for generations. It would hardly be an exaggeration to say that the dominant personality in Belgrade was not King Peter, nor yet M. Pachitch, but the brilliant, energetic, unscrupulous Russian Minister, the late M. de Hartwig. He formed the Balkan League, and he also encouraged the Servians to tear up the Treaty of Partition, which the Tsar had guaranteed. There were several reasons why Russian policy regarded the Servians as its favoured foster-children, and willingly aggrandised them at the expense of the Bulgarians. The Servians, in the first place, have always been the more pliable, the less independent of the Balkan Slav peoples. But while the Bulgarians were useful as a piece in an anti-Turkish policy, the Servians were doubly valuable, for they were indispensable to any move against Austria. The annexation of Bosnia, so far from being accepted by the Servians as a final and irrevocable fact, had actually been the starting point of an agitation more conscious, more open, and more reckless than any which had preceded it. The triumph of Servian arms in Macedonia, first over the Turks and then over the Bulgarians, was accepted by most Servians as the presage of a greater victory to come. There was evident a tremendous heightening of the national consciousness. Some of its effects worked uncompensated mischief. It showed itself as brutal intolerance towards the Albanians and the Bulgars in Macedonia. The Servians are an attractive race, imaginative, quick-witted, excitable, and richly endowed with the artistic temperament. But their morals and their politics belong to the Middle Ages. They were judged more harshly than they deserved for the murder of that neurotic despot, King Alexander. But the officers who at the same time murdered his queen, mutilated her corpse, and flung it naked into the streets of Belgrade, gave the measure of their own social development. Their record in Macedonia reveals their political immaturity. By exile and imprisonment they forced the conquered Bulgarians to sign documents in which they declared themselves not merely loyal Servian subjects, but Servians by race and choice. They totally suppressed the Bulgarian Church, and exiled its bishops. They forbade the public use of the Bulgarian language. They denied the conquered population all political and some civil rights. They have ruled by the harshest form of martial law. This revival of patriotism created a militarism wholly alien to the democratic traditions of the Balkan races. But it also set the nation to the work of organising itself for the future with a new seriousness and a new devotion. Under her two last Obrenovitch Kings, Servia had been nothing but a meaningless and isolated *enclave* in the Balkans, wedged between Austria and Bulgaria, without a future and without a mission. Her national life was stagnant and corrupt. The coming of the new dynasty, and still more the breach between Austria and Russia, opened a brilliant path before her. She believed at last that the re-union of all the Servian peoples was possible, and she resolved that it should come about under her leadership. She saw herself destined to do for the Serbs what Piedmont had done for the Italians. The adventure might seem to sober minds impossible. Servia in isolation could hardly dream of challenging Austria with success, even if she had the moral and material resources which enabled Piedmont to expand into the Kingdom of Italy. But the Servians remembered that Piedmont did not overcome Austria by her own resources. She had Louis Napoleon behind her. If the Servians armed and plotted for the liberation of Bosnia and the other Serb lands under the Austrian yoke, it was with the firm conviction that when the hour of destiny struck, Russia would stand behind them.[3]

Russia Behind Servia.

When historians come to deal with the real causes of this general war, it is possible that exact documentary evidence may show how far Russian diplomacy stood behind the Greater Servian propaganda. The general presumption is strong. No one doubts that Russian influence was supreme in Belgrade. The Serbs owed much to their own arms, but on the whole they owed more to Russian diplomacy. But for Russia, the Austrians would have crushed them in 1909; but for Russia, Austria would certainly not have remained neutral during the two Balkan wars. To Russian pressure Servia owed such of her conquests in Albania as she was allowed to retain, and but for Russia, Austria would have torn up the iniquitous Treaty of Bucharest. There were more material bonds between the Great Power and her satellite. The Servian soldiers made the winter campaign of 1912–1913 in Russian greatcoats, and the second Balkan War was financed by the French banks which do nothing in the Balkans that would run counter to Russian policy. When the full tide of Servian aspirations set towards Bosnia, and the National Union (Narodya Odbrana) began to turn against Austria all the criminal "comitadji" methods of agitation consecrated by long usage in Macedonia, Russia, had she chosen, might have set her veto on a development of Servian policy which threatened European peace. It is this absolute dependence of Servia upon Russian countenance and support, which makes it probable that when Servia openly launched and assisted the Great Servian propaganda, she did this with Russia's approval. This propaganda involved much more than a mental disturbance in the minds of the Servian population of Bosnia and Herzegovina, who were organised in patriotic leagues and clubs with a view to an insurrection in the future. It had begun to smuggle arms, and it had been guilty of a series of assassinations of Austrian officials, to which the murder of the Archduke Francis Ferdinand and his Consort came as the climax. The Archduke was singled out for vengeance, not at all because he was the enemy, or oppressor of the Slavs. He was feared by Servians because his aim was to reconcile the Slavs to Austria. The historical memorandum in the German White Paper declares bluntly that this reckless and provocative attitude was possible for Servia "only because she believed that she had Russian support in her activities." The memorandum goes on to make an even graver statement. After referring to the original creation of the Balkan League under Russian auspices, it continues:—

> "Russian Statesmen planned the rise of a new Balkan League under Russian protection, a league which was aimed not at Turkey—now vanished from the Balkans—but against the Austro-Hungarian monarchy. The idea was that Servia should be compensated for the cession of its Macedonian acquisitions to Bulgaria by receiving Bosnia and Herzegovina at Austro-Hungary's expense."

There is nothing improbable in this statement. The original Serbo-Bulgarian alliance of 1912, afterwards expanded into the Balkan League, was directed against Austria as well as Turkey. The treaty, as more than one Balkan diplomatist has told me, required Bulgaria to put all her forces at Servia's disposal in the event of a war against Austria. These preparations for a united Slav assault upon Austria explain the determination of the German Powers to challenge Russia. Nor should it be forgotten that Pan-Slavism was busy in Galicia as well as in the Serbian lands. An active propaganda, disclosed in some famous State trials, was endeavouring, in Russian interests, to win the Ruthenians for the Orthodox Church. At its head stood the Russian reactionary politician, Count Bobrinsky, who, as Governor of Galicia, is now officially promoting the conversion of the Catholic Ruthenians to Orthodoxy.

It is not easy in the midst of the horrors and resentments of war to view such a situation as this in cold retrospect. The peril in front of Austria was grave, but it was not immediate. Russia had not at the first essay succeeded in restoring the Balkan League. Bulgaria could not forget her resentment, and had become a loosely attached associate of the Triple Alliance. If the Slavs were to choose their own hour, they would wait presumably until the Balkan armies had somewhat recovered from the exhaustion of two campaigns, and until the Russian military re-organisation was completed. But there was good reason to infer that, sooner or later, the blow would be struck. A rising in Bosnia, organised by Servian comitadjis, would bring Servia herself into the field, and behind Servia would be the Balkan League and the Russian Empire. Such conspiracies as this are so remote from Western habits of life and thought, so inconceivable in our own experience, that we are apt to dismiss them as fantastic. They are the stuff of daily life in the Balkans, and we may do Austrian statesmen the justice of supposing that their fears were sincere. "The country," wrote Sir Maurice de Bunsen in his final dispatch, "certainly believed that it had before it only the alternative of subduing Servia, or of submitting sooner or later to mutilation at her hands." An enlightened Power in Austria's place would not have acted as she did. The "Great Servian" idea is dangerous to Austria, because she lacks the courage to be liberal without reserves. Servia may compare herself to Piedmont, but the parallel is imperfect. Her culture is so backward, her politics so corrupt, her economic life so primitive, that she has little to commend her to the Austrian Serbs save the community of blood. Our fathers sympathised with Italian aspirations, because the Italians were a race with a great past and a living culture, subject to an Empire which was not their superior in civilisation, and which denied them any species of autonomy. Austria does not deny Home Rule to their Serbs, though she gives it grudgingly, and she represents an older and maturer civilisation. The Italians, moreover, were a homogeneous people. Of the Austrian Serbs one third are Catholics, who have no reason to hope for equal treatment from an Orthodox State, whose record in Macedonia is a defiance of toleration, and another third are Moslems, who will emigrate *en masse* if the Servians should conquer Bosnia. Even the remaining third, who are Orthodox Serbs, would not have been ready-made material for a Servian propaganda, if Austria had known how to treat them with generosity. Faced by this Great Servian danger, and forced to realise at last that it was serious, a big man in Count Berchtold's place would have resolved to make Austria a home so attractive even to Servian idealists, that the half-civilised kingdom over the border, with its backward culture and Oriental morals, would have lured and beckoned them in vain. He would have made them feel, as the Poles have long felt, that they are Austrians with a share in the fortunes of the Empire. He would have made their autonomy a handsome reality. He would have banished the spies and the policemen, enemies of the Austrian idea more dangerous than all the Servian bomb-throwers and comitadjis. He would have released the Croatians from the Magyar yoke, and bidden Dalmatians, Croatians, and Bosnians realise their Great Servia to their heart's content within the Austrian Empire itself. That was the policy which the dead Archduke was supposed to favour. Against such a policy, conceived with some boldness of imagination and executed with good faith and tact, the incitements and conspiracies of Belgrade would have been powerless. Count Berchtold is neither a Liberal nor a man of genius. He acted after the Serajevo murder as the average Imperialist bureaucrat commonly does act in such cases. He tightened his police system. He made Austrian rule a little more than usually hateful to men of Servian race. He determined

THE ORIGINS OF THE GREAT WAR

to crush and humiliate Servia, and realising that behind Servia stood Russia, he turned to his ally for aid.

A Preventive War.

The policy on which Austria and Germany determined is a matter of history, and the German White Paper describes it with an approach to frankness. This interesting document has not been fairly reproduced by our daily newspapers, and the main passage may be worth translating at length:—

> "In these circumstances Austria was driven to the conclusion that the dignity and self-preservation of the Monarchy alike forbade her to watch this movement from across the frontier any longer in passivity. She communicated her view to us and asked our advice. We were able with all our hearts to inform our ally that we shared her opinion of the situation, and we assured her of our approval for any action which she might take to put an end to the movement in Servia directed against the integrity of the Monarchy. We were well aware that any military action by Austria against Servia might bring Russia on the scene, and involve us in war by reason of the obligations of our alliance. Realising, as we did, that the vital interests of Austria-Hungary were at stake, we could neither counsel our ally to a pliability inconsistent with her dignity, nor refuse her our aid in this difficult moment. Nor could we forget that our own interests were nearly threatened by this continual Servian agitation. Had the Servians been allowed, with the help of Russia and France, to endanger the integrity of the neighbouring Monarchy much longer, the consequence must have been the gradual disruption of Austria, and the subjection of the whole Slav world to the Russian sceptre, with the result that the position of the German race in central Europe would have become untenable."

There lies, in its naked simplicity, the German case for this war. The provocations followed in an alternating series. Russia encouraged the Great Servian movement, which aimed at the break-up of Austria, whereupon Austria struck at Servia, and thereby challenged Russia. The issue now was, in plain words, whether Servia should become an Austrian vassal or remain a Russian tool. While a diplomatic accommodation was still possible, Russia took the menacing step of proclaiming a general mobilisation, and Germany replied with an ultimatum, followed in a few hours by war. This war is a co-operative crime. To its making have gone Russian ambitions and German fears. It would be as just to say that the real aggressor was the Power which stood behind Servia, as it would be to say that it was the Power which first lit the conflagration by hurling its shells at Belgrade. On their own showing, the Germans had planned a bold challenging stroke, which might lead them into a preventive war. The last thing which they wanted was a universal war. They tried to buy our neutrality. They even appealed to us to keep

France neutral. There is evidence enough in our own White Paper that they did not believe that Russia would fight. They thought that they had defied her in good time before her armaments were ready. They had bullied her with success in the similar crisis of 1909, and with the characteristic clumsiness of Bismarckian psychology, they did not realise that a public act of bullying can never be repeated. It was precisely because Russia had yielded in 1909, that she could not yield again. It is nonsense to say, as M. Sazonoff said, that the prestige of Russia as a Great Power would be gone if Servia became an Austrian vassal. Servia had been an Austrian vassal throughout the lifetime of King Milan, and for many a year after his abdication. But it may be true to say that Russia would have lost in prestige, if Servia had been torn from her orbit by Austrian arms and German threats. It is more to the point that such a humiliation would have ended the dream of a Great Servia for ever. That was the real issue. What Russia dreaded was not so much the humiliation of her little Slav brothers, the Serbs; she had watched the humiliation of her other little brothers in Bulgaria with equanimity, and even with satisfaction. The Servians, however, were more than brothers; they were tools. They were an indispensable piece in the game of chess for the Empire of the East.

The Russian Mobilisation.

The historian of the future will be in one sense more biassed in his judgment of this moving chapter of history than we are ourselves. He will give his verdict, as historians commonly do, to the side that wins. To us the issue is unknown, and we must divide our wonder and our censures. The Pan-Slavists have brought the whole of European civilisation to a test which may come near submerging it, in order to accomplish their dream of racial unity. The Germans, by rashly precipitating an issue which might never, in fact, have been forced upon them, may well have brought upon themselves the very catastrophe which they dreaded. A preventive war, if it is not a crime as inexcusable as a war of naked aggression, is always a folly. Nothing obliged Austria to fight now. From Servia she might have had ample reparation, with pledges for her future good behaviour. The crime of Serajevo was far from raising Servia's prestige among the Austrian Slavs; it had, on the contrary, lowered and besmirched it. A policy of conciliation might have rendered any insurrection impossible. Nor was Russia's star in the ascendant in the counsels of Europe. Persian affairs had led to a marked cooling in Sir Edward Grey's hitherto uncritical regard for Russia. The Anglo-German friendship was deepening, and something like the "Utopian" proposal of our White Paper (Sir Edward Grey's conception of a collective guarantee by the Triple Entente that it would allow no aggression against the Triple Alliance) might have isolated Russia in the future, if, in fact, she meditated a war of Slav against Teuton. What is clear to-day is, that Germany, reasoning in cold blood amid profound peace, that Austria's future status was threatened by this Pan-Servian danger, has made a war in which the chief issue may soon be whether Austria can continue to exist. The event will probably show that Germany, when she forced the quarrel to a trial of armed strength, acted with folly. Her violation of Belgian neutrality was certainly as imprudent as it was iniquitous. It cannot be honestly argued that the Russian mobilisation justified her declaration of war. The answer to mobilisation is not war, but a counter mobilisation. But when this overwhelming case against German policy is stated, the fact remains that Germany could fairly plead that Russian policy was provocative. Russia was backing Servia in manœuvres which threatened to break up Germany's ally, Austria. Russia was, moreover, the first of the Great Powers to order a general mobilisation. This capital fact is ignored in nearly all the statements of the British case against Germany. It is slurred over in Sir Maurice de Bunsen's final despatch. It is omitted altogether in the historical preface to the cheap edition of the White Paper. That is not the way to write candid history. The dates are given in the White Paper. Russia, after a partial mobilisation in her Southern provinces against Austria, made her mobilisation general (*i.e.,* called out the reserves in the Northern provinces for use against Germany) on July 31 (No. 113). Austria and Germany ordered their general mobilisations on August 1 (Nos. 127 and 142). Up to the first day of August Austria had only partially mobilised; Germany had not mobilised at all; Austria in this last phase of the negotiations was showing moderation, and had conceded, as Sir Maurice de Bunsen has recognised, the main point at issue. The Kaiser was offering his personal services as mediator, and there can be no doubt that at the last moment, when she realised that the Austro-Serbian War could not be localised, Germany did use her influence with success to induce Austria to be moderate. She now saw in the Russian mobilisation a threat to herself, and she replied to the threat with a defiance. The Tsar's order to mobilise compromised the hope of peace; the Kaiser's ultimatum ruined it. The moral responsibility for the universal war must be shared between Germany and Russia.

The Eastern Melting-Pot.

If the Triple Entente should be victorious, and if Russian policy is allowed to dominate the settlement, it is hard to draw a fortunate horoscope for Austria. A Russian proclamation has already snatched from Germany the Polish province of Posen, and from Austria the loyal and contented Poles of Galicia. We may be sure, if Servian arms should meet with any measure of success, that Russia will aim at creating a Greater Servia by amalgamating Croatia, Dalmatia, Bosnia, and Herzegovina with Servia and Montenegro. The *tertius gaudens,* as the Balkan struggle shows, is apt to exact a heavy price for his neutrality. Italy will not forget that Trent is peopled by Italians, and that the miserable Albanians will require some strong hand to restore their wretched country to order and peace. Roumania is a formidable military power, and at the moment when the struggle becomes desperate, her weight might be decisive in one or other of the Eastern scales of power. She has no love for either Empire, though her king is a Hohenzollern. Russia took Bessarabia from her, and Hungary is the mistress of a large Roumanian population in Transylvania. She may elect to move her armies into one or the other of these provinces, but more probably she will sell her neutrality for an assurance that the victor will reward her. Bulgaria is in the same case. An armed neutrality will pay her best. If Russia wins, then Servia, rich in her new acquisitions, can well afford to give up a part at least of Macedonia. The whole of the Near East is in the melting-pot, but the central question of all is in what shape Austria will emerge from the tremendous test. A decisive victory would mean for her that Russian hegemony would be ended in Europe. She would have become herself the rival Slavonic Power. She anticipated Russia by promising the restoration of Polish unity. She would either annex Servia outright, or reduce her to vassalage, while Roumania, Bulgaria, and Turkey, each aggrandised somewhat by the pursuit of a profitable neutrality, would be attached to her as grateful satellites. She would dominate the Balkans, and in the act she would have solved triumphantly the problem of her own internal cohesion. A beaten Russia would no longer attract the Southern Slavs. The other alternative is, if possible, still more cataclysmic. If Russia wins and has her way, little will be left of Austria save her German provinces, and these might be incorporated at length in a German Empire which had lost Posen and Alsace-Lorraine. Roumania and Servia would emerge as big States, attached by interest to the Russian system. Bulgaria would be reconciled by the gift of Macedonia. The doubtful points would be the future of the Czechs and Magyars. But whatever their fate might be, the German Powers would have been cut off for ever from the East, and Russia with some millions of Poles and Ruthenians added to her territories, and the Southern Slavs enlisted as her allies and vanguard, would dominate the Eastern Mediterranean and overshadow Turkey, as to-day she overshadows Persia.

Defence or Conquest?

We are taking a parochial view of Armageddon if we allow ourselves to imagine that it is primarily a struggle for the independence of Belgium and the future of France. The Germans are nearer the truth when they regard it as a Russo-German war. It began in a struggle for the hegemony of the Near East, with its pivotal point at Belgrade. It will end logically, if either side achieves a decisive success, in a melting of all the frontiers of the East, and the settlement by force of arms of the question whether its destinies shall be governed by Germany or by Russia. It is, to my mind, an issue so barbarous, so remote from any real interest or concern of our daily life in these islands, that I can only marvel at the illusions, and curse the fatality which have made us belligerents in this struggle. We are neither Slavs nor Germans. How many of us, high or low, dare form a decided opinion as to whether Bosnia would in the end be happier under the native but intolerant and semi-civilised rule of the Serbs, or the alien but relatively civilised rule of Austria? How many of us would dare to answer one by one the questions whether Poles and Ruthenians and Slovacks would be the happier for passing from Austrian to Russian rule? We have not even debated these questions, yet our arms are helping to settle them. Our fleet in the North Sea, our army in France

THE ORIGINS OF THE GREAT WAR

may be winning for the Tsar millions of fresh subjects, and for the familiar process of forcible Russification unnumbered victims. They will pass from a higher to a lower civilisation, from a system usually tolerant and fitfully Liberal, to one which has not even begun to grasp the idea of toleration, and whose answer to Liberalism is the censorship, the prison, and the "truly Russian" pogrom. The Russian exiles who ask us to believe in the Liberal Russia of to-morrow can only repeat their pathetic, instinctive hopes. They admit, with a candour which enlists our respect, that nothing is changed as yet. One may hope for some slow evolution in Russian politics. One may dream of a future federal organisation of its many nationalities. But are we so secure in our anticipation of that brighter future that we will back it by our arms? On the lower level of self-interest and Imperial expediency have we reason to desire a world in which the Balance of Power will lurch violently to the side of this unscrupulous and incalculable Empire? Within a year from the breaking of Germany's power (if that is the result of this war), as Russia forces her way through the Dardanelles, dominates Turkey, overruns Persia, and bestrides the road to India, our Imperialists will be calling out for a strong Germany to balance a threatening Russia. A mechanical fatality has forced France into this struggle, and a comradeship, translated by secret commitments into a defensive alliance, has brought us into the war in her wake. It is no real concern of hers or of ours. It is a war for the Empire of the East. If our statesmanship is clear-sighted, it will stop the war before it has passed from a struggle for the defence of France and Belgium, into a colossal wrangle for the dominion of the Balkans and the mastery of the Slavs. When the campaign in the West has ended, as we all hope that it soon will end, in the liberation of French and Belgian soil from a deplorable invasion, the moment will have come to pause. To back our Western friends in a war of defence is one thing, to fling ourselves into the further struggle for the Empire of the East quite another. No call of the blood, no imperious calculation of self-interest, no hope for the future of mankind requires us to side with Slav against Teuton. We cannot wish that either Austria or Russia should dominate the Balkans, but if we had to make the choice in cold blood, most of us would prefer the more tolerant and more civilised German influence. Our orators talk of the cause of nationality. Two months ago what man in his senses would have suggested that the best way to serve the cause of nationality was to bring fresh subject races under the Russian yoke? The Poles and Ruthenians are Slavs indeed, but they are not Russians. One might as well propose to further the cause of nationality by annexing Holland to the German Empire. If in the heat of battle, we allow ourselves to rush onward without reflection from a war of defence to a war of conquest, we shall find that all the old problems confront us anew. Enthusiasts for this hateful war may applaud it as an effort to "destroy German militarism." That is a meaningless phrase. The Allies may indeed destroy the German armies, but no one can destroy German militarism, save the German people itself. Militarism seizes a nation only when the prophets of the gospel of force can preach to ears prepared by fear. We are about to make new fears for the German people. Crush that people, load it with indemnities, lop it of its provinces, encircle

361

it with triumphant allies, and so far from turning to depose its Prussian leaders, it will rally behind them in a national struggle to recover its standing, its integrity, its power of free movement. Not France but Germany will arm to recover lost provinces, and weave new alliances to adjust the ever-shifting balance of power. If once the world begins to play at map-making, it will create unsatisfied appetites; there will be States enough to join with Germany in an effort to upset the settlement. The future will stretch before us, a new phase of the ruinous armed peace, destined to end, after further years of anger and waste, in another war of revenge. It lies with public opinion to limit the duration of this quarrel, and to impose on our diplomacy, when victory in the West is won, a return to its natural *rôle* of moderator in a quarrel no longer its own.

Notes

1 Read, for example, this typical declaration by the *Volkstimme,* one of the German Socialist Party organs: "All must set aside the aims and purposes of their party, and bear in mind one fact—Germany, and in a larger sense all Europe, is endangered by Russian despotism. At this moment we all feel the duty to fight chiefly and exclusively against Russian despotism. Germany's women and children must not become the prey of Russian bestiality; the German country must not be the spoil of Cossacks; because if the Allies should be victorious, not an English governor or a French republican would rule over Germany, but the Russian Tsar. Therefore we must defend at this moment everything that means German culture and German liberty against a merciless and barbaric enemy."

2 In an article entitled "Europe Under Arms" (June 3, 1914), the military correspondent of the *Times* explained how well founded were these German fears of Russian preparations. Russia, he explained, had raised her peace-effectives by 150,000 men, "making a total peace strength of about 1,700,000, or approximately double that of Germany." . . . "The Russian reply to Germany is next door to a mobilisation in time of peace, and it quite accounts for the embittered outburst of the *Cologne Gazette,* and for the German pot calling the Russian kettle black. . . . There are signs that Russia has done with defensive strategy. . . . The increased number of guns in the Russian Army Corps, the growing efficiency of the Army, and the improvements made or planned in strategic railways are, again, matters which cannot be left out of account. These things are well calculated to make the Germans anxious."

3 My statement has since been confirmed by a distinguished historian, who writes as a friend and admirer of the Serbs. "Last year," writes Mr. G. M. Trevelyan in the *Times* of September 18, "when I was among them, they looked forward to this [a war with Austria] as the grand national object, and they regarded the then impending war with Bulgaria as an unfortunate but necessary prelude to the war of liberation against Austria. . . . The young men in Serbia, many of them, spoke of themselves as belonging to the 'Piedmontese Party,' and books about Piedmont's part in the Italian *risorgimento* were the commonest 'serious literature' in the Belgrade shops, and lay on the table in the waiting-room of their Foreign Office." I may add that an influential daily newspaper was called *Piemonte*. Can we wonder that Austria first shuddered and then struck out?

BIBLIOGRAPHY

Barker, Rodney. 1997. *Political Ideas in Modern Britain in and after the 20th Century*, 2nd edition, London: Routledge.

Barnes, John. 2005. "Gentleman Crusader: Henry Hyde Champion in the Early Socialist Movement". *History Workshop Journal* 60: 116–138.

Bealey, Frank. 1956. "The Electoral Arrangement Between the Labour Representation Committee and the Liberal Party". *The Journal of Modern History* 28 (4): 353–373.

Beaumont, Matthew. 2003. "William Reeves and Late-Victorian Radical Publishing: Unpacking the Bellamy Library". *History Workshop Journal*, no. 55 (Spring): 91–110.

Beech, Matt, and Hickson, Kevin. 2007. *Labour's Thinkers: The Intellectual Roots of Labour from Tawney to Gordon Brown*. London: Tauris.

Beer, Max. 1929. *A History of British Socialism*, Volume II. London: G. Bell and Sons.

Besant, Annie. 1886. "Why I am a Socialist". *Our Corner*, September: 157–163.

Besant, Annie, and Nairn, W.J. 1892. *What is Socialism? A Discussion Between Mrs. Annie Besant and Mr W. J. Nairn*. Glasgow: SDF.

Bevir, Mark. 1996. "Fabianism, Permeation and Independent Labour". *The Historical Journal* 39 (1): 179–196.

Bevir, Mark. 2011. *The Making of British Socialism*. Princeton N.J.: Princeton University Press.

Bhattacharaya, Sumangala. 2017. "The Victorian Occult Atom: Annie Besant and Clairvoyant Atomic Research". In *Investigating the Limits of Knowledge in the Victorian Age*, edited by Lara Karpenko and Shalyn Claggett, 197–214. Ann Arbor, Mich.: University of Michigan Press.

Blair, T. 1994. *Socialism*. London: Fabian Society.

Bland, Hubert. 1889. "The Outlook". In *Fabian Essays in Socialism*, edited by George Bernard Shaw, 202–221. London: The Fabian Society.

Blatchford, Robert. 1897. *The New Religion*, 2nd edition. London: Clarion Press.

Blatchford, Robert. 1902. *Britain for the British*. London: Clarion Press.

Bondfield, Margaret. 1899. "Conditions Under which Shop Assistants Work". *The Economic Journal* 9 (34): 277–286.

Bondfield, Margaret. 1905. *The Women's Suffrage Controversy*. London: Adult Suffrage Society.

Brailsford, Henry Noel. 1914. *The Origins of the Great War*. London: Union of Democratic Control.

Brown, Kenneth D. 1971. "The Labour Party and the Unemployment Question, 1906–1910". *The Historical Journal* 14 (3): 599–616.

BIBLIOGRAPHY

Bruce Glasier, Katherine. 1909. *Socialism and the Home*. London: Independent Labour Party.

Caine, Barbara. 1982. "Beatrice Webb and the 'Woman Question'". *History Workshop* 14: 23–43.

Callaghan, John. 1990. *Socialism in Britain Since 1884*. Oxford: Basil Blackwell.

Cowman, Krista. 2002. "'Incipient Toryism'? The Women's Social and Political Union and the Independent Labour Party, 1903–14". *History Workshop Journal* 53: 128–148.

Davis, Mary. 2009. *Comrade or Brother? A History of the British Labour Movement*. London: Pluto Press.

Derfel, R.J. 1891. *On the Importance of Right Methods in Teaching Socialism: A Paper Read to the Manchester and District Fabian Society*. Manchester: R.J. Derfel.

Dubery, Harry, c. 1913. *A Labour Case Against Conscription*. Manchester: National Labour Press.

Duffy, A.E.P. 1961. "New Unionism in Britain, 1889–1890: A Reappraisal". *The Economic History Review* 14 (2): 306–319.

Duffy, A.E.P. 1962. "Differing Policies and Personal Rivalries in the Origins of the Independent Labour Party". *Victorian Studies* 6 (1): 43–65.

Durand, E. Dana. 1902. "The British Trade Union Congress of 1902". *The Quarterly Journal of Economics* 17 (1): 181–184.

El-Amin, Mohammed Nuri. 1977. "Sydney Olivier on Socialism and the Colonies". *The Review of Politics* 39 (4): 521–539.

Elliott, Gregory. 1993. *Labourism and the English Genius: The Strange Death of Labour England?* London: Verso.

Fabian Society. 1884. *A Manifesto*, Fabian Tracts No. 2. London: Geo Standring.

Fabian Society. 1890. *What Socialism Is*. London: Fabian Society.

Freeden, Michael. 1979. "Eugenics and Progressive Thought: A Study in Ideological Affinity". *The Historical Journal* 22 (3): 645–671.

Gilbert, Bentley Brinkerhoff. 1976. "David Lloyd George: Land, The Budget, and Social Reform". *The American Historical Review* 81 (5): 1058–1066.

Gomme, Robert. 2003. "George Herbert Perris 1866–1920: A Case Study of an Ethicist and a Radical". *Ethical Record* 108 (7): 12–21.

Greenleaf, W.H. 1983. *The British Political Tradition, Volume Two: The Ideological Heritage*. London: Routledge.

Hammill, Fred. c. 1894. *The Claims and Progress of Labour Representation*. Newcastle-on-Tyne: Labour Literature Society (North England).

Hardie, James Keir. 1893. "Introductory Letter". In *The Independent Labour Party, Its Programme and Policy*, by Russell H. Smart. Manchester: Labour Press Society Ltd.

Hardie, Keir. 1902. *Miners' Eight Hours' Bill*. London: John Penny.

Hardie, J. Keir. 1903. "Federated Labor as a New Factor in British Politics". *The North American Review* 177 (561): 233–241.

Hardie, J. Keir. 1904. "Dealing with the Unemployed: A Hint from the Past". *Nineteenth Century*, December: 1–14.

Hardie, Keir. 1906. *The Citizenship of Women: A Plea for Women's Suffrage*, 3rd edition. London: Independent Labour Party.

Hardie, Keir. 1910. *The Party Pledge and the Osborne Judgement*. Manchester: The National Press Ltd.

Hardie, Keir. 2015. *From Serfdom to Socialism*. London: Lawrence and Wishart.

BIBLIOGRAPHY

Hardie, J. Keir, and MacDonald, J.R. 1899. "The Liberal Collapse, III: The Independent Labour Party's Programme". *The Nineteenth Century: A Monthly Review* 45 (263): 20–38.

Harrison, Brian. 1989. "Class and Gender in Modern British Labour History". *Past and Present* 124: 121–158.

Higgs, Richard. 1908. *Socialism and Agriculture*. London: Independent Labour Party.

Hobson, John M. 2012. *The Eurocentric Conception of World Politics: Western International Theory, 1760–2010*. Cambridge: Cambridge University Press.

Howell, David. 1980. *British Social Democracy: A Study in Development and Decay*, 2nd edition. London: Croom Helm.

Hunt, E.H., and Pam, S.J. 2001. "Managerial Failure in Late Victorian Britain?: Land Use and English Agriculture". *The Economic History Review* 54, (2): 240–266.

Independent Labour Party. 1894. "To the Workers of Great Britain and Ireland, Greeting". *The Economic Journal* 4 (14): 368–371.

Jackson, Ben. 2007. *Equality and the British Left: A Study in Progressive Political Thought, 1900–64*. Manchester: Manchester University Press.

Jameson, William. 1896. *Land Lessons for Town Folk*. London: Clarion.

Johnson, Graham. 2000. "'Making Reform the Instrument of Revolution': British Social Democracy, 1881–1911". *The Historical Journal* 43 (4): 977–1002.

Joint Committee of Socialist Bodies. 1893. *Manifesto of the Joint Committee of Socialist Bodies*. London: Twentieth Century Press.

Kingston, Beverley. 1975. "Yours Very Truly, Marion Phillips". *Labour History* 29: 123–131.

Klarman, Michael J. 1989a. "The Judges Versus the Unions: The Development of British Labor Law, 1867–1913". *Virginia Law Review* 75 (8): 1487–1602.

Klarman, Michael J. 1989b. "Parliamentary Reversal of the Osborne Judgement". *The Historical Journal* 32 (4): 893–924.

Labour Party. c. 1907. *Labour and Politics: Why Trade Unionists Should Support the Labour Party*. London: Labour Party.

Labour Party. 1918. *Labour and the New Social Order: A Report on Reconstruction*. London: The Labour Party.

Labour Representation Committee. 1903. *Why We Are Independent*. London: Labour Representation Committee.

Labour Representation Committee. c. 1905. *Why is the L.R.C. Independent?* London: Labour Representation Committee.

Lamb, Peter. 2011. "Henry Noel Brailsford's Radical International Relations Theory". *International Relations* 25 (4): 479–498.

Lamb, Peter. 2017. "Henry Noel Brailsford: Neglected Cosmopolitan". *International Politics* 54 (1): 104–117.

Lamb, Peter. 2019. *Socialism*. Cambridge: Polity Press.

Lawrence, Jon. 1992. "Popular Radicalism and the Socialist Revival in Britain". *Journal of British Studies* 31 (2): 163–186.

Lawrence, Jon. 2006. "The Transformation of British Public Politics after the First World War". *Past and Present* 190: 185–216.

Laybourn, Keith. 1994. "The Failure of Socialist Unity in Britain c. 1893–1914". *Transactions of the Royal Historical Society* 4: 153–175.

Leventhal, F.M. 1985. *The Last Dissenter: Henry Noel Brailsford and His World*. Oxford: Clarendon Press.

BIBLIOGRAPHY

Livesey, Ruth. 2004. "The Politics of Work: Feminism, Professionalisation and Women Inspectors of Factories and Workshops". *Women's History Review* 13 (2): 233–262.

Lloyd, C.M. 1912. *The New Children's Charter*. London: Independent Labour Party and Fabian Society.

MacDonald, J. Ramsay. 1903. *The Law and Trade Union Funds. A Plea for "Ante-Taff Vale"*. London: Independent Labour Party.

MacDonald, J. Ramsay. 1904. "The International Socialist Congress". *The Speaker*, 77, August.

MacDonald, J. Ramsay. c. 1907. *The New Unemployed Bill of the Labour Party*. London: Independent Labour Party.

MacDonald, J. Ramsay. 1910. "The Trade Union Unrest". *The English Review*, November: 728–739.

Mackay, Carol Hanbery. 2009. "A Journal of Her Own: The Rise of Annie Besant's *Our Corner*". *Victorian Periodicals Review* 42 (4): 324–358.

Mackenzie, Norman, ed. 2008. *The Letters of Sidney and Beatrice Webb: Volume I, Apprenticeships 1873–1892*. Cambridge: Cambridge University Press.

Mann, Tom. 1896. *A Socialist's View of Religion and the Churches*. London: Clarion.

Manton, Kevin. 2003. "The Fellowship of the New Life: English Ethical Socialism Reconsidered". *History of Political Thought* 24 (2): 282–304.

Marcus, Jane. 1978. "Transatlantic Sisterhood: Labor and Suffrage Links in the Letters of Elizabeth Robins and Emmeline Pankhurst". *Signs* 3 (3): 744–755.

Marx, Karl. 1976. *Capital, Volume One*. Harmondsworth: Penguin.

McCormick, B., and Williams, J.E. 1959. "The Miners and the Eight-Hour Day, 1863–1910". *The Economic History Review*, New Series, 12 (2): 222–238.

McNeilly, E. 2009. "Labour and the Politics of Internationalism, 1906–1914". *Twentieth Century British History* 20 (4): 431–453.

Middlemas, Keith. 1970. *Politics in Industrial Society: The Experience of the British System Since 1911*. London: André Deutsch.

Miliband, Ralph. 1972. *Parliamentary Democracy: A Study in the Politics of Labour*, 2nd edition. London: Merlin Press.

Minkin, Lewis. 1978. *The Labour Party Conference: A Study in the Politics of Intra-Party Democracy*. London: Allen Lane.

Morgan, Kevin. 2006. *Ramsay MacDonald*. London: Haus.

Morgan, Kevin. 2009. "Militarism and Anti-Militarism: Socialists, Communists and Conscription in France and Britain 1900–1940". *Past and Present* 202: 207–244.

Partington, John S. 2008. "H. G. Wells: A Political Life". *Utopian Studies* 19 (3): 517–576.

Paul, Diane. 1984. "Eugenics and the Left". *Journal of the History of Ideas* 45 (4): 567–590.

Pearson, Robert, and Williams, Geraint. 1984. *Political Thought and Public Policy in the Nineteenth Century*. London: Longman.

Pease, Edward R. 1916. *The History of the Fabian Society*. New York: E.P. Dutton and Company.

Pelling, Henry. 1976. *A History of British Trade Unionism*, 3rd edition. Harmondsworth: Penguin.

Pelling, Henry. 1982. "The Politics of the Osborne Judgement". *The Historical Journal* 25 (4): 888–909.

Perris, G.H. c. 1910. *Hands Across the Sea: Labour's Pleas for International Peace*. Manchester: The National Labour Press.

Powell, David. 1986. "The New Liberalism and the Rise of Labour, 1886–1906". *The Historical Journal* 29 (2): 369–393.

Prynn, David. 1976. "The Clarion Clubs, Rambling and the Holiday Associations in Britain since the 1890s". *Journal of Contemporary History* 11 (2–3): 65–77.

Pugh, Martin, 1988. "Popular Conservatism in Britain: Continuity and Change, 1880–1987". *Journal of British Studies* 27 (3): 254–282.

Pugh, Martin. 2002. "The Rise of Labour and the Political Culture of Conservatism, 1890–1945". *History* 87 (288): 514–537.

Ricci, David M. 1969. "Fabian Socialism: A Theory of Rent as Exploitation". *Journal of British Studies* 9 (1): 105–121.

Ritchie, David G. 1891. *Principles of State Interference*. London: Swan Sonnenschein & Co.

Rowan, Caroline. 1982. "Women in the Labour Party, 1906–1920". *Feminist Review* 12: 74–91.

Sassoon, Donald. 2014. *One Hundred Years of Socialism: The West European Left in the Twentieth Century*, new edition. London: I.B. Tauris.

Shaw, G. Bernard. 1889. "Preface". In *Fabian Essays in Socialism*, edited by George Bernard Shaw. London: Fabian Society.

Skidelsky, Robert. 1994. *Politicians and the Slump: The Labour Government of 1929–1931*, 2nd edition. London: Macmillan.

Smart, H. Russell. 1893. *The Independent Labour Party, Its Programme and Policy*. Manchester: Labour Press Society Ltd.

Smart, H. Russell. c. 1908. *The Right to Work*. London: Independent Labour Party.

Snowden, Philip. c. 1908. *The Individual under Socialism: A Lecture*. London: ILP.

Stewart, John. 1993. "Ramsay MacDonald, the Labour Party, and Child Welfare, 1900–1914". *Twentieth Century British History* 4 (2): 105–125.

Thackeray, David. 2010. "Home and Politics: Women and Conservative Activism in Early Twentieth-Century Britain". *Journal of British Studies* 49 (4): 826–848.

Thackeray, David. 2011. "Rethinking the Edwardian Crisis of Conservatism". *The Historical Journal* 54 (1): 191–213.

Thoburn, Nicholas. 2016. *Anti-Book: On the Art and Politics of Radical Publishing*. Minneapolis: University of Minnesota Press.

Thompson, James. 2014. "The Great Labour Unrest and Political Thought in Britain, 1911–1914". *Labour History Review* 79 (1): 37–54.

Tichelar, Michael. 1997. "Socialists, Labour and the Land: The Response of the Labour Party to the Land Campaign of Lloyd George before the First World War". *Twentieth Century British History* 8 (2): 127–144.

Toye, Richard. 2008. "H.G. Wells and the New Liberalism". *Twentieth Century British History* 19 (2): 156–185.

Ward, Paul, and Wright, Martin. 2010. "Mirrors of Wales – Life Story as National Metaphor: Case Studies of R. J. Derfel (1824–1905) and Huw T. Edwards (1892–1970)". *History* 95 (317): 45–63.

Webb, Beatrice. 1896. *Women and the Factory Acts*. London: Fabian Society.

Webb, Sidney. c. 1888a. *The Progress of Socialism*. London: Modern Press, William Reeves and Freethought Publishing Company.

Webb, Sidney. c. 1888b. *What Socialism Means: A Call to the Unconverted*, 3rd edition. London: William Reeves.

Webb, Sidney. 1890. Lecture: *Socialism!* Poster for lecture scheduled for Tuesday, Nov. 4, 1890.

Webb, Sidney. 1891. "The Difficulties of Individualism". *The Economic Journal* 1 (2): 360–381.

BIBLIOGRAPHY

Webb, Sidney. 1896. *The Difficulties of Individualism*. London: Fabian Society.

Webb, Sidney. 1901. *Twentieth Century Politics: A Policy of National Efficiency*. London: Fabian Society.

Webb, Sidney. 1911. "The Osborne Revolution". *The English Review*, January: 380–393.

Webb, Sidney. 1918. *The New Constitution of the Labour Party*. London: Labour Party.

Webb, Sidney. 1931. "Introduction to the 1920 edition". In *Fabian Essays in Socialism*, edited by George Bernard Shaw, 5th edition, xvii–xxxi. London: Fabian Society and George Allen and Unwin.

Webb, Sidney, and Webb, Beatrice. 1918. *The Principles of the Labour Party*. London: Labour Party.

Weinroth, Howard S. 1970. "The British Radicals and the Balance of Power, 1902–1914". *The Historical Journal* 13 (4): 653–682.

Wells, H.G. 1906a. "Socialism and the Middle Classes". *Fortnightly Review*, November: 785–798.

Wells, H.G. 1906b. *Socialism and the Family*. London: A.C. Fifield.

Wells, H.G. c. 1907. *Will Socialism Destroy the Home?* London: Independent Labour Party.

Yeo, Stephen. 1977. "A New Life: The Religion of Socialism in Britain, 1883–1896". *History Workshop* no. 4: 5–56.